W9-CIC-545

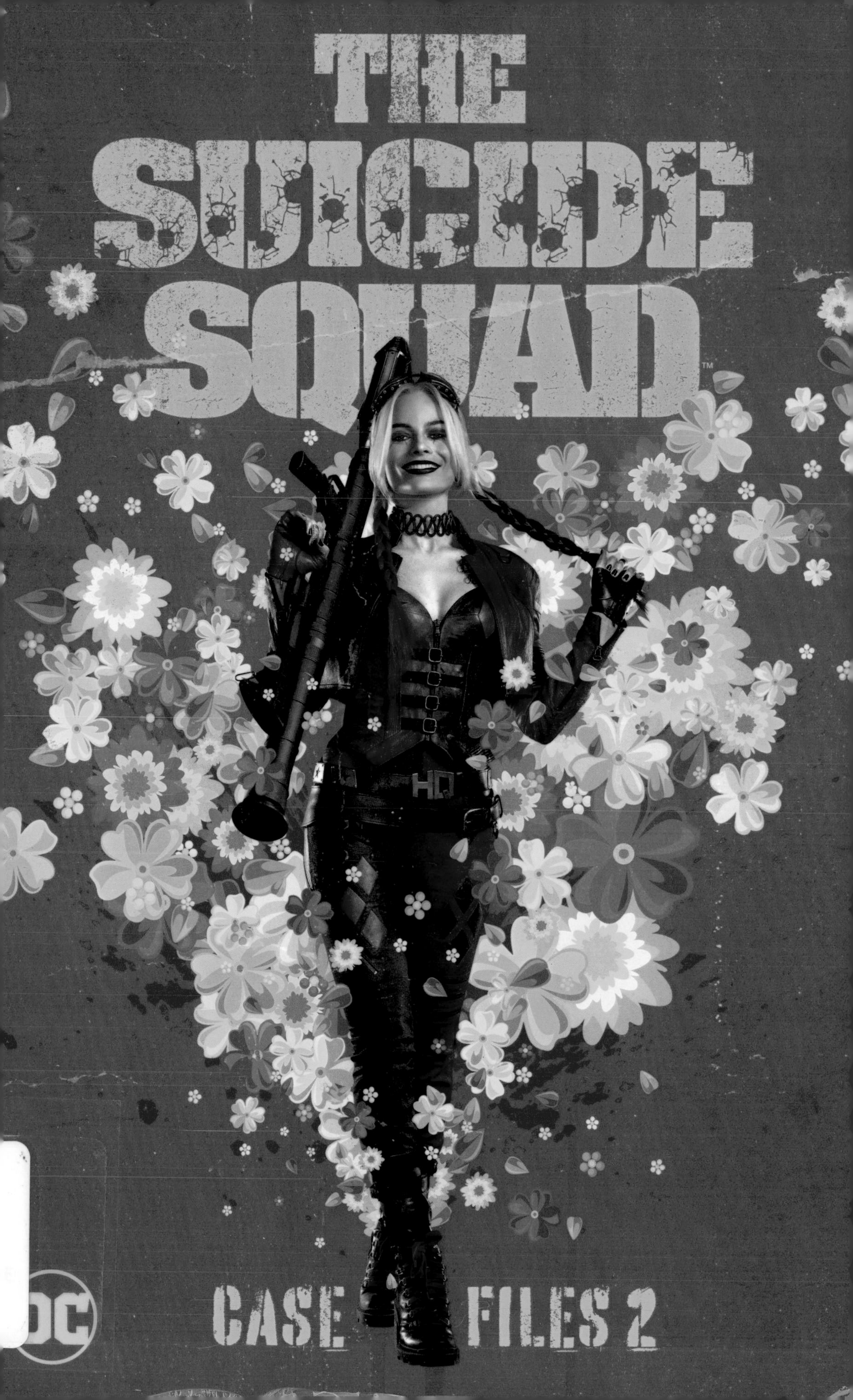
THE SUICIDE SQUAD™
DC
CASE FILES 2

THE SUICIDE SQUAD

CASE FILES 2

THE SUICIDE SQUAD

CASE FILES 2

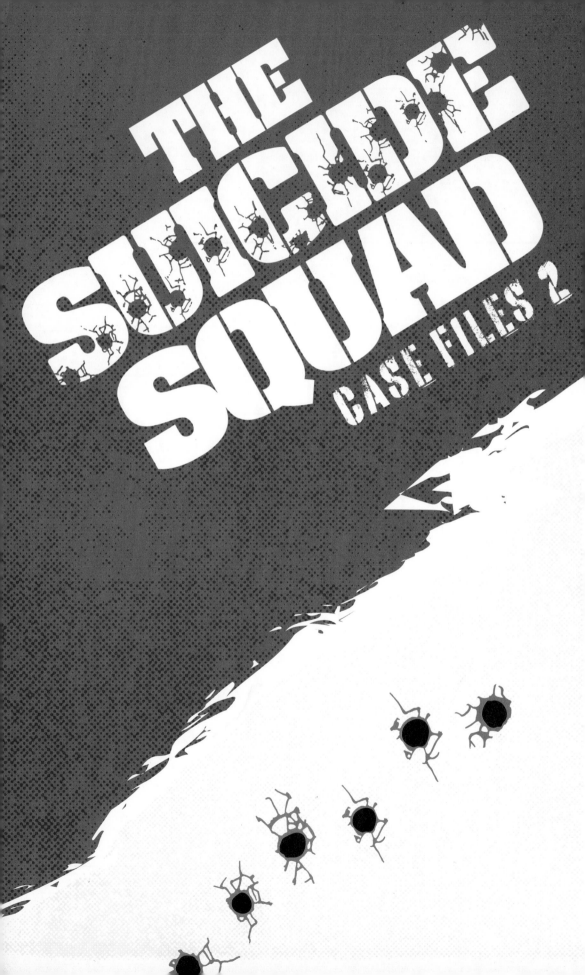

AARON SOWD
DAVE HUNT
MIKE DeCARLO
DAVE GIBBONS
ALEX LEI
LUKE McDONNELL
RICARDO VILLAGRÁN
inkers

CARL GAFFORD
RICHARD HORIE
TANYA HORIE
HI-FI
ADRIENNE ROY
ANTHONY TOLLIN
TOM ZIUKO
colorists

JOHN OSTRANDER
PAUL DINI
DAVID M. DeVRIES
ALAN GRANT
DAN JURGENS
JOHN WAGNER
GAIL SIMONE
LEN WEIN
writers

WILLIE SCHUBERT
ALBERT DeGUZMAN
TODD KLEIN
DAVE GIBBONS
AGUSTIN MAS
JOHN E. WORKMAN
letterers

YVEL GUICHET
LUKE McDONNELL
ED BENES
NORM BREYFOGLE
DAVE GIBBONS
DAN JURGENS
pencillers

JORDAN B. GORFINKEL
ROBERT GREENBERGER
DENNIS O'NEIL
JANICE RACE
DAN RASPLER
ROY THOMAS
DARREN VINCENZO
LEN WEIN
Editors - Original Series

JOSEPH ILLIDGE
Associate Editor - Original Series

FRANK BERRIOS
Assistant Editor - Original Series

ALEX GALER
Editor - Collected Edition

STEVE COOK
Design Director - Books

MEGEN BELLERSEN
Publication Design

TOM VALENTE
Publication Production

MARIE JAVINS
Editor-in-Chief, DC Comics

DANIEL CHERRY III
Senior VP - General Manager

JIM LEE
Publisher & Chief Creative Officer

JOEN CHOE
VP - Global Brand & Creative Services

DON FALLETTI
VP - Manufacturing Operations & Workflow Management

LAWRENCE GANEM
VP - Talent Services

ALISON GILL
Senior VP - Manufacturing & Operations

NICK J. NAPOLITANO
VP - Manufacturing Administration & Design

NANCY SPEARS
VP - Revenue

THE SUICIDE SQUAD CASE FILES 2

DC Comics, 2900 West Alameda Ave., Burbank, CA 91505
Printed by Solisco Printers, Scott, QC, Canada. 6/18/21. First Printing.
ISBN: 978-1-77951-156-0

Library of Congress Cataloging-in-Publication Data is available.

PEFC Certified
This product is from sustainably managed forests, recycled and controlled sources
PEFC/26-31-02
www.pefc.org

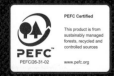

TABLE OF CONTENTS
MEET THE SQUAD

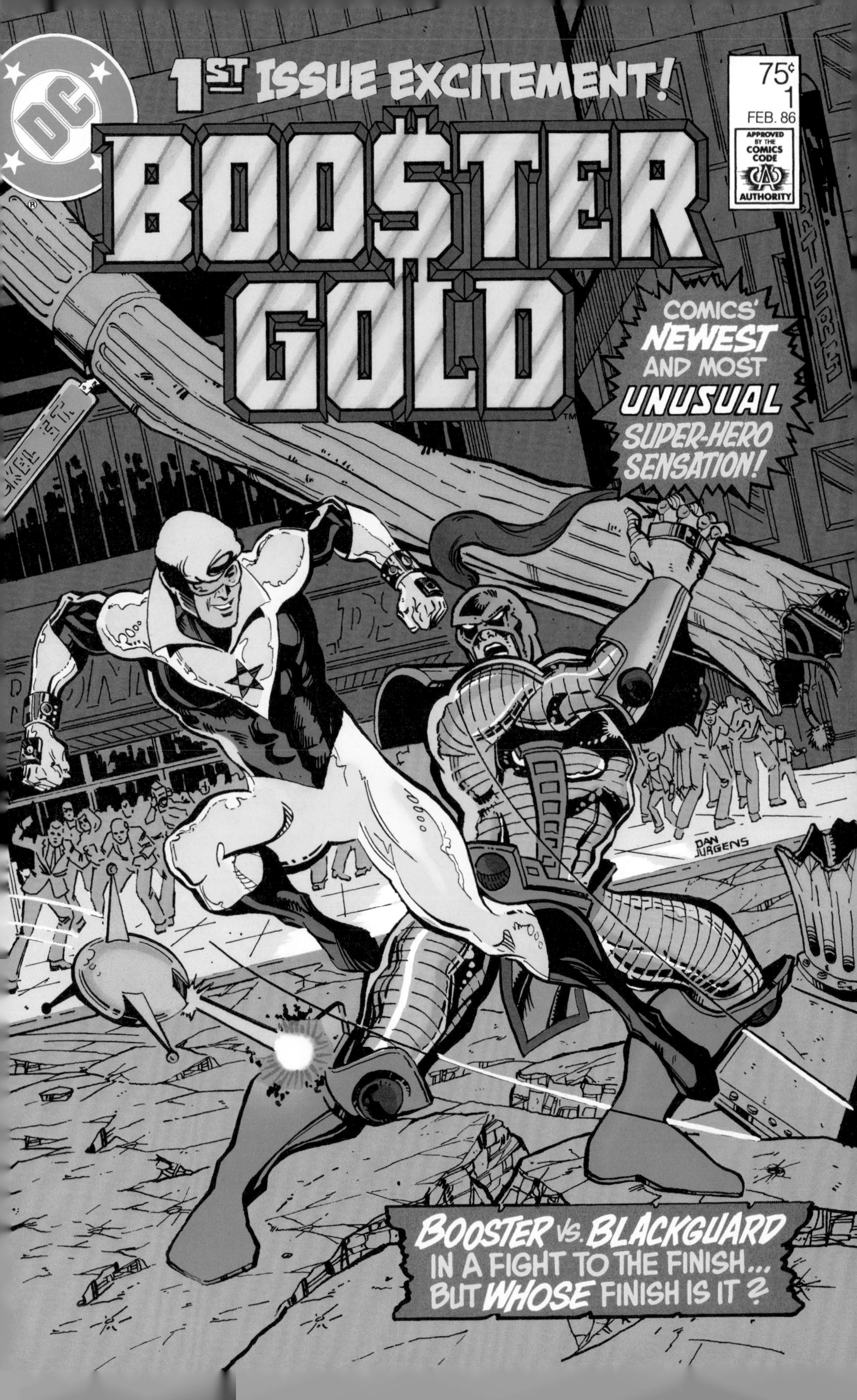
1ST ISSUE EXCITEMENT!
75¢
1
FEB. 86
APPROVED BY THE COMICS CODE AUTHORITY
BOO$TER GOLD
COMICS' NEWEST AND MOST UNUSUAL SUPER-HERO SENSATION!
DAN JURGENS
BOOSTER VS. BLACKGUARD
IN A FIGHT TO THE FINISH...
BUT WHOSE FINISH IS IT?

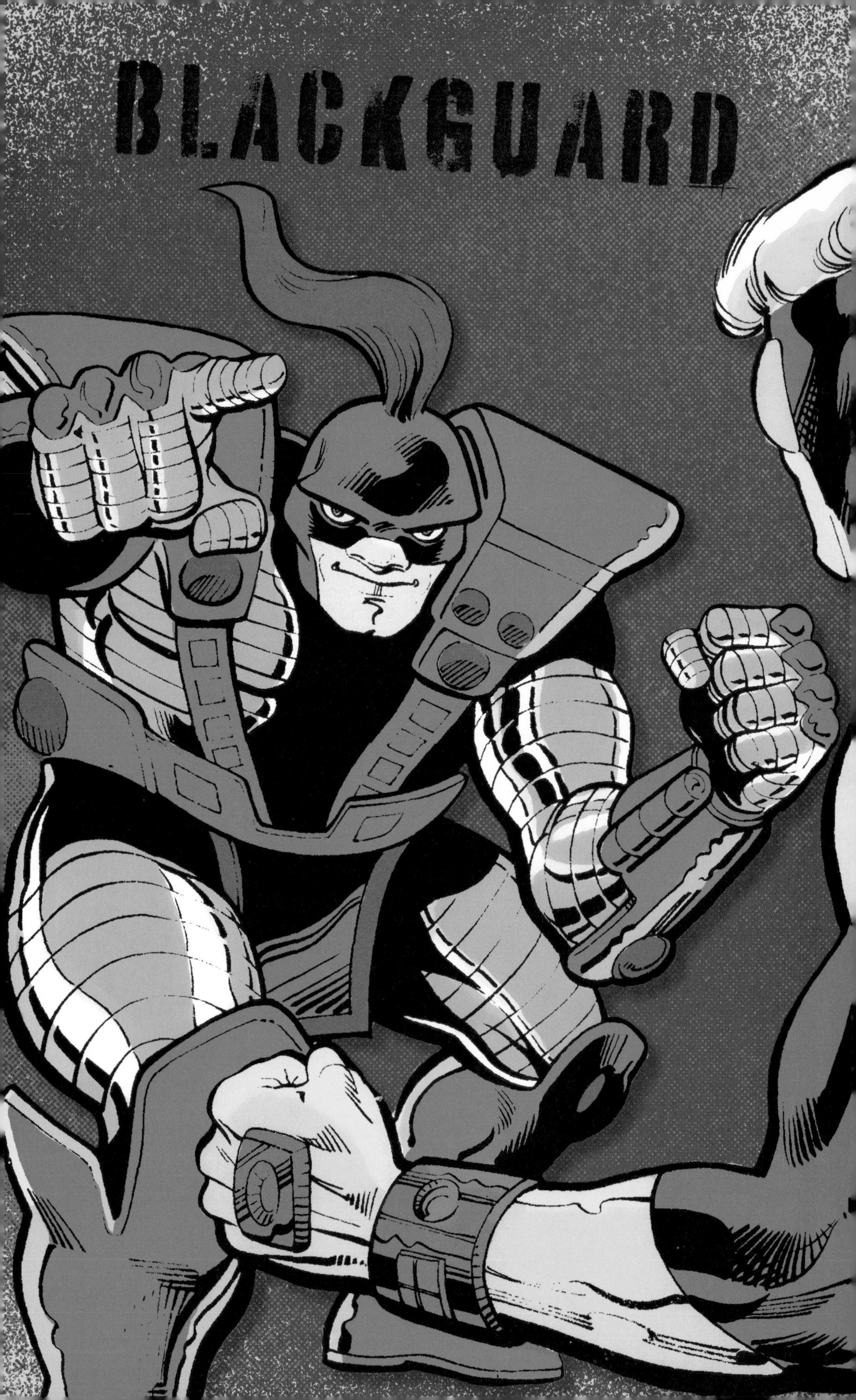
BLACKGUARD

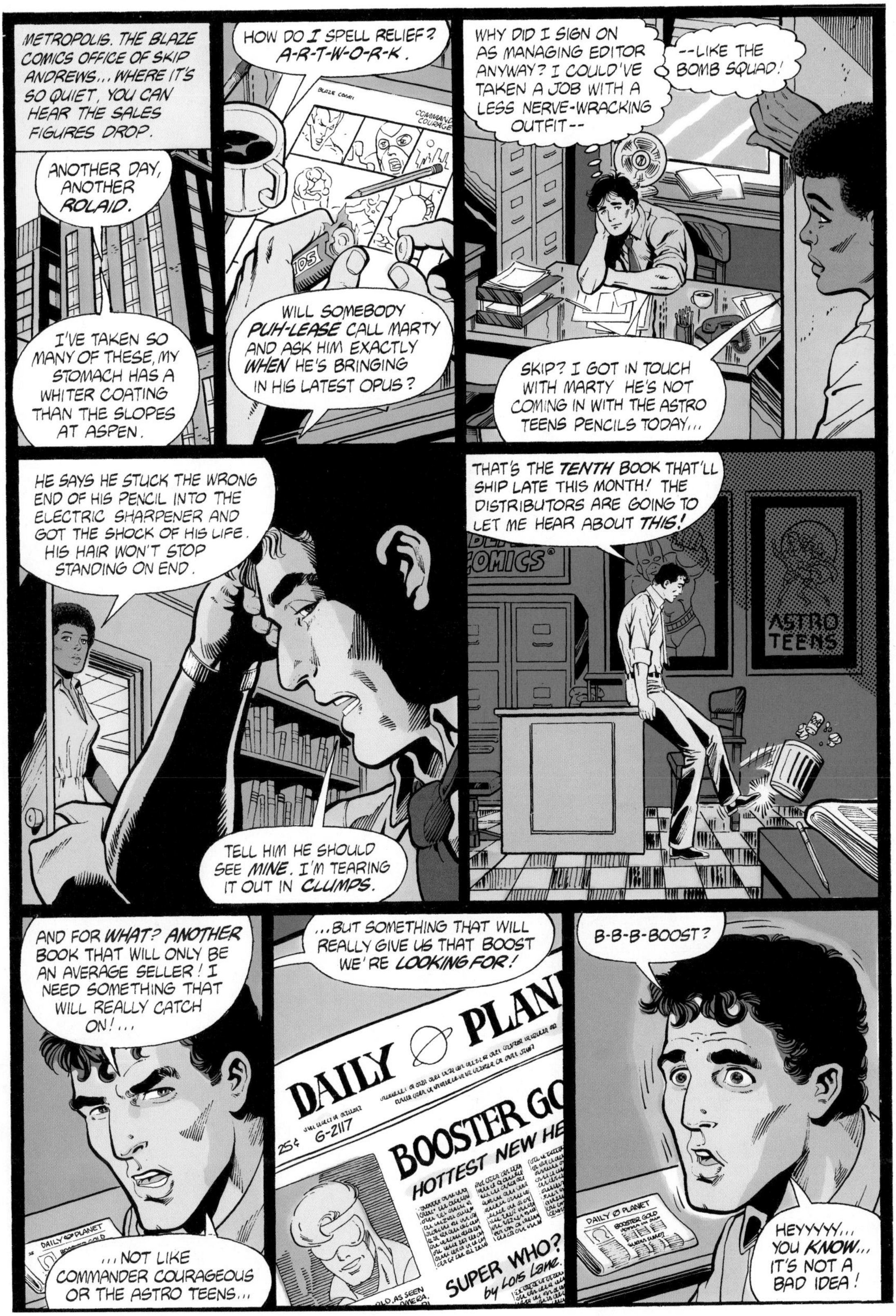
METROPOLIS. THE BLAZE COMICS OFFICE OF SKIP ANDREWS... WHERE IT'S SO QUIET, YOU CAN HEAR THE SALES FIGURES DROP.
HOW DO I SPELL RELIEF? A-R-T-W-O-R-K.
ANOTHER DAY, ANOTHER ROLAID.
I'VE TAKEN SO MANY OF THESE, MY STOMACH HAS A WHITER COATING THAN THE SLOPES AT ASPEN.
WILL SOMEBODY PUH-LEASE CALL MARTY AND ASK HIM EXACTLY WHEN HE'S BRINGING IN HIS LATEST OPUS?
WHY DID I SIGN ON AS MANAGING EDITOR ANYWAY? I COULD'VE TAKEN A JOB WITH A LESS NERVE-WRACKING OUTFIT--
--LIKE THE BOMB SQUAD!
SKIP? I GOT IN TOUCH WITH MARTY HE'S NOT COMING IN WITH THE ASTRO TEENS PENCILS TODAY...
HE SAYS HE STUCK THE WRONG END OF HIS PENCIL INTO THE ELECTRIC SHARPENER AND GOT THE SHOCK OF HIS LIFE. HIS HAIR WON'T STOP STANDING ON END.
TELL HIM HE SHOULD SEE MINE. I'M TEARING IT OUT IN CLUMPS.
THAT'S THE TENTH BOOK THAT'LL SHIP LATE THIS MONTH! THE DISTRIBUTORS ARE GOING TO LET ME HEAR ABOUT THIS!
ASTRO TEENS
AND FOR WHAT? ANOTHER BOOK THAT WILL ONLY BE AN AVERAGE SELLER! I NEED SOMETHING THAT WILL REALLY CATCH ON!...
...NOT LIKE COMMANDER COURAGEOUS OR THE ASTRO TEENS...
...BUT SOMETHING THAT WILL REALLY GIVE US THAT BOOST WE'RE LOOKING FOR!
DAILY
25¢ G-2117
HOTTEST NEW
SUPER WHO? by Lois Lane.
B-B-B-BOOST?
DAILY PLANET
BOOSTER GOLD
HEYYYYY... YOU KNOW... IT'S NOT A BAD IDEA!

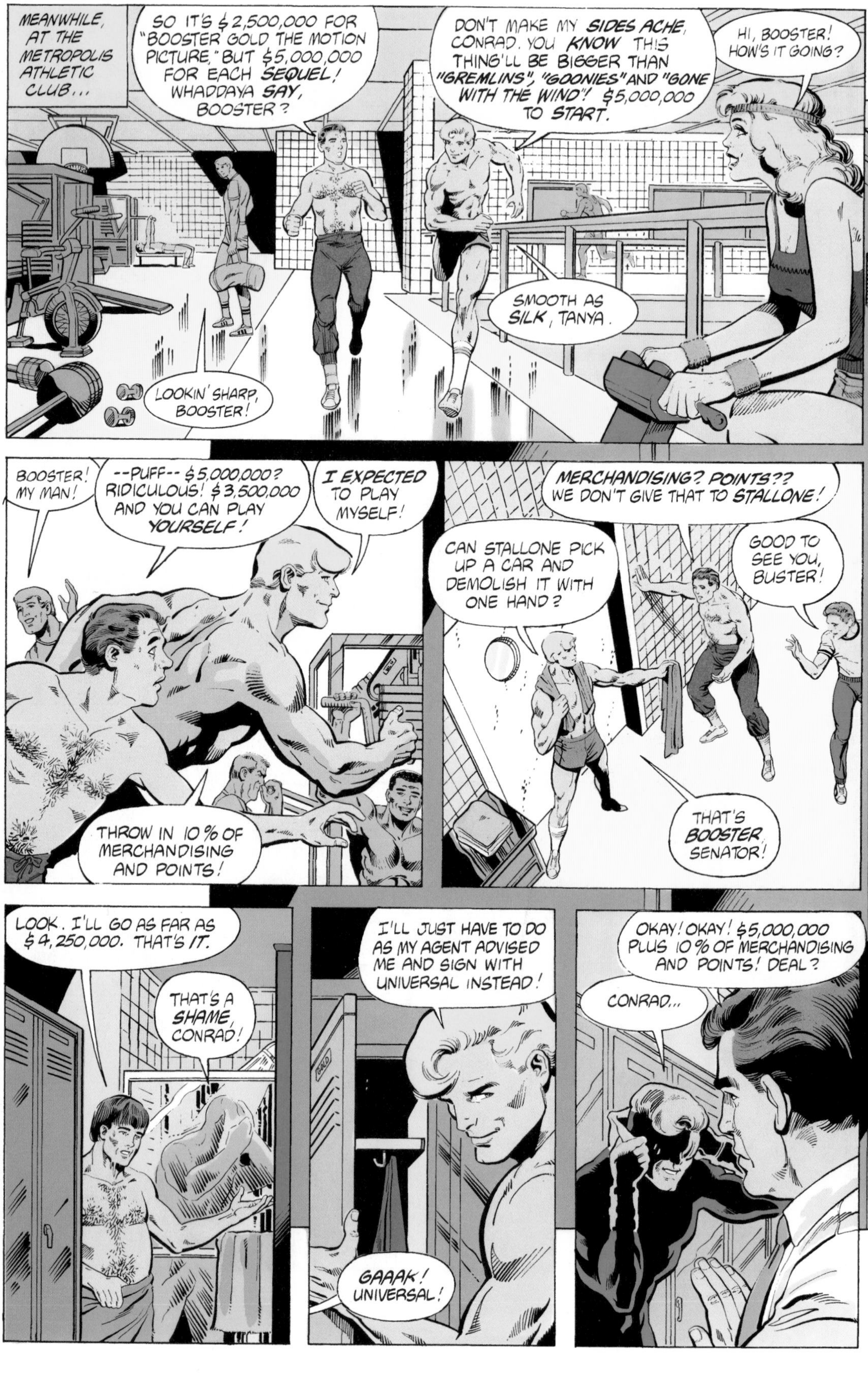

MEANWHILE, AT THE METROPOLIS ATHLETIC CLUB...
SO IT'S $2,500,000 FOR "BOOSTER GOLD THE MOTION PICTURE," BUT $5,000,000 FOR EACH SEQUEL! WHADDAYA SAY, BOOSTER?
DON'T MAKE MY SIDES ACHE, CONRAD. YOU KNOW THIS THING'LL BE BIGGER THAN "GREMLINS", "GOONIES" AND "GONE WITH THE WIND"! $5,000,000 TO START.
HI, BOOSTER! HOW'S IT GOING?
SMOOTH AS SILK, TANYA.
LOOKIN' SHARP, BOOSTER!
BOOSTER! MY MAN!
--PUFF-- $5,000,000? RIDICULOUS! $3,500,000 AND YOU CAN PLAY YOURSELF!
I EXPECTED TO PLAY MYSELF!
THROW IN 10% OF MERCHANDISING AND POINTS!
MERCHANDISING? POINTS?? WE DON'T GIVE THAT TO STALLONE!
CAN STALLONE PICK UP A CAR AND DEMOLISH IT WITH ONE HAND?
GOOD TO SEE YOU, BUSTER!
THAT'S BOOSTER, SENATOR!
LOOK. I'LL GO AS FAR AS $4,250,000. THAT'S IT.
THAT'S A SHAME, CONRAD!
I'LL JUST HAVE TO DO AS MY AGENT ADVISED ME AND SIGN WITH UNIVERSAL INSTEAD!
GAAAK! UNIVERSAL!
OKAY! OKAY! $5,000,000 PLUS 10% OF MERCHANDISING AND POINTS! DEAL?
CONRAD...

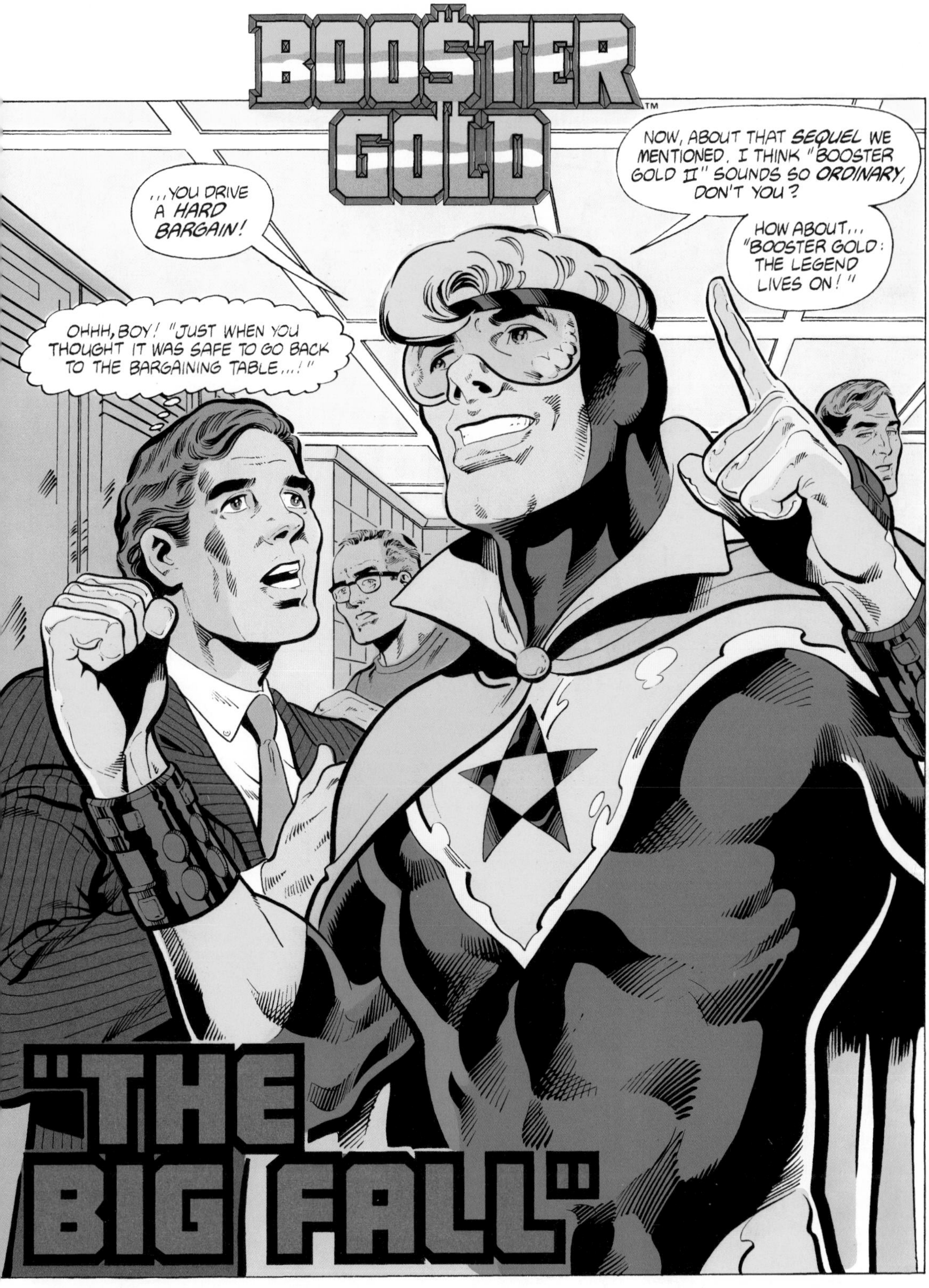
BOO$TER GOLD™
...YOU DRIVE A HARD BARGAIN!
NOW, ABOUT THAT SEQUEL WE MENTIONED. I THINK "BOOSTER GOLD II" SOUNDS SO ORDINARY, DON'T YOU?
HOW ABOUT... "BOOSTER GOLD: THE LEGEND LIVES ON!"
OHHH, BOY! "JUST WHEN YOU THOUGHT IT WAS SAFE TO GO BACK TO THE BARGAINING TABLE...!"
"THE BIG FALL"

CREATED, PLOTTED AND WRITTEN BY *DAN JURGENS* • INKED BY *MIKE DeCARLO* • COLORED BY *TOM ZIUKO* • LETTERED BY *AGUSTIN MAS* • EDITED BY *JANICE RACE*

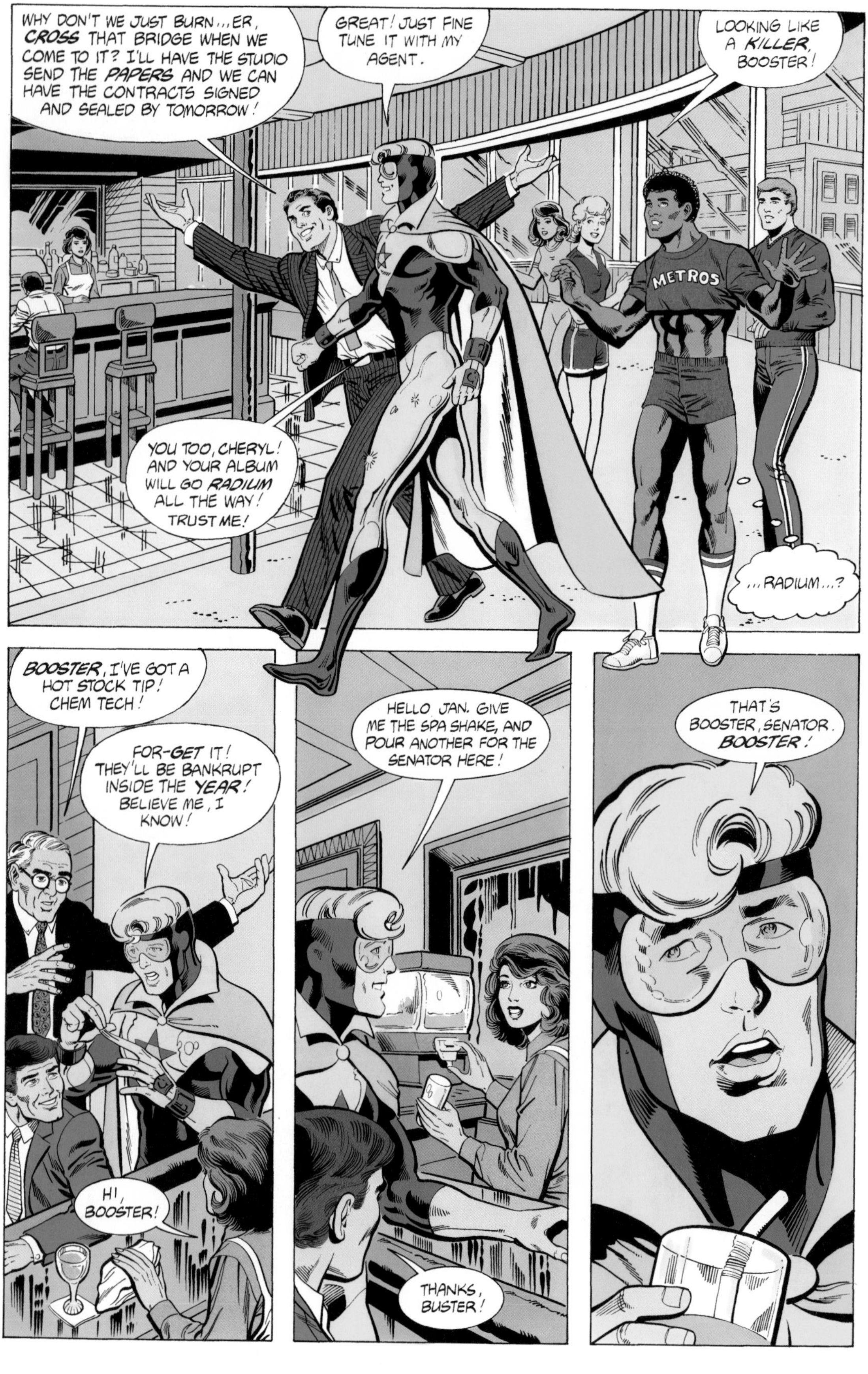
WHY DON'T WE JUST BURN... ER, CROSS THAT BRIDGE WHEN WE COME TO IT? I'LL HAVE THE STUDIO SEND THE PAPERS AND WE CAN HAVE THE CONTRACTS SIGNED AND SEALED BY TOMORROW!
GREAT! JUST FINE TUNE IT WITH MY AGENT.
LOOKING LIKE A KILLER, BOOSTER!
YOU TOO, CHERYL! AND YOUR ALBUM WILL GO RADIUM ALL THE WAY! TRUST ME!
...RADIUM...?
BOOSTER, I'VE GOT A HOT STOCK TIP! CHEM TECH!
FOR-GET IT! THEY'LL BE BANKRUPT INSIDE THE YEAR! BELIEVE ME, I KNOW!
HI, BOOSTER!
HELLO JAN. GIVE ME THE SPA SHAKE, AND POUR ANOTHER FOR THE SENATOR HERE!
THANKS, BUSTER!
THAT'S BOOSTER, SENATOR. BOOSTER!

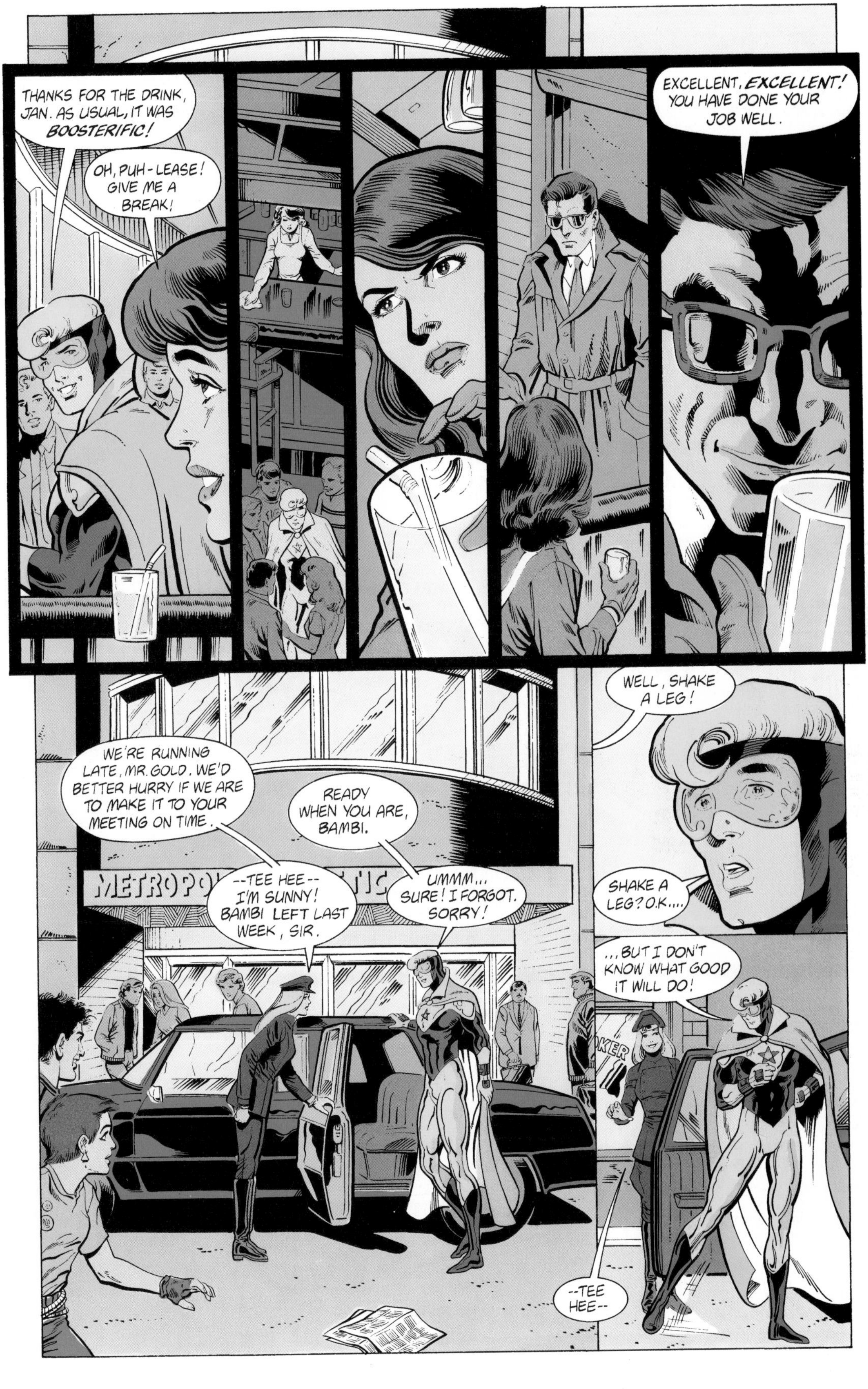
THANKS FOR THE DRINK, JAN. AS USUAL, IT WAS BOOSTERIFIC!
OH, PUH-LEASE! GIVE ME A BREAK!
EXCELLENT, EXCELLENT! YOU HAVE DONE YOUR JOB WELL.
WE'RE RUNNING LATE, MR. GOLD. WE'D BETTER HURRY IF WE ARE TO MAKE IT TO YOUR MEETING ON TIME.
READY WHEN YOU ARE, BAMBI.
--TEE HEE-- I'M SUNNY! BAMBI LEFT LAST WEEK, SIR.
UMMM... SURE! I FORGOT. SORRY!
WELL, SHAKE A LEG!
SHAKE A LEG? O.K....
...BUT I DON'T KNOW WHAT GOOD IT WILL DO!
--TEE HEE--

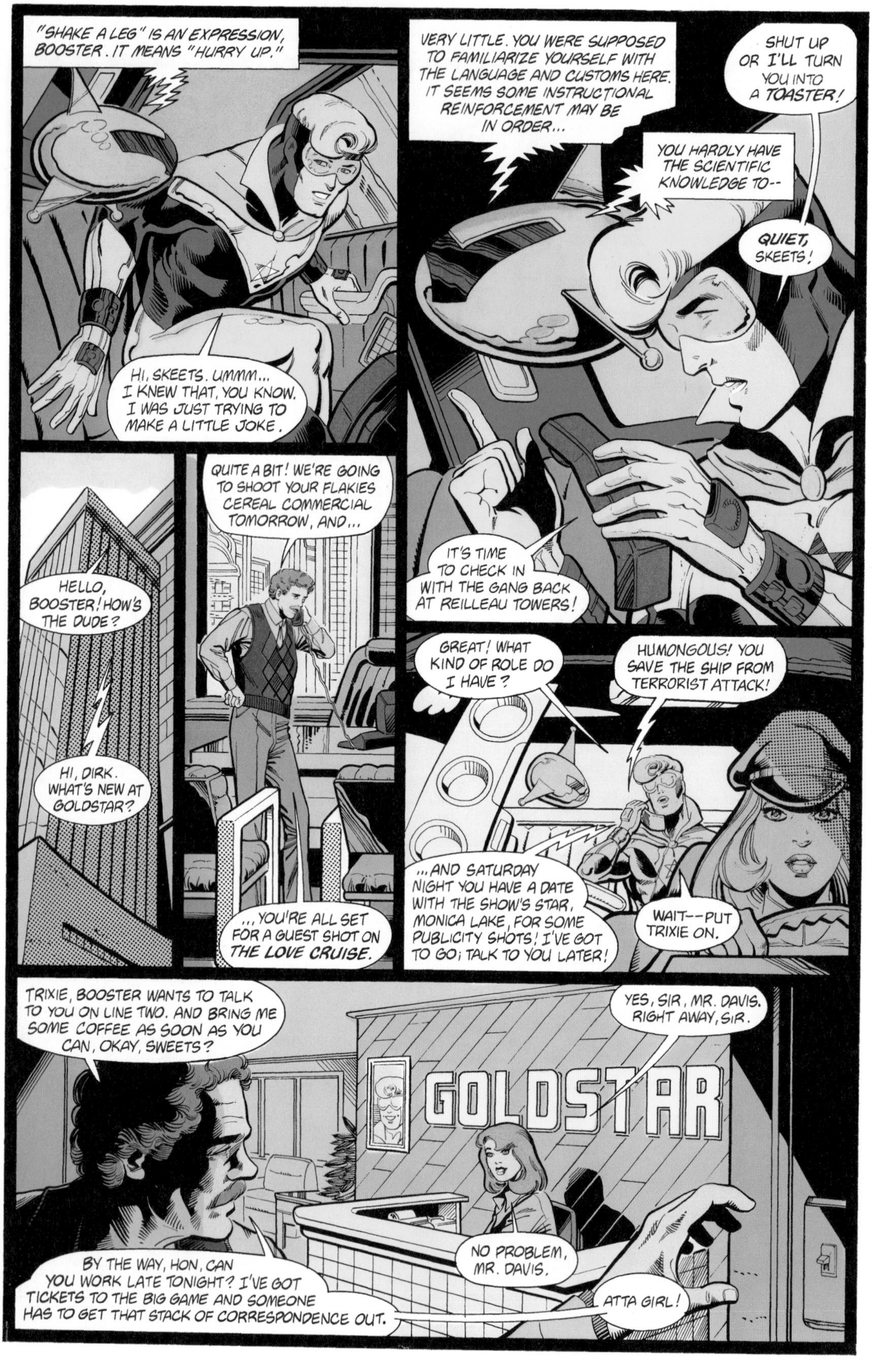

"SHAKE A LEG" IS AN EXPRESSION, BOOSTER. IT MEANS "HURRY UP."
HI, SKEETS. UMMM... I KNEW THAT, YOU KNOW. I WAS JUST TRYING TO MAKE A LITTLE JOKE.
VERY LITTLE. YOU WERE SUPPOSED TO FAMILIARIZE YOURSELF WITH THE LANGUAGE AND CUSTOMS HERE. IT SEEMS SOME INSTRUCTIONAL REINFORCEMENT MAY BE IN ORDER...
SHUT UP OR I'LL TURN YOU INTO A TOASTER!
YOU HARDLY HAVE THE SCIENTIFIC KNOWLEDGE TO--
QUIET, SKEETS!
IT'S TIME TO CHECK IN WITH THE GANG BACK AT REILLEAU TOWERS!
HELLO, BOOSTER! HOW'S THE DUDE?
HI, DIRK. WHAT'S NEW AT GOLDSTAR?
QUITE A BIT! WE'RE GOING TO SHOOT YOUR FLAKIES CEREAL COMMERCIAL TOMORROW, AND...
...YOU'RE ALL SET FOR A GUEST SHOT ON THE LOVE CRUISE.
GREAT! WHAT KIND OF ROLE DO I HAVE?
HUMONGOUS! YOU SAVE THE SHIP FROM TERRORIST ATTACK!
...AND SATURDAY NIGHT YOU HAVE A DATE WITH THE SHOW'S STAR, MONICA LAKE, FOR SOME PUBLICITY SHOTS! I'VE GOT TO GO; TALK TO YOU LATER!
WAIT--PUT TRIXIE ON.
TRIXIE, BOOSTER WANTS TO TALK TO YOU ON LINE TWO. AND BRING ME SOME COFFEE AS SOON AS YOU CAN, OKAY, SWEETS?
YES, SIR, MR. DAVIS. RIGHT AWAY, SIR.
GOLDSTAR
BY THE WAY, HON, CAN YOU WORK LATE TONIGHT? I'VE GOT TICKETS TO THE BIG GAME AND SOMEONE HAS TO GET THAT STACK OF CORRESPONDENCE OUT.
NO PROBLEM, MR. DAVIS.
ATTA GIRL!

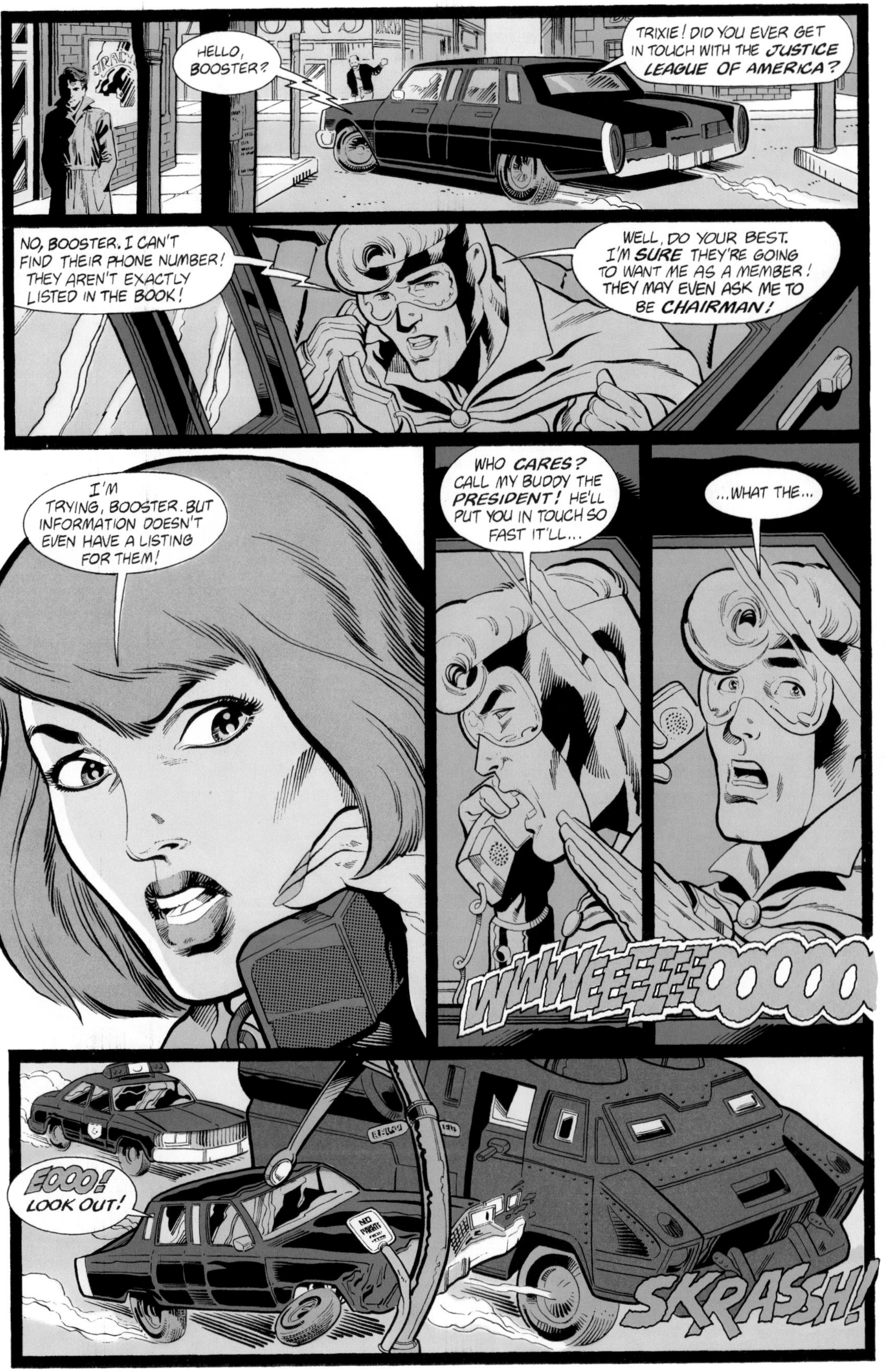
HELLO, BOOSTER?
TRIXIE! DID YOU EVER GET IN TOUCH WITH THE JUSTICE LEAGUE OF AMERICA?
NO, BOOSTER. I CAN'T FIND THEIR PHONE NUMBER! THEY AREN'T EXACTLY LISTED IN THE BOOK!
WELL, DO YOUR BEST. I'M SURE THEY'RE GOING TO WANT ME AS A MEMBER! THEY MAY EVEN ASK ME TO BE CHAIRMAN!
I'M TRYING, BOOSTER. BUT INFORMATION DOESN'T EVEN HAVE A LISTING FOR THEM!
WHO CARES? CALL MY BUDDY THE PRESIDENT! HE'LL PUT YOU IN TOUCH SO FAST IT'LL...
...WHAT THE...
WWWEEEEEOOOOO
EOOO! LOOK OUT!
SKRASSH!

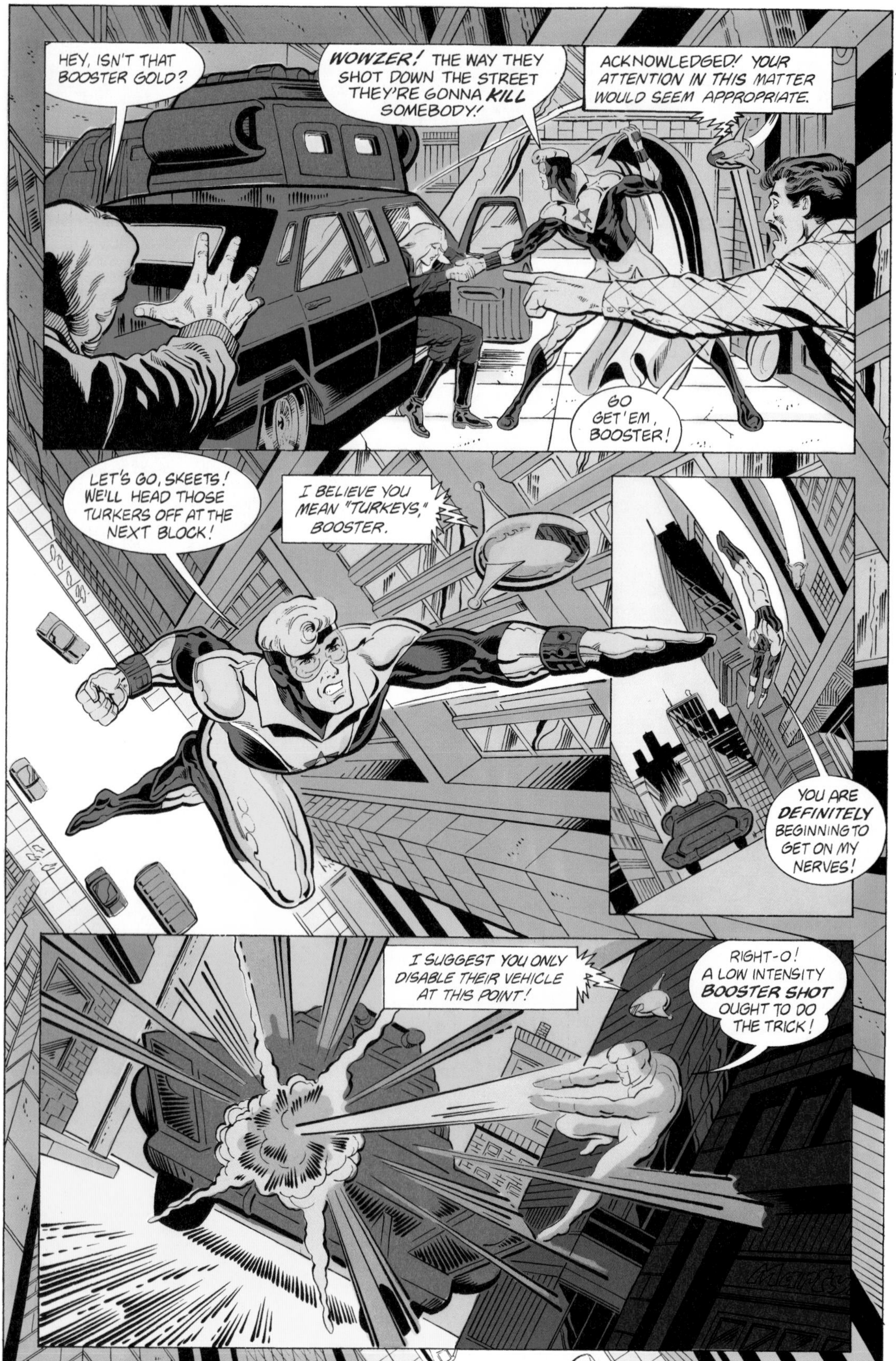
HEY, ISN'T THAT BOOSTER GOLD?
WOWZER! THE WAY THEY SHOT DOWN THE STREET THEY'RE GONNA KILL SOMEBODY!
ACKNOWLEDGED! YOUR ATTENTION IN THIS MATTER WOULD SEEM APPROPRIATE.
GO GET'EM, BOOSTER!
LET'S GO, SKEETS! WE'LL HEAD THOSE TURKERS OFF AT THE NEXT BLOCK!
I BELIEVE YOU MEAN "TURKEYS," BOOSTER.
YOU ARE DEFINITELY BEGINNING TO GET ON MY NERVES!
I SUGGEST YOU ONLY DISABLE THEIR VEHICLE AT THIS POINT!
RIGHT-O! A LOW INTENSITY BOOSTER SHOT OUGHT TO DO THE TRICK!

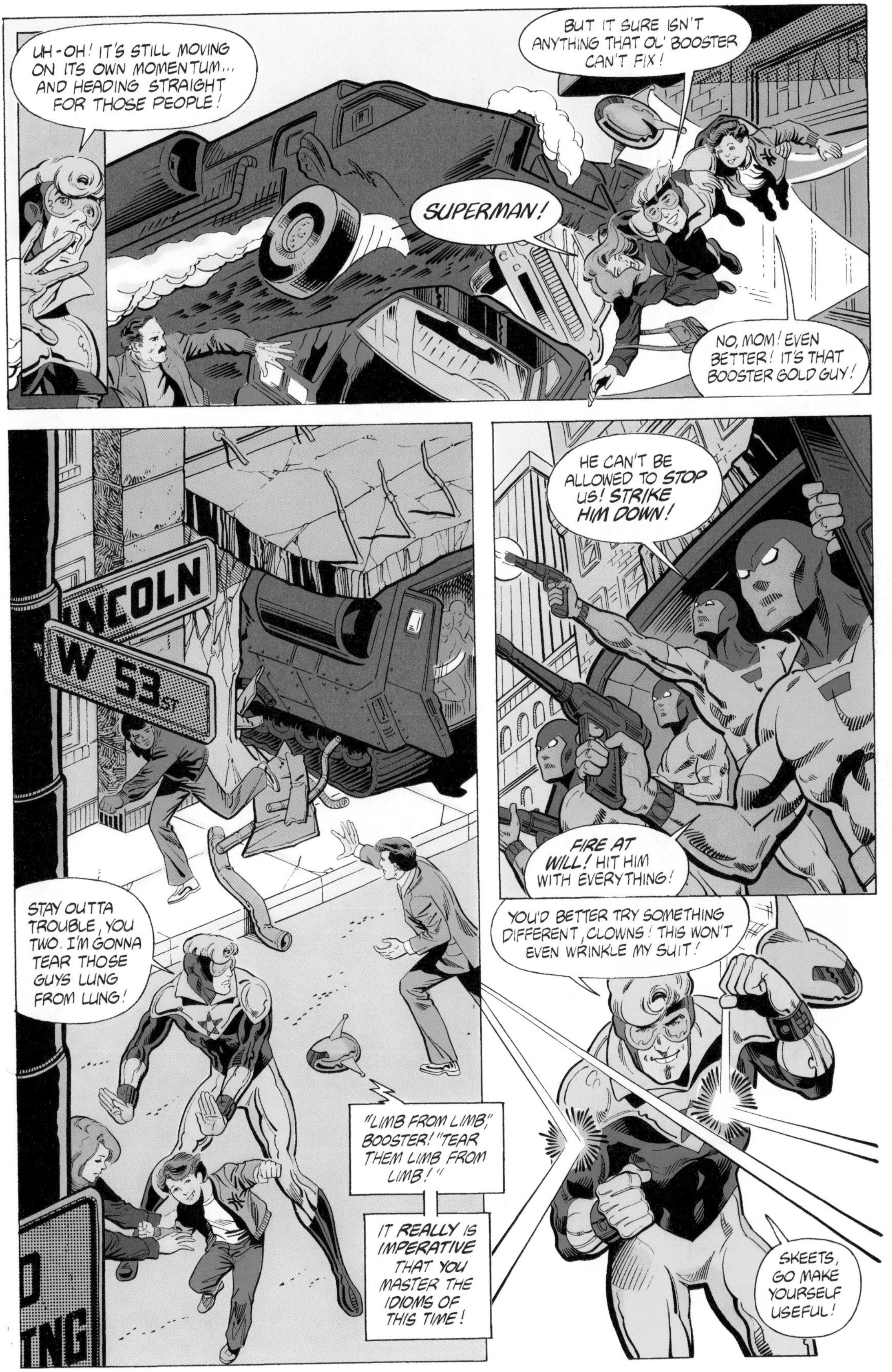

UH-OH! IT'S STILL MOVING ON ITS OWN MOMENTUM... AND HEADING STRAIGHT FOR THOSE PEOPLE!
BUT IT SURE ISN'T ANYTHING THAT OL' BOOSTER CAN'T FIX!
SUPERMAN!
NO, MOM! EVEN BETTER! IT'S THAT BOOSTER GOLD GUY!
LINCOLN
W 53 ST
HE CAN'T BE ALLOWED TO STOP US! STRIKE HIM DOWN!
FIRE AT WILL! HIT HIM WITH EVERYTHING!
STAY OUTTA TROUBLE, YOU TWO. I'M GONNA TEAR THOSE GUYS LUNG FROM LUNG!
"LIMB FROM LIMB," BOOSTER! "TEAR THEM LIMB FROM LIMB!"
IT REALLY IS IMPERATIVE THAT YOU MASTER THE IDIOMS OF THIS TIME!
YOU'D BETTER TRY SOMETHING DIFFERENT, CLOWNS! THIS WON'T EVEN WRINKLE MY SUIT!
SKEETS, GO MAKE YOURSELF USEFUL!

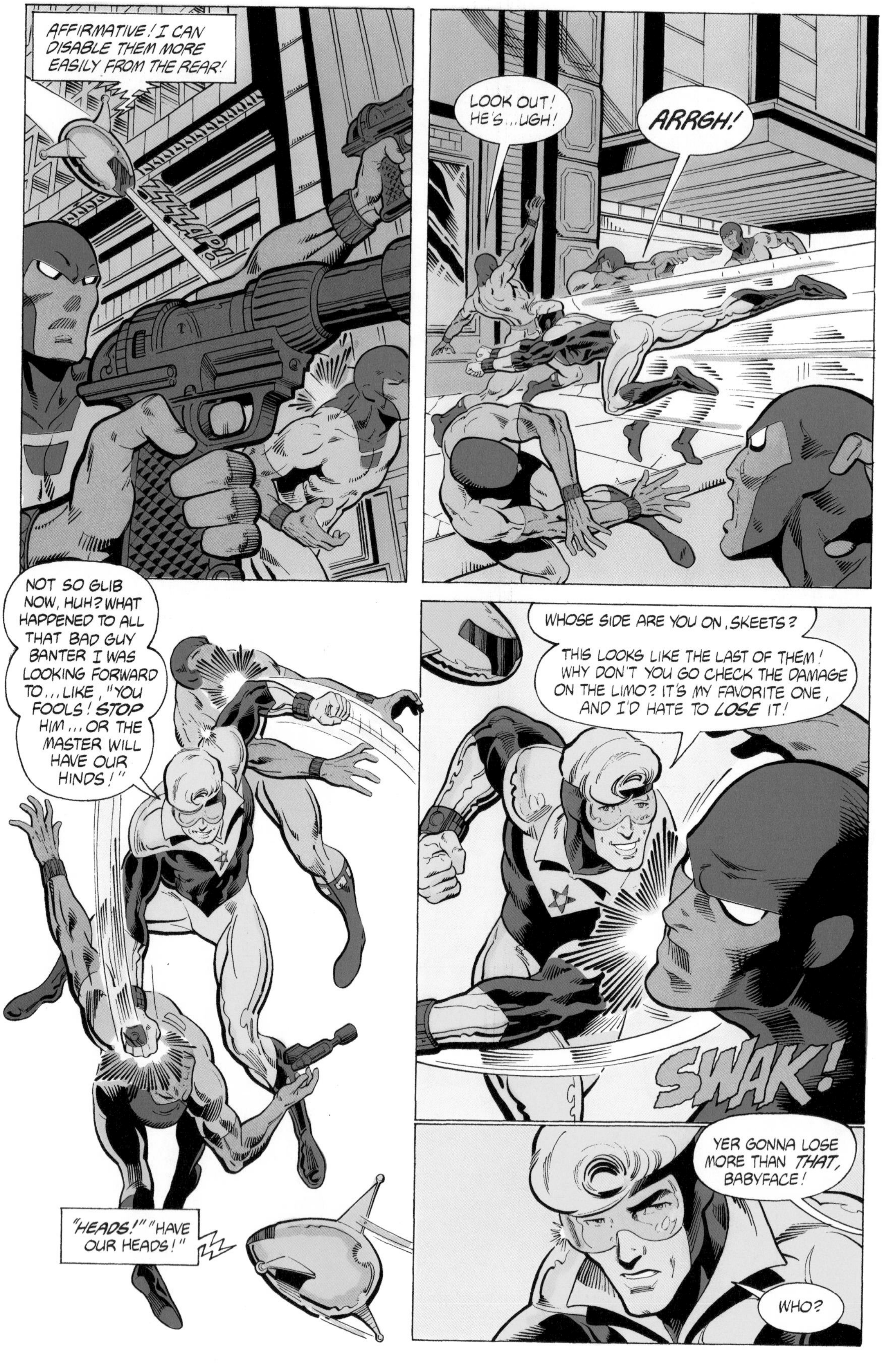
AFFIRMATIVE! I CAN DISABLE THEM MORE EASILY FROM THE REAR!
LOOK OUT! HE'S...UGH!
ARRGH!
NOT SO GLIB NOW, HUH? WHAT HAPPENED TO ALL THAT BAD GUY BANTER I WAS LOOKING FORWARD TO...LIKE, "YOU FOOLS! STOP HIM...OR THE MASTER WILL HAVE OUR HINDS!"
"HEADS!" "HAVE OUR HEADS!"
WHOSE SIDE ARE YOU ON, SKEETS?
THIS LOOKS LIKE THE LAST OF THEM! WHY DON'T YOU GO CHECK THE DAMAGE ON THE LIMO? IT'S MY FAVORITE ONE, AND I'D HATE TO LOSE IT!
SWAK!
YER GONNA LOSE MORE THAN THAT, BABYFACE!
WHO?

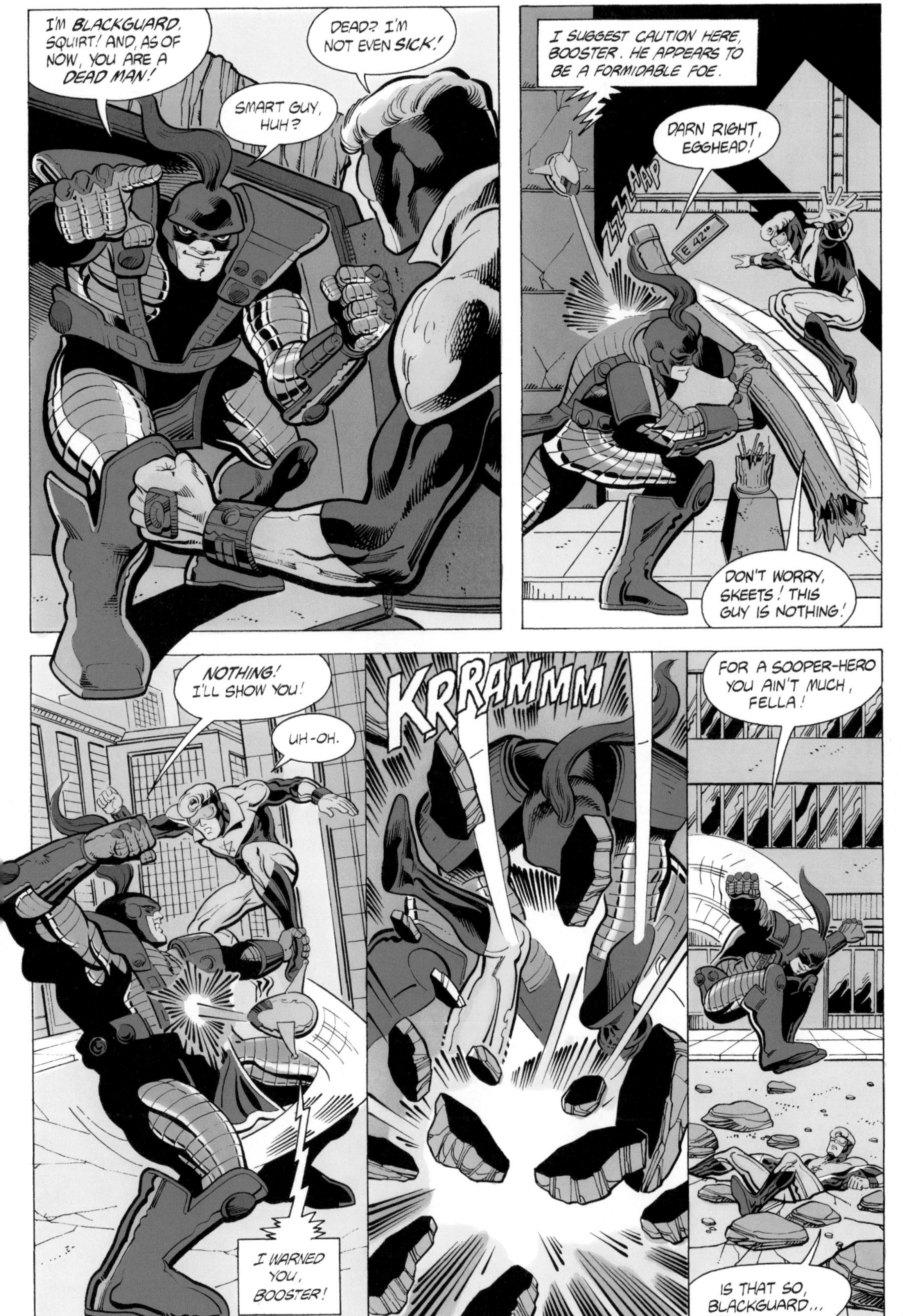
I'M BLACKGUARD, SQUIRT! AND, AS OF NOW, YOU ARE A DEAD MAN!
DEAD? I'M NOT EVEN SICK!
SMART GUY, HUH?
I SUGGEST CAUTION HERE, BOOSTER. HE APPEARS TO BE A FORMIDABLE FOE.
DARN RIGHT, EGGHEAD!
E 42
DON'T WORRY, SKEETS! THIS GUY IS NOTHING!
NOTHING! I'LL SHOW YOU!
UH-OH.
I WARNED YOU, BOOSTER!
KRRAMMM
FOR A SOOPER-HERO YOU AIN'T MUCH, FELLA!
IS THAT SO, BLACKGUARD...

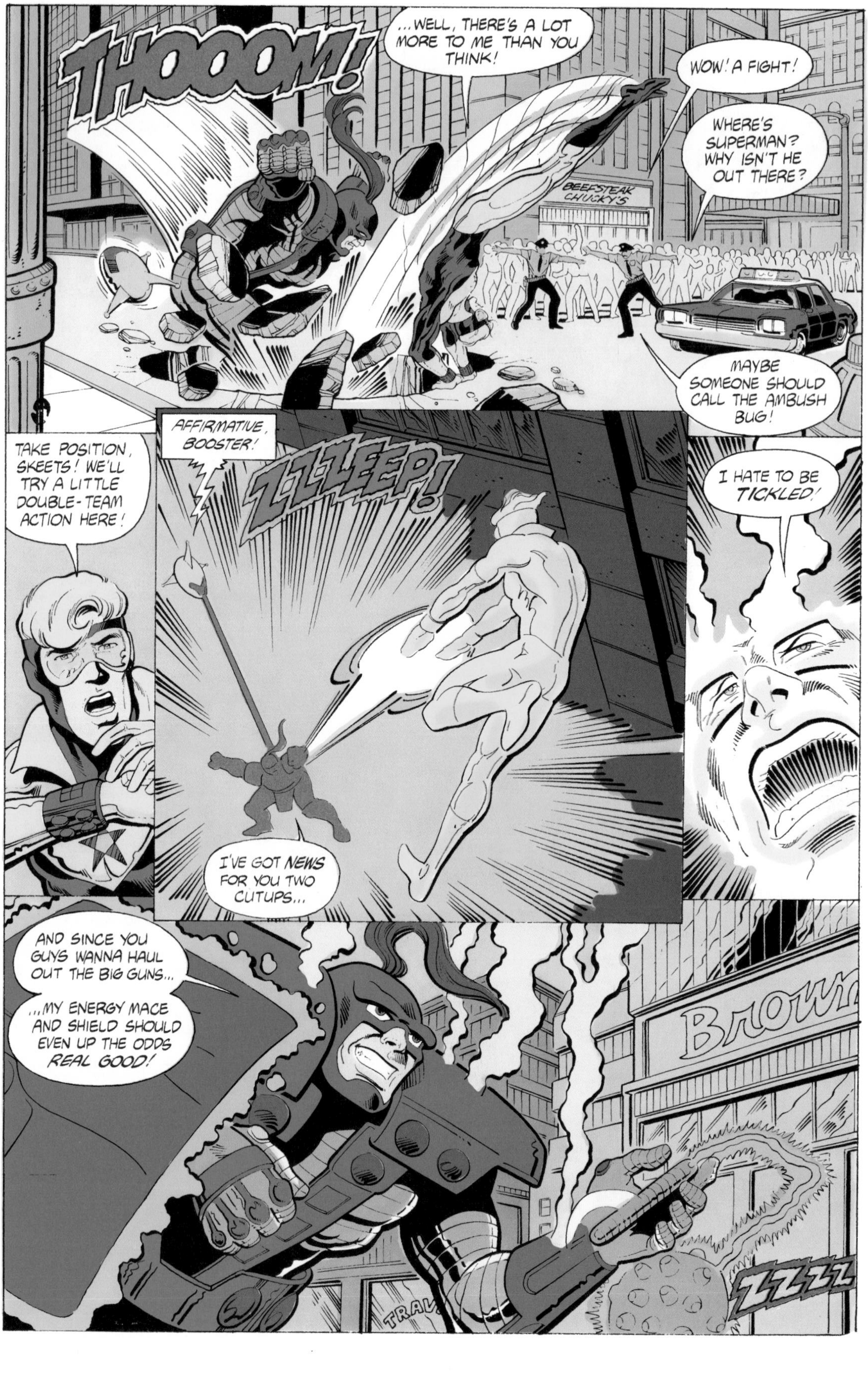
THOOOM!
...WELL, THERE'S A LOT MORE TO ME THAN YOU THINK!
WOW! A FIGHT!
WHERE'S SUPERMAN? WHY ISN'T HE OUT THERE?
BEEFSTEAK CHUCKY'S
MAYBE SOMEONE SHOULD CALL THE AMBUSH BUG!
TAKE POSITION, SKEETS! WE'LL TRY A LITTLE DOUBLE-TEAM ACTION HERE!
AFFIRMATIVE, BOOSTER!
ZZZEEP!
I'VE GOT NEWS FOR YOU TWO CUTUPS...
I HATE TO BE TICKLED!
AND SINCE YOU GUYS WANNA HAUL OUT THE BIG GUNS...
...MY ENERGY MACE AND SHIELD SHOULD EVEN UP THE ODDS REAL GOOD!
ZZZZ

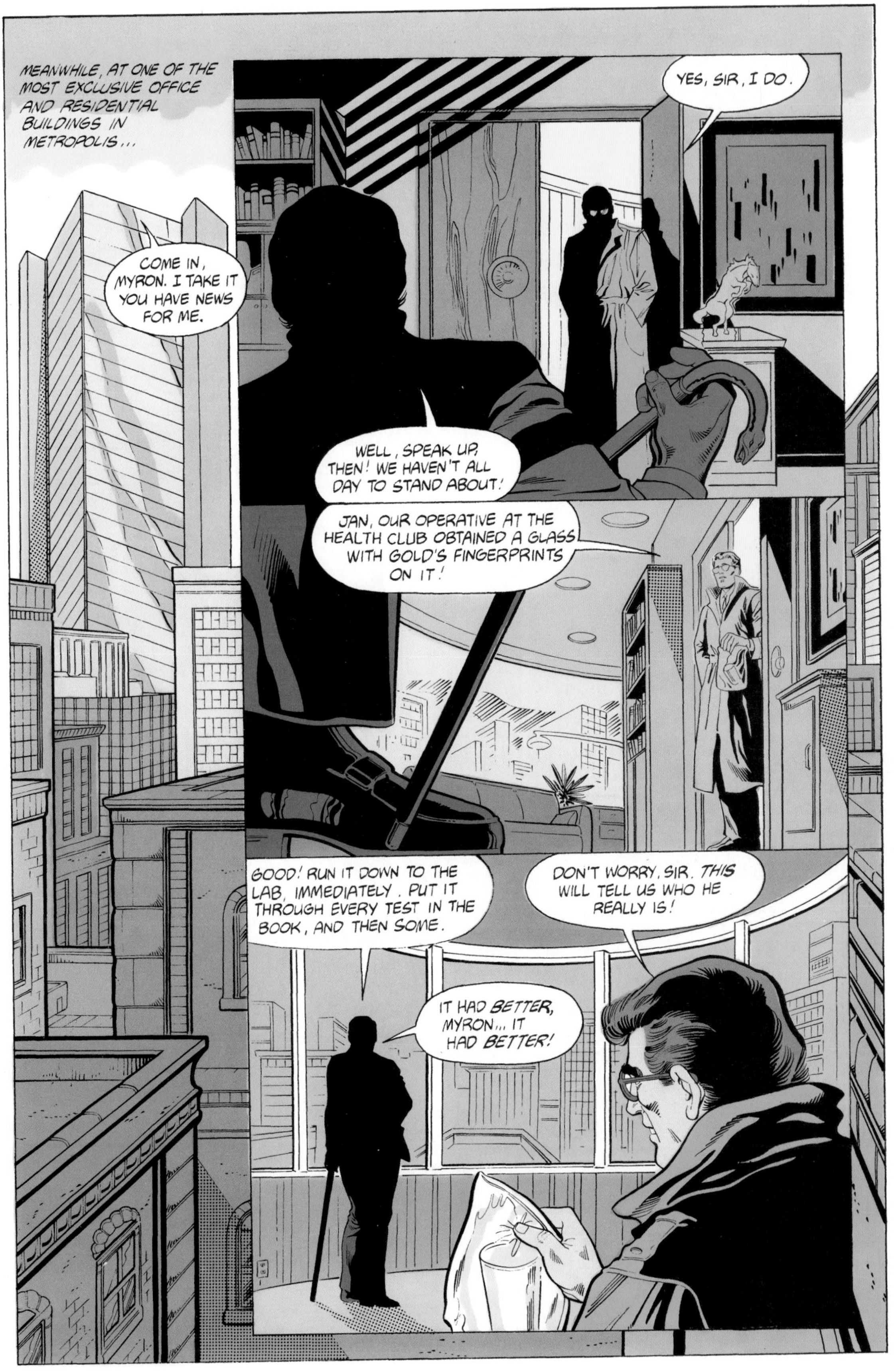
MEANWHILE, AT ONE OF THE MOST EXCLUSIVE OFFICE AND RESIDENTIAL BUILDINGS IN METROPOLIS...
COME IN, MYRON. I TAKE IT YOU HAVE NEWS FOR ME.
YES, SIR, I DO.
WELL, SPEAK UP, THEN! WE HAVEN'T ALL DAY TO STAND ABOUT!
JAN, OUR OPERATIVE AT THE HEALTH CLUB OBTAINED A GLASS WITH GOLD'S FINGERPRINTS ON IT!
GOOD! RUN IT DOWN TO THE LAB, IMMEDIATELY. PUT IT THROUGH EVERY TEST IN THE BOOK, AND THEN SOME.
DON'T WORRY, SIR. THIS WILL TELL US WHO HE REALLY IS!
IT HAD BETTER, MYRON... IT HAD BETTER!

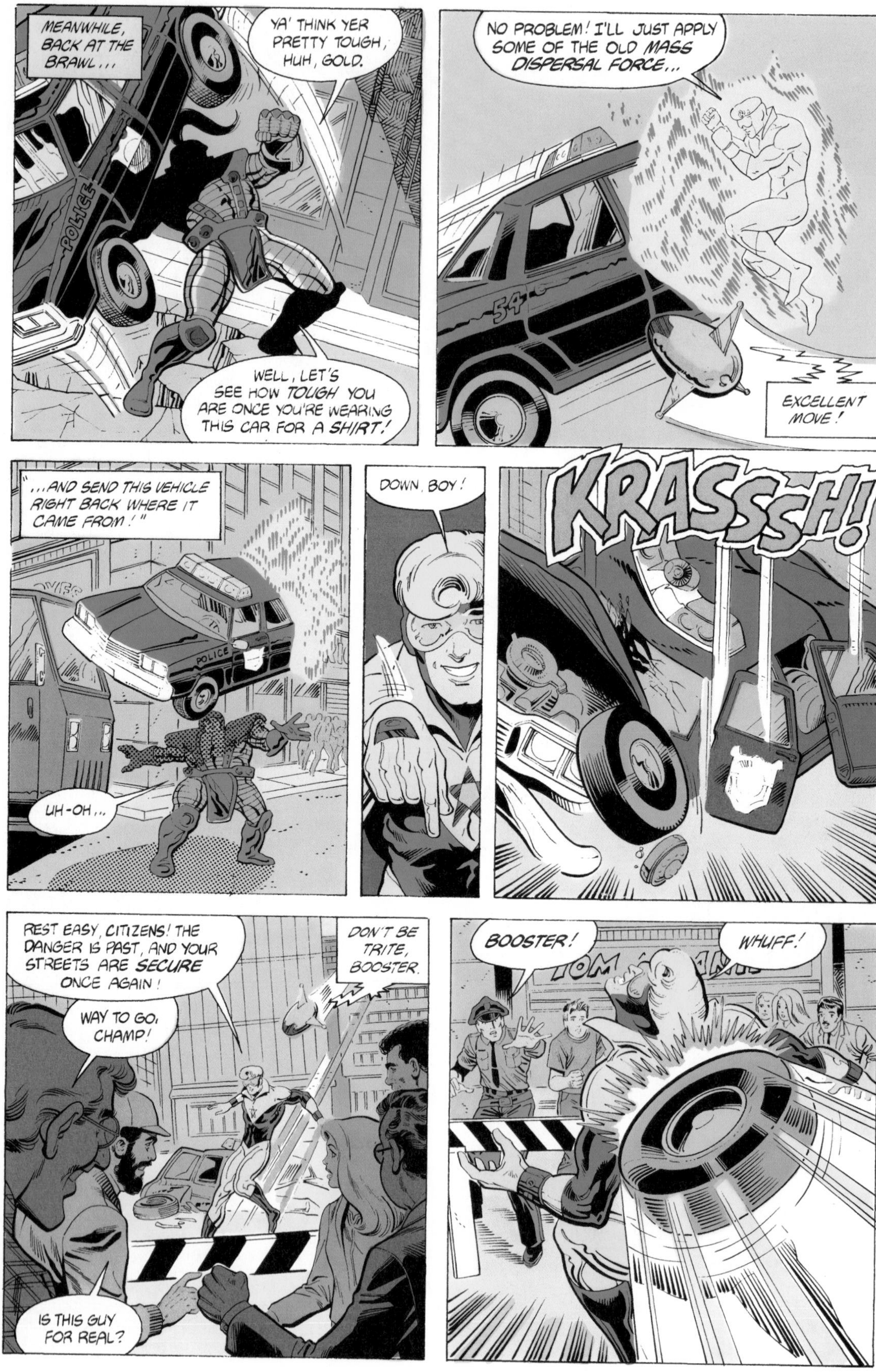
MEANWHILE, BACK AT THE BRAWL...
YA' THINK YER PRETTY TOUGH, HUH, GOLD.
WELL, LET'S SEE HOW TOUGH YOU ARE ONCE YOU'RE WEARING THIS CAR FOR A SHIRT!
NO PROBLEM! I'LL JUST APPLY SOME OF THE OLD MASS DISPERSAL FORCE...
EXCELLENT MOVE!
"...AND SEND THIS VEHICLE RIGHT BACK WHERE IT CAME FROM!"
POLICE
UH-OH...
DOWN, BOY!
KRASSSH!
REST EASY, CITIZENS! THE DANGER IS PAST, AND YOUR STREETS ARE SECURE ONCE AGAIN!
DON'T BE TRITE, BOOSTER.
WAY TO GO, CHAMP!
IS THIS GUY FOR REAL?
BOOSTER!
WHUFF!

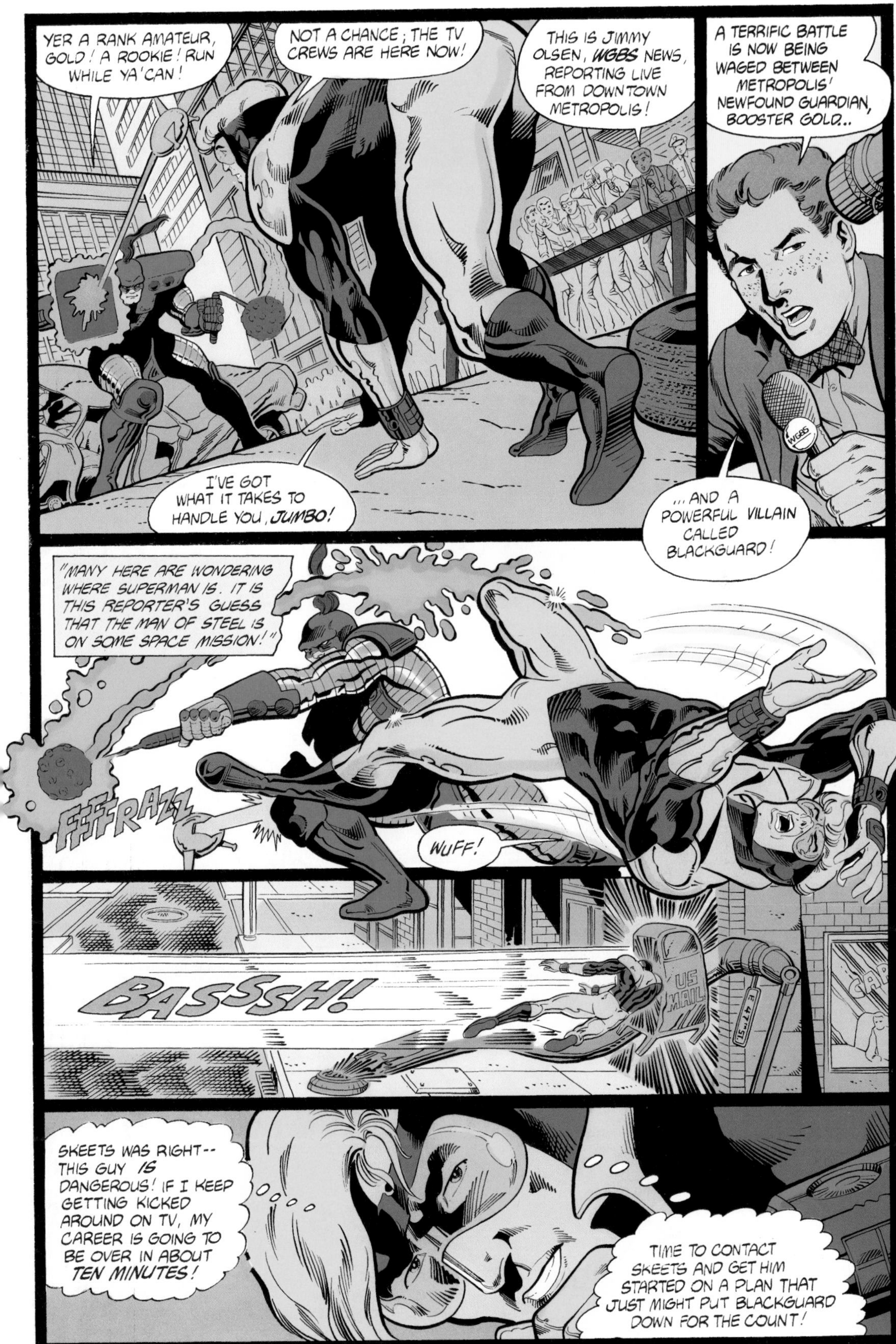
YER A RANK AMATEUR, GOLD! A ROOKIE! RUN WHILE YA'CAN!
NOT A CHANCE; THE TV CREWS ARE HERE NOW!
THIS IS JIMMY OLSEN, WGBS NEWS, REPORTING LIVE FROM DOWNTOWN METROPOLIS!
A TERRIFIC BATTLE IS NOW BEING WAGED BETWEEN METROPOLIS' NEWFOUND GUARDIAN, BOOSTER GOLD...
I'VE GOT WHAT IT TAKES TO HANDLE YOU, JUMBO!
...AND A POWERFUL VILLAIN CALLED BLACKGUARD!
"MANY HERE ARE WONDERING WHERE SUPERMAN IS. IT IS THIS REPORTER'S GUESS THAT THE MAN OF STEEL IS ON SOME SPACE MISSION!"
FFFRAZZ
WUFF!
BASSSH!
US MAIL
SKEETS WAS RIGHT-- THIS GUY IS DANGEROUS! IF I KEEP GETTING KICKED AROUND ON TV, MY CAREER IS GOING TO BE OVER IN ABOUT TEN MINUTES!
TIME TO CONTACT SKEETS AND GET HIM STARTED ON A PLAN THAT JUST MIGHT PUT BLACKGUARD DOWN FOR THE COUNT!

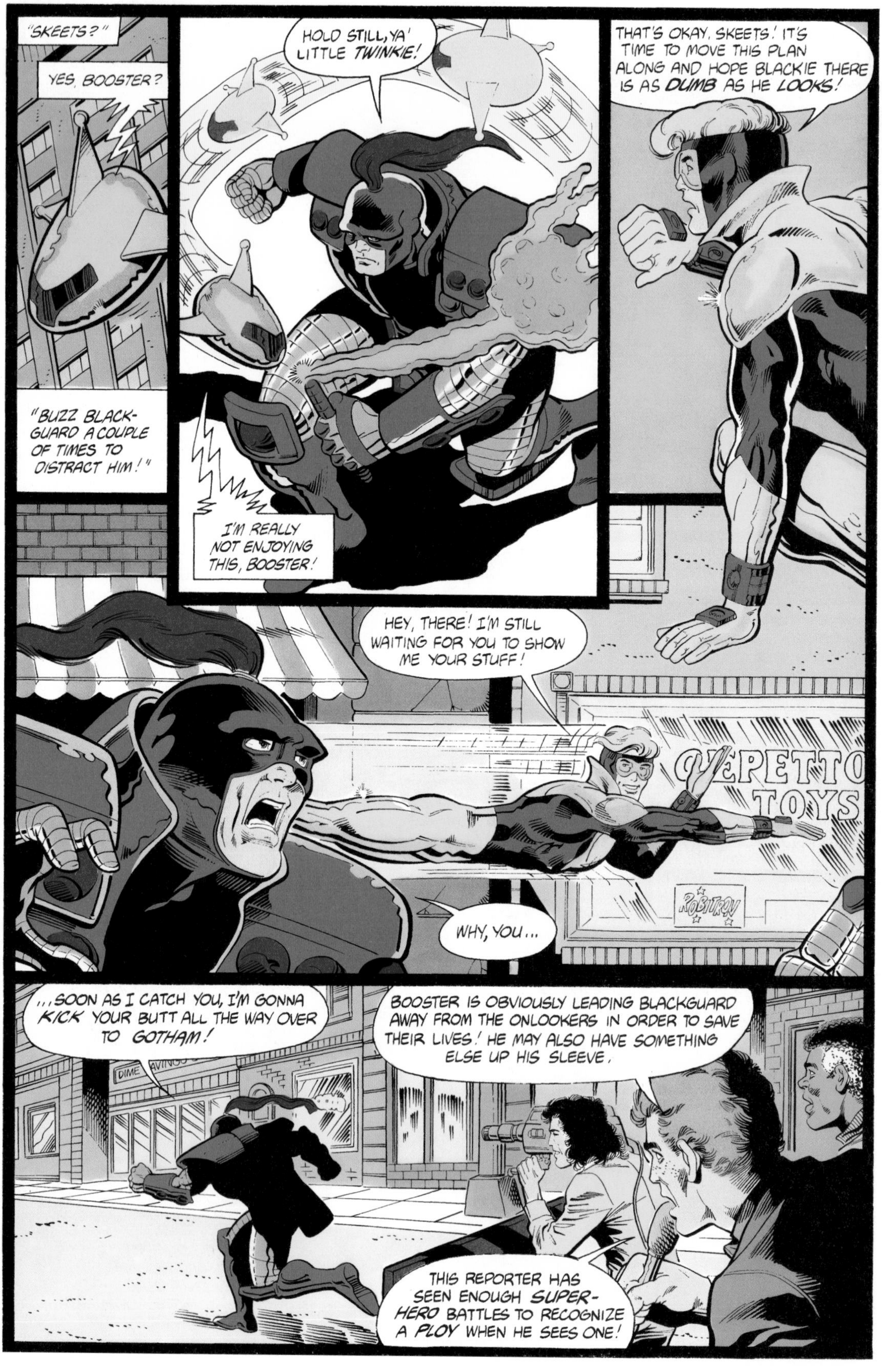
"SKEETS?"
YES, BOOSTER?
HOLD STILL, YA' LITTLE TWINKIE!
"BUZZ BLACKGUARD A COUPLE OF TIMES TO DISTRACT HIM!"
I'M REALLY NOT ENJOYING THIS, BOOSTER!
THAT'S OKAY, SKEETS! IT'S TIME TO MOVE THIS PLAN ALONG AND HOPE BLACKIE THERE IS AS DUMB AS HE LOOKS!
HEY, THERE! I'M STILL WAITING FOR YOU TO SHOW ME YOUR STUFF!
GEPETTO TOYS
ROBITRON
WHY, YOU...
...SOON AS I CATCH YOU, I'M GONNA KICK YOUR BUTT ALL THE WAY OVER TO GOTHAM!
BOOSTER IS OBVIOUSLY LEADING BLACKGUARD AWAY FROM THE ONLOOKERS IN ORDER TO SAVE THEIR LIVES! HE MAY ALSO HAVE SOMETHING ELSE UP HIS SLEEVE.
DIME
THIS REPORTER HAS SEEN ENOUGH SUPER-HERO BATTLES TO RECOGNIZE A PLOY WHEN HE SEES ONE!

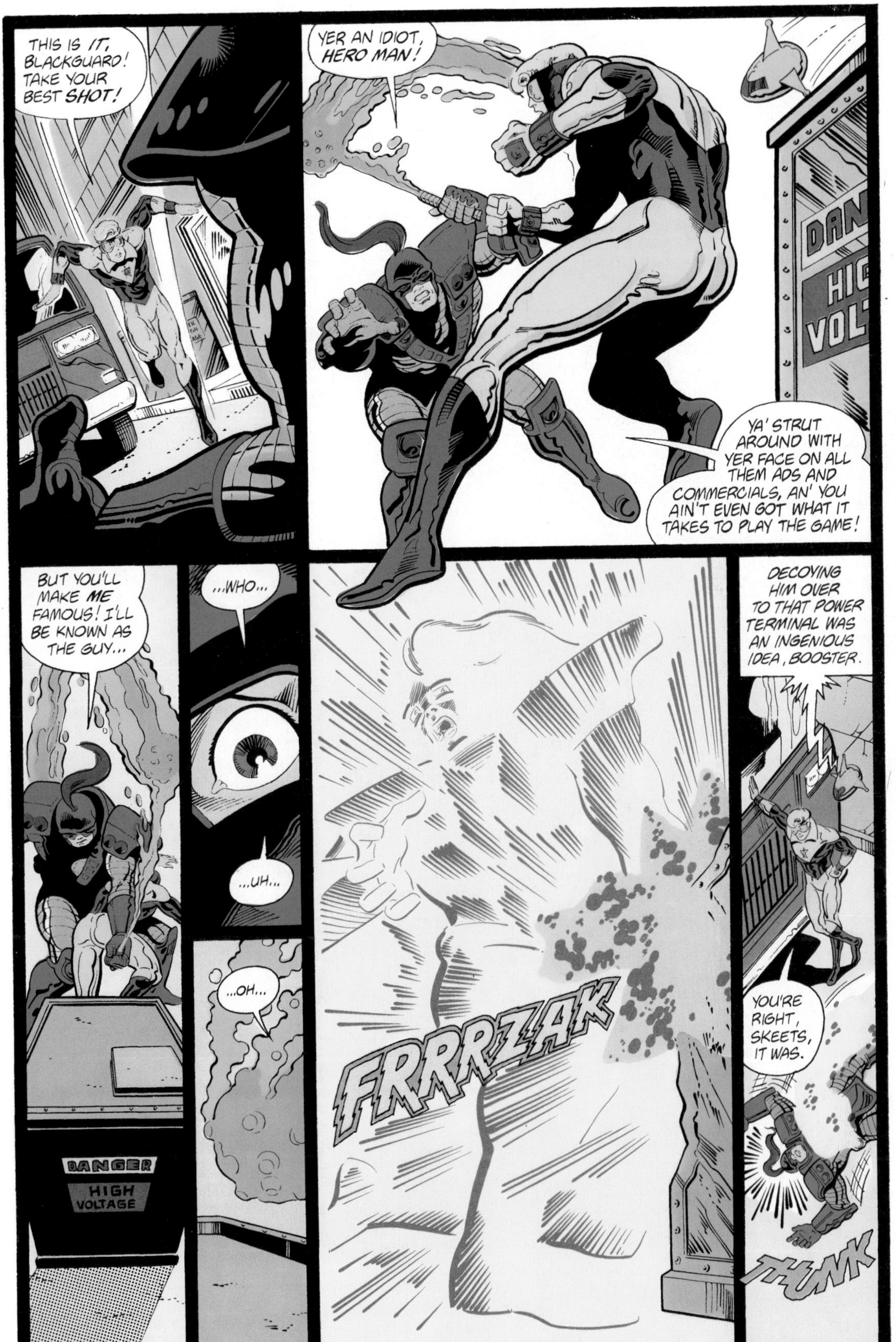
THIS IS *IT*, BLACKGUARD! TAKE YOUR BEST **SHOT**!
YER AN IDIOT, **HERO MAN**!
DAN
HIG
VOLT
YA' STRUT AROUND WITH YER FACE ON ALL THEM ADS AND COMMERCIALS, AN' YOU AIN'T EVEN GOT WHAT IT TAKES TO PLAY THE GAME!
BUT YOU'LL MAKE **ME** FAMOUS! I'LL BE KNOWN AS THE GUY...
...WHO...
...UH...
...OH...
DANGER
HIGH
VOLTAGE
FRRRZAK
DECOYING HIM OVER TO THAT POWER TERMINAL WAS AN INGENIOUS IDEA, BOOSTER.
YOU'RE RIGHT, SKEETS, IT WAS.
THUNK

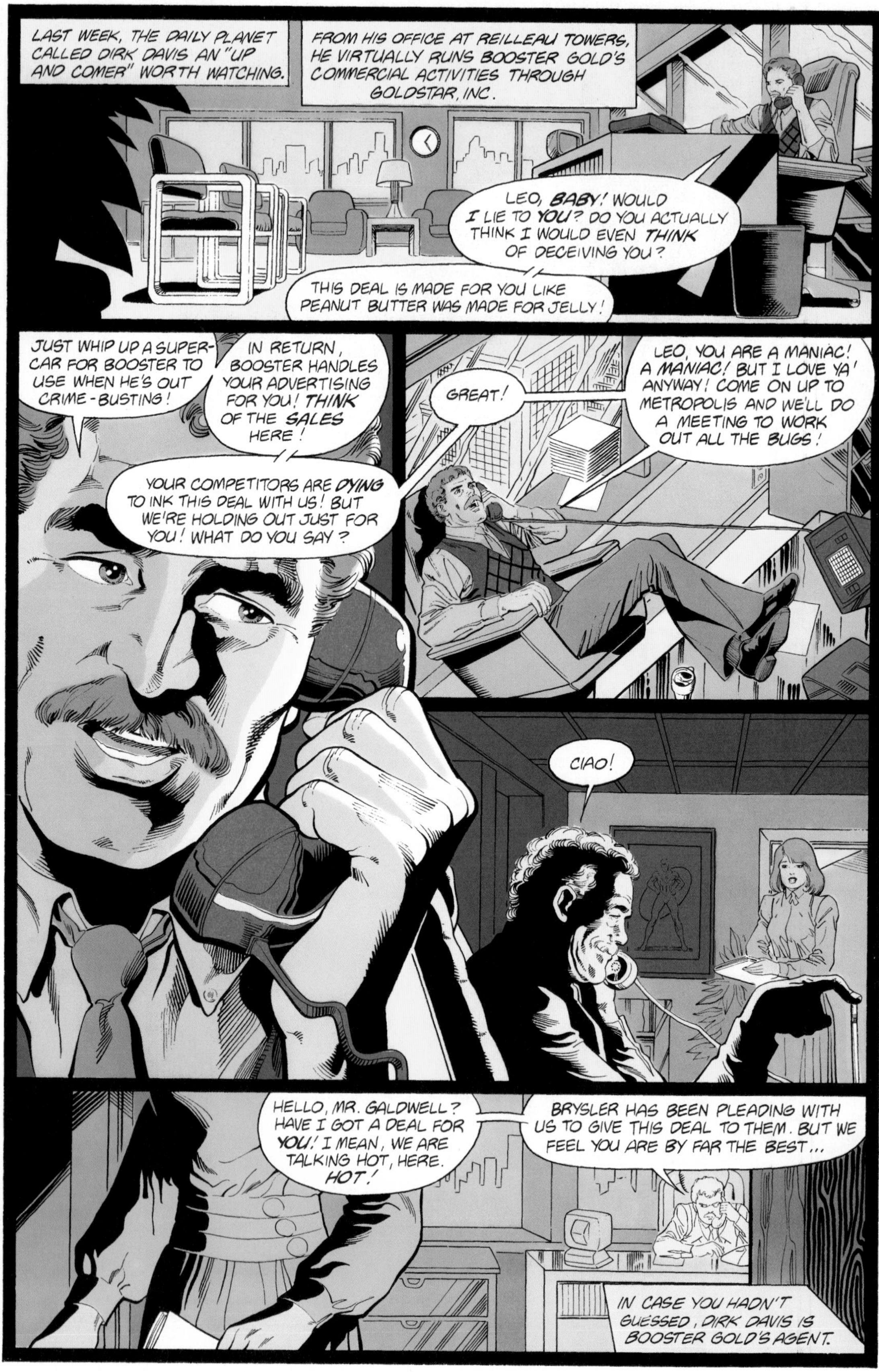
LAST WEEK, THE DAILY PLANET CALLED DIRK DAVIS AN "UP AND COMER" WORTH WATCHING.
FROM HIS OFFICE AT REILLEAU TOWERS, HE VIRTUALLY RUNS BOOSTER GOLD'S COMMERCIAL ACTIVITIES THROUGH GOLDSTAR, INC.
LEO, BABY! WOULD I LIE TO YOU? DO YOU ACTUALLY THINK I WOULD EVEN THINK OF DECEIVING YOU?
THIS DEAL IS MADE FOR YOU LIKE PEANUT BUTTER WAS MADE FOR JELLY!
JUST WHIP UP A SUPER-CAR FOR BOOSTER TO USE WHEN HE'S OUT CRIME-BUSTING!
IN RETURN, BOOSTER HANDLES YOUR ADVERTISING FOR YOU! THINK OF THE SALES HERE!
YOUR COMPETITORS ARE DYING TO INK THIS DEAL WITH US! BUT WE'RE HOLDING OUT JUST FOR YOU! WHAT DO YOU SAY?
GREAT!
LEO, YOU ARE A MANIAC! A MANIAC! BUT I LOVE YA' ANYWAY! COME ON UP TO METROPOLIS AND WE'LL DO A MEETING TO WORK OUT ALL THE BUGS!
CIAO!
HELLO, MR. GALDWELL? HAVE I GOT A DEAL FOR YOU! I MEAN, WE ARE TALKING HOT, HERE. HOT!
BRYSLER HAS BEEN PLEADING WITH US TO GIVE THIS DEAL TO THEM. BUT WE FEEL YOU ARE BY FAR THE BEST...
IN CASE YOU HADN'T GUESSED, DIRK DAVIS IS BOOSTER GOLD'S AGENT.

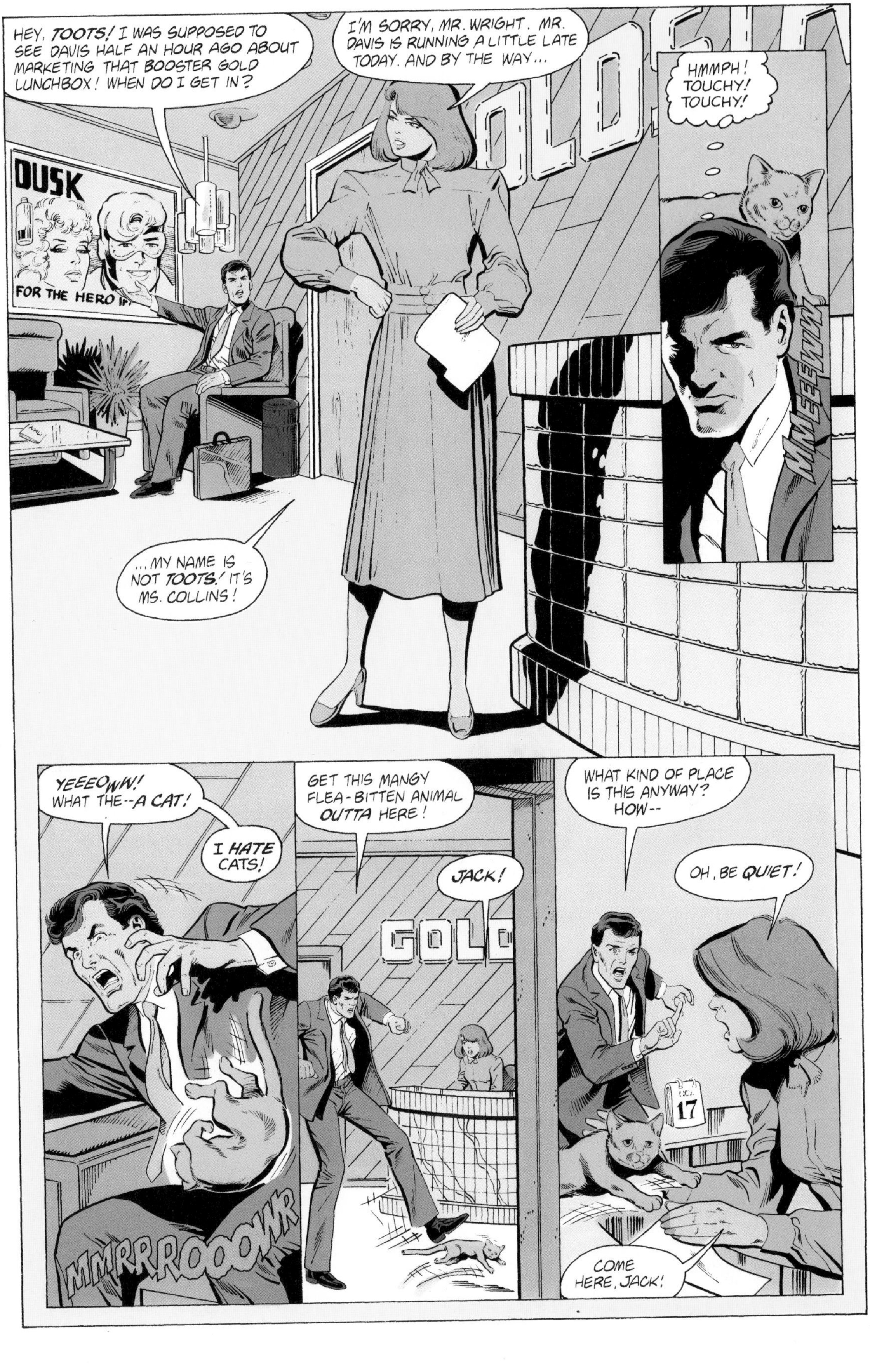
HEY, TOOTS! I WAS SUPPOSED TO SEE DAVIS HALF AN HOUR AGO ABOUT MARKETING THAT BOOSTER GOLD LUNCHBOX! WHEN DO I GET IN?
I'M SORRY, MR. WRIGHT. MR. DAVIS IS RUNNING A LITTLE LATE TODAY. AND BY THE WAY...
DUSK
FOR THE HERO IN
...MY NAME IS NOT TOOTS! IT'S MS. COLLINS!
HMMPH! TOUCHY! TOUCHY!
MMEEEWW
YEEEOWW! WHAT THE--A CAT!
I HATE CATS!
MMRRROOOWR
GET THIS MANGY FLEA-BITTEN ANIMAL OUTTA HERE!
JACK!
WHAT KIND OF PLACE IS THIS ANYWAY? HOW--
OH, BE QUIET!
17
COME HERE, JACK!

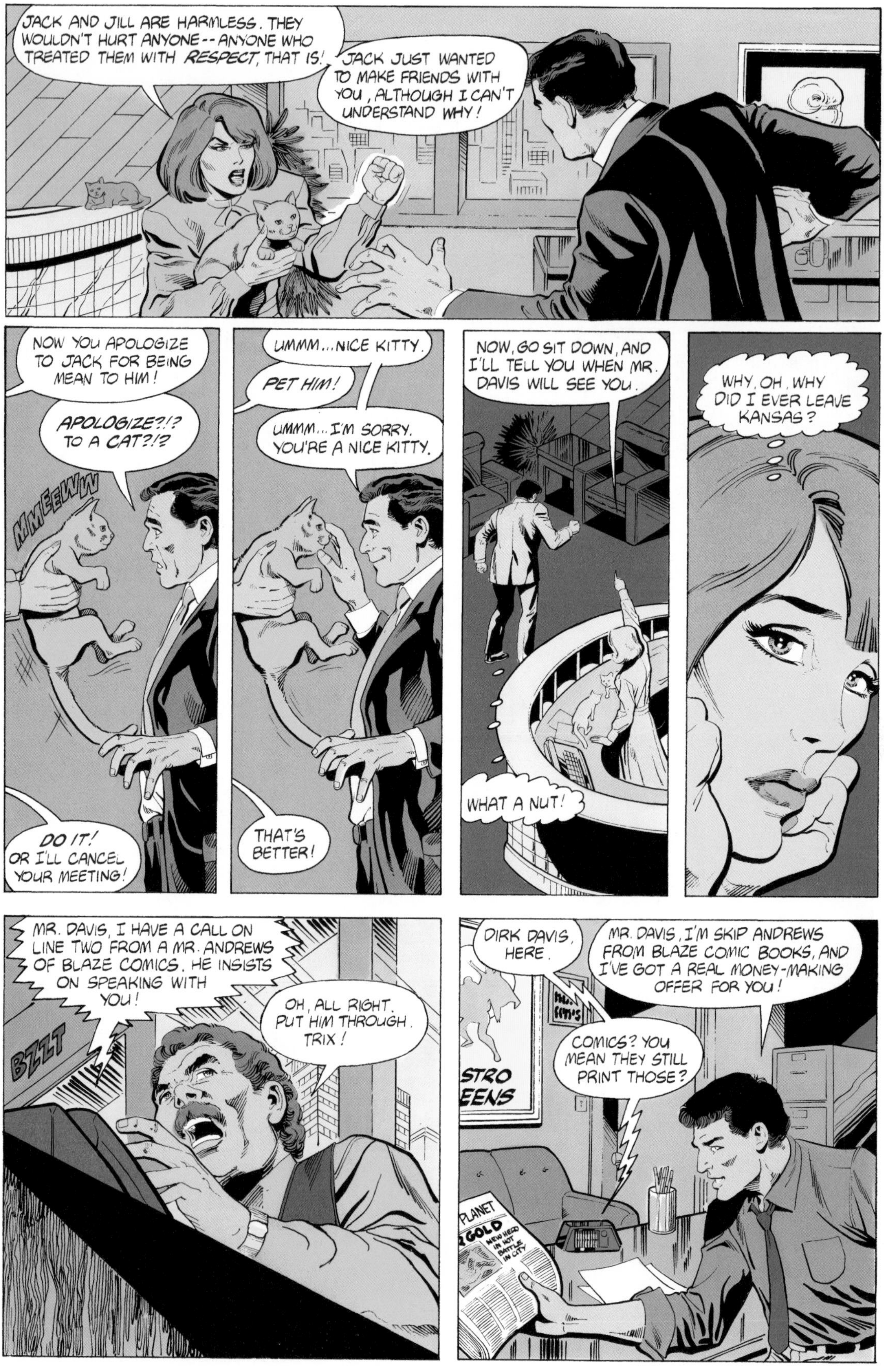
JACK AND JILL ARE HARMLESS. THEY WOULDN'T HURT ANYONE-- ANYONE WHO TREATED THEM WITH RESPECT, THAT IS!
JACK JUST WANTED TO MAKE FRIENDS WITH YOU, ALTHOUGH I CAN'T UNDERSTAND WHY!
NOW YOU APOLOGIZE TO JACK FOR BEING MEAN TO HIM!
APOLOGIZE?!? TO A CAT?!?
MMEEWW
DO IT! OR I'LL CANCEL YOUR MEETING!
UMMM... NICE KITTY.
PET HIM!
UMMM... I'M SORRY. YOU'RE A NICE KITTY.
THAT'S BETTER!
NOW, GO SIT DOWN, AND I'LL TELL YOU WHEN MR. DAVIS WILL SEE YOU.
WHAT A NUT!
WHY, OH, WHY DID I EVER LEAVE KANSAS?
MR. DAVIS, I HAVE A CALL ON LINE TWO FROM A MR. ANDREWS OF BLAZE COMICS. HE INSISTS ON SPEAKING WITH YOU!
BZZT
OH, ALL RIGHT. PUT HIM THROUGH, TRIX!
DIRK DAVIS, HERE.
MR. DAVIS, I'M SKIP ANDREWS FROM BLAZE COMIC BOOKS, AND I'VE GOT A REAL MONEY-MAKING OFFER FOR YOU!
COMICS? YOU MEAN THEY STILL PRINT THOSE?
STRO
EENS
PLANET
R GOLD
NEW HERO IN HOT BATTLE IN CITY

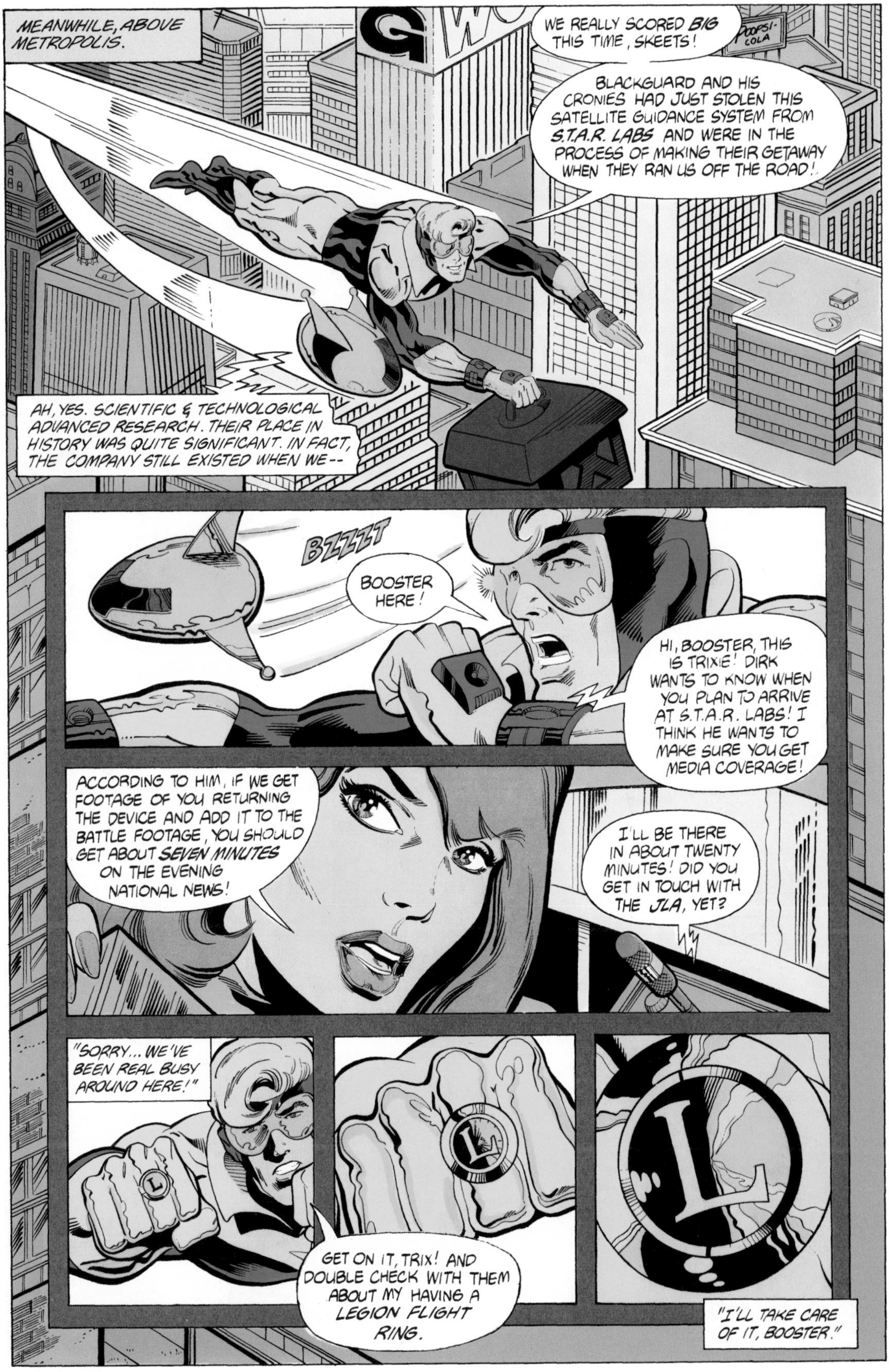

MEANWHILE, ABOVE METROPOLIS.
WE REALLY SCORED BIG THIS TIME, SKEETS!
POOPSI-COLA
BLACKGUARD AND HIS CRONIES HAD JUST STOLEN THIS SATELLITE GUIDANCE SYSTEM FROM S.T.A.R. LABS AND WERE IN THE PROCESS OF MAKING THEIR GETAWAY WHEN THEY RAN US OFF THE ROAD!
AH, YES. SCIENTIFIC & TECHNOLOGICAL ADVANCED RESEARCH. THEIR PLACE IN HISTORY WAS QUITE SIGNIFICANT. IN FACT, THE COMPANY STILL EXISTED WHEN WE--
BZZZT
BOOSTER HERE!
HI, BOOSTER, THIS IS TRIXIE! DIRK WANTS TO KNOW WHEN YOU PLAN TO ARRIVE AT S.T.A.R. LABS! I THINK HE WANTS TO MAKE SURE YOU GET MEDIA COVERAGE!
ACCORDING TO HIM, IF WE GET FOOTAGE OF YOU RETURNING THE DEVICE AND ADD IT TO THE BATTLE FOOTAGE, YOU SHOULD GET ABOUT SEVEN MINUTES ON THE EVENING NATIONAL NEWS!
I'LL BE THERE IN ABOUT TWENTY MINUTES! DID YOU GET IN TOUCH WITH THE JLA, YET?
"SORRY... WE'VE BEEN REAL BUSY AROUND HERE!"
GET ON IT, TRIX! AND DOUBLE CHECK WITH THEM ABOUT MY HAVING A LEGION FLIGHT RING.
"I'LL TAKE CARE OF IT, BOOSTER."

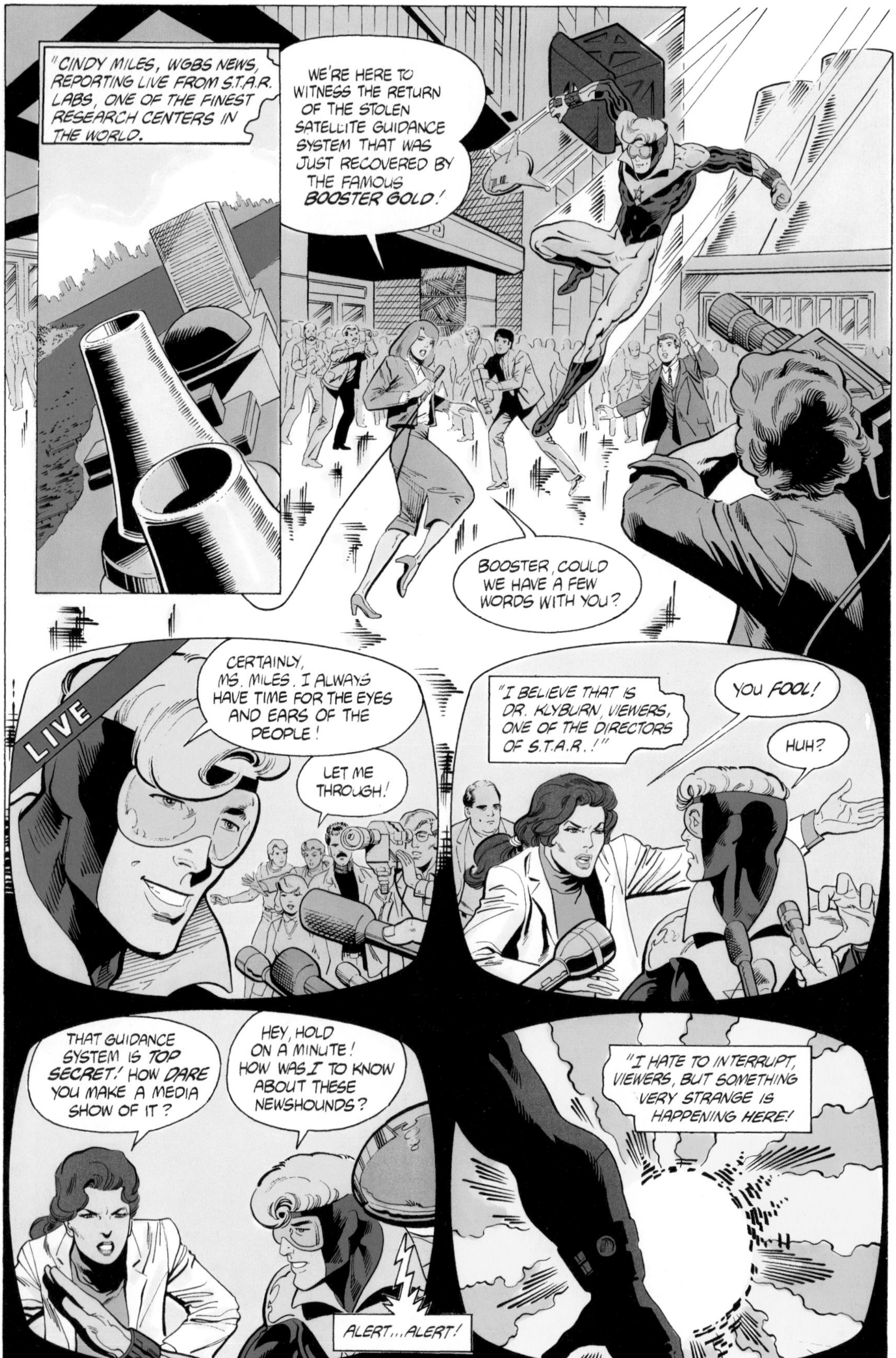
"CINDY MILES, WGBS NEWS, REPORTING LIVE FROM S.T.A.R. LABS, ONE OF THE FINEST RESEARCH CENTERS IN THE WORLD.
WE'RE HERE TO WITNESS THE RETURN OF THE STOLEN SATELLITE GUIDANCE SYSTEM THAT WAS JUST RECOVERED BY THE FAMOUS BOOSTER GOLD!
BOOSTER, COULD WE HAVE A FEW WORDS WITH YOU?
LIVE
CERTAINLY, MS. MILES. I ALWAYS HAVE TIME FOR THE EYES AND EARS OF THE PEOPLE!
LET ME THROUGH!
"I BELIEVE THAT IS DR. KLYBURN, VIEWERS, ONE OF THE DIRECTORS OF S.T.A.R.!"
YOU FOOL!
HUH?
THAT GUIDANCE SYSTEM IS TOP SECRET! HOW DARE YOU MAKE A MEDIA SHOW OF IT?
HEY, HOLD ON A MINUTE! HOW WAS I TO KNOW ABOUT THESE NEWSHOUNDS?
ALERT... ALERT!
"I HATE TO INTERRUPT, VIEWERS, BUT SOMETHING VERY STRANGE IS HAPPENING HERE!

"I DON'T KNOW IF YOU SAW IT, FOLKS, BUT THERE WAS JUST AN *INCREDIBLE* BURST OF LIGHT HERE!' THE SITUATION IS CHAOTIC.

"JOHNSON, PICK UP THAT CAMERA AND GET ME A SHOT OF *BOOSTER!*

"I CAN'T GET A MICROPHONE TO HIM, FOLKS, BUT *BOOSTER GOLD* IS TRYING TO GET EVERYONE *OUT* OF THE PLAZA AREA--

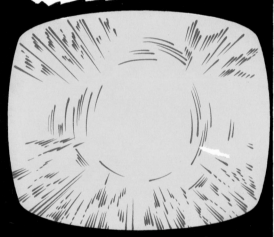

"OH, MY *GOD!* BOOSTER WAS JUST *HIT* BY SOME TYPE OF BEAM...

"...WHAT IS GOING *ON* HERE? WE SEEM TO BE LOSING--"

PLEASE STAND BY

Thankyou   WGBS

ARE WE BACK ON THE AIR? *GOOD!*

JUST MINUTES AGO THERE WAS AN ATTACK OF SOME SORT HERE AT S.T.A.R. LABS...

31

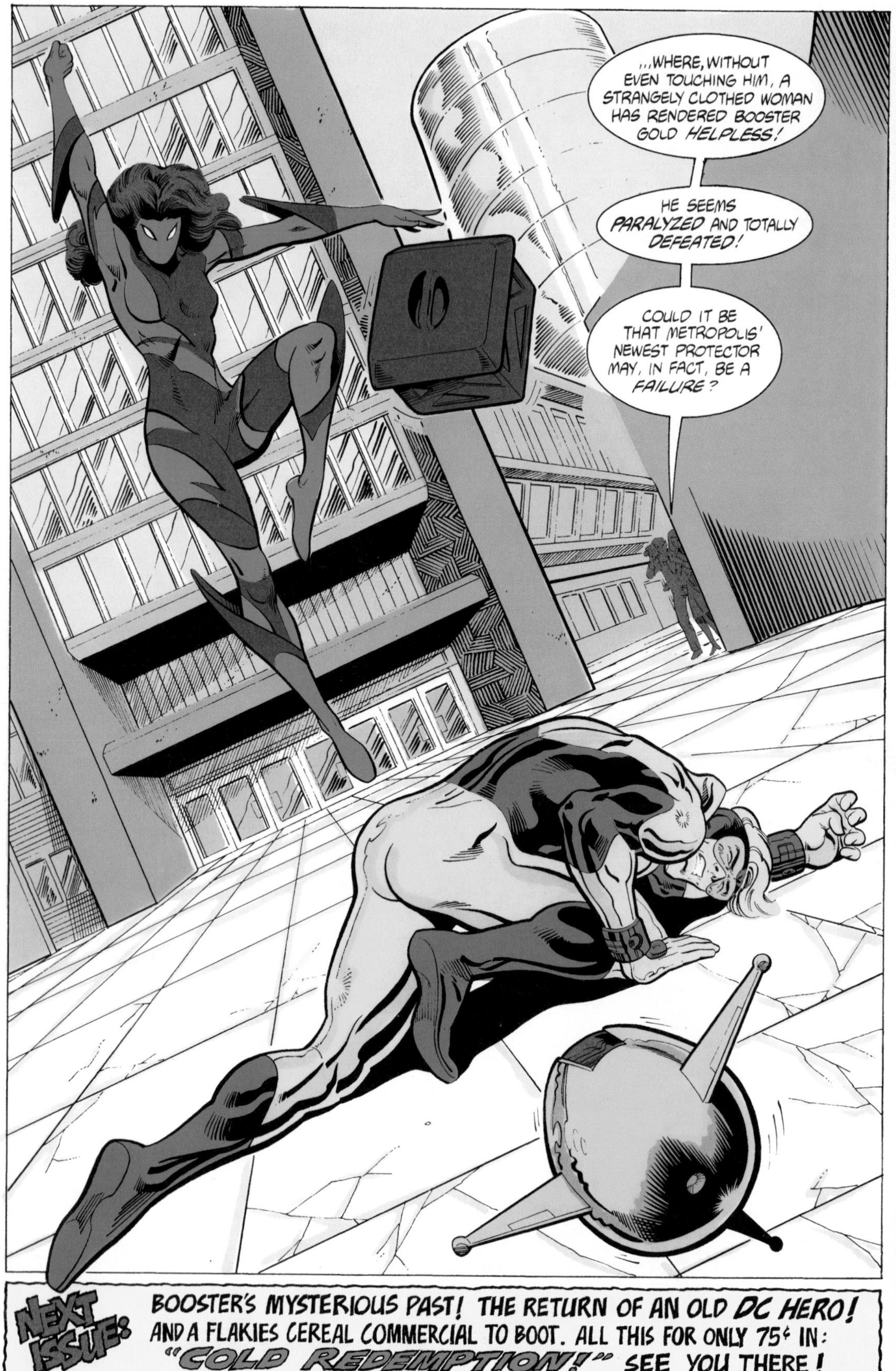
...WHERE, WITHOUT EVEN TOUCHING HIM, A STRANGELY CLOTHED WOMAN HAS RENDERED BOOSTER GOLD HELPLESS!
HE SEEMS PARALYZED AND TOTALLY DEFEATED!
COULD IT BE THAT METROPOLIS' NEWEST PROTECTOR MAY, IN FACT, BE A FAILURE?
NEXT ISSUE: BOOSTER'S MYSTERIOUS PAST! THE RETURN OF AN OLD DC HERO! AND A FLAKIES CEREAL COMMERCIAL TO BOOT. ALL THIS FOR ONLY 75¢ IN: "GOLD REDEMPTION!" SEE YOU THERE!

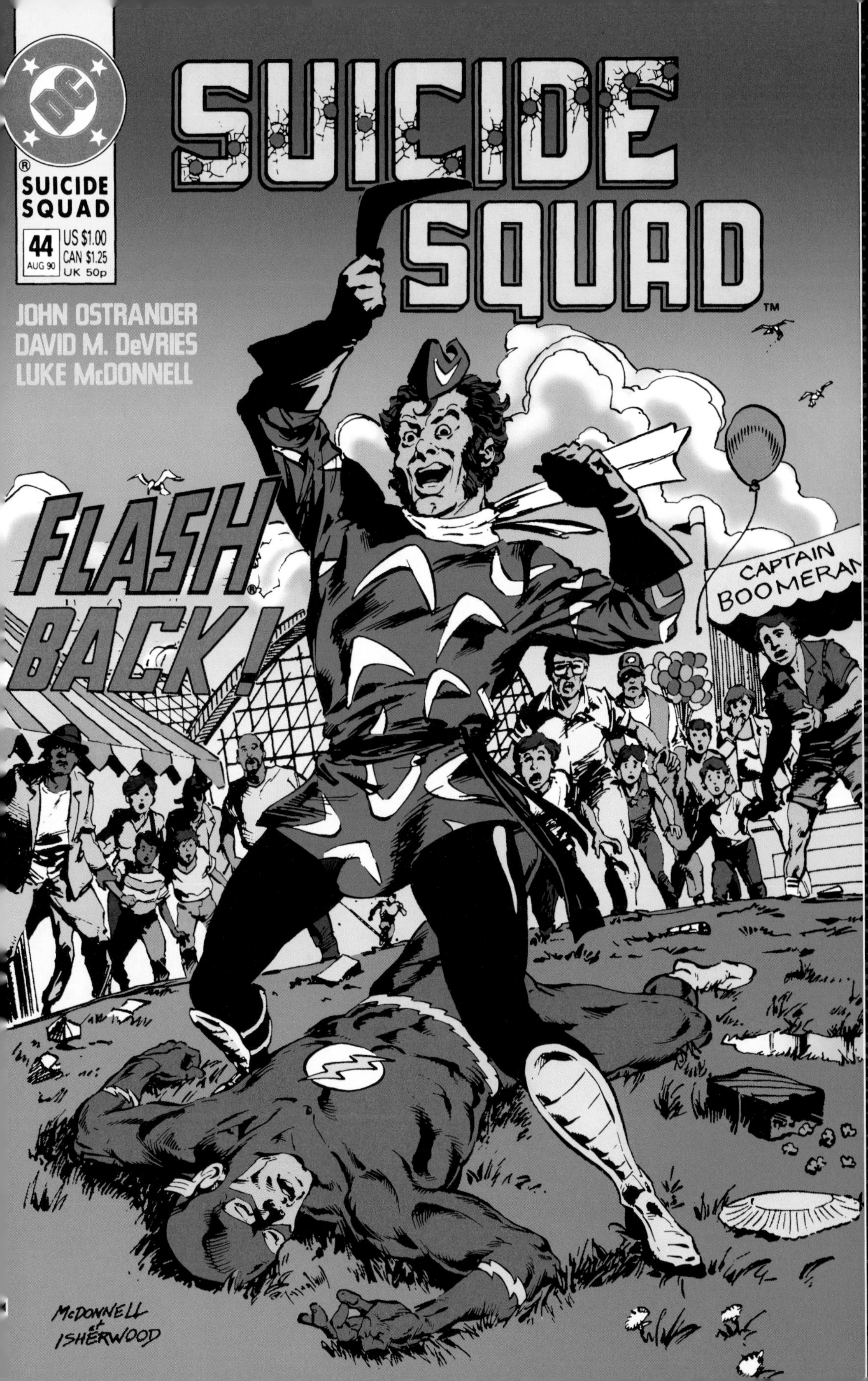
SUICIDE SQUAD
44
AUG 90
US $1.00
CAN $1.25
UK 50p
SUICIDE SQUAD™
JOHN OSTRANDER
DAVID M. DeVRIES
LUKE McDONNELL
FLASH® BACK!
CAPTAIN BOOMERAN
McDONNELL et ISHERWOOD

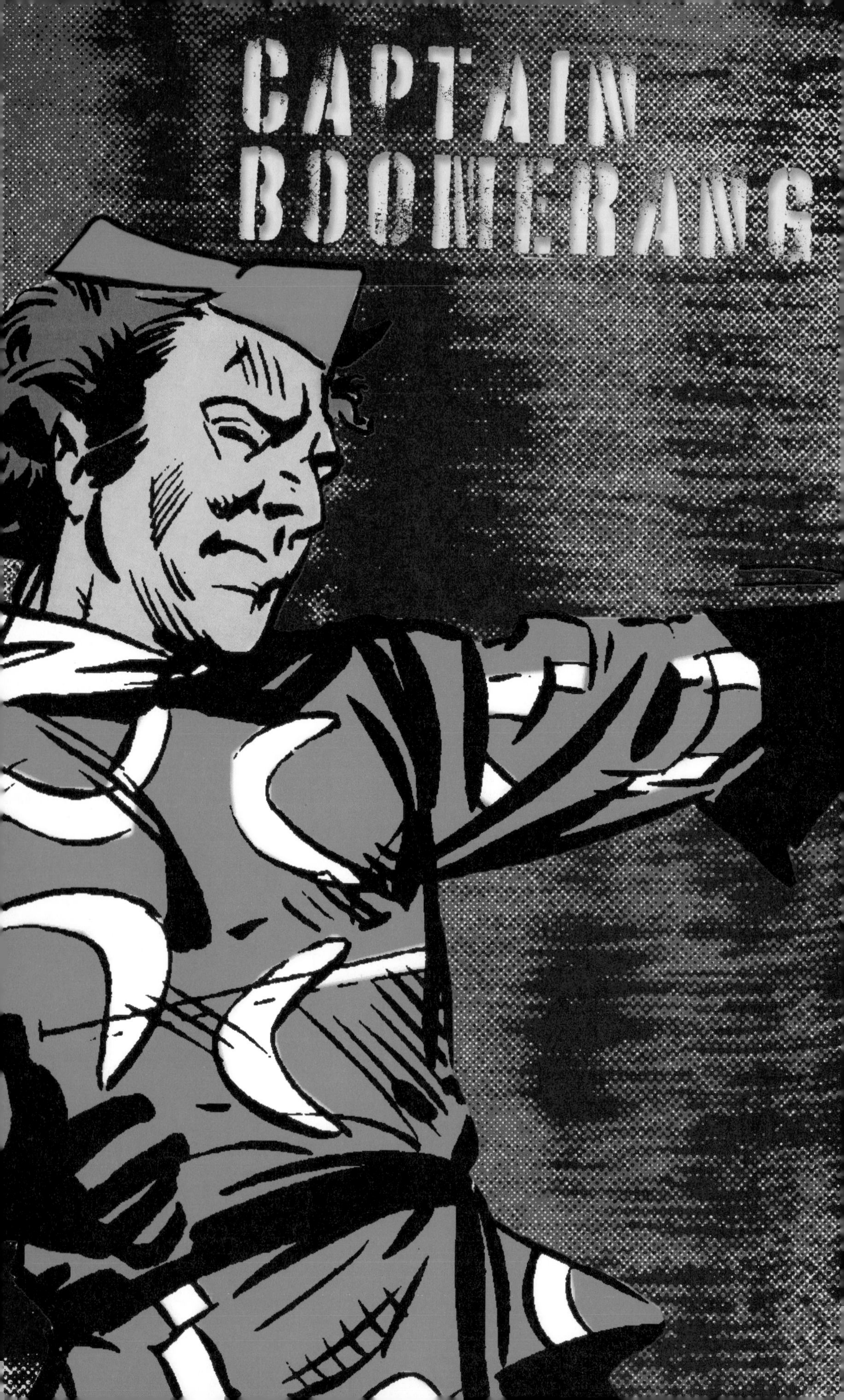
CAPTAIN
BOOMERANG

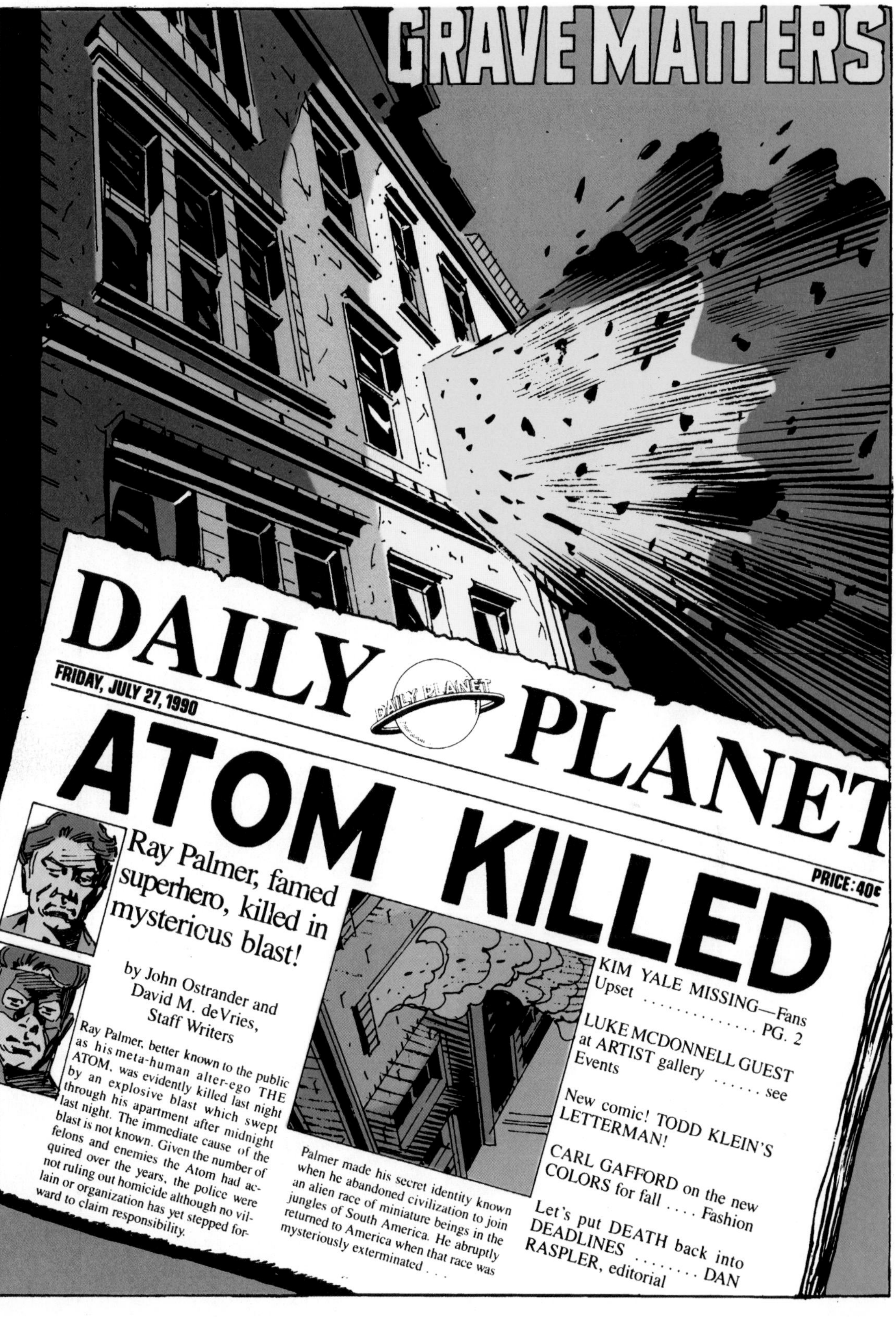
GRAVE MATTERS
DAILY PLANET
FRIDAY, JULY 27, 1990
ATOM KILLED
PRICE: 40¢
Ray Palmer, famed superhero, killed in mysterious blast!
by John Ostrander and David M. deVries, Staff Writers
Ray Palmer, better known to the public as his meta-human alter-ego THE ATOM, was evidently killed last night by an explosive blast which swept through his apartment after midnight last night. The immediate cause of the blast is not known. Given the number of felons and enemies the Atom had acquired over the years, the police were not ruling out homicide although no villain or organization has yet stepped forward to claim responsibility.
Palmer made his secret identity known when he abandoned civilization to join an alien race of miniature beings in the jungles of South America. He abruptly returned to America when that race was mysteriously exterminated . . .
KIM YALE MISSING—Fans Upset . . . . PG. 2
LUKE MCDONNELL GUEST at ARTIST gallery . . . . . . see Events
New comic! TODD KLEIN'S LETTERMAN!
CARL GAFFORD on the new COLORS for fall . . . . Fashion
Let's put DEATH back into DEADLINES . . . . DAN RASPLER, editorial

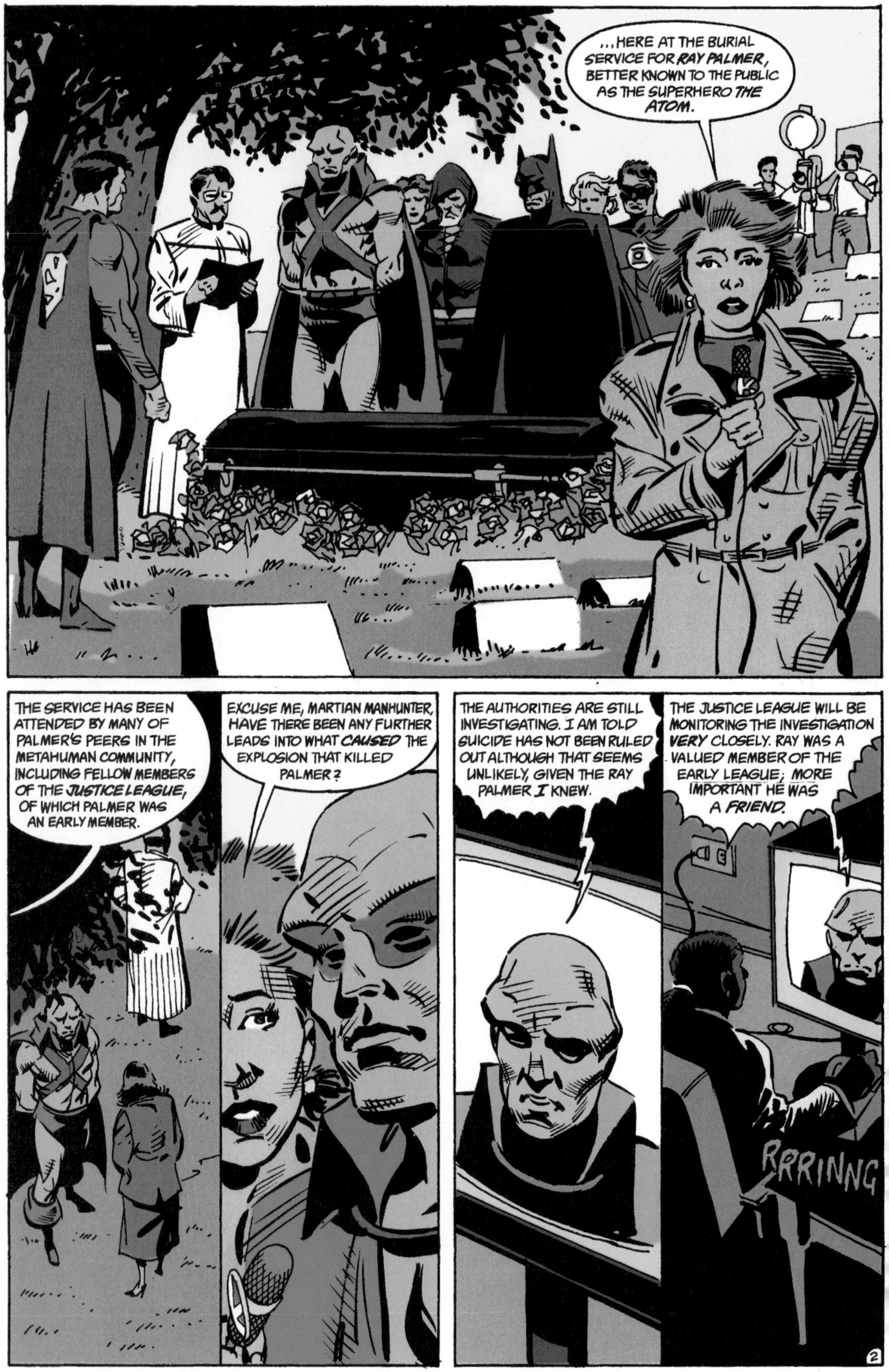
...HERE AT THE BURIAL SERVICE FOR RAY PALMER, BETTER KNOWN TO THE PUBLIC AS THE SUPERHERO THE ATOM.
THE SERVICE HAS BEEN ATTENDED BY MANY OF PALMER'S PEERS IN THE METAHUMAN COMMUNITY, INCLUDING FELLOW MEMBERS OF THE JUSTICE LEAGUE, OF WHICH PALMER WAS AN EARLY MEMBER.
EXCUSE ME, MARTIAN MANHUNTER, HAVE THERE BEEN ANY FURTHER LEADS INTO WHAT CAUSED THE EXPLOSION THAT KILLED PALMER?
THE AUTHORITIES ARE STILL INVESTIGATING. I AM TOLD SUICIDE HAS NOT BEEN RULED OUT ALTHOUGH THAT SEEMS UNLIKELY, GIVEN THE RAY PALMER I KNEW.
THE JUSTICE LEAGUE WILL BE MONITORING THE INVESTIGATION VERY CLOSELY. RAY WAS A VALUED MEMBER OF THE EARLY LEAGUE; MORE IMPORTANT HE WAS A FRIEND.
RRRINNG
2

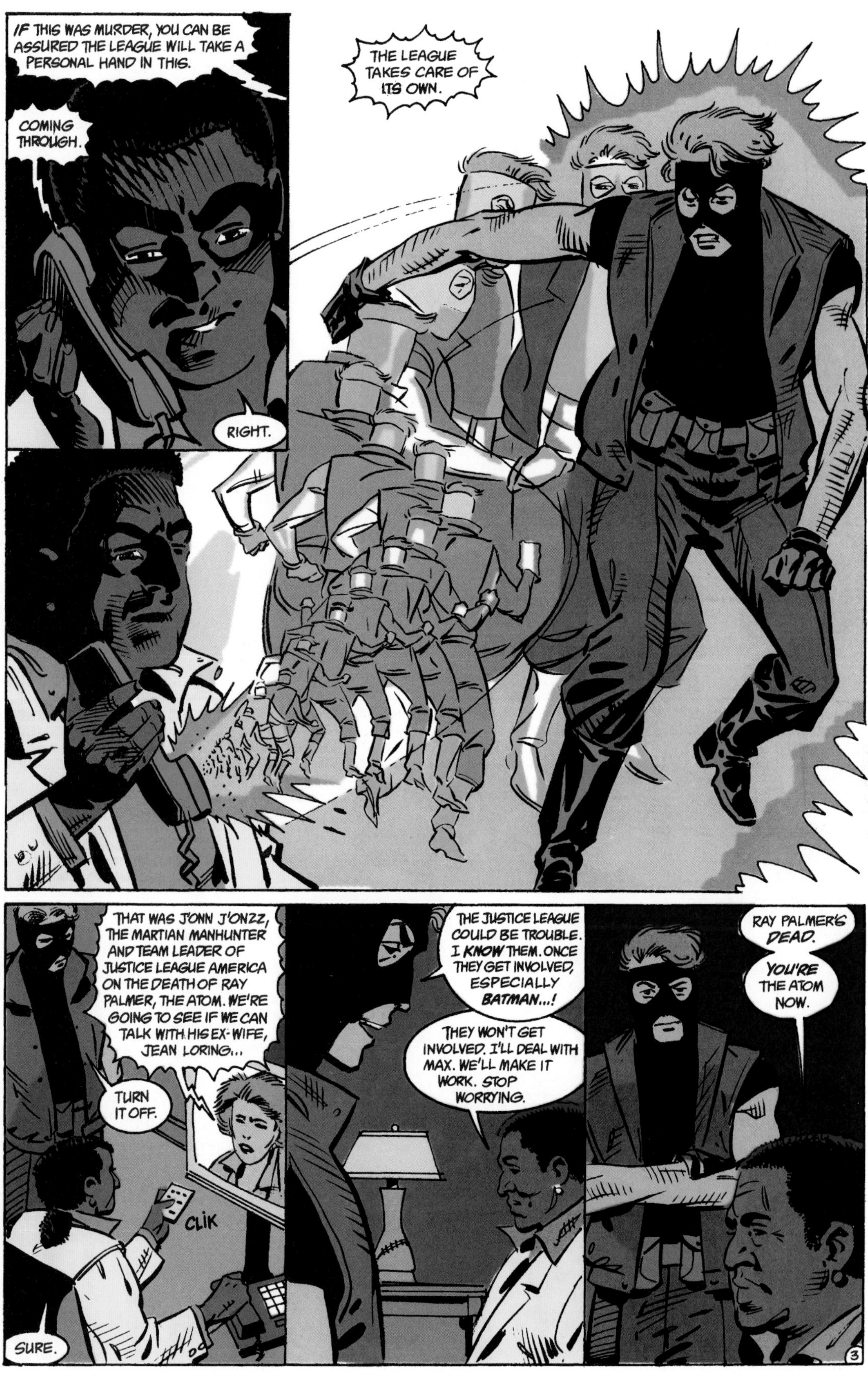

IF THIS WAS MURDER, YOU CAN BE ASSURED THE LEAGUE WILL TAKE A PERSONAL HAND IN THIS.
COMING THROUGH.
THE LEAGUE TAKES CARE OF ITS OWN.
RIGHT.
THAT WAS J'ONN J'ONZZ, THE MARTIAN MANHUNTER AND TEAM LEADER OF JUSTICE LEAGUE AMERICA ON THE DEATH OF RAY PALMER, THE ATOM. WE'RE GOING TO SEE IF WE CAN TALK WITH HIS EX-WIFE, JEAN LORING...
TURN IT OFF.
CLIK
SURE.
THE JUSTICE LEAGUE COULD BE TROUBLE. I KNOW THEM. ONCE THEY GET INVOLVED, ESPECIALLY BATMAN...!
THEY WON'T GET INVOLVED. I'LL DEAL WITH MAX. WE'LL MAKE IT WORK. STOP WORRYING.
RAY PALMER'S DEAD.
YOU'RE THE ATOM NOW.
3

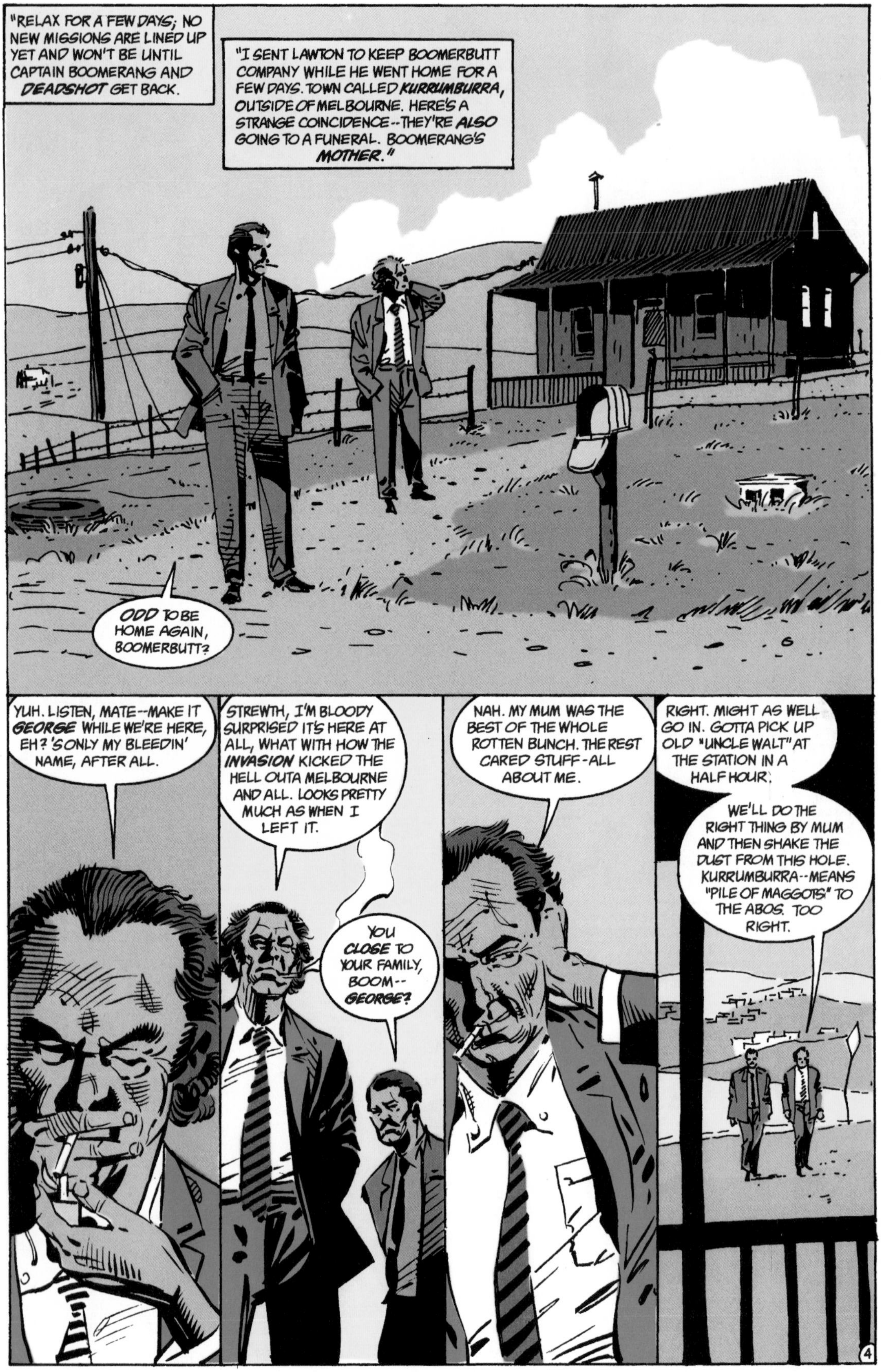
"RELAX FOR A FEW DAYS; NO NEW MISSIONS ARE LINED UP YET AND WON'T BE UNTIL CAPTAIN BOOMERANG AND DEADSHOT GET BACK.
"I SENT LAWTON TO KEEP BOOMERBUTT COMPANY WHILE HE WENT HOME FOR A FEW DAYS. TOWN CALLED KURRUMBURRA, OUTSIDE OF MELBOURNE. HERE'S A STRANGE COINCIDENCE--THEY'RE ALSO GOING TO A FUNERAL. BOOMERANG'S MOTHER."
ODD TO BE HOME AGAIN, BOOMERBUTT?
YUH. LISTEN, MATE--MAKE IT GEORGE WHILE WE'RE HERE, EH? 'S ONLY MY BLEEDIN' NAME, AFTER ALL.
STREWTH, I'M BLOODY SURPRISED IT'S HERE AT ALL, WHAT WITH HOW THE INVASION KICKED THE HELL OUTA MELBOURNE AND ALL. LOOKS PRETTY MUCH AS WHEN I LEFT IT.
YOU CLOSE TO YOUR FAMILY, BOOM-- GEORGE?
NAH. MY MUM WAS THE BEST OF THE WHOLE ROTTEN BUNCH. THE REST CARED STUFF-ALL ABOUT ME.
RIGHT. MIGHT AS WELL GO IN. GOTTA PICK UP OLD "UNCLE WALT" AT THE STATION IN A HALF HOUR.
WE'LL DO THE RIGHT THING BY MUM AND THEN SHAKE THE DUST FROM THIS HOLE. KURRUMBURRA--MEANS "PILE OF MAGGOTS" TO THE ABOS. TOO RIGHT.
4

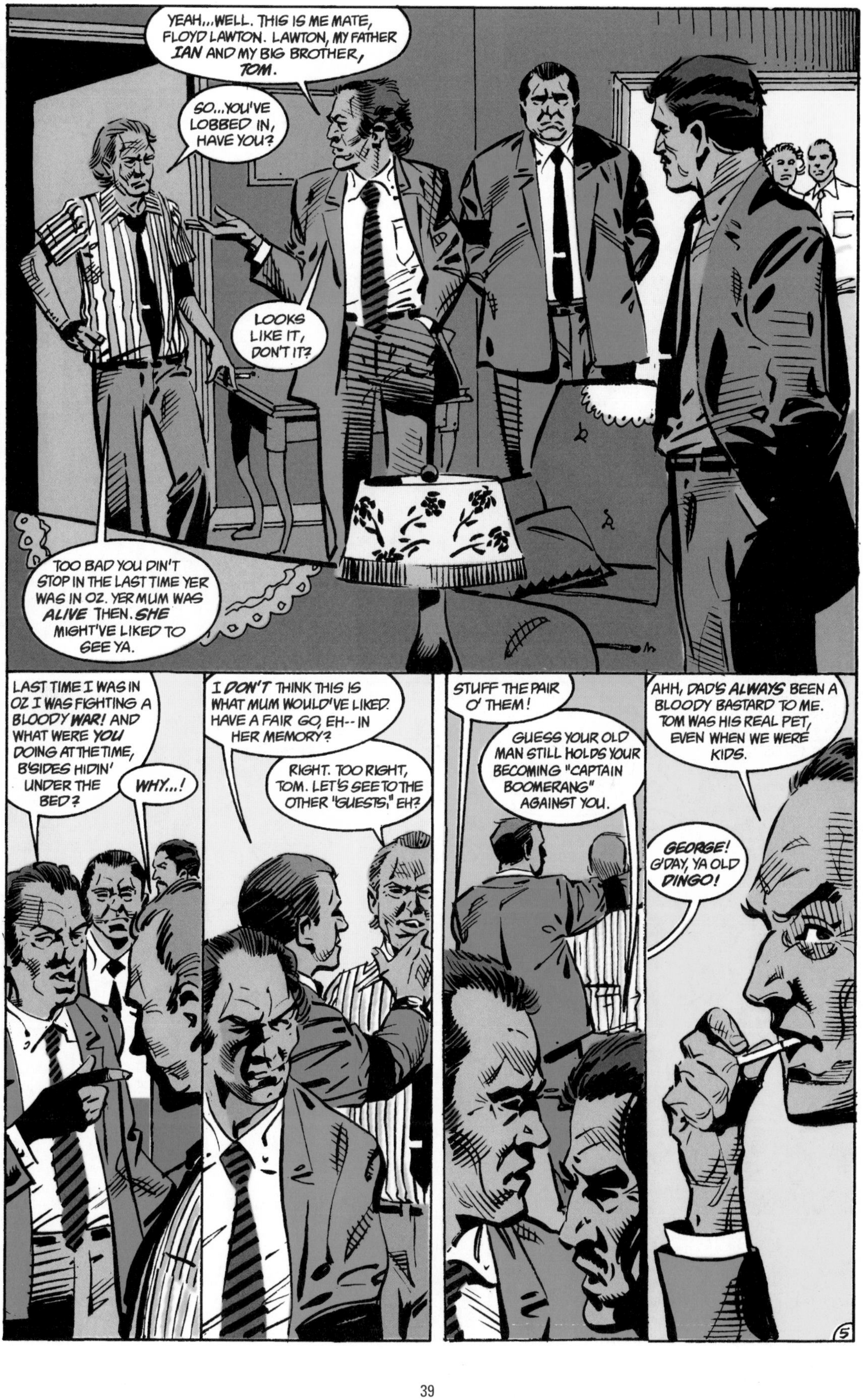
YEAH...WELL. THIS IS ME MATE, FLOYD LAWTON. LAWTON, MY FATHER IAN AND MY BIG BROTHER, TOM.
SO...YOU'VE LOBBED IN, HAVE YOU?
LOOKS LIKE IT, DON'T IT?
TOO BAD YOU DIN'T STOP IN THE LAST TIME YER WAS IN OZ. YER MUM WAS ALIVE THEN. SHE MIGHT'VE LIKED TO SEE YA.
LAST TIME I WAS IN OZ I WAS FIGHTING A BLOODY WAR! AND WHAT WERE YOU DOING AT THE TIME, B'SIDES HIDIN' UNDER THE BED?
WHY...!
I DON'T THINK THIS IS WHAT MUM WOULD'VE LIKED. HAVE A FAIR GO, EH-- IN HER MEMORY?
RIGHT. TOO RIGHT, TOM. LET'S SEE TO THE OTHER "GUESTS," EH?
STUFF THE PAIR O' THEM!
GUESS YOUR OLD MAN STILL HOLDS YOUR BECOMING "CAPTAIN BOOMERANG" AGAINST YOU.
AHH, DAD'S ALWAYS BEEN A BLOODY BASTARD TO ME. TOM WAS HIS REAL PET, EVEN WHEN WE WERE KIDS.
GEORGE! G'DAY, YA OLD DINGO!
5

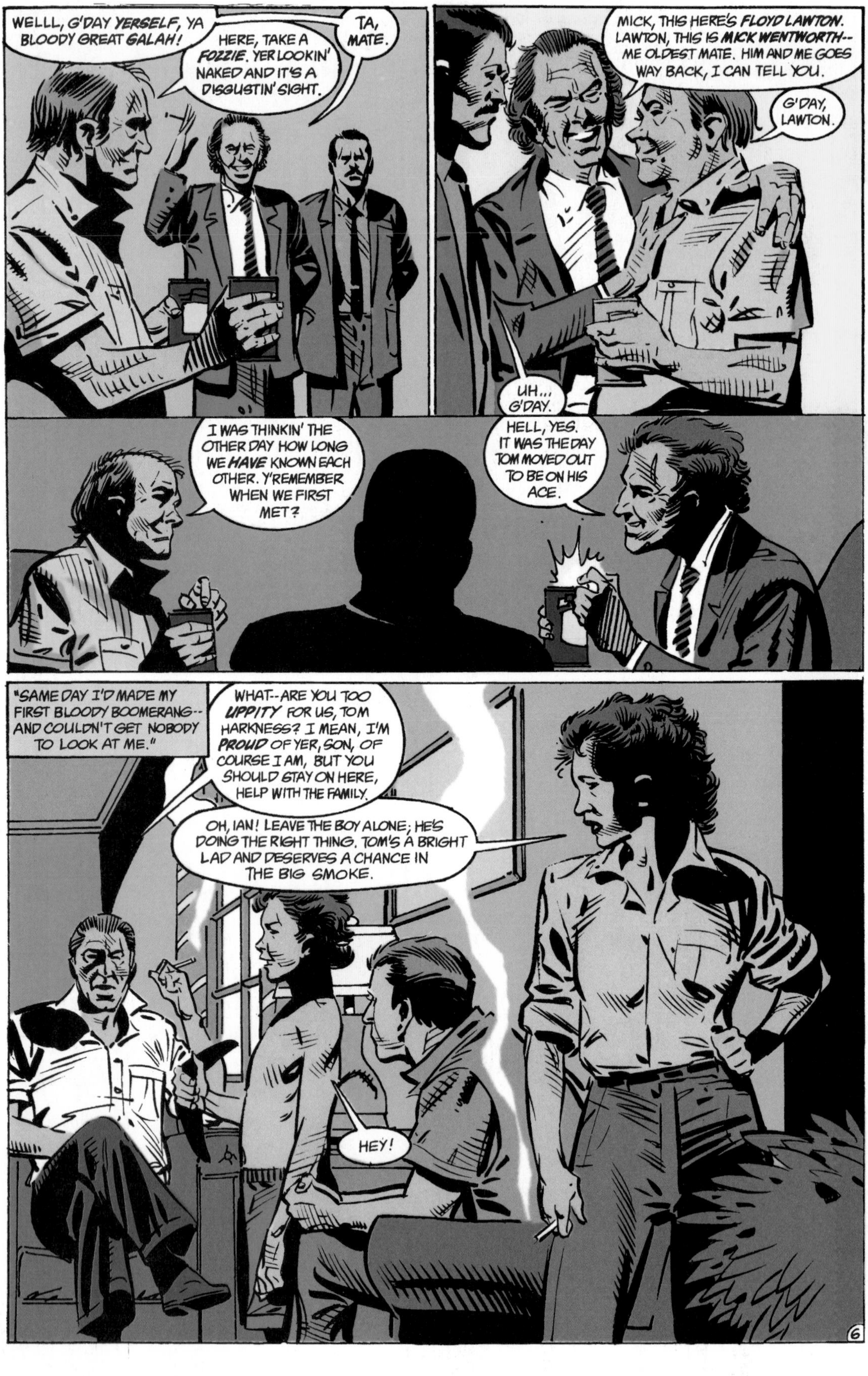
WELLL, G'DAY YERSELF, YA BLOODY GREAT GALAH!
HERE, TAKE A FOZZIE. YER LOOKIN' NAKED AND IT'S A DISGUSTIN' SIGHT.
TA, MATE.
MICK, THIS HERE'S FLOYD LAWTON. LAWTON, THIS IS MICK WENTWORTH-- ME OLDEST MATE. HIM AND ME GOES WAY BACK, I CAN TELL YOU.
G'DAY, LAWTON.
UH... G'DAY.
I WAS THINKIN' THE OTHER DAY HOW LONG WE HAVE KNOWN EACH OTHER. Y'REMEMBER WHEN WE FIRST MET?
HELL, YES. IT WAS THE DAY TOM MOVED OUT TO BE ON HIS ACE.
"SAME DAY I'D MADE MY FIRST BLOODY BOOMERANG-- AND COULDN'T GET NOBODY TO LOOK AT ME."
WHAT--ARE YOU TOO UPPITY FOR US, TOM HARKNESS? I MEAN, I'M PROUD OF YER, SON, OF COURSE I AM, BUT YOU SHOULD STAY ON HERE, HELP WITH THE FAMILY.
OH, IAN! LEAVE THE BOY ALONE; HE'S DOING THE RIGHT THING. TOM'S A BRIGHT LAD AND DESERVES A CHANCE IN THE BIG SMOKE.
HEY!
6

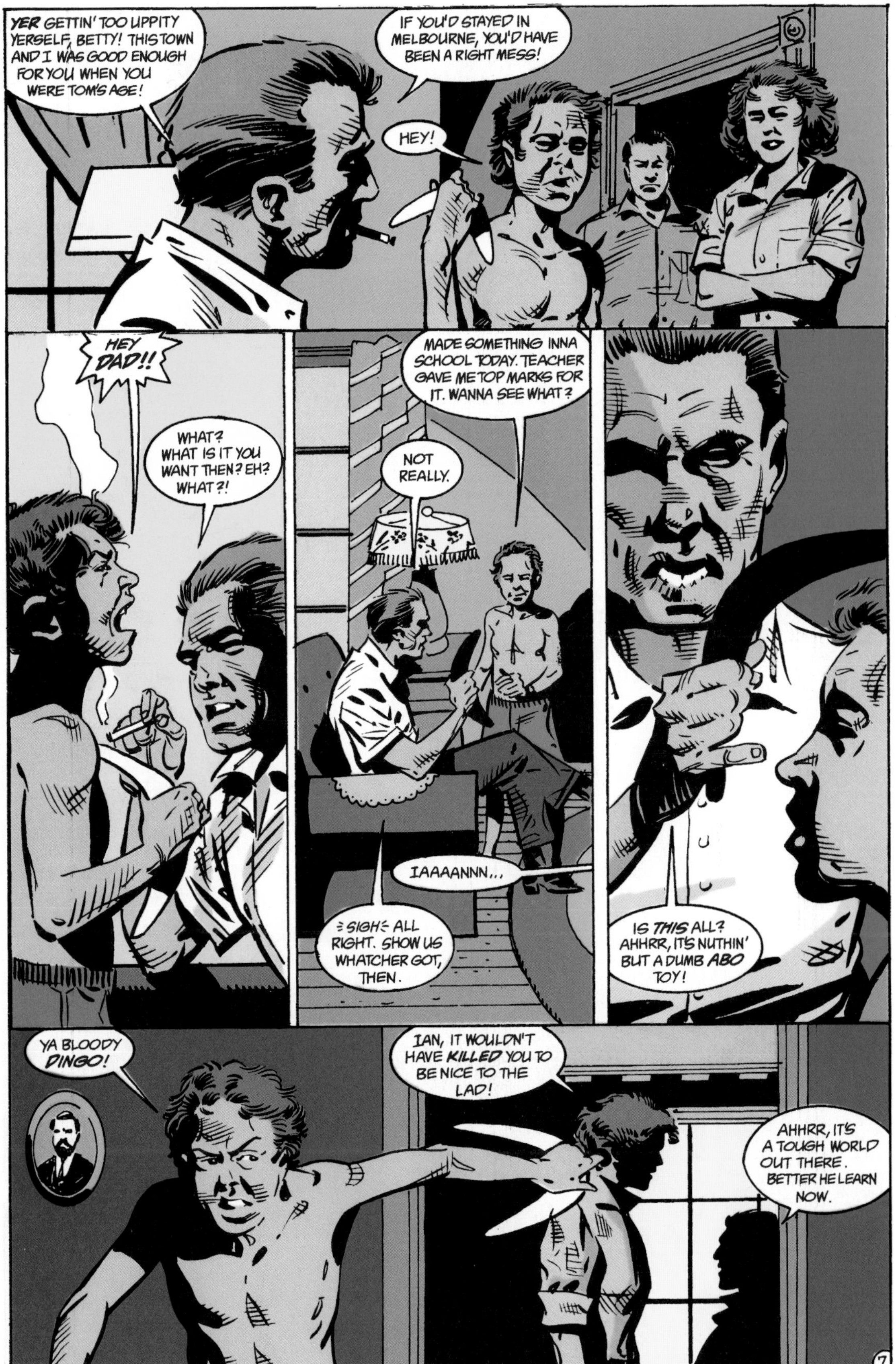
YER GETTIN' TOO UPPITY YERSELF, BETTY! THIS TOWN AND I WAS GOOD ENOUGH FOR YOU WHEN YOU WERE TOM'S AGE!
IF YOU'D STAYED IN MELBOURNE, YOU'D HAVE BEEN A RIGHT MESS!
HEY!
HEY DAD!!
WHAT? WHAT IS IT YOU WANT THEN? EH? WHAT?!
MADE SOMETHING INNA SCHOOL TODAY. TEACHER GAVE ME TOP MARKS FOR IT. WANNA SEE WHAT?
NOT REALLY.
IAAAANNN...
SIGH ALL RIGHT. SHOW US WHATCHER GOT, THEN.
IS THIS ALL? AHHRR, IT'S NUTHIN' BUT A DUMB ABO TOY!
YA BLOODY DINGO!
IAN, IT WOULDN'T HAVE KILLED YOU TO BE NICE TO THE LAD!
AHHRR, IT'S A TOUGH WORLD OUT THERE. BETTER HE LEARN NOW.
7

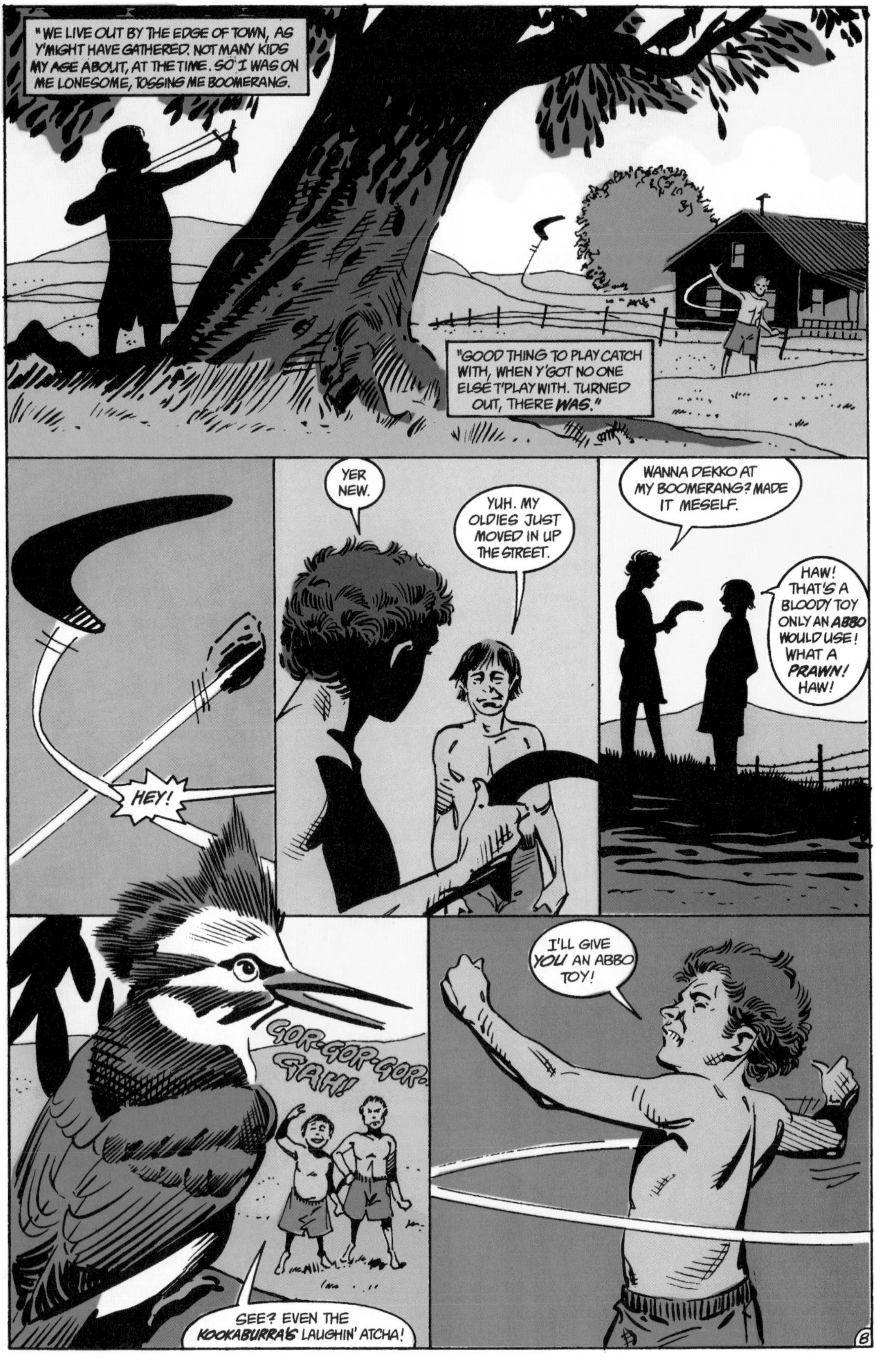
"WE LIVE OUT BY THE EDGE OF TOWN, AS Y'MIGHT HAVE GATHERED. NOT MANY KIDS MY AGE ABOUT, AT THE TIME. SO I WAS ON ME LONESOME, TOSSING ME BOOMERANG.
"GOOD THING TO PLAY CATCH WITH, WHEN Y'GOT NO ONE ELSE T'PLAY WITH. TURNED OUT, THERE WAS."
HEY!
YER NEW.
YUH. MY OLDIES JUST MOVED IN UP THE STREET.
WANNA DEKKO AT MY BOOMERANG? MADE IT MESELF.
HAW! THAT'S A BLOODY TOY ONLY AN ABBO WOULD USE! WHAT A PRAWN! HAW!
GOR-GOR-GOR-GAH!
SEE? EVEN THE KOOKABURRA'S LAUGHIN' ATCHA!
I'LL GIVE YOU AN ABBO TOY!
8

KRAK!

WHUP

FWUMP!

STREWTH! 'S *DEAD!* YUH *KILLED* IT!

WHAT A RIPPER!

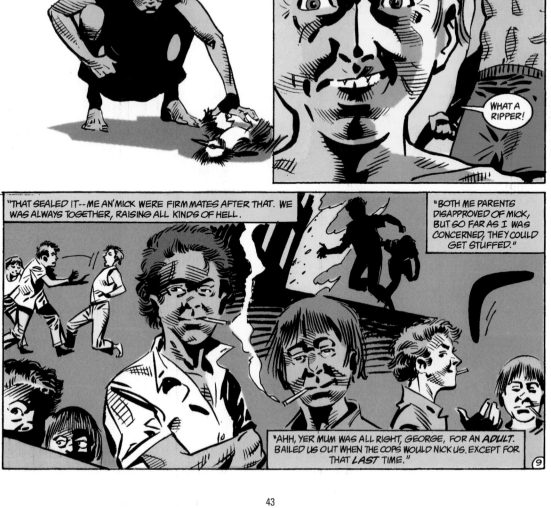

"THAT SEALED IT-- ME AN' MICK WERE FIRM MATES AFTER THAT. WE WAS ALWAYS TOGETHER, RAISING ALL KINDS OF HELL.

"BOTH ME PARENTS DISAPPROVED OF MICK, BUT SO FAR AS I WAS CONCERNED, THEY COULD GET STUFFED."

"AHH, YER MUM WAS ALL RIGHT, GEORGE, FOR AN *ADULT.* BAILED US OUT WHEN THE COPS WOULD NICK US. EXCEPT FOR THAT *LAST* TIME."

9

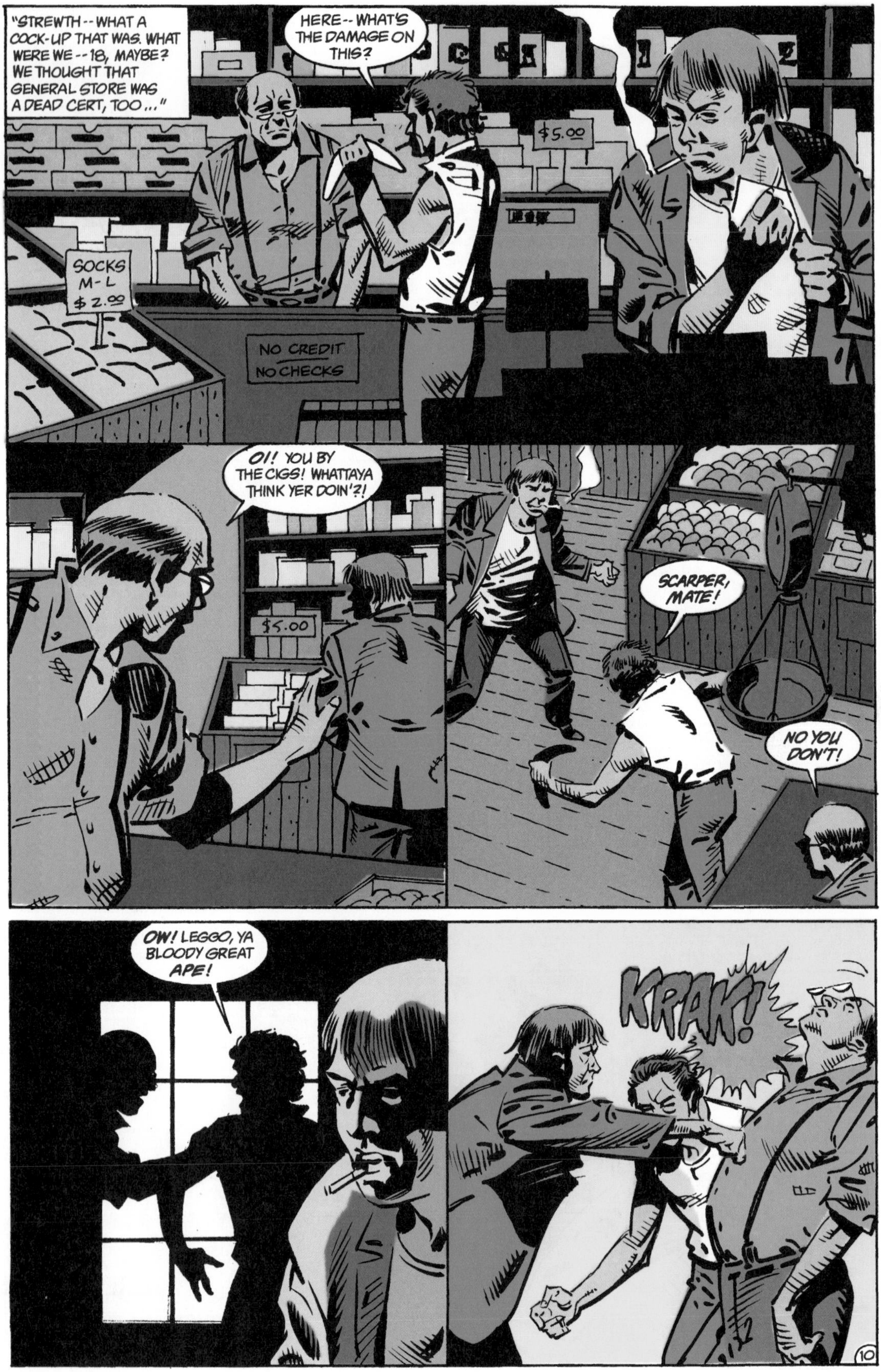
"STREWTH -- WHAT A COCK-UP THAT WAS. WHAT WERE WE -- 18, MAYBE? WE THOUGHT THAT GENERAL STORE WAS A DEAD CERT, TOO ..."
HERE -- WHAT'S THE DAMAGE ON THIS?
$5.00
SOCKS M-L $2.00
NO CREDIT NO CHECKS
OI! YOU BY THE CIGS! WHATTAYA THINK YER DOIN'?!
$5.00
SCARPER, MATE!
NO YOU DON'T!
OW! LEGGO, YA BLOODY GREAT APE!
KRAK!
10

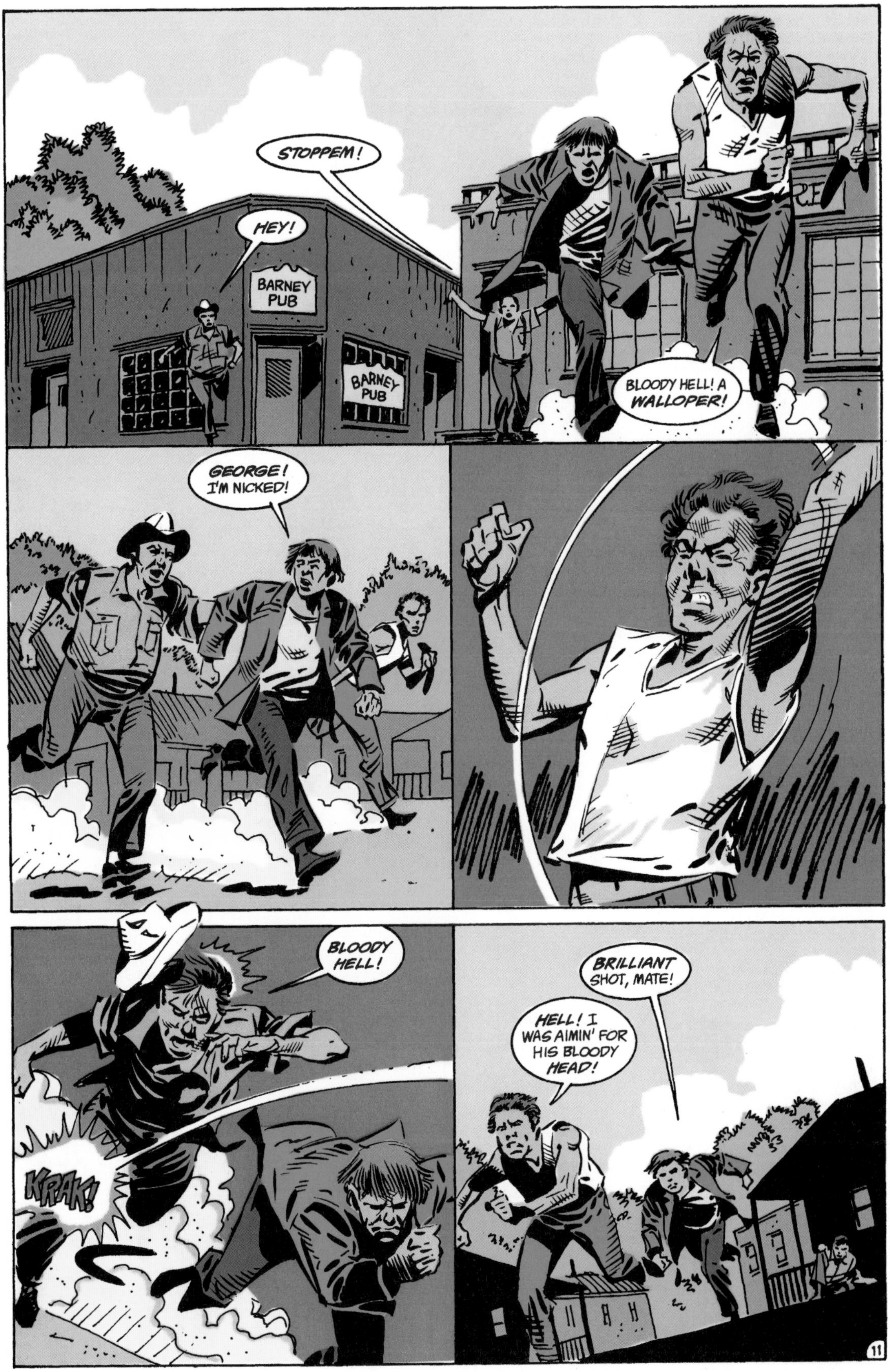
STOPPEM!
HEY!
BARNEY PUB
BARNEY PUB
BLOODY HELL! A WALLOPER!
GEORGE! I'M NICKED!
BLOODY HELL!
KRAK!
BRILLIANT SHOT, MATE!
HELL! I WAS AIMIN' FOR HIS BLOODY HEAD!
11

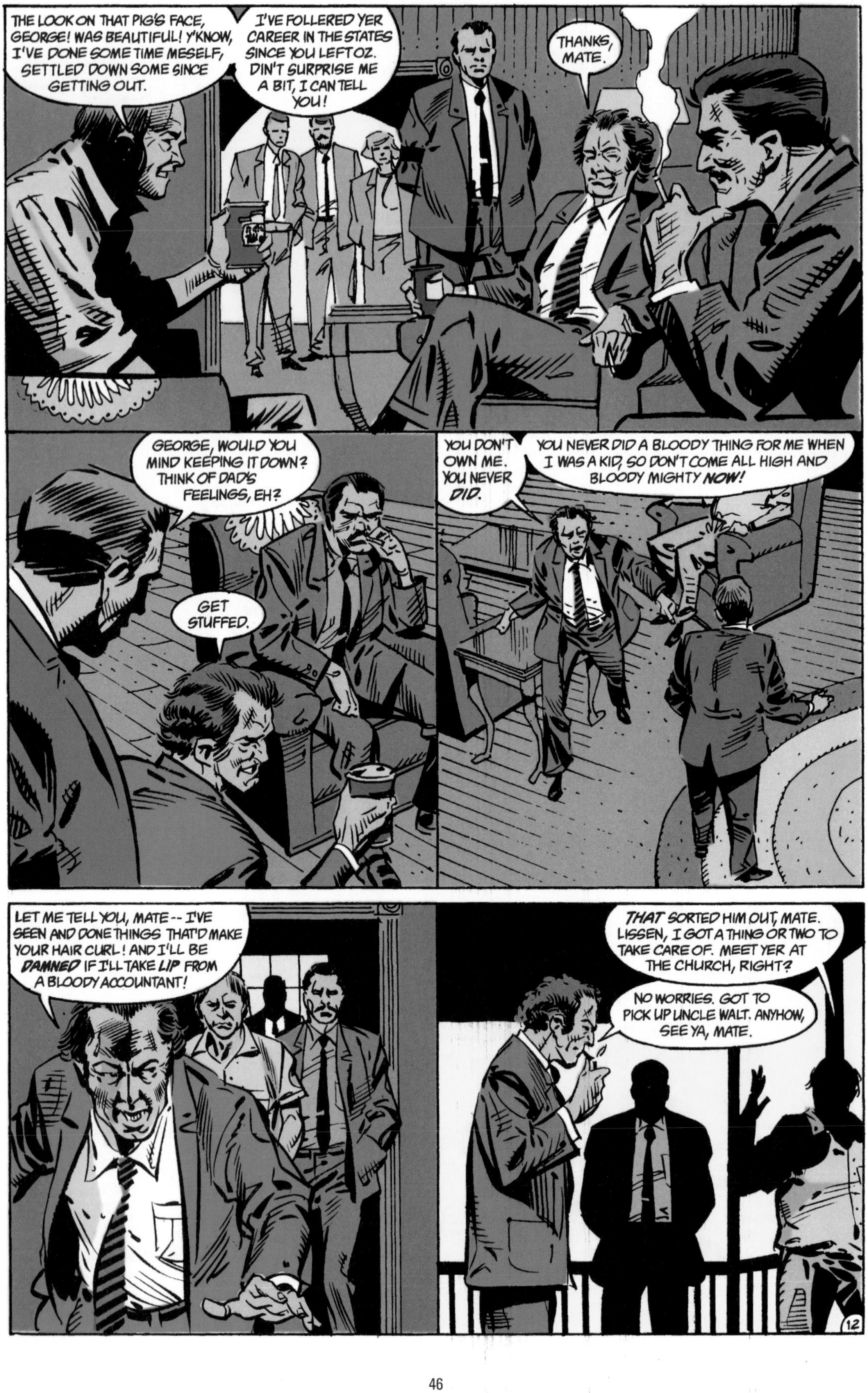
THE LOOK ON THAT PIG'S FACE, GEORGE! WAS BEAUTIFUL! Y'KNOW, I'VE DONE SOME TIME MESELF, SETTLED DOWN SOME SINCE GETTING OUT.
I'VE FOLLERED YER CAREER IN THE STATES SINCE YOU LEFT OZ. DIN'T SURPRISE ME A BIT, I CAN TELL YOU!
THANKS, MATE.
GEORGE, WOULD YOU MIND KEEPING IT DOWN? THINK OF DAD'S FEELINGS, EH?
GET STUFFED.
YOU DON'T OWN ME. YOU NEVER DID.
YOU NEVER DID A BLOODY THING FOR ME WHEN I WAS A KID, SO DON'T COME ALL HIGH AND BLOODY MIGHTY NOW!
LET ME TELL YOU, MATE -- I'VE SEEN AND DONE THINGS THAT'D MAKE YOUR HAIR CURL! AND I'LL BE DAMNED IF I'LL TAKE LIP FROM A BLOODY ACCOUNTANT!
THAT SORTED HIM OUT, MATE. LISSEN, I GOT A THING OR TWO TO TAKE CARE OF. MEET YER AT THE CHURCH, RIGHT?
NO WORRIES. GOT TO PICK UP UNCLE WALT. ANYHOW, SEE YA, MATE.
12

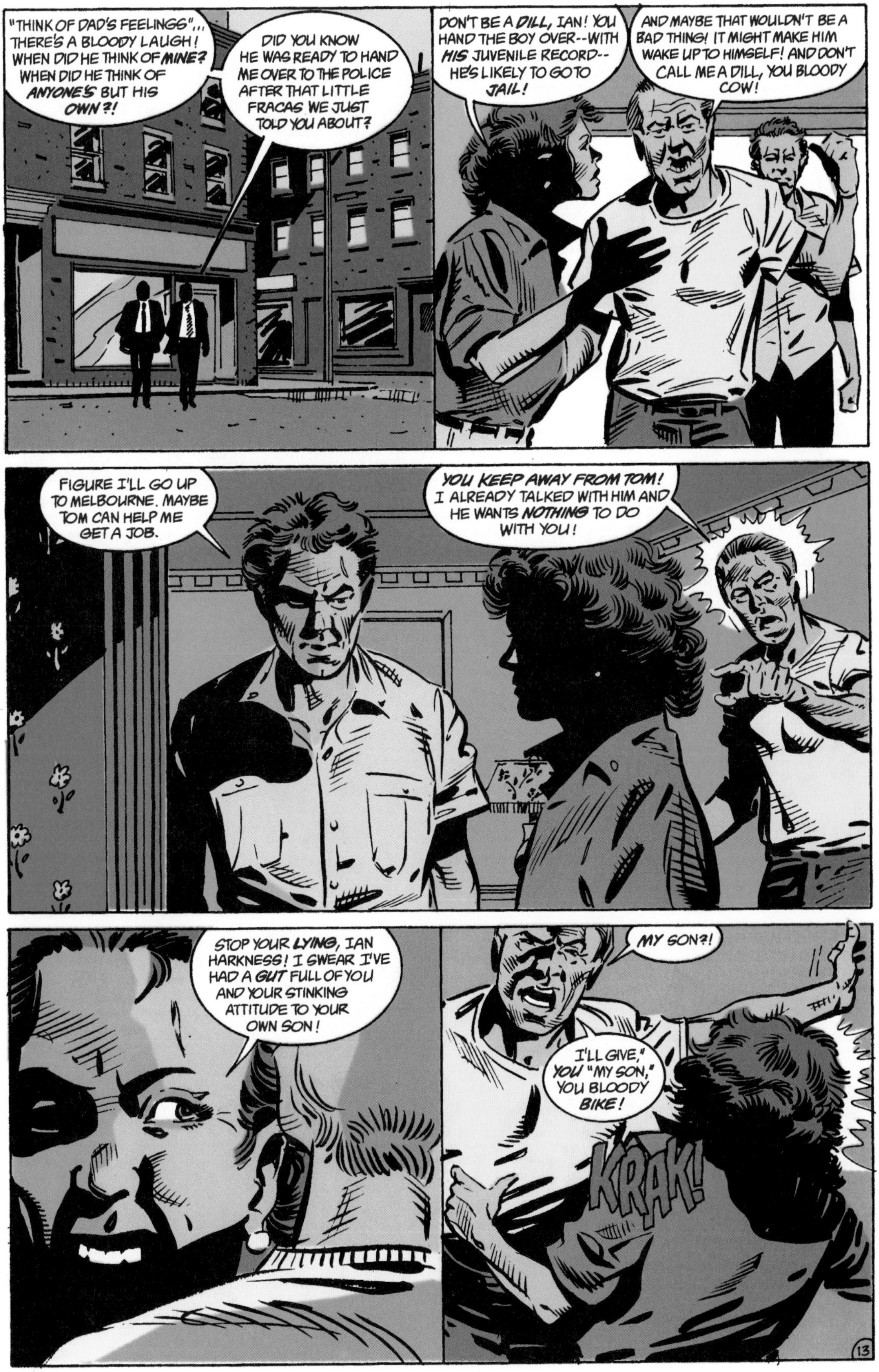
"THINK OF DAD'S FEELINGS"... THERE'S A BLOODY LAUGH! WHEN DID HE THINK OF MINE? WHEN DID HE THINK OF ANYONE'S BUT HIS OWN?!
DID YOU KNOW HE WAS READY TO HAND ME OVER TO THE POLICE AFTER THAT LITTLE FRACAS WE JUST TOLD YOU ABOUT?
DON'T BE A DILL, IAN! YOU HAND THE BOY OVER--WITH HIS JUVENILE RECORD--HE'S LIKELY TO GO TO JAIL!
AND MAYBE THAT WOULDN'T BE A BAD THING! IT MIGHT MAKE HIM WAKE UP TO HIMSELF! AND DON'T CALL ME A DILL, YOU BLOODY COW!
FIGURE I'LL GO UP TO MELBOURNE. MAYBE TOM CAN HELP ME GET A JOB.
YOU KEEP AWAY FROM TOM! I ALREADY TALKED WITH HIM AND HE WANTS NOTHING TO DO WITH YOU!
STOP YOUR LYING, IAN HARKNESS! I SWEAR I'VE HAD A GUT FULL OF YOU AND YOUR STINKING ATTITUDE TO YOUR OWN SON!
MY SON?!
I'LL GIVE," YOU "MY SON," YOU BLOODY BIKE!
KRAK!
13

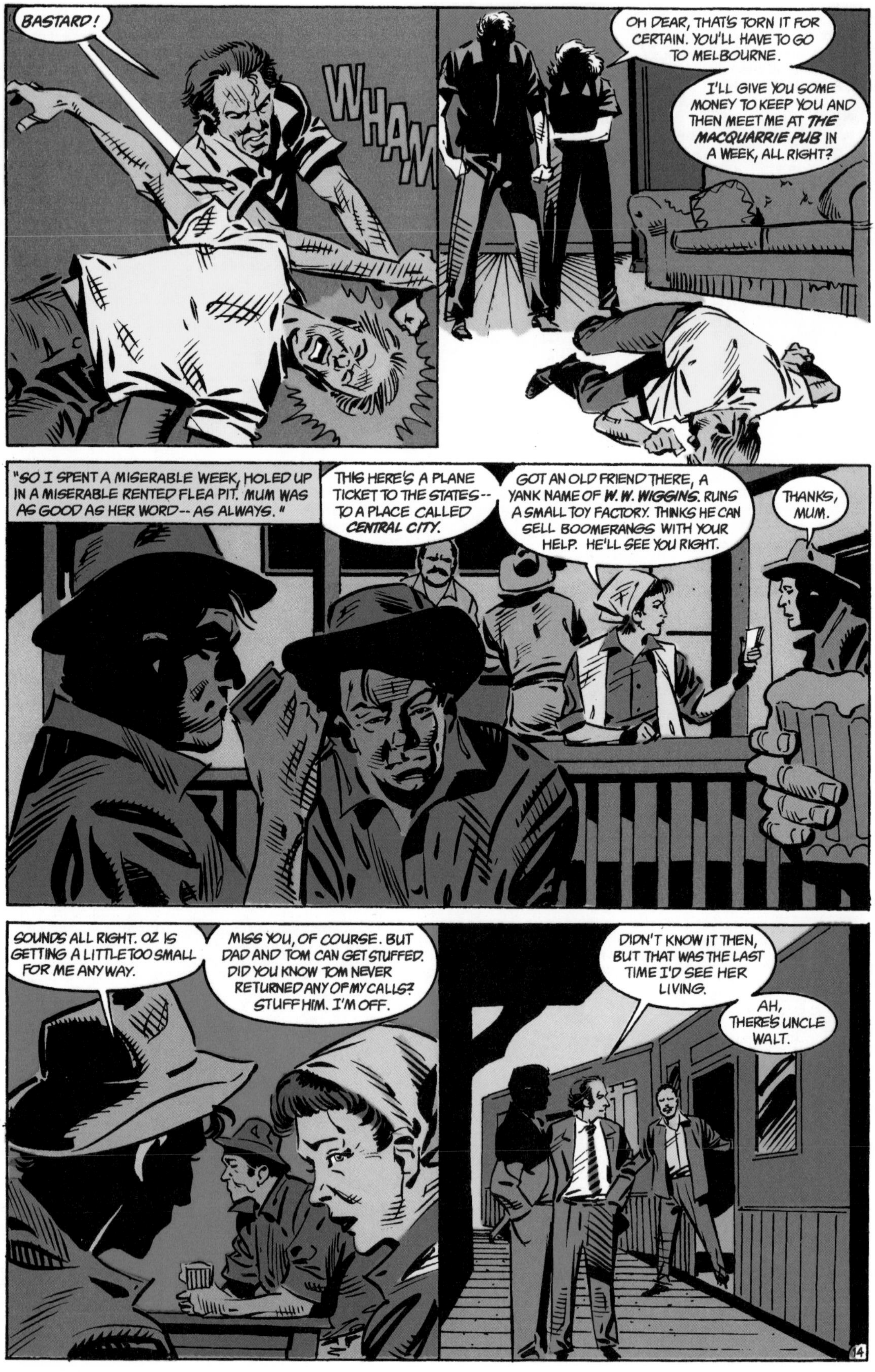
BASTARD!
WHAM
OH DEAR, THAT'S TORN IT FOR CERTAIN. YOU'LL HAVE TO GO TO MELBOURNE.
I'LL GIVE YOU SOME MONEY TO KEEP YOU AND THEN MEET ME AT THE MACQUARRIE PUB IN A WEEK, ALL RIGHT?
"SO I SPENT A MISERABLE WEEK, HOLED UP IN A MISERABLE RENTED FLEA PIT. MUM WAS AS GOOD AS HER WORD-- AS ALWAYS."
THIS HERE'S A PLANE TICKET TO THE STATES-- TO A PLACE CALLED CENTRAL CITY.
GOT AN OLD FRIEND THERE, A YANK NAME OF W. W. WIGGINS. RUNS A SMALL TOY FACTORY. THINKS HE CAN SELL BOOMERANGS WITH YOUR HELP. HE'LL SEE YOU RIGHT.
THANKS, MUM.
SOUNDS ALL RIGHT. OZ IS GETTING A LITTLE TOO SMALL FOR ME ANYWAY.
MISS YOU, OF COURSE. BUT DAD AND TOM CAN GET STUFFED. DID YOU KNOW TOM NEVER RETURNED ANY OF MY CALLS? STUFF HIM. I'M OFF.
DIDN'T KNOW IT THEN, BUT THAT WAS THE LAST TIME I'D SEE HER LIVING.
AH, THERE'S UNCLE WALT.
14

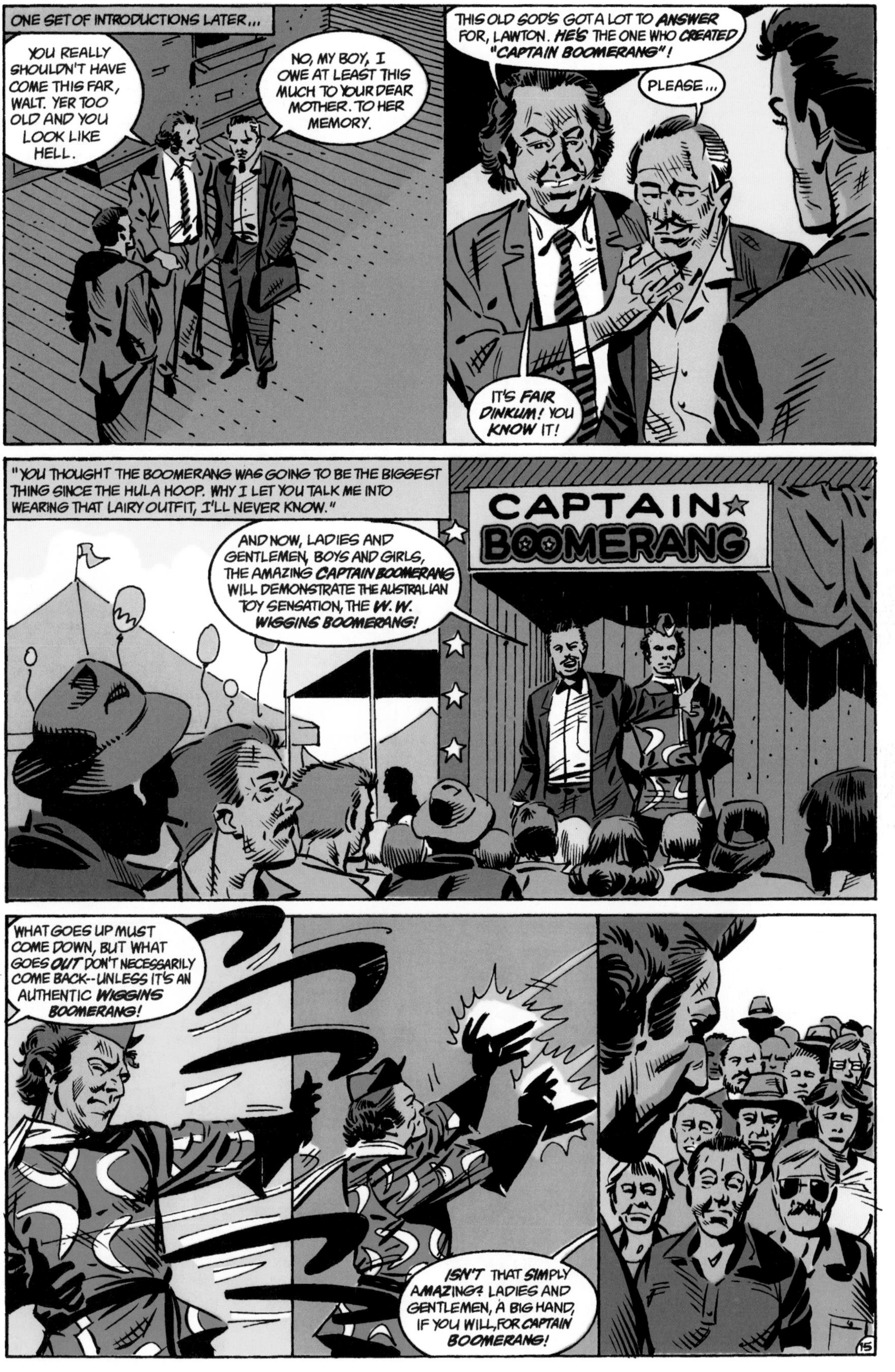
ONE SET OF INTRODUCTIONS LATER...
YOU REALLY SHOULDN'T HAVE COME THIS FAR, WALT. YER TOO OLD AND YOU LOOK LIKE HELL.
NO, MY BOY, I OWE AT LEAST THIS MUCH TO YOUR DEAR MOTHER. TO HER MEMORY.
THIS OLD SOD'S GOT A LOT TO ANSWER FOR, LAWTON. HE'S THE ONE WHO CREATED "CAPTAIN BOOMERANG"!
PLEASE...
IT'S FAIR DINKUM! YOU KNOW IT!
"YOU THOUGHT THE BOOMERANG WAS GOING TO BE THE BIGGEST THING SINCE THE HULA HOOP. WHY I LET YOU TALK ME INTO WEARING THAT LAIRY OUTFIT, I'LL NEVER KNOW."
CAPTAIN BOOMERANG
AND NOW, LADIES AND GENTLEMEN, BOYS AND GIRLS, THE AMAZING CAPTAIN BOOMERANG WILL DEMONSTRATE THE AUSTRALIAN TOY SENSATION, THE W. W. WIGGINS BOOMERANG!
WHAT GOES UP MUST COME DOWN, BUT WHAT GOES OUT DON'T NECESSARILY COME BACK--UNLESS IT'S AN AUTHENTIC WIGGINS BOOMERANG!
ISN'T THAT SIMPLY AMAZING? LADIES AND GENTLEMEN, A BIG HAND, IF YOU WILL, FOR CAPTAIN BOOMERANG!
15

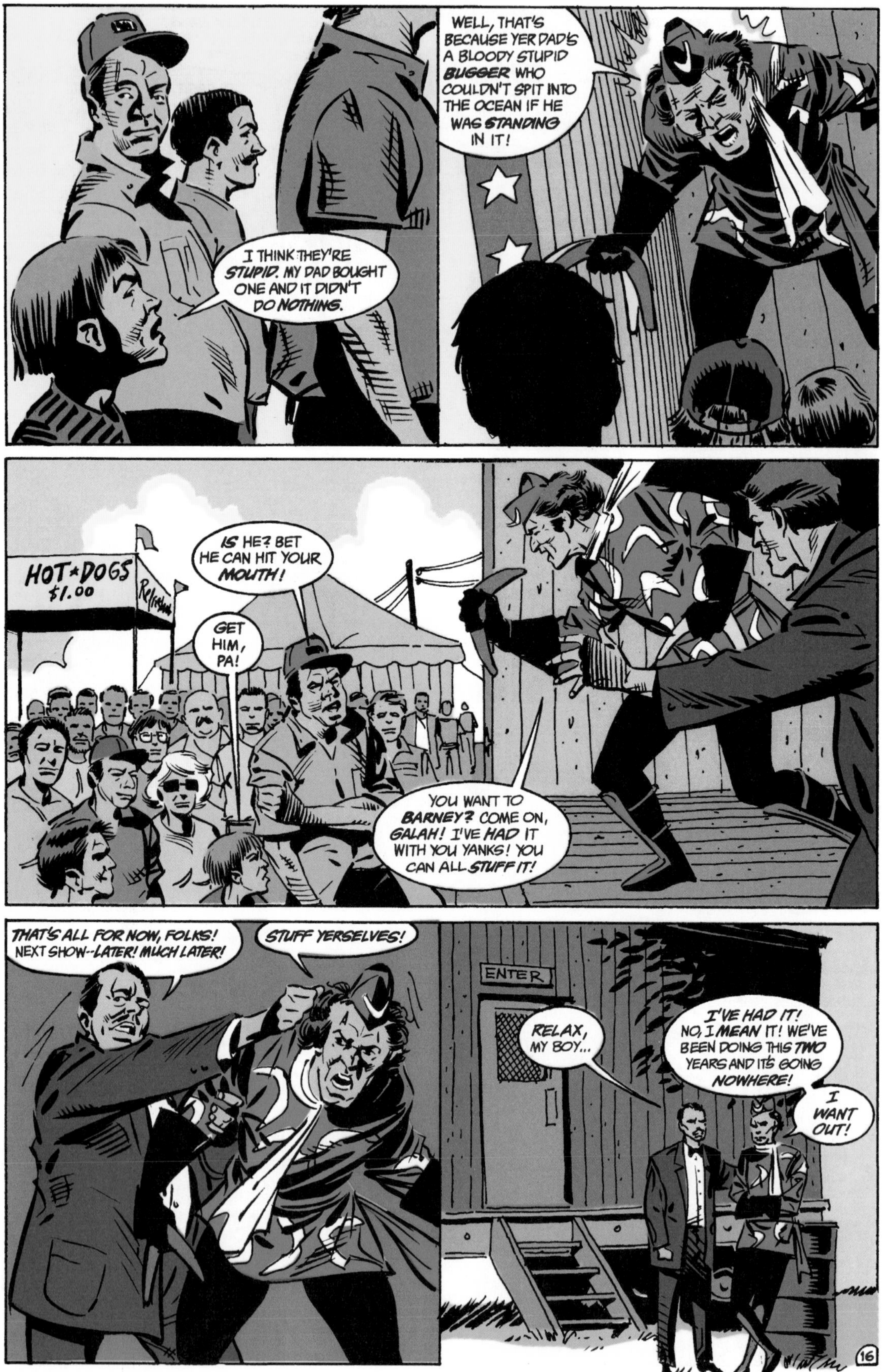
I THINK THEY'RE STUPID. MY DAD BOUGHT ONE AND IT DIDN'T DO NOTHING.
WELL, THAT'S BECAUSE YER DAD'S A BLOODY STUPID BUGGER WHO COULDN'T SPIT INTO THE OCEAN IF HE WAS STANDING IN IT!
HOT★DOGS $1.00
IS HE? BET HE CAN HIT YOUR MOUTH!
GET HIM, PA!
YOU WANT TO BARNEY? COME ON, GALAH! I'VE HAD IT WITH YOU YANKS! YOU CAN ALL STUFF IT!
THAT'S ALL FOR NOW, FOLKS! NEXT SHOW--LATER! MUCH LATER!
STUFF YERSELVES!
ENTER
RELAX, MY BOY...
I'VE HAD IT! NO, I MEAN IT! WE'VE BEEN DOING THIS TWO YEARS AND IT'S GOING NOWHERE!
I WANT OUT!
16

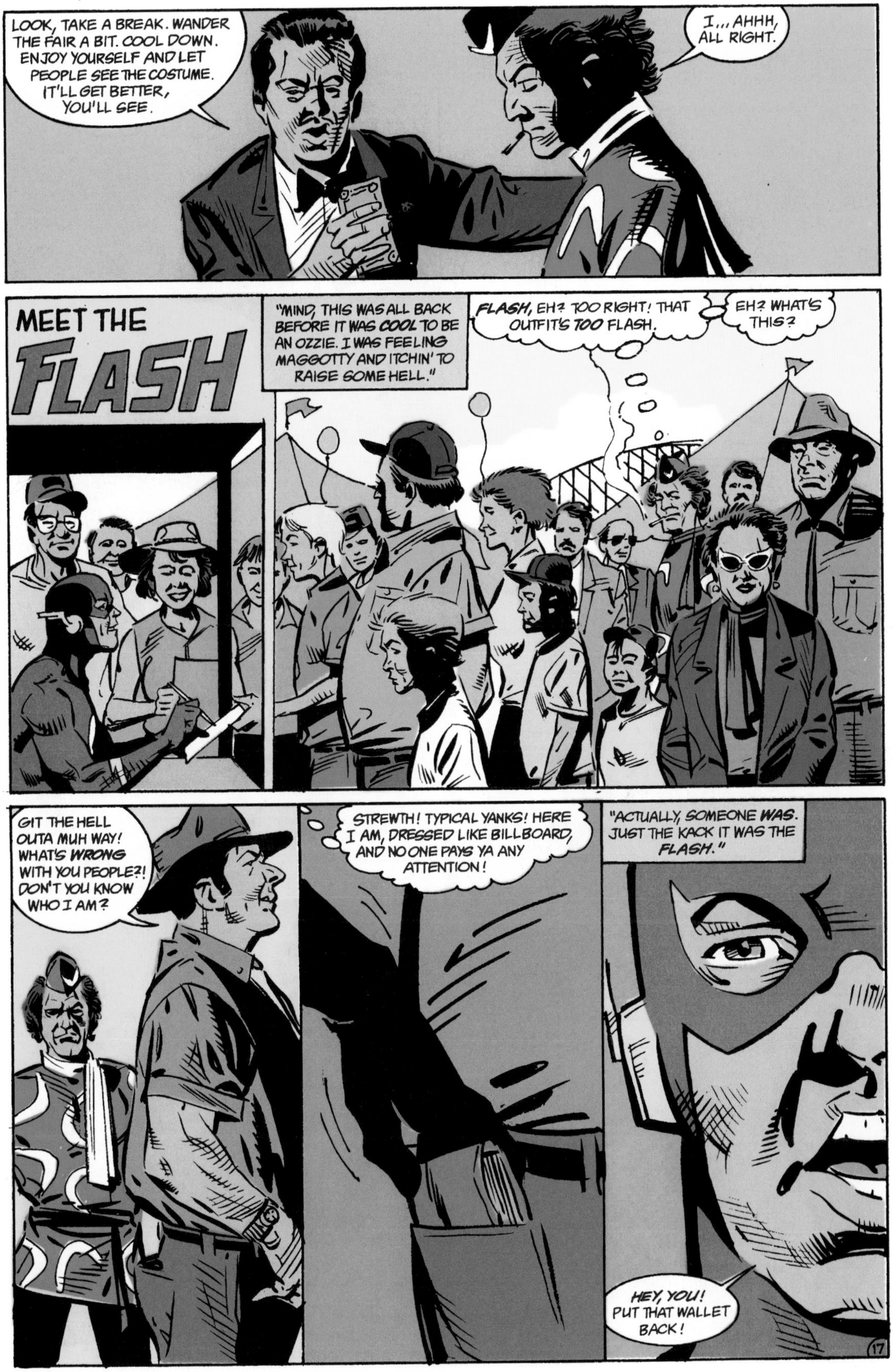
LOOK, TAKE A BREAK. WANDER THE FAIR A BIT. COOL DOWN. ENJOY YOURSELF AND LET PEOPLE SEE THE COSTUME. IT'LL GET BETTER, YOU'LL SEE.
I... AHHH, ALL RIGHT.
MEET THE FLASH
"MIND, THIS WAS ALL BACK BEFORE IT WAS COOL TO BE AN OZZIE. I WAS FEELING MAGGOTTY AND ITCHIN' TO RAISE SOME HELL."
FLASH, EH? TOO RIGHT! THAT OUTFIT'S TOO FLASH.
EH? WHAT'S THIS?
GIT THE HELL OUTA MUH WAY! WHAT'S WRONG WITH YOU PEOPLE?! DON'T YOU KNOW WHO I AM?
STREWTH! TYPICAL YANKS! HERE I AM, DRESSED LIKE BILLBOARD, AND NO ONE PAYS YA ANY ATTENTION!
"ACTUALLY, SOMEONE WAS. JUST THE KACK IT WAS THE FLASH."
HEY, YOU! PUT THAT WALLET BACK!
17

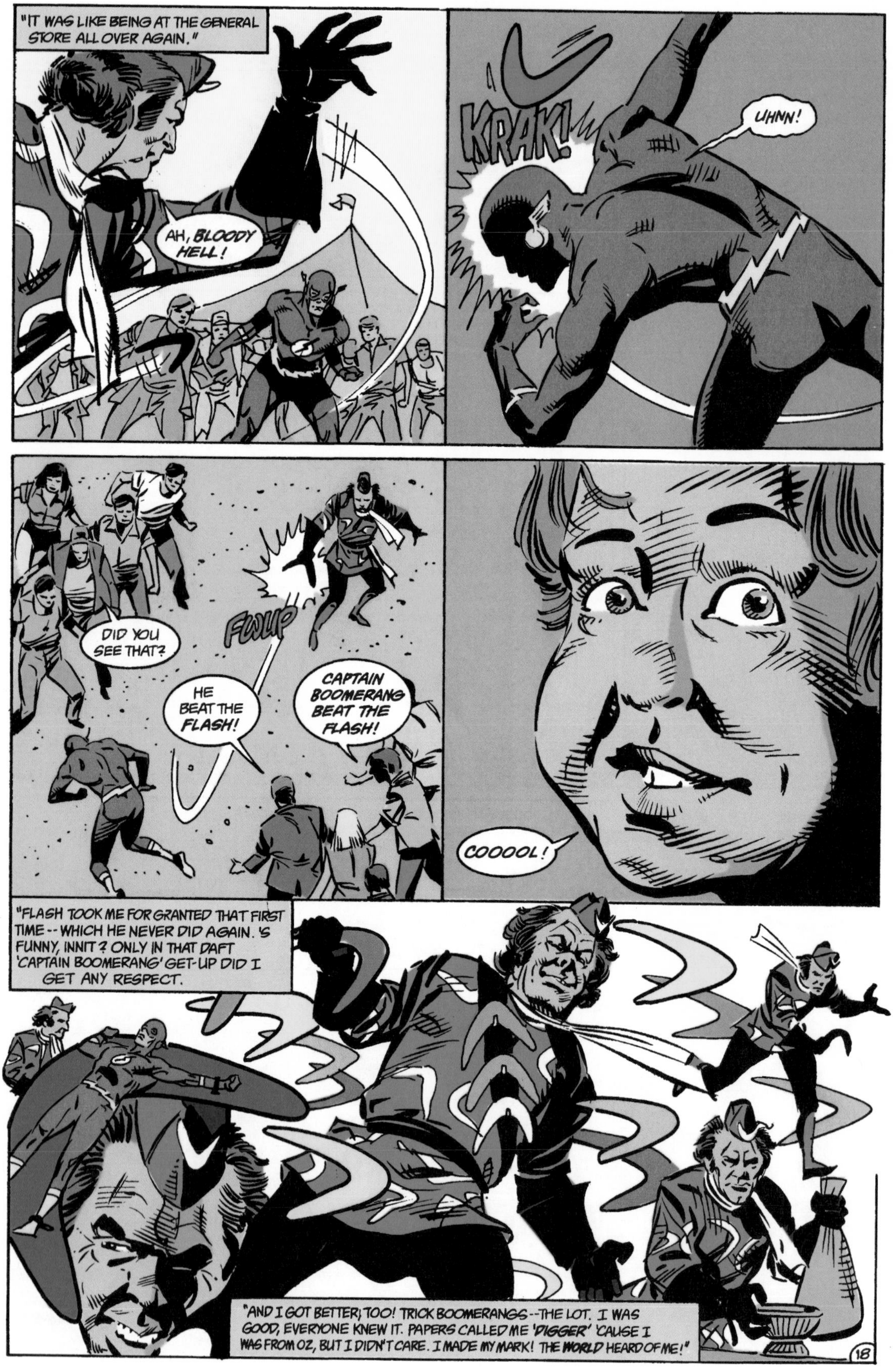
"IT WAS LIKE BEING AT THE GENERAL STORE ALL OVER AGAIN."
AH, BLOODY HELL!
KRAK!
UHNN!
FWUP
DID YOU SEE THAT?
HE BEAT THE FLASH!
CAPTAIN BOOMERANG BEAT THE FLASH!
COOOOL!
"FLASH TOOK ME FOR GRANTED THAT FIRST TIME -- WHICH HE NEVER DID AGAIN. 'S FUNNY, INNIT? ONLY IN THAT DAFT 'CAPTAIN BOOMERANG' GET-UP DID I GET ANY RESPECT.
"AND I GOT BETTER, TOO! TRICK BOOMERANGS -- THE LOT. I WAS GOOD, EVERYONE KNEW IT. PAPERS CALLED ME 'DIGGER' 'CAUSE I WAS FROM OZ, BUT I DIDN'T CARE. I MADE MY MARK! THE WORLD HEARD OF ME!"
18

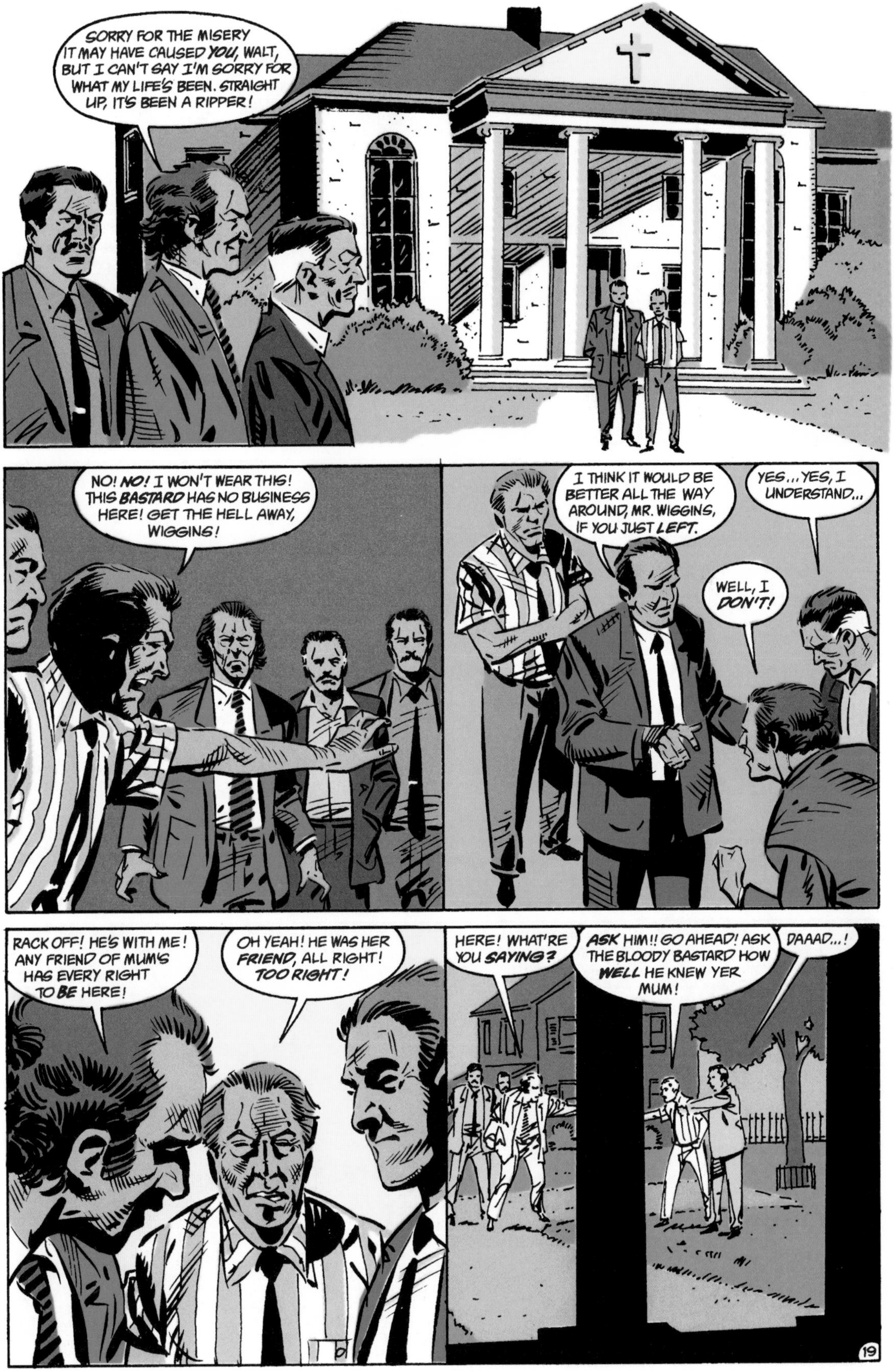

SORRY FOR THE MISERY IT MAY HAVE CAUSED YOU, WALT, BUT I CAN'T SAY I'M SORRY FOR WHAT MY LIFE'S BEEN. STRAIGHT UP, IT'S BEEN A RIPPER!
NO! NO! I WON'T WEAR THIS! THIS BASTARD HAS NO BUSINESS HERE! GET THE HELL AWAY, WIGGINS!
I THINK IT WOULD BE BETTER ALL THE WAY AROUND, MR. WIGGINS, IF YOU JUST LEFT.
YES... YES, I UNDERSTAND...
WELL, I DON'T!
RACK OFF! HE'S WITH ME! ANY FRIEND OF MUM'S HAS EVERY RIGHT TO BE HERE!
OH YEAH! HE WAS HER FRIEND, ALL RIGHT! TOO RIGHT!
HERE! WHAT'RE YOU SAYING?
ASK HIM!! GO AHEAD! ASK THE BLOODY BASTARD HOW WELL HE KNEW YER MUM!
DAAAD...!
19

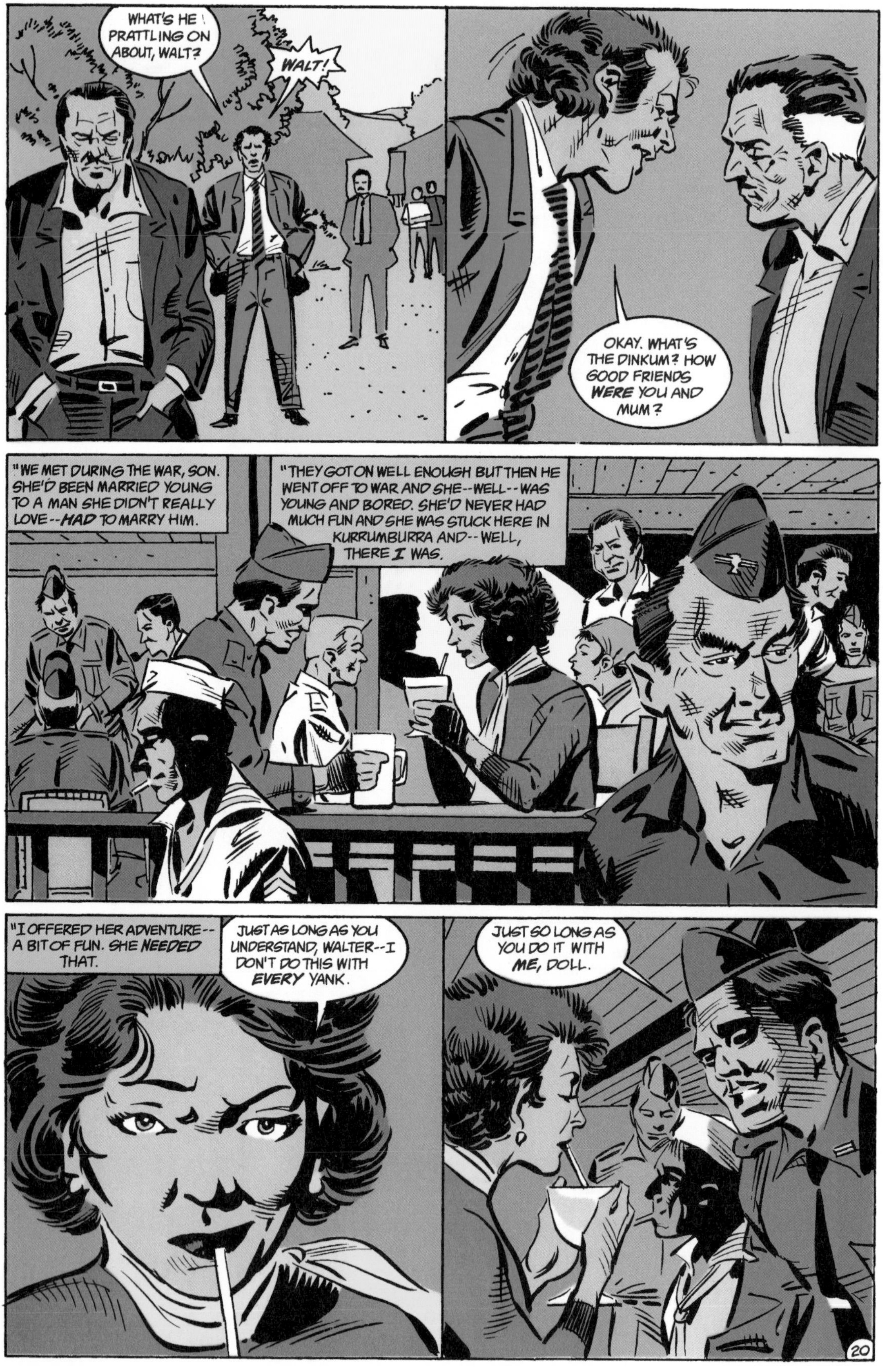
WHAT'S HE PRATTLING ON ABOUT, WALT?
WALT!
OKAY. WHAT'S THE DINKUM? HOW GOOD FRIENDS *WERE* YOU AND MUM?
"WE MET DURING THE WAR, SON. SHE'D BEEN MARRIED YOUNG TO A MAN SHE DIDN'T REALLY LOVE--*HAD* TO MARRY HIM.
"THEY GOT ON WELL ENOUGH BUT THEN HE WENT OFF TO WAR AND SHE--WELL--WAS YOUNG AND BORED. SHE'D NEVER HAD MUCH FUN AND SHE WAS STUCK HERE IN KURRUMBURRA AND--WELL, THERE *I* WAS.
"I OFFERED HER ADVENTURE-- A BIT OF FUN. SHE *NEEDED* THAT.
JUST AS LONG AS YOU UNDERSTAND, WALTER--I DON'T DO THIS WITH *EVERY* YANK.
JUST SO LONG AS YOU DO IT WITH *ME*, DOLL.
20

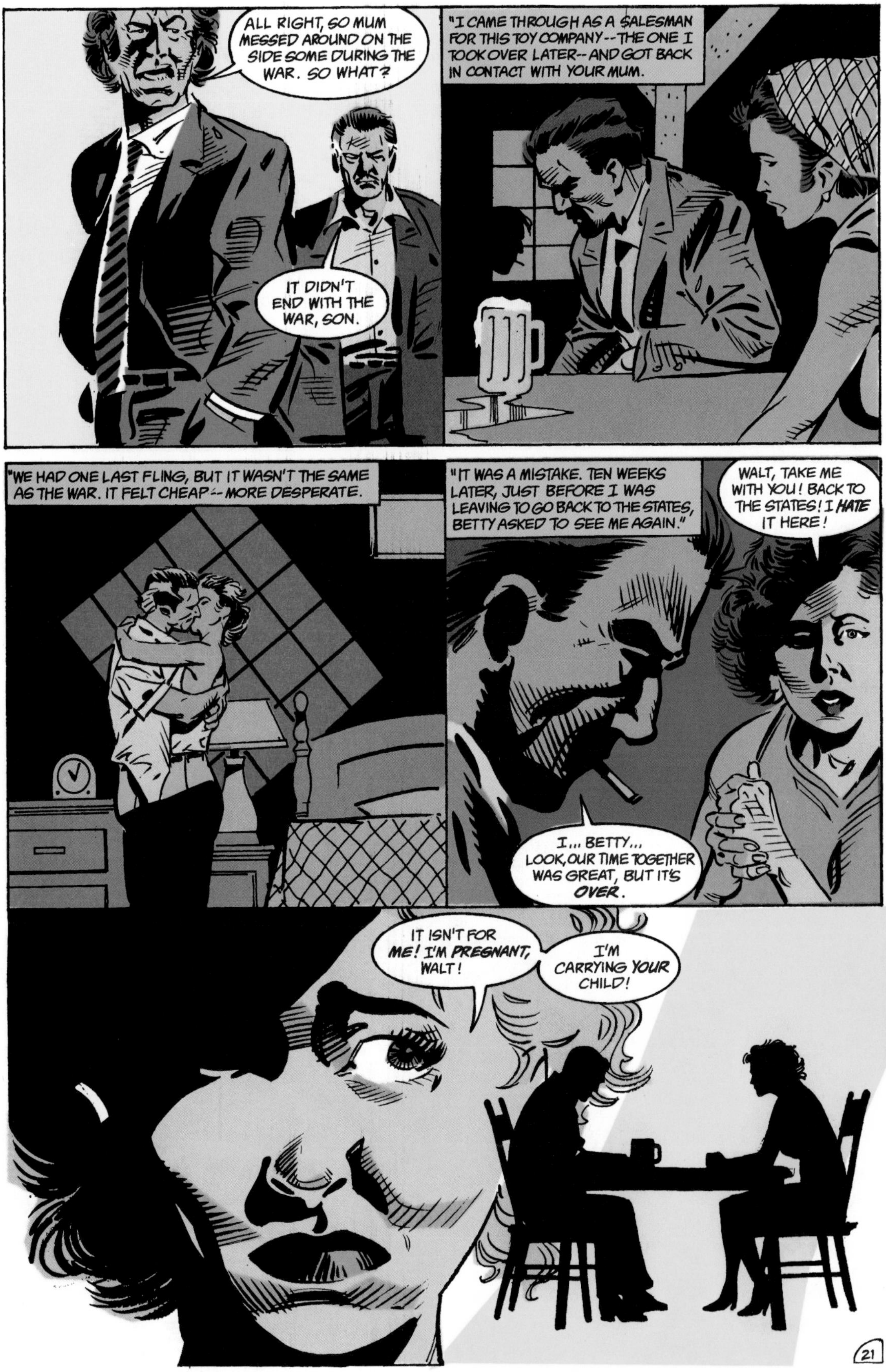
ALL RIGHT, SO MUM MESSED AROUND ON THE SIDE SOME DURING THE WAR. SO WHAT?
IT DIDN'T END WITH THE WAR, SON.
"I CAME THROUGH AS A SALESMAN FOR THIS TOY COMPANY--THE ONE I TOOK OVER LATER--AND GOT BACK IN CONTACT WITH YOUR MUM.
"WE HAD ONE LAST FLING, BUT IT WASN'T THE SAME AS THE WAR. IT FELT CHEAP--MORE DESPERATE.
"IT WAS A MISTAKE. TEN WEEKS LATER, JUST BEFORE I WAS LEAVING TO GO BACK TO THE STATES, BETTY ASKED TO SEE ME AGAIN."
WALT, TAKE ME WITH YOU! BACK TO THE STATES! I HATE IT HERE!
I... BETTY... LOOK, OUR TIME TOGETHER WAS GREAT, BUT IT'S OVER.
IT ISN'T FOR ME! I'M PREGNANT, WALT!
I'M CARRYING YOUR CHILD!
21

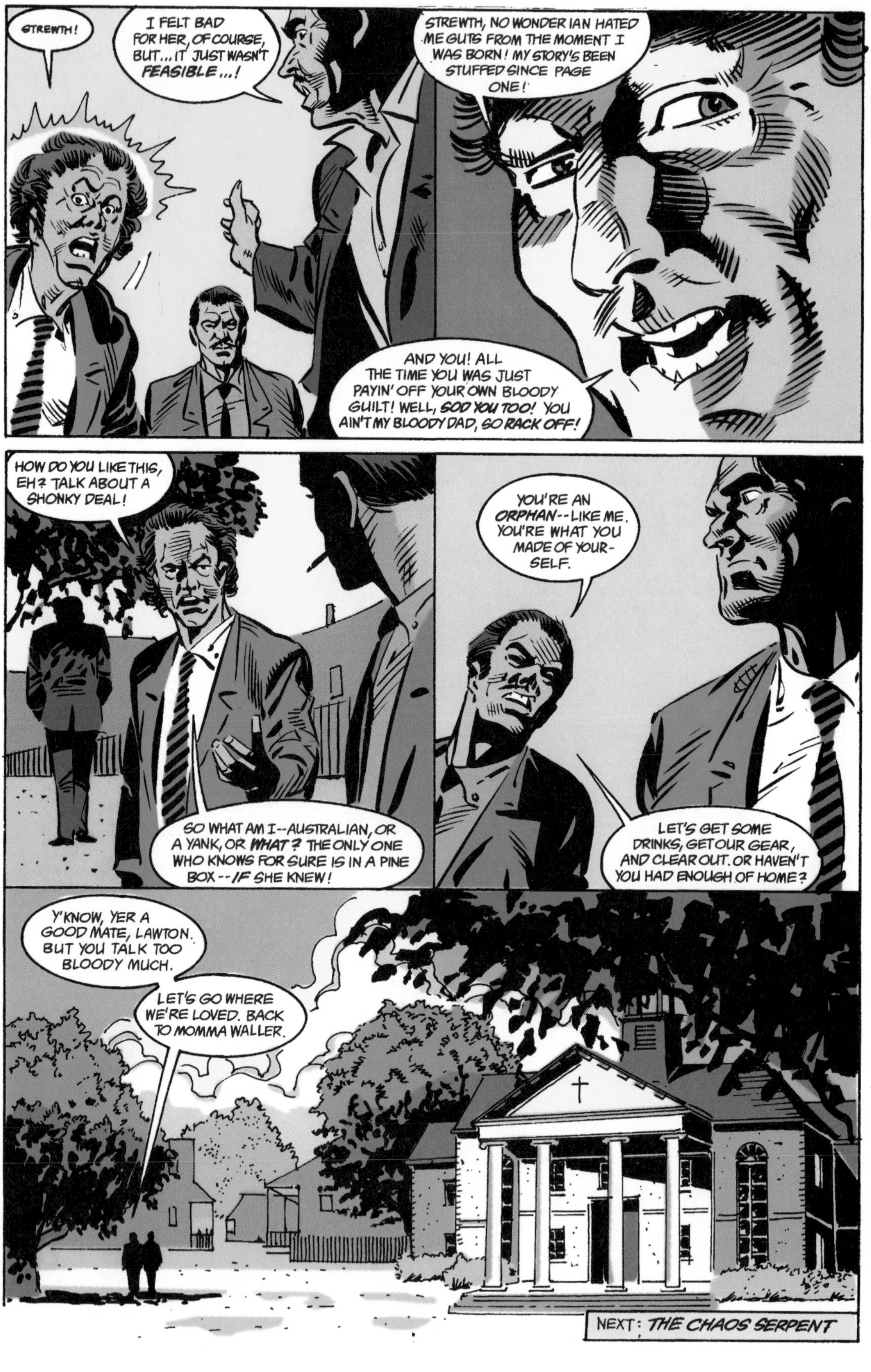
STREWTH!
I FELT BAD FOR HER, OF COURSE, BUT... IT JUST WASN'T *FEASIBLE*...!
STREWTH, NO WONDER IAN HATED ME GUTS FROM THE MOMENT I WAS BORN! MY STORY'S BEEN STUFFED SINCE PAGE ONE!
AND YOU! ALL THE TIME YOU WAS JUST PAYIN' OFF YOUR OWN BLOODY GUILT! WELL, *SOD YOU TOO!* YOU AIN'T MY BLOODY DAD, SO *RACK OFF!*
HOW DO YOU LIKE THIS, EH? TALK ABOUT A SHONKY DEAL!
SO WHAT AM I--AUSTRALIAN, OR A YANK, OR *WHAT?* THE ONLY ONE WHO KNOWS FOR SURE IS IN A PINE BOX--*IF* SHE KNEW!
YOU'RE AN *ORPHAN*--LIKE ME. YOU'RE WHAT YOU MADE OF YOURSELF.
LET'S GET SOME DRINKS, GET OUR GEAR, AND CLEAR OUT. OR HAVEN'T YOU HAD ENOUGH OF HOME?
Y'KNOW, YER A GOOD MATE, LAWTON. BUT YOU TALK TOO BLOODY MUCH.
LET'S GO WHERE WE'RE LOVED. BACK TO MOMMA WALLER.
NEXT: *THE CHAOS SERPENT*

Cover by **Alex Ross**

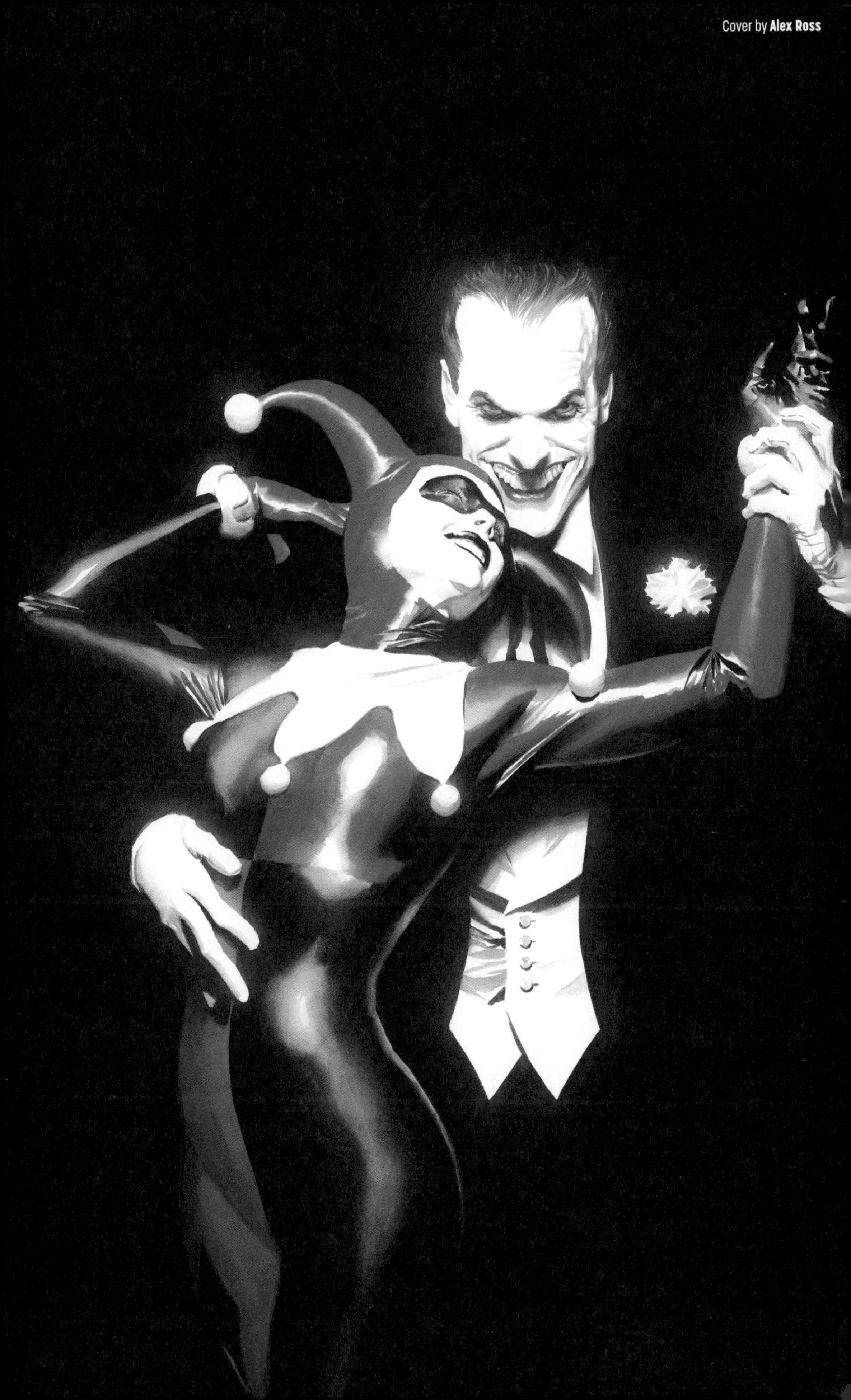

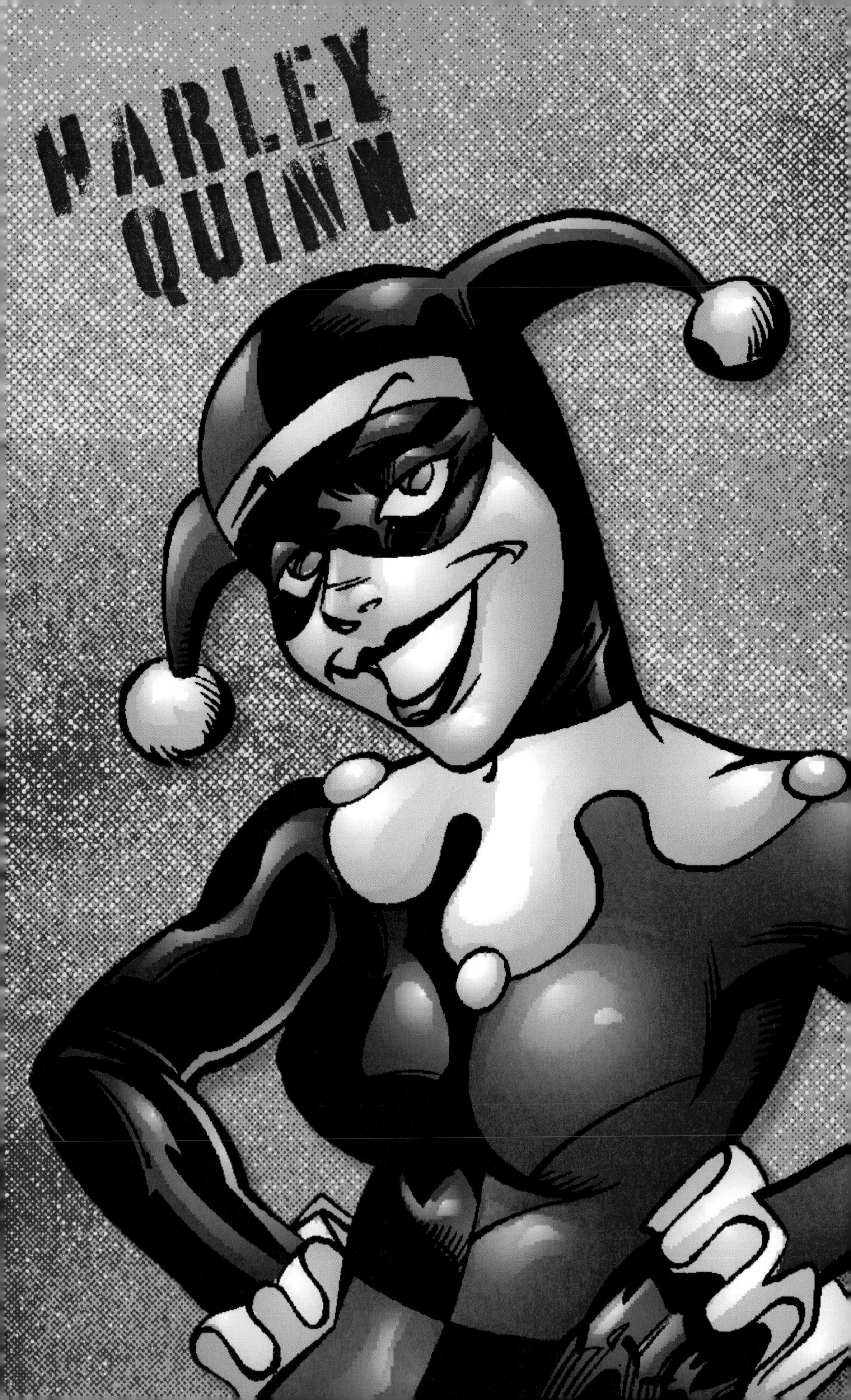
HARLEY
QUINN

BATMAN
HARLEY QUINN

written by **PAUL DINI**

pencilled by **YVEL GUICHET**

inked by **AARON SOWD**

lettered by **WILLIE SCHUBERT**

colored and separated by **RICHARD** and **TANYA HORIE**

Batman created by **BOB KANE**

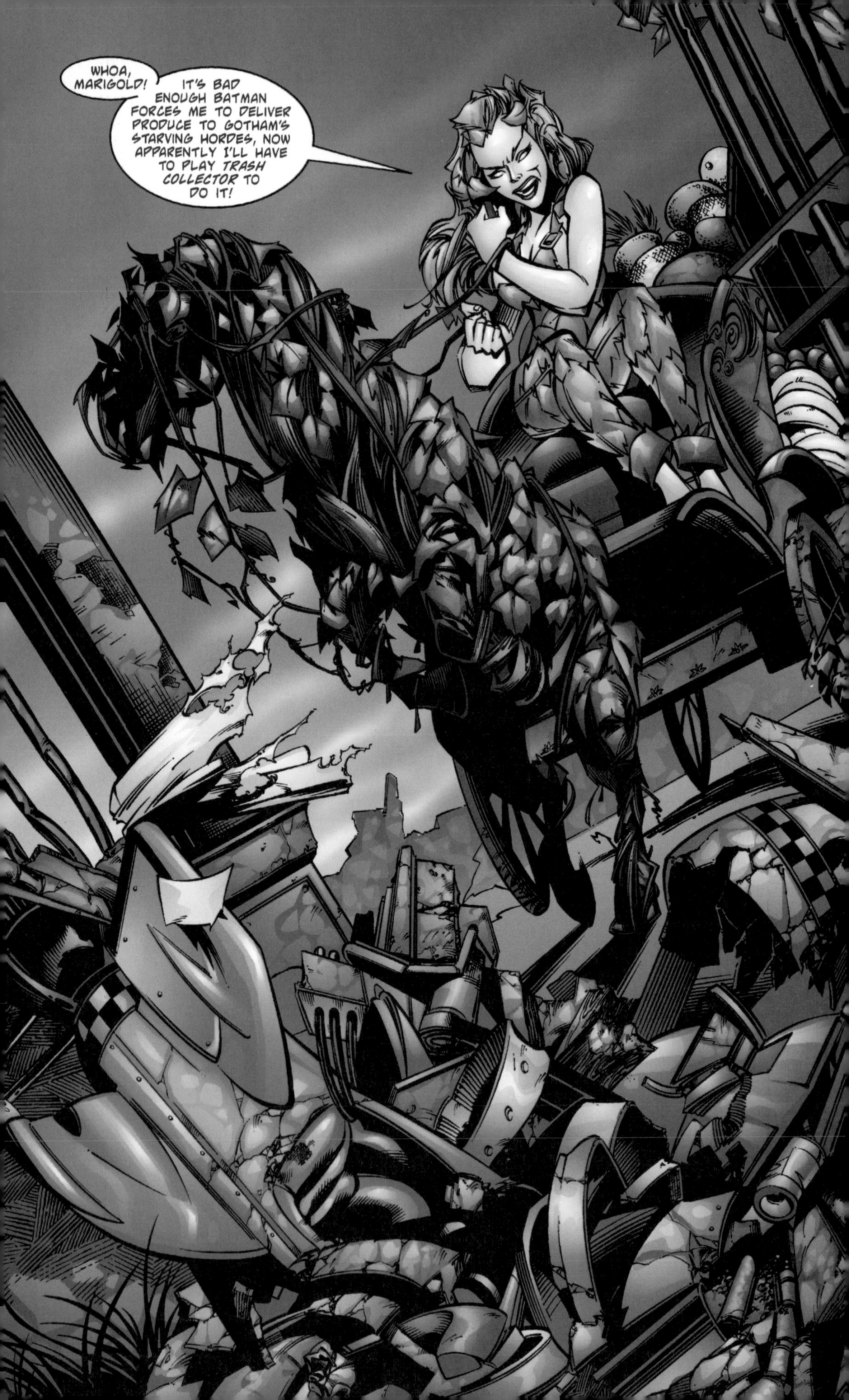
WHOA, MARIGOLD!
IT'S BAD ENOUGH BATMAN FORCES ME TO DELIVER PRODUCE TO GOTHAM'S STARVING HORDES, NOW APPARENTLY I'LL HAVE TO PLAY *TRASH COLLECTOR* TO DO IT!

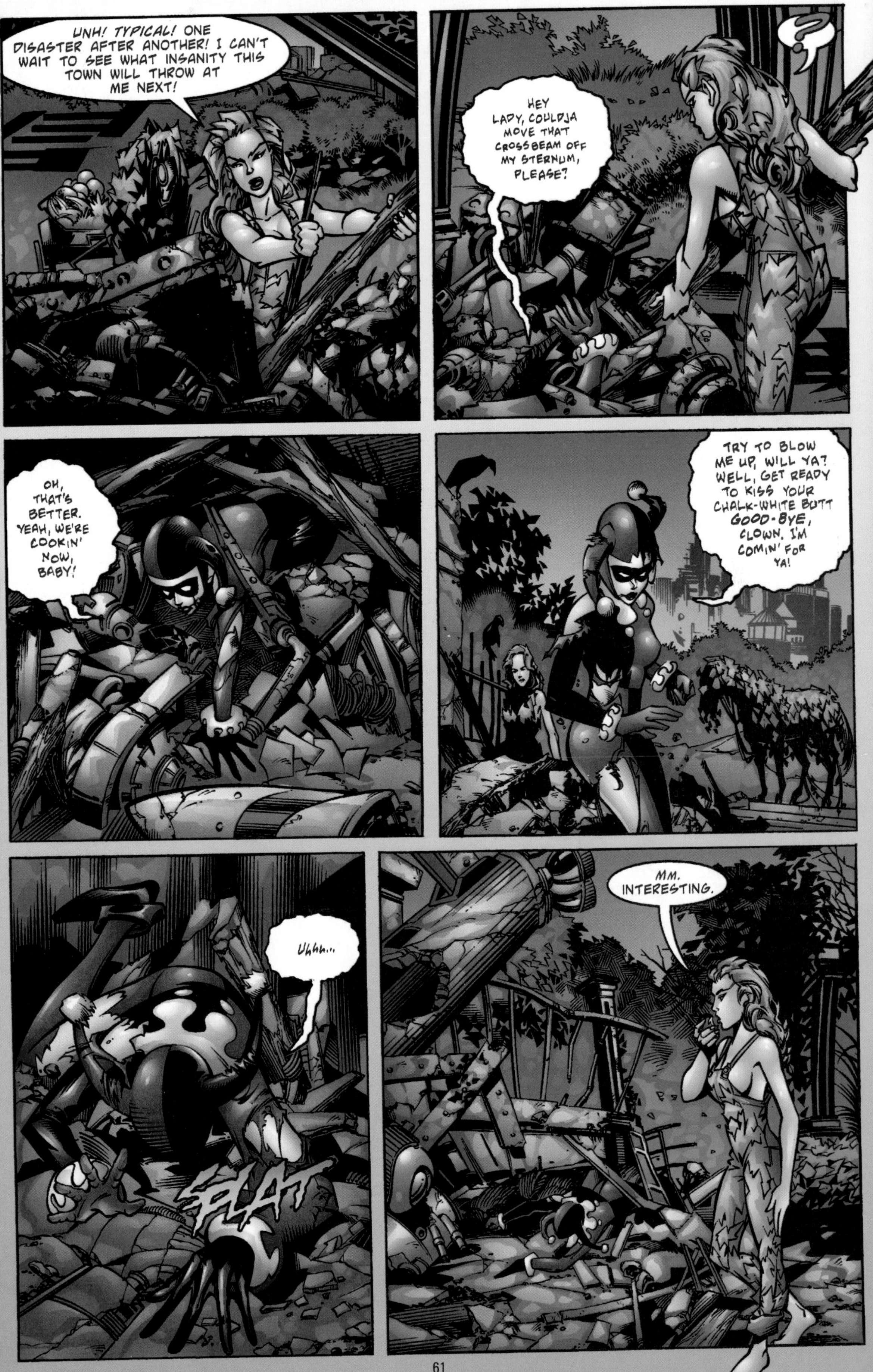
UNH! TYPICAL! ONE DISASTER AFTER ANOTHER! I CAN'T WAIT TO SEE WHAT INSANITY THIS TOWN WILL THROW AT ME NEXT!
?
HEY LADY, COULDJA MOVE THAT CROSSBEAM OFF MY STERNUM, PLEASE?
OH, THAT'S BETTER. YEAH, WE'RE COOKIN' NOW, BABY!
TRY TO BLOW ME UP, WILL YA? WELL, GET READY TO KISS YOUR CHALK-WHITE BUTT GOOD-BYE, CLOWN. I'M COMIN' FOR YA!
Uhhh...
SPLAT
MM. INTERESTING.

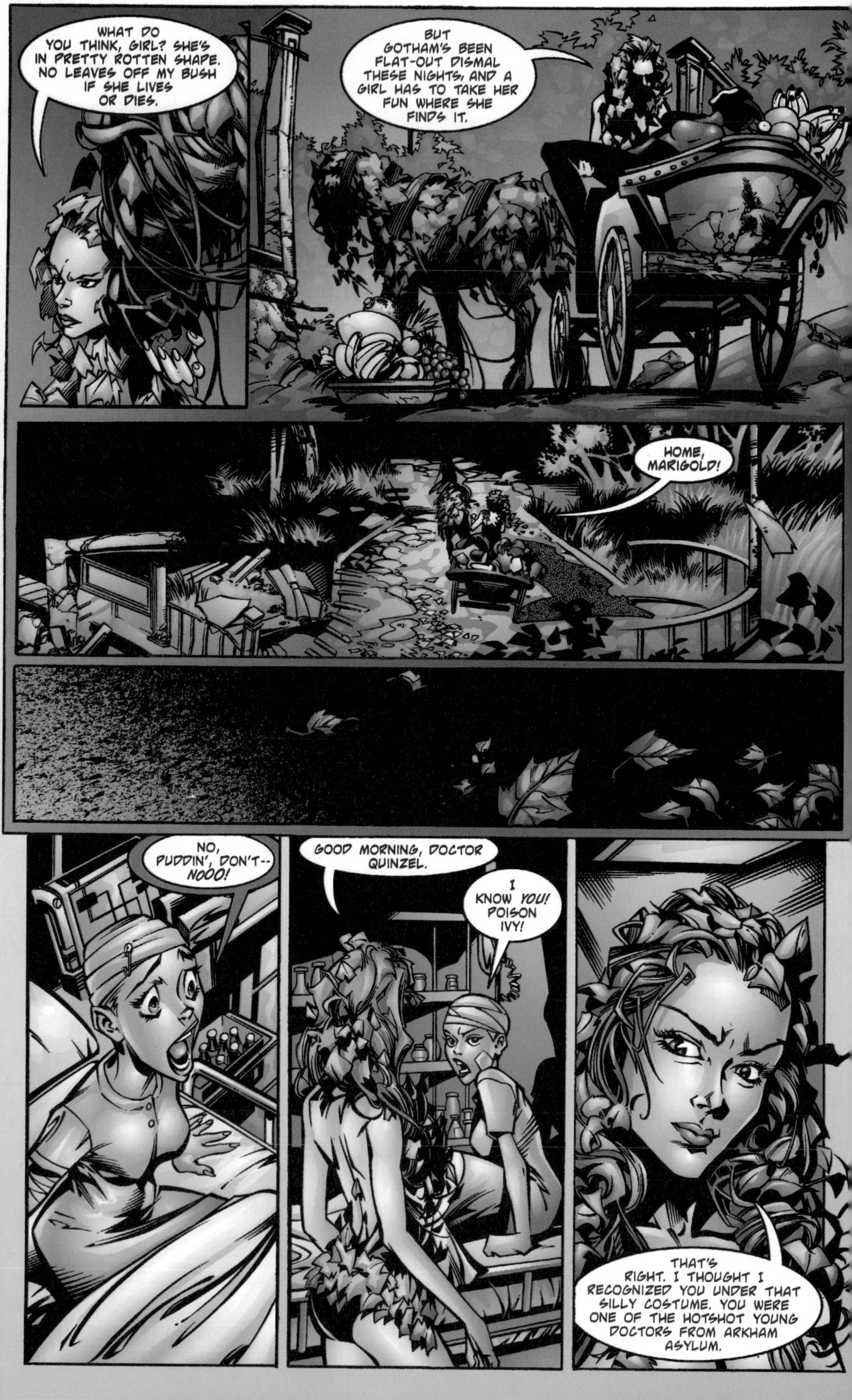
WHAT DO YOU THINK, GIRL? SHE'S IN PRETTY ROTTEN SHAPE. NO LEAVES OFF MY BUSH IF SHE LIVES OR DIES.
BUT GOTHAM'S BEEN FLAT-OUT DISMAL THESE NIGHTS, AND A GIRL HAS TO TAKE HER FUN WHERE SHE FINDS IT.
HOME, MARIGOLD!
NO, PUDDIN', DON'T-- NOOO!
GOOD MORNING, DOCTOR QUINZEL.
I KNOW YOU! POISON IVY!
THAT'S RIGHT. I THOUGHT I RECOGNIZED YOU UNDER THAT SILLY COSTUME. YOU WERE ONE OF THE HOTSHOT YOUNG DOCTORS FROM ARKHAM ASYLUM.

THAT ALONE IS ALL THE REASON I NEED TO KILL YOU!

SURE! BE MY GUEST! I DON'T CARE ANYMORE.

I GOT NOTHING TO LIVE FOR NOW! HERE, THIS GUNK LOOKS GOOD 'N NASTY. KNOWING YOU, ONE SIP AND IT'S FOOD-FOR-WORMS-TIME, RIGHT?

NOT SO FAST! YOU'RE ACTING IRRATIONALLY AND OUT OF GRIEF. THERE'S OBVIOUSLY A GOOD STORY HERE, AND I WANT TO HEAR IT.

WHY NOT? NOTHING LIKE A GOOD LAUGH AT SOME-ONE ELSE'S EXPENSE, RIGHT?

WELL, IF YOU REMEMBER ANYTHING AT ALL ABOUT ME, IT WAS PROBABLY THAT I WAS JUST ANOTHER NO-FUN INTERN DOING MY FIRST-YEAR RESIDENCY AT ARKHAM.

"AND THAT YOU WERE TRYING TO CONVINCE THE HIGHER-UPS TO LET YOU HOLD PRIVATE SESSIONS WITH THE JOKER. TALK ABOUT LIVING DANGEROUSLY."

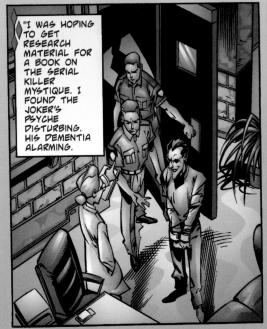

"I WAS HOPING TO GET RESEARCH MATERIAL FOR A BOOK ON THE SERIAL KILLER MYSTIQUE. I FOUND THE JOKER'S PSYCHE DISTURBING, HIS DEMENTIA ALARMING.

"AND HIS CHARM IRRESISTIBLE!

"WHAT CAN I TELL YA? THE GUY JUST DID IT FOR ME.

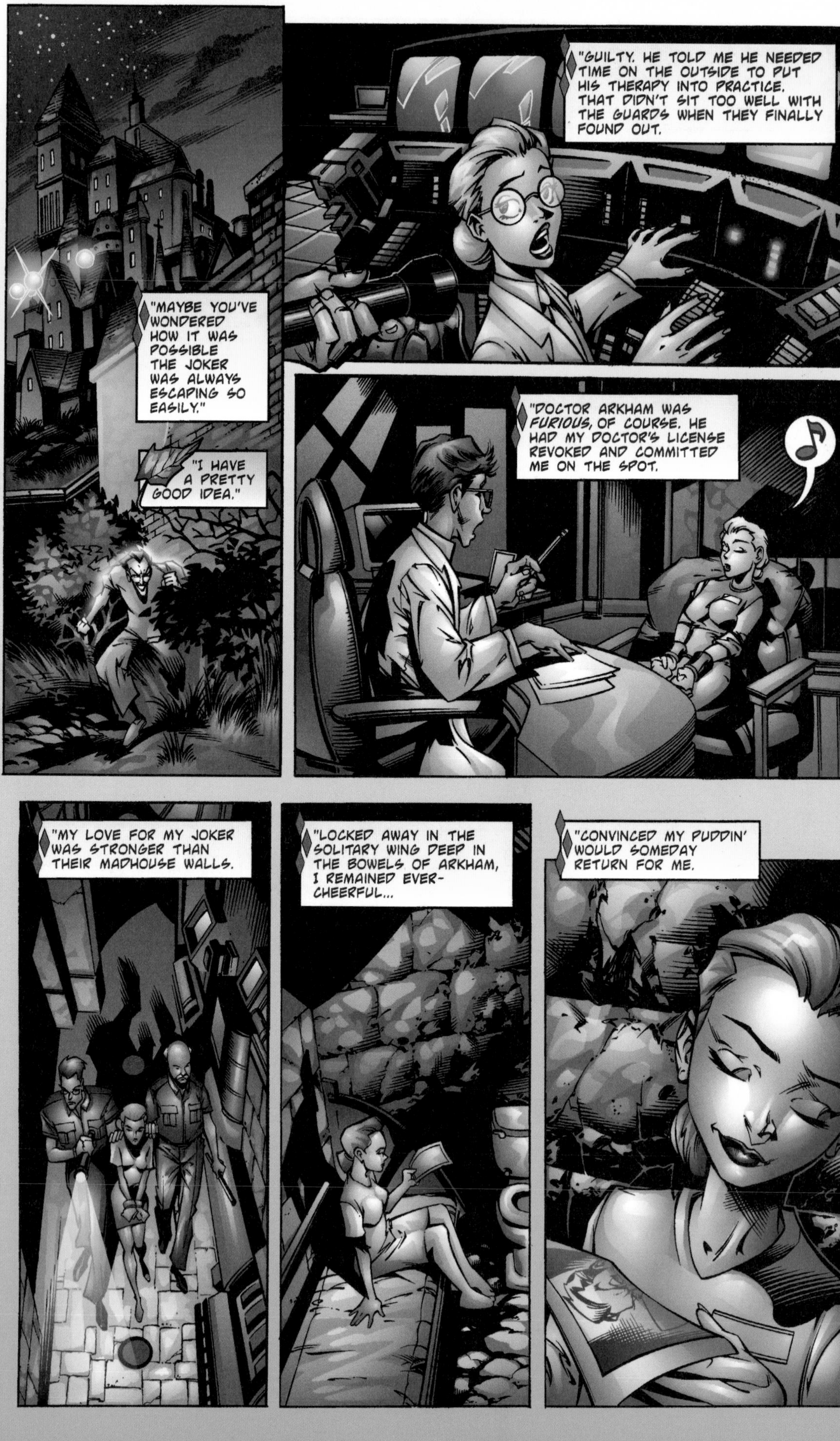
"MAYBE YOU'VE WONDERED HOW IT WAS POSSIBLE THE JOKER WAS ALWAYS ESCAPING SO EASILY."
"I HAVE A PRETTY GOOD IDEA."
"GUILTY. HE TOLD ME HE NEEDED TIME ON THE OUTSIDE TO PUT HIS THERAPY INTO PRACTICE. THAT DIDN'T SIT TOO WELL WITH THE GUARDS WHEN THEY FINALLY FOUND OUT.
"DOCTOR ARKHAM WAS FURIOUS, OF COURSE. HE HAD MY DOCTOR'S LICENSE REVOKED AND COMMITTED ME ON THE SPOT.
"MY LOVE FOR MY JOKER WAS STRONGER THAN THEIR MADHOUSE WALLS.
"LOCKED AWAY IN THE SOLITARY WING DEEP IN THE BOWELS OF ARKHAM, I REMAINED EVER-CHEERFUL...
"CONVINCED MY PUDDIN' WOULD SOMEDAY RETURN FOR ME.

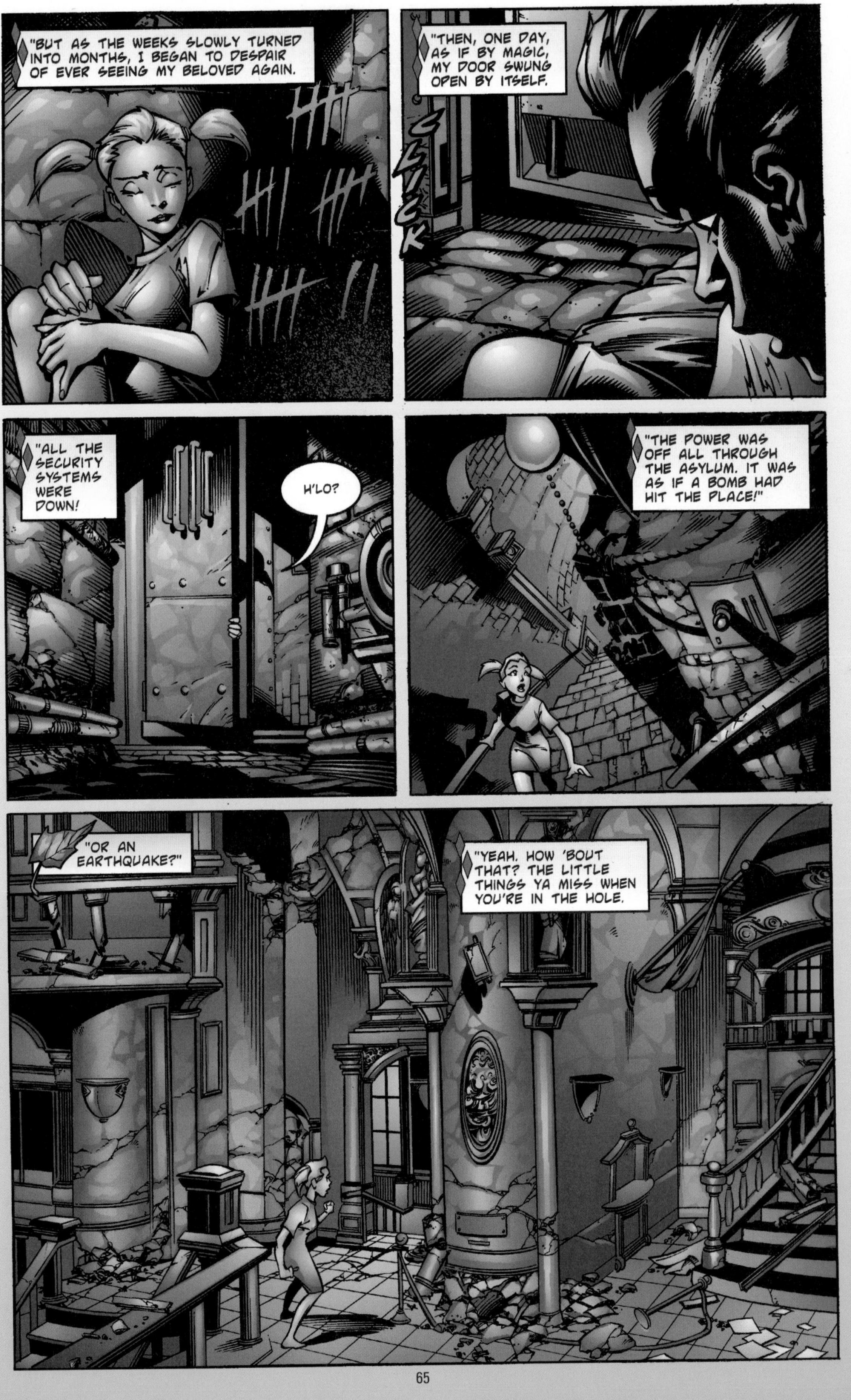
"BUT AS THE WEEKS SLOWLY TURNED INTO MONTHS, I BEGAN TO DESPAIR OF EVER SEEING MY BELOVED AGAIN.
"THEN, ONE DAY, AS IF BY MAGIC, MY DOOR SWUNG OPEN BY ITSELF.
CLICK
"ALL THE SECURITY SYSTEMS WERE DOWN!
H'LO?
"THE POWER WAS OFF ALL THROUGH THE ASYLUM. IT WAS AS IF A BOMB HAD HIT THE PLACE!"
"OR AN EARTHQUAKE?"
"YEAH. HOW 'BOUT THAT? THE LITTLE THINGS YA MISS WHEN YOU'RE IN THE HOLE.

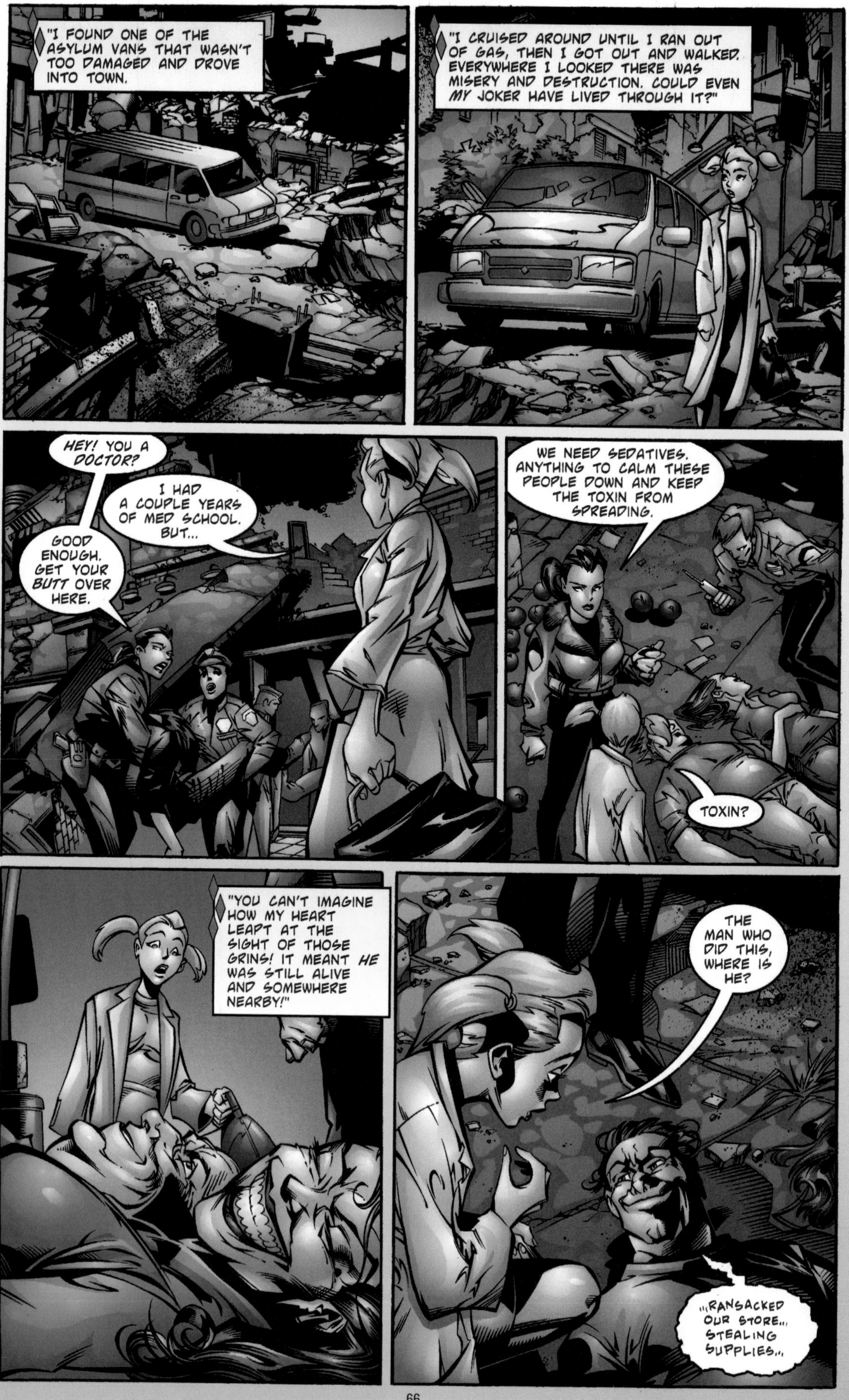
"I FOUND ONE OF THE ASYLUM VANS THAT WASN'T TOO DAMAGED AND DROVE INTO TOWN.
"I CRUISED AROUND UNTIL I RAN OUT OF GAS, THEN I GOT OUT AND WALKED. EVERYWHERE I LOOKED THERE WAS MISERY AND DESTRUCTION. COULD EVEN *MY* JOKER HAVE LIVED THROUGH IT?"
HEY! YOU A *DOCTOR?*
I HAD A COUPLE YEARS OF MED SCHOOL. BUT...
GOOD ENOUGH. GET YOUR *BUTT* OVER HERE.
WE NEED SEDATIVES. ANYTHING TO CALM THESE PEOPLE DOWN AND KEEP THE TOXIN FROM SPREADING.
TOXIN?
"YOU CAN'T IMAGINE HOW MY HEART LEAPT AT THE SIGHT OF THOSE GRINS! IT MEANT *HE* WAS STILL ALIVE AND SOMEWHERE NEARBY!"
THE MAN WHO DID THIS, WHERE IS HE?
...RANSACKED OUR STORE... STEALING SUPPLIES...

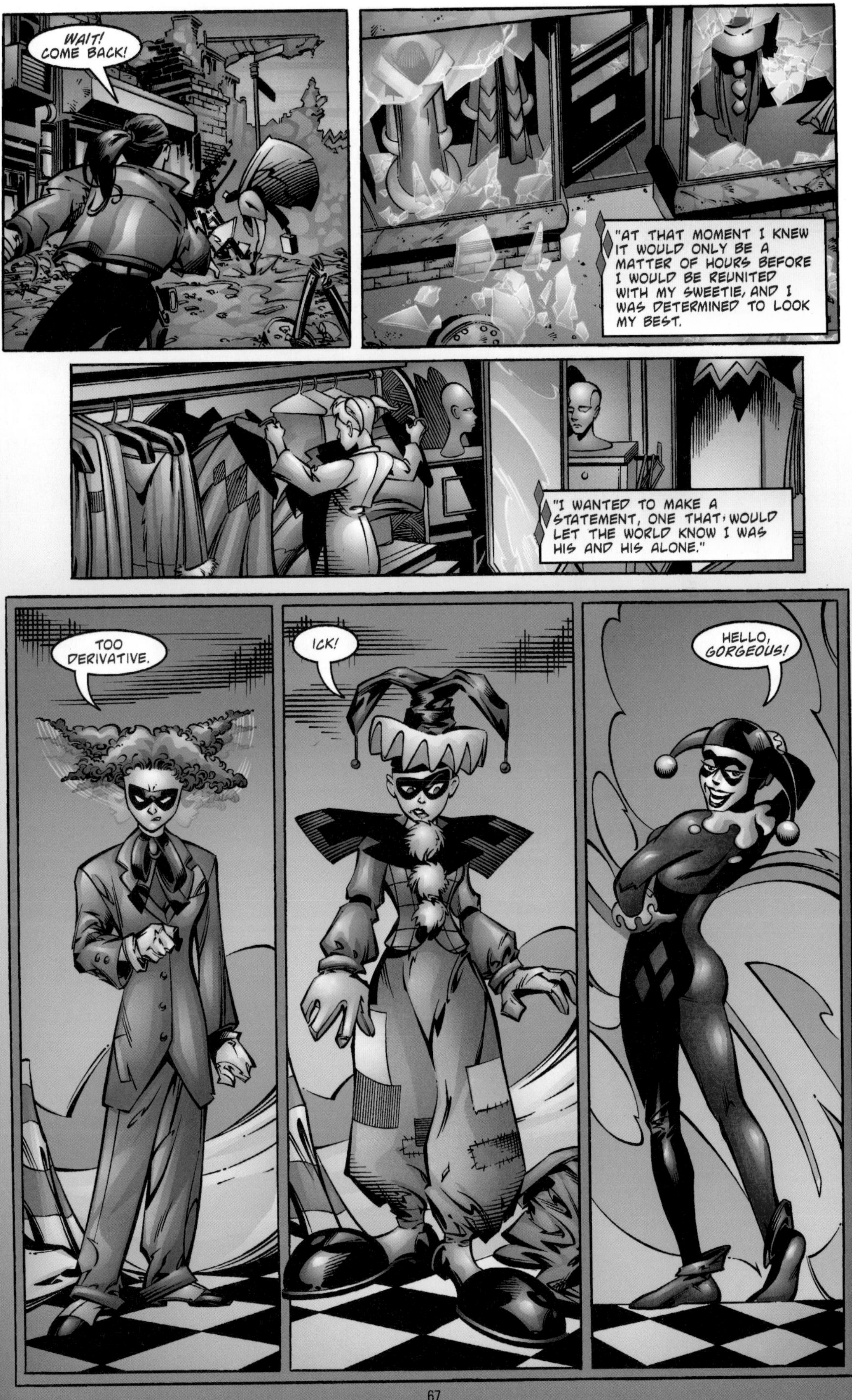
WAIT! COME BACK!
"AT THAT MOMENT I KNEW IT WOULD ONLY BE A MATTER OF HOURS BEFORE I WOULD BE REUNITED WITH MY SWEETIE, AND I WAS DETERMINED TO LOOK MY BEST.
"I WANTED TO MAKE A STATEMENT, ONE THAT WOULD LET THE WORLD KNOW I WAS HIS AND HIS ALONE."
TOO DERIVATIVE.
ICK!
HELLO, GORGEOUS!

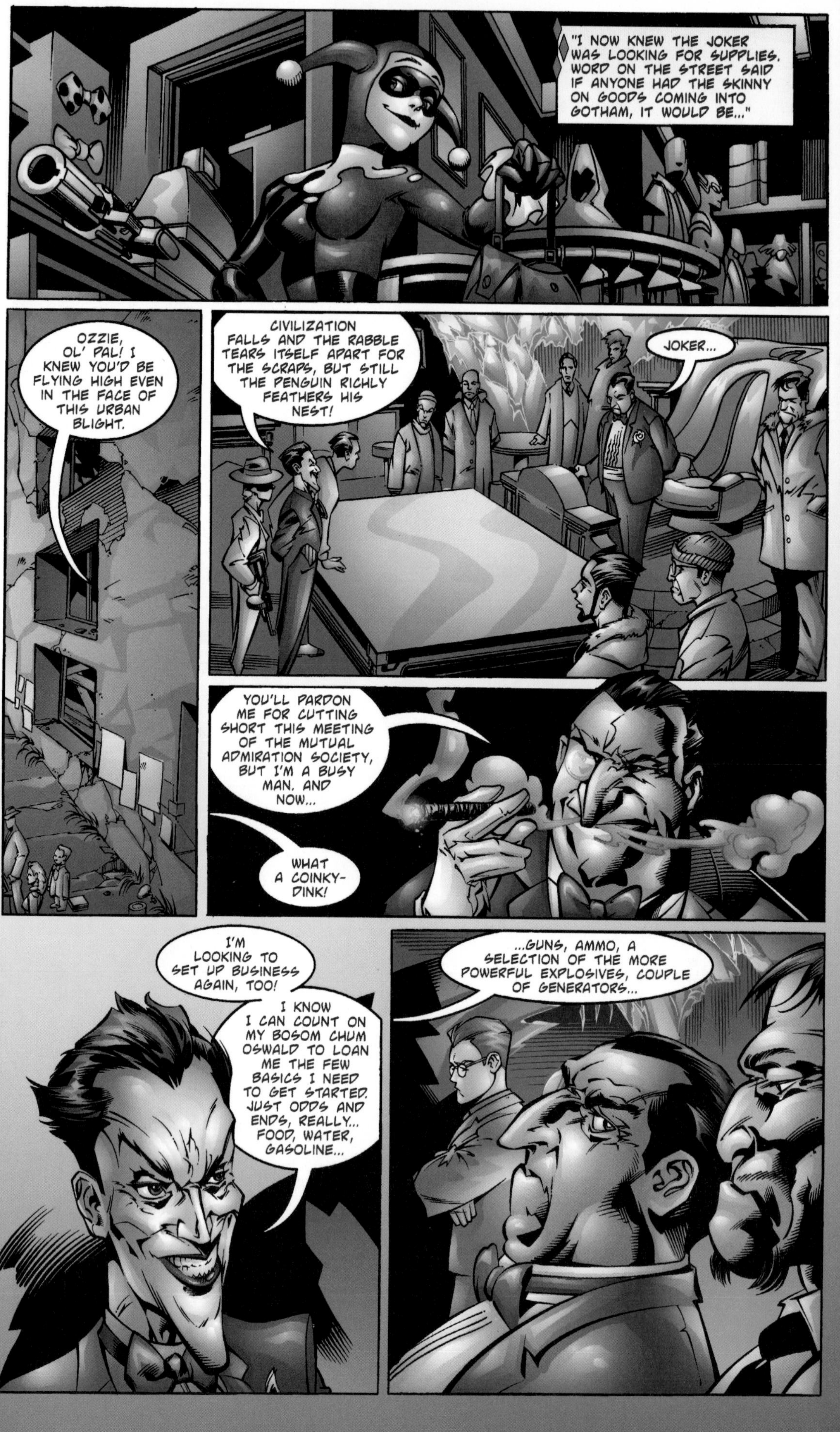
"I NOW KNEW THE JOKER WAS LOOKING FOR SUPPLIES. WORD ON THE STREET SAID IF ANYONE HAD THE SKINNY ON GOODS COMING INTO GOTHAM, IT WOULD BE..."
OZZIE, OL' PAL! I KNEW YOU'D BE FLYING HIGH EVEN IN THE FACE OF THIS URBAN BLIGHT.
CIVILIZATION FALLS AND THE RABBLE TEARS ITSELF APART FOR THE SCRAPS, BUT STILL THE PENGUIN RICHLY FEATHERS HIS NEST!
JOKER...
YOU'LL PARDON ME FOR CUTTING SHORT THIS MEETING OF THE MUTUAL ADMIRATION SOCIETY, BUT I'M A BUSY MAN. AND NOW...
WHAT A COINKY-DINK!
I'M LOOKING TO SET UP BUSINESS AGAIN, TOO!
I KNOW I CAN COUNT ON MY BOSOM CHUM OSWALD TO LOAN ME THE FEW BASICS I NEED TO GET STARTED. JUST ODDS AND ENDS, REALLY... FOOD, WATER, GASOLINE...
...GUNS, AMMO, A SELECTION OF THE MORE POWERFUL EXPLOSIVES, COUPLE OF GENERATORS...

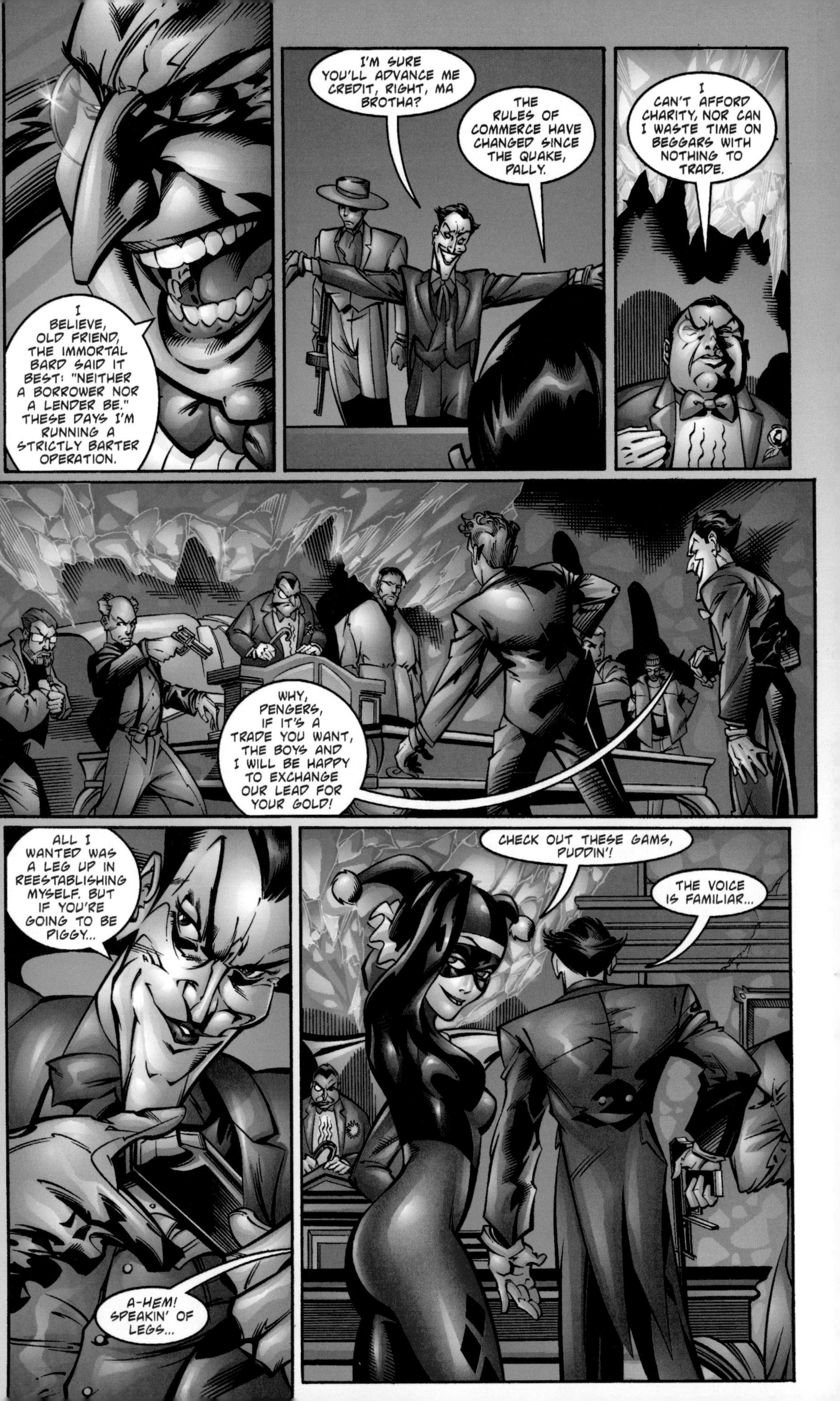
I BELIEVE, OLD FRIEND, THE IMMORTAL BARD SAID IT BEST: "NEITHER A BORROWER NOR A LENDER BE." THESE DAYS I'M RUNNING A STRICTLY BARTER OPERATION.
I'M SURE YOU'LL ADVANCE ME CREDIT, RIGHT, MA BROTHA?
THE RULES OF COMMERCE HAVE CHANGED SINCE THE QUAKE, PALLY.
I CAN'T AFFORD CHARITY, NOR CAN I WASTE TIME ON BEGGARS WITH NOTHING TO TRADE.
WHY, PENGERS, IF IT'S A TRADE YOU WANT, THE BOYS AND I WILL BE HAPPY TO EXCHANGE OUR LEAD FOR YOUR GOLD!
ALL I WANTED WAS A LEG UP IN REESTABLISHING MYSELF. BUT IF YOU'RE GOING TO BE PIGGY...
A-HEM! SPEAKIN' OF LEGS...
CHECK OUT THESE GAMS, PUDDIN'!
THE VOICE IS FAMILIAR...

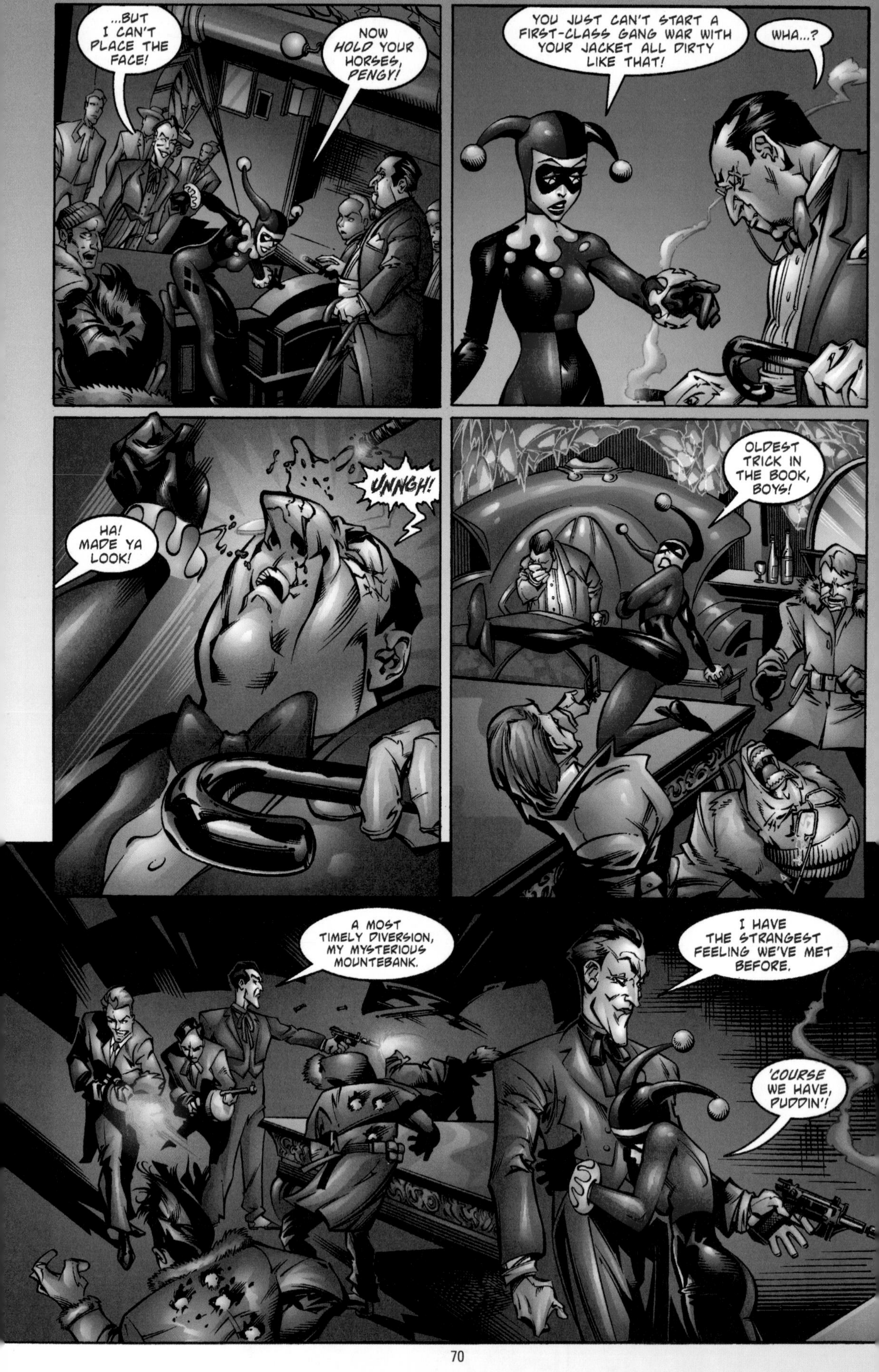
...BUT I CAN'T PLACE THE FACE!
NOW HOLD YOUR HORSES, PENGY!
YOU JUST CAN'T START A FIRST-CLASS GANG WAR WITH YOUR JACKET ALL DIRTY LIKE THAT!
WHA...?
HA! MADE YA LOOK!
UNNGH!
OLDEST TRICK IN THE BOOK, BOYS!
A MOST TIMELY DIVERSION, MY MYSTERIOUS MOUNTEBANK.
I HAVE THE STRANGEST FEELING WE'VE MET BEFORE.
'COURSE WE HAVE, PUDDIN'!

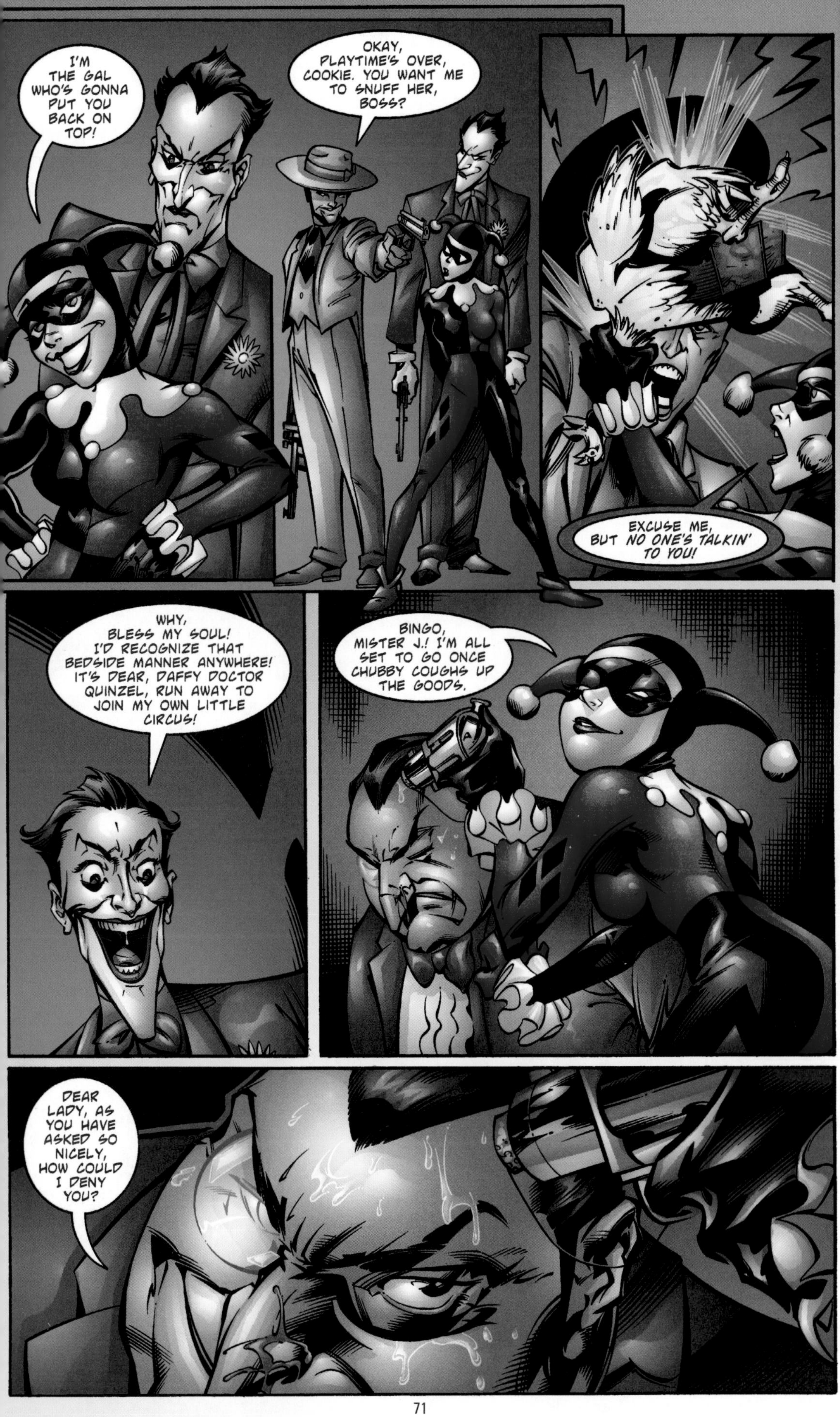
I'M THE GAL WHO'S GONNA PUT YOU BACK ON TOP!
OKAY, PLAYTIME'S OVER, COOKIE. YOU WANT ME TO SNUFF HER, BOSS?
EXCUSE ME, BUT NO ONE'S TALKIN' TO YOU!
WHY, BLESS MY SOUL! I'D RECOGNIZE THAT BEDSIDE MANNER ANYWHERE! IT'S DEAR, DAFFY DOCTOR QUINZEL, RUN AWAY TO JOIN MY OWN LITTLE CIRCUS!
BINGO, MISTER J.! I'M ALL SET TO GO ONCE CHUBBY COUGHS UP THE GOODS.
DEAR LADY, AS YOU HAVE ASKED SO NICELY, HOW COULD I DENY YOU?

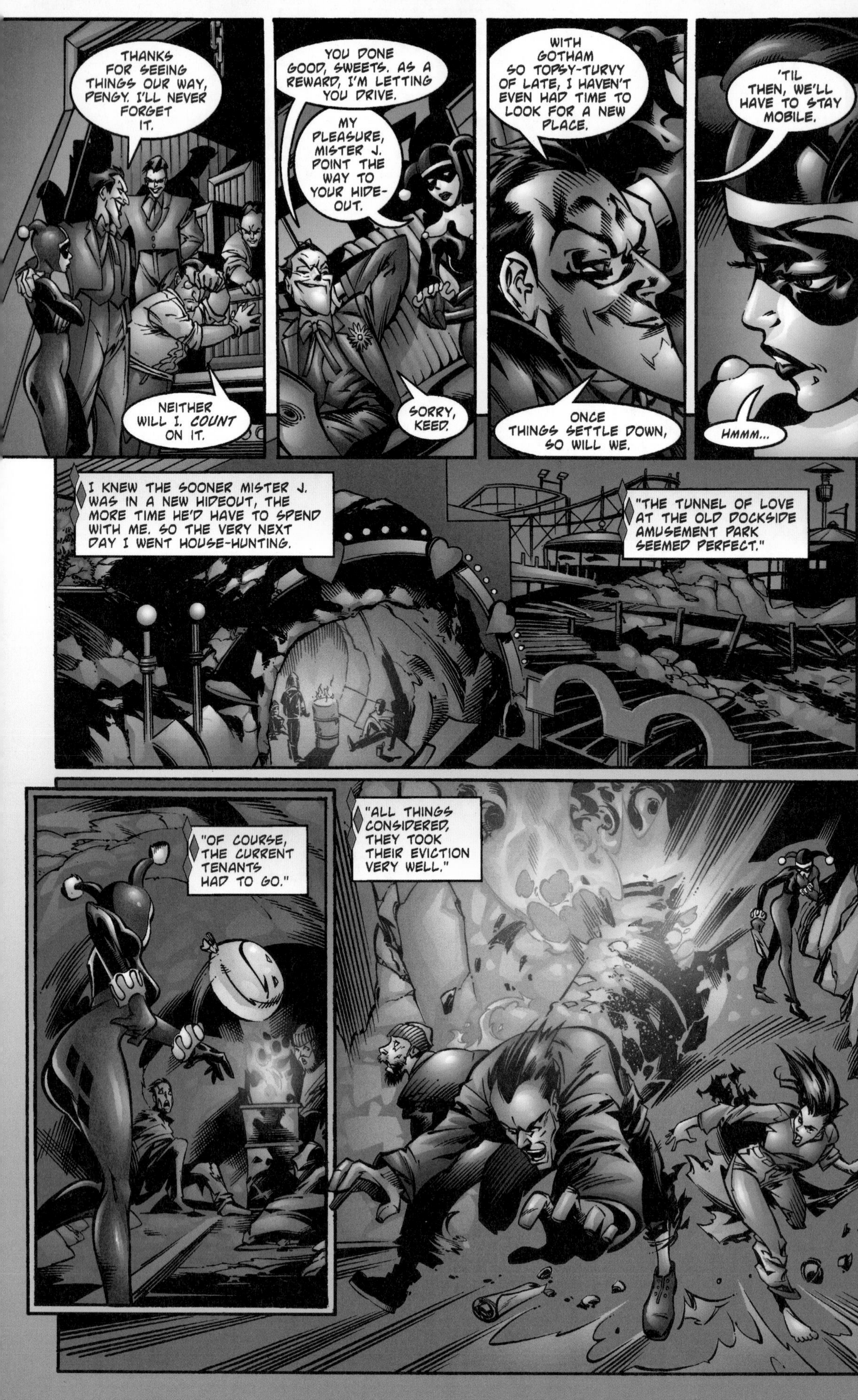
THANKS FOR SEEING THINGS OUR WAY, PENGY. I'LL NEVER FORGET IT.
NEITHER WILL I. COUNT ON IT.
YOU DONE GOOD, SWEETS. AS A REWARD, I'M LETTING YOU DRIVE.
MY PLEASURE, MISTER J. POINT THE WAY TO YOUR HIDE-OUT.
SORRY, KEED.
WITH GOTHAM SO TOPSY-TURVY OF LATE, I HAVEN'T EVEN HAD TIME TO LOOK FOR A NEW PLACE.
ONCE THINGS SETTLE DOWN, SO WILL WE.
'TIL THEN, WE'LL HAVE TO STAY MOBILE.
HMMM...
I KNEW THE SOONER MISTER J. WAS IN A NEW HIDEOUT, THE MORE TIME HE'D HAVE TO SPEND WITH ME. SO THE VERY NEXT DAY I WENT HOUSE-HUNTING.
"THE TUNNEL OF LOVE AT THE OLD DOCKSIDE AMUSEMENT PARK SEEMED PERFECT."
"OF COURSE, THE CURRENT TENANTS HAD TO GO."
"ALL THINGS CONSIDERED, THEY TOOK THEIR EVICTION VERY WELL."

"THE PLACE WAS A REAL FIXER-UPPER, BUT IT HAD GREAT POTENTIAL. I THREW MYSELF INTO IT, DETERMINED TO SPARE NO EXPENSE NOR OVERLOOK ANY DETAIL.

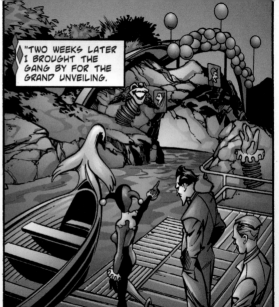

"TWO WEEKS LATER I BROUGHT THE GANG BY FOR THE GRAND UNVEILING.

"MISTER J. NEVER STOPPED LAUGHING AS WE SAILED THROUGH THE CANAL...

"...AND I THINK THE BOYS LIKED IT, TOO.

"AT LAST WE ARRIVED AT OUR LOVE NEST. WHEN HE SAW HOW I HAD TRANSFORMED THE PLACE, MISTER J. WAS OVERCOME WITH DELIGHT! YOU SHOULDA HEARD HIM RAVE!

DOABLE.

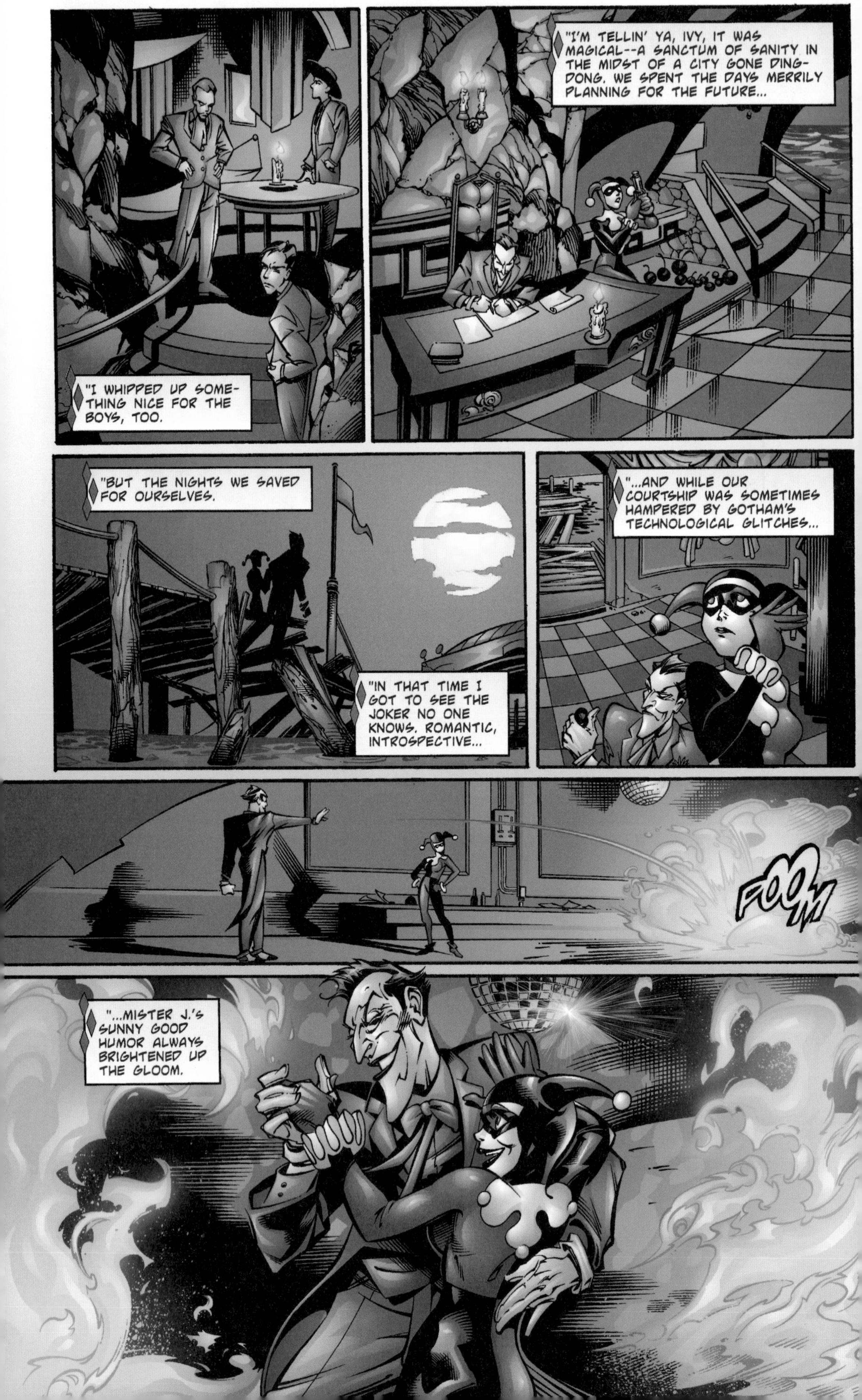
"I'M TELLIN' YA, IVY, IT WAS MAGICAL--A SANCTUM OF SANITY IN THE MIDST OF A CITY GONE DING-DONG. WE SPENT THE DAYS MERRILY PLANNING FOR THE FUTURE...
"I WHIPPED UP SOME-THING NICE FOR THE BOYS, TOO.
"BUT THE NIGHTS WE SAVED FOR OURSELVES.
"IN THAT TIME I GOT TO SEE THE JOKER NO ONE KNOWS. ROMANTIC, INTROSPECTIVE...
"...AND WHILE OUR COURTSHIP WAS SOMETIMES HAMPERED BY GOTHAM'S TECHNOLOGICAL GLITCHES...
FOOM
"...MISTER J.'S SUNNY GOOD HUMOR ALWAYS BRIGHTENED UP THE GLOOM.

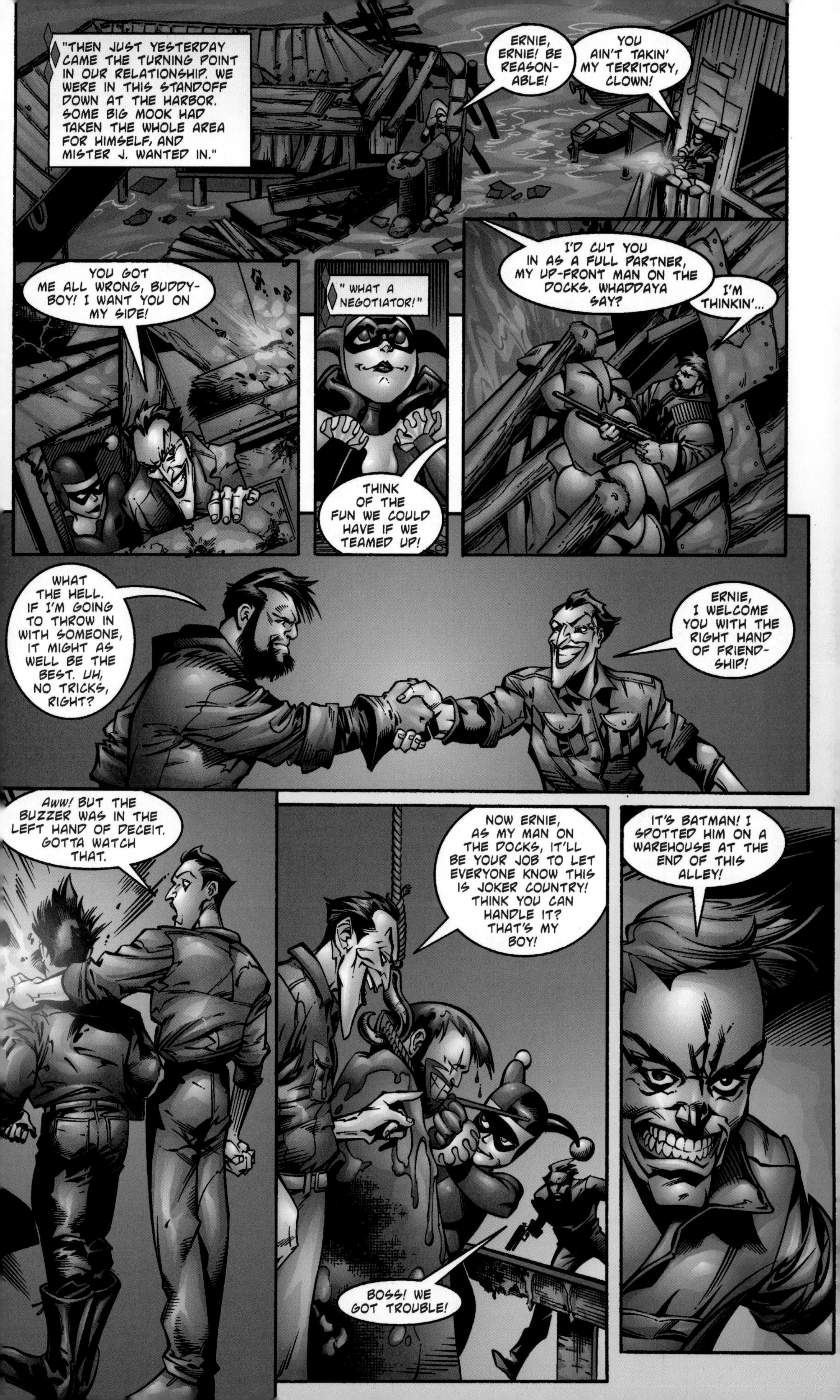
"THEN JUST YESTERDAY CAME THE TURNING POINT IN OUR RELATIONSHIP. WE WERE IN THIS STANDOFF DOWN AT THE HARBOR. SOME BIG MOOK HAD TAKEN THE WHOLE AREA FOR HIMSELF, AND MISTER J. WANTED IN."
ERNIE, ERNIE! BE REASON-ABLE!
YOU AIN'T TAKIN' MY TERRITORY, CLOWN!
YOU GOT ME ALL WRONG, BUDDY-BOY! I WANT YOU ON MY SIDE!
" WHAT A NEGOTIATOR!"
THINK OF THE FUN WE COULD HAVE IF WE TEAMED UP!
I'D CUT YOU IN AS A FULL PARTNER, MY UP-FRONT MAN ON THE DOCKS. WHADDAYA SAY?
I'M THINKIN'...
WHAT THE HELL. IF I'M GOING TO THROW IN WITH SOMEONE, IT MIGHT AS WELL BE THE BEST. UH, NO TRICKS, RIGHT?
ERNIE, I WELCOME YOU WITH THE RIGHT HAND OF FRIEND-SHIP!
AWW! BUT THE BUZZER WAS IN THE LEFT HAND OF DECEIT. GOTTA WATCH THAT.
NOW ERNIE, AS MY MAN ON THE DOCKS, IT'LL BE YOUR JOB TO LET EVERYONE KNOW THIS IS JOKER COUNTRY! THINK YOU CAN HANDLE IT? THAT'S MY BOY!
BOSS! WE GOT TROUBLE!
IT'S BATMAN! I SPOTTED HIM ON A WAREHOUSE AT THE END OF THIS ALLEY!

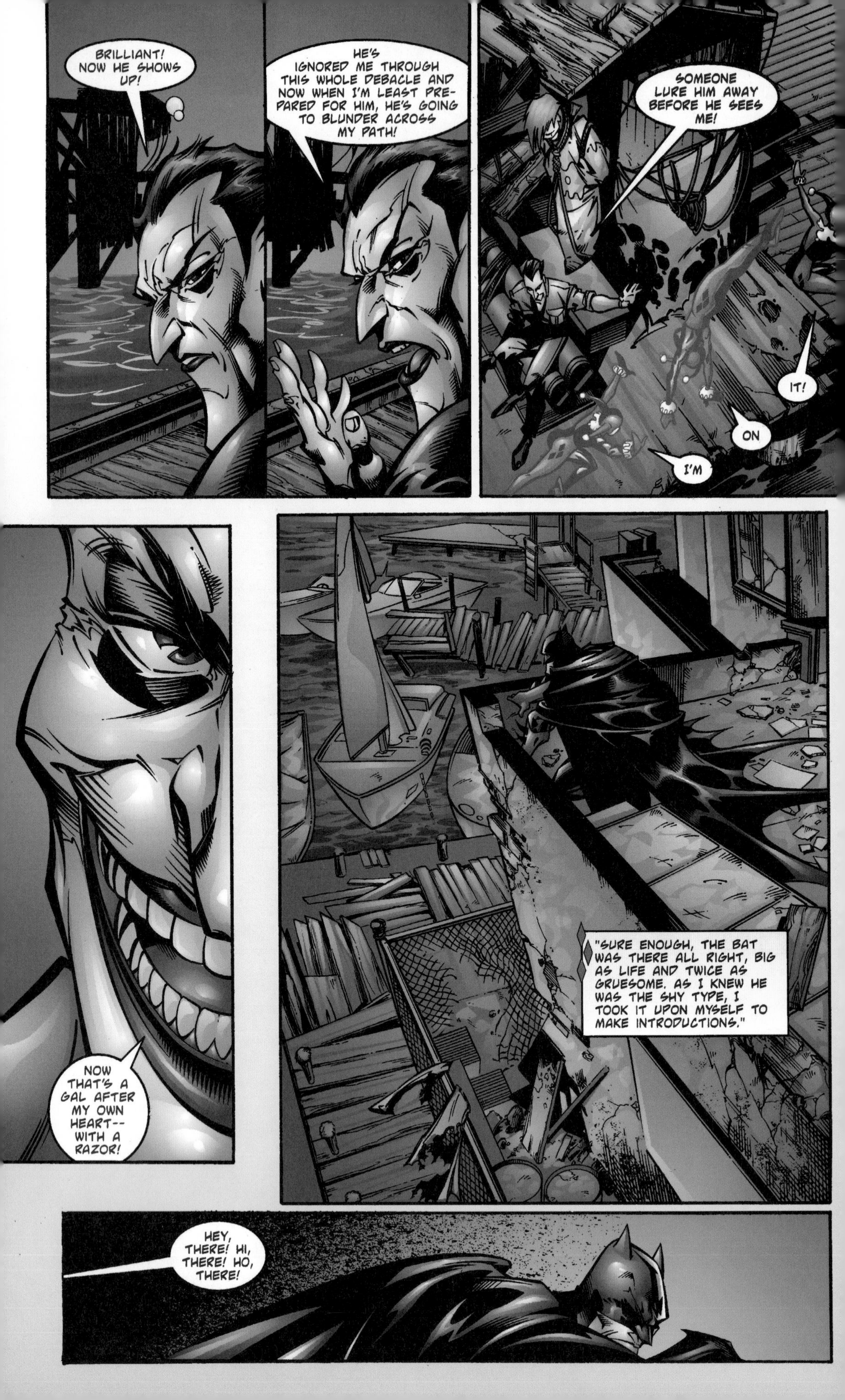
BRILLIANT! NOW HE SHOWS UP!
HE'S IGNORED ME THROUGH THIS WHOLE DEBACLE AND NOW WHEN I'M LEAST PRE-PARED FOR HIM, HE'S GOING TO BLUNDER ACROSS MY PATH!
SOMEONE LURE HIM AWAY BEFORE HE SEES ME!
I'M
ON
IT!
NOW THAT'S A GAL AFTER MY OWN HEART-- WITH A RAZOR!
"SURE ENOUGH, THE BAT WAS THERE ALL RIGHT, BIG AS LIFE AND TWICE AS GRUESOME. AS I KNEW HE WAS THE SHY TYPE, I TOOK IT UPON MYSELF TO MAKE INTRODUCTIONS."
HEY, THERE! HI, THERE! HO, THERE!

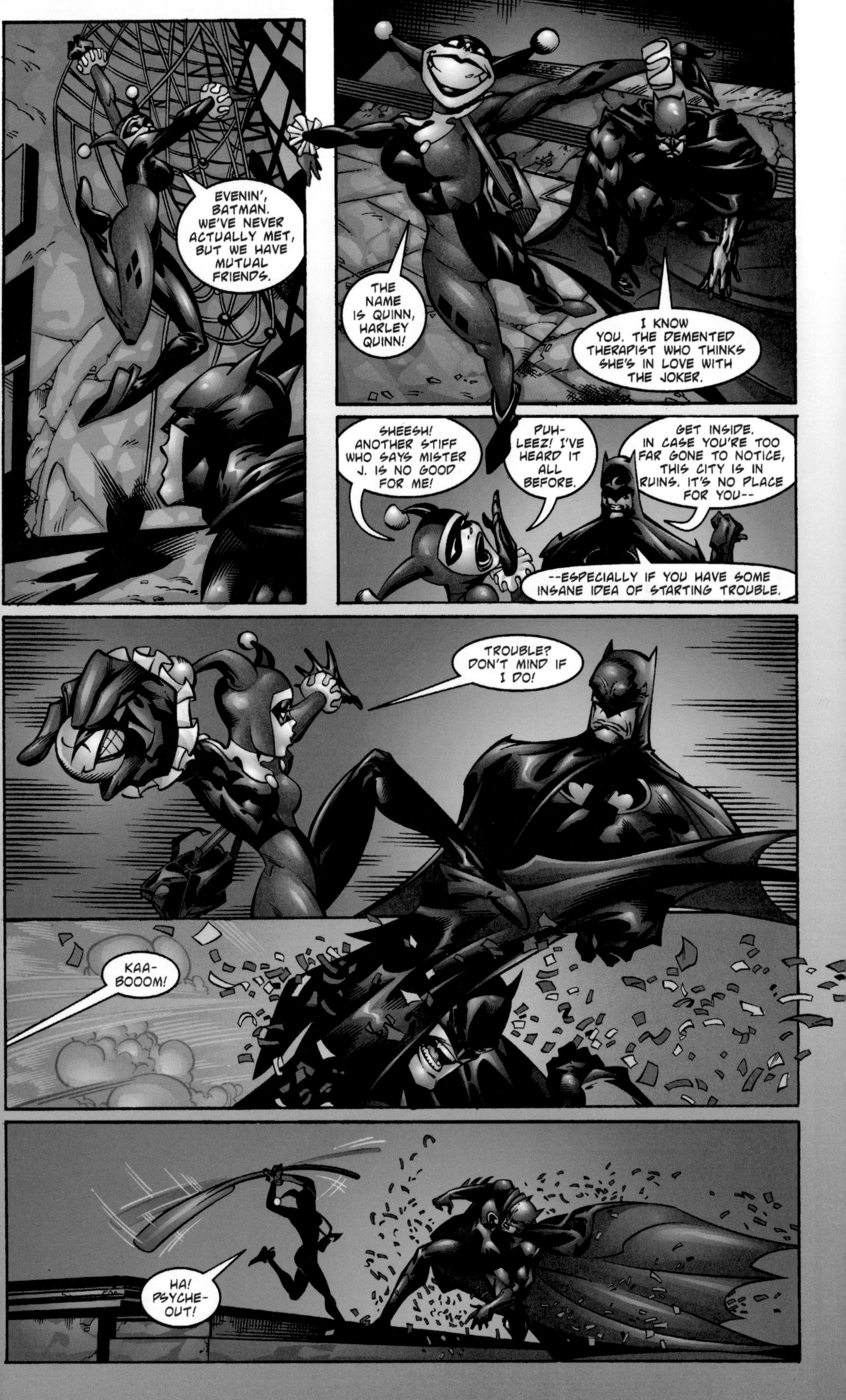
EVENIN', BATMAN. WE'VE NEVER ACTUALLY MET, BUT WE HAVE MUTUAL FRIENDS.
THE NAME IS QUINN, HARLEY QUINN!
I KNOW YOU. THE DEMENTED THERAPIST WHO THINKS SHE'S IN LOVE WITH THE JOKER.
SHEESH! ANOTHER STIFF WHO SAYS MISTER J. IS NO GOOD FOR ME!
PUH-LEEZ! I'VE HEARD IT ALL BEFORE.
GET INSIDE. IN CASE YOU'RE TOO FAR GONE TO NOTICE, THIS CITY IS IN RUINS. IT'S NO PLACE FOR YOU--
--ESPECIALLY IF YOU HAVE SOME INSANE IDEA OF STARTING TROUBLE.
TROUBLE? DON'T MIND IF I DO!
KAA-BOOOM!
HA! PSYCHE-OUT!

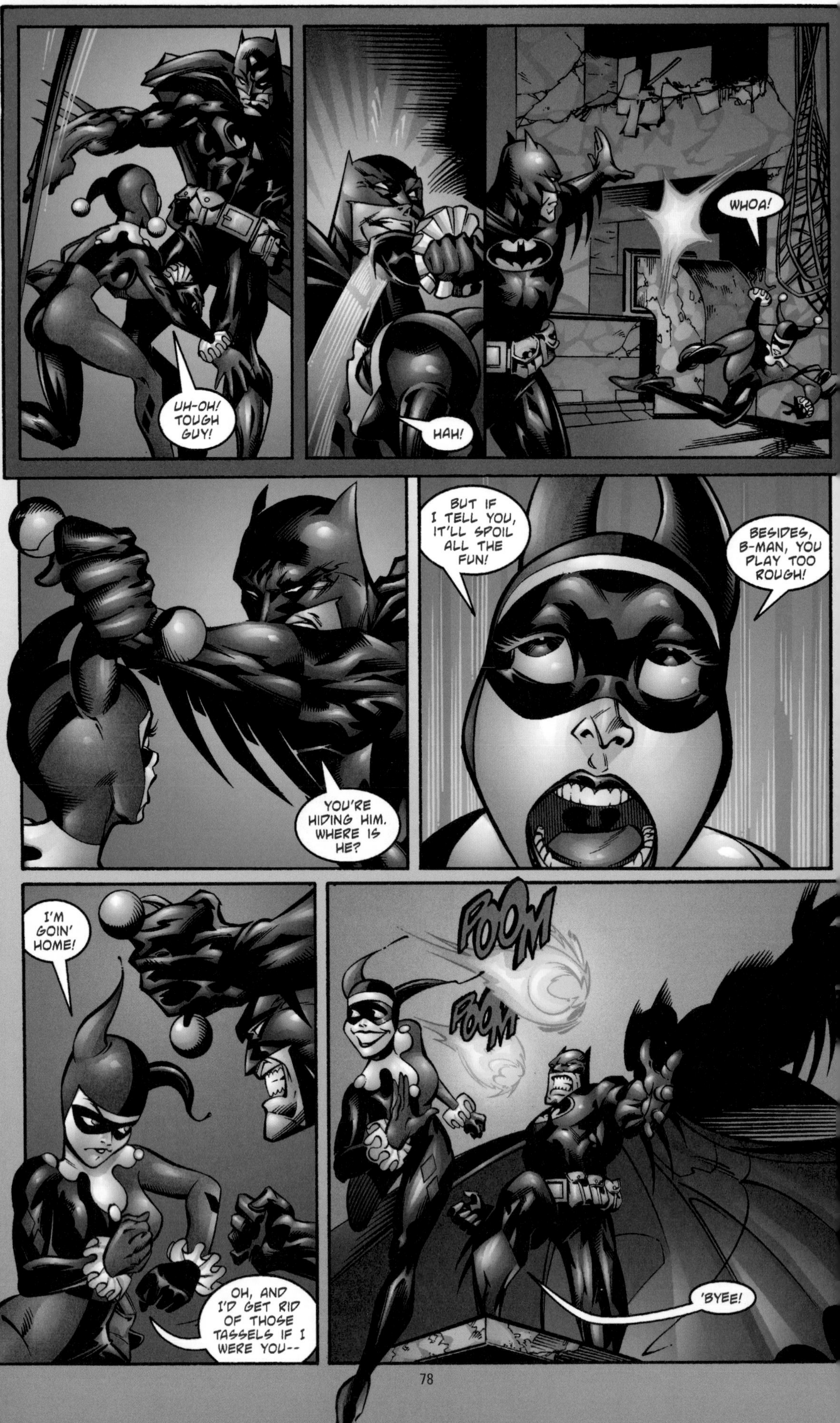
UH-OH! TOUGH GUY!
HAH!
WHOA!
YOU'RE HIDING HIM. WHERE IS HE?
BUT IF I TELL YOU, IT'LL SPOIL ALL THE FUN!
BESIDES, B-MAN, YOU PLAY TOO ROUGH!
I'M GOIN' HOME!
OH, AND I'D GET RID OF THOSE TASSELS IF I WERE YOU--
FOOM
FOOM
'BYEE!

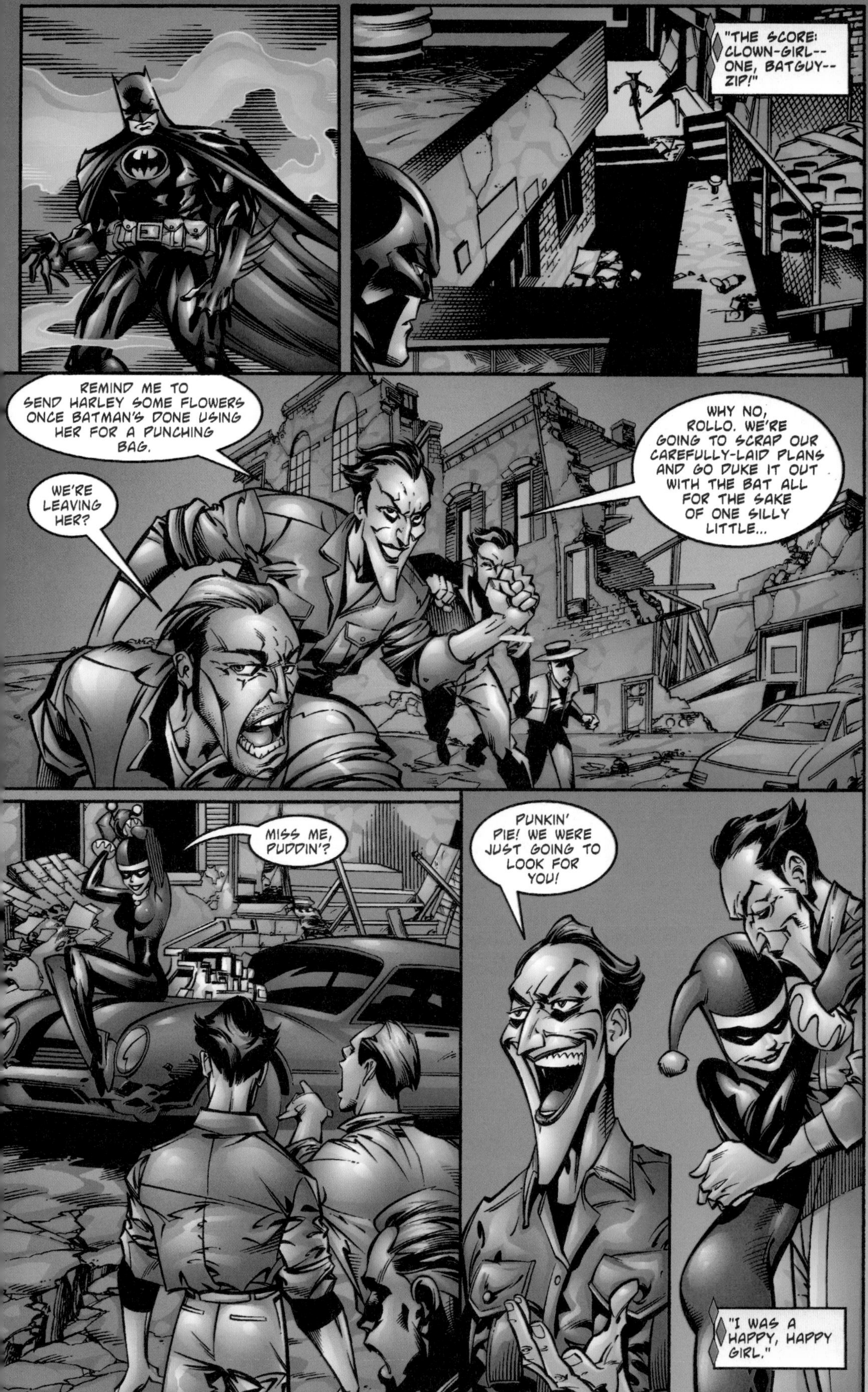
"THE SCORE: CLOWN-GIRL-- ONE, BATGUY-- ZIP!"
REMIND ME TO SEND HARLEY SOME FLOWERS ONCE BATMAN'S DONE USING HER FOR A PUNCHING BAG.
WE'RE LEAVING HER?
WHY NO, ROLLO. WE'RE GOING TO SCRAP OUR CAREFULLY-LAID PLANS AND GO DUKE IT OUT WITH THE BAT ALL FOR THE SAKE OF ONE SILLY LITTLE...
MISS ME, PUDDIN'?
PUNKIN' PIE! WE WERE JUST GOING TO LOOK FOR YOU!
"I WAS A HAPPY, HAPPY GIRL."

THEN WE WENT BACK TO THE HIDEOUT FOR A NIGHT OF SHEER JOY.

OH, COME ON. THE JOKER MAY BE MANY THINGS, BUT SEXY ISN'T ON THE LIST.

I'LL HAVE YOU KNOW IT WAS A MAGICAL EVENING!

WE DRANK A TOAST, THEN HE HELD ME TIGHT. I FELT MY HEART DO FLIP-FLOPS! I WAS FAINTING! SWOONING! SENSELESS WITH DELIGHT! EVERYTHING AFTER THAT WAS A BLISSFUL BLUR!

DRUGGED YOU, HUH?

"THIS MORNING I WOKE UP ALL AGLOW. STRANGELY, MISTER J. WAS NOWHERE TO BE FOUND."

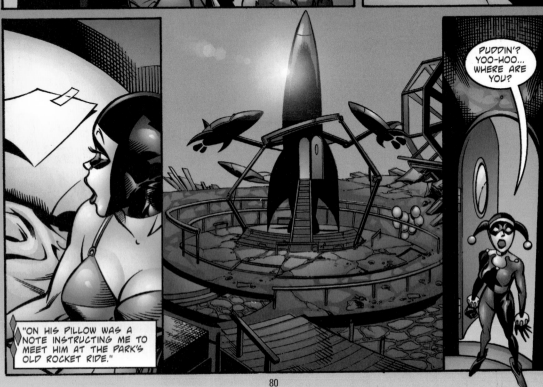

"ON HIS PILLOW WAS A NOTE INSTRUCTING ME TO MEET HIM AT THE PARK'S OLD ROCKET RIDE."

PUDDIN'? YOO-HOO... WHERE ARE YOU?

SLAM

HEY! WHAT GIVES?

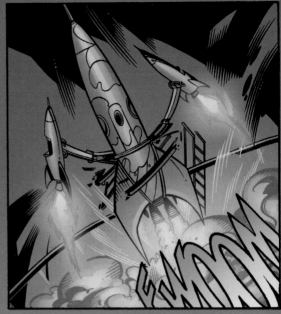

KABOOM

HOUSTON, WE HAVE LIFTOFF!

THIS ISN'T FUNNY, PUDDIN'! LET ME OUT!

ALL KIDDING ASIDE, HARL'! I JUST WANTED TO TAKE SOME TIME AND TALK ABOUT WHERE OUR RELATIONSHIP IS GOING.

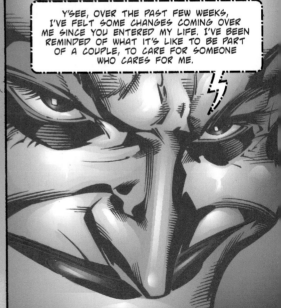

Y'SEE, OVER THE PAST FEW WEEKS, I'VE FELT SOME CHANGES COMING OVER ME SINCE YOU ENTERED MY LIFE. I'VE BEEN REMINDED OF WHAT IT'S LIKE TO BE PART OF A COUPLE, TO CARE FOR SOMEONE WHO CARES FOR ME.

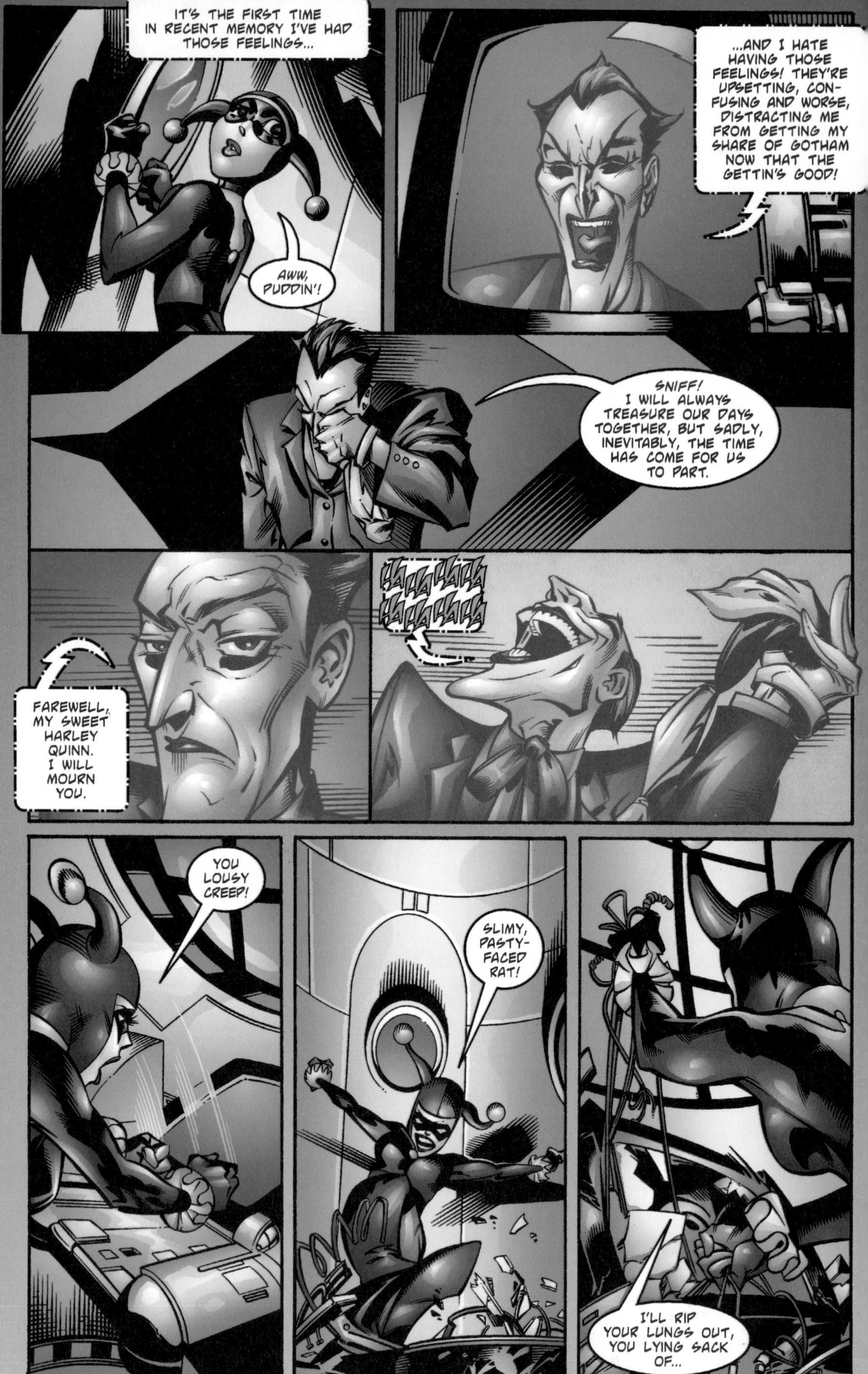
IT'S THE FIRST TIME IN RECENT MEMORY I'VE HAD THOSE FEELINGS...
AWW, PUDDIN'!
...AND I HATE HAVING THOSE FEELINGS! THEY'RE UPSETTING, CON-FUSING AND WORSE, DISTRACTING ME FROM GETTING MY SHARE OF GOTHAM NOW THAT THE GETTIN'S GOOD!
SNIFF! I WILL ALWAYS TREASURE OUR DAYS TOGETHER, BUT SADLY, INEVITABLY, THE TIME HAS COME FOR US TO PART.
FAREWELL, MY SWEET HARLEY QUINN. I WILL MOURN YOU.
HAHAHAHA HAHAHAHA
YOU LOUSY CREEP!
SLIMY, PASTY-FACED RAT!
I'LL RIP YOUR LUNGS OUT, YOU LYING SACK OF...

YAAAA!

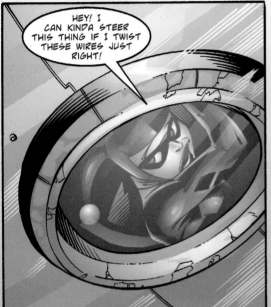

HEY! I CAN KINDA STEER THIS THING IF I TWIST THESE WIRES JUST RIGHT!

THAT'S THE PARK DOWN THERE! GREAT BIG LAKE, LOTSA SOFT, CUSHY TREES!

PLENTY OF PLACES TO LAND THIS BABY NICE 'N' EASY!

LOOKS LIKE I GOT THE LAST LAUGH ON YOU, MISTER J.! HA, HA...

OY!

BOOM

GENERAL GORFUNKEL

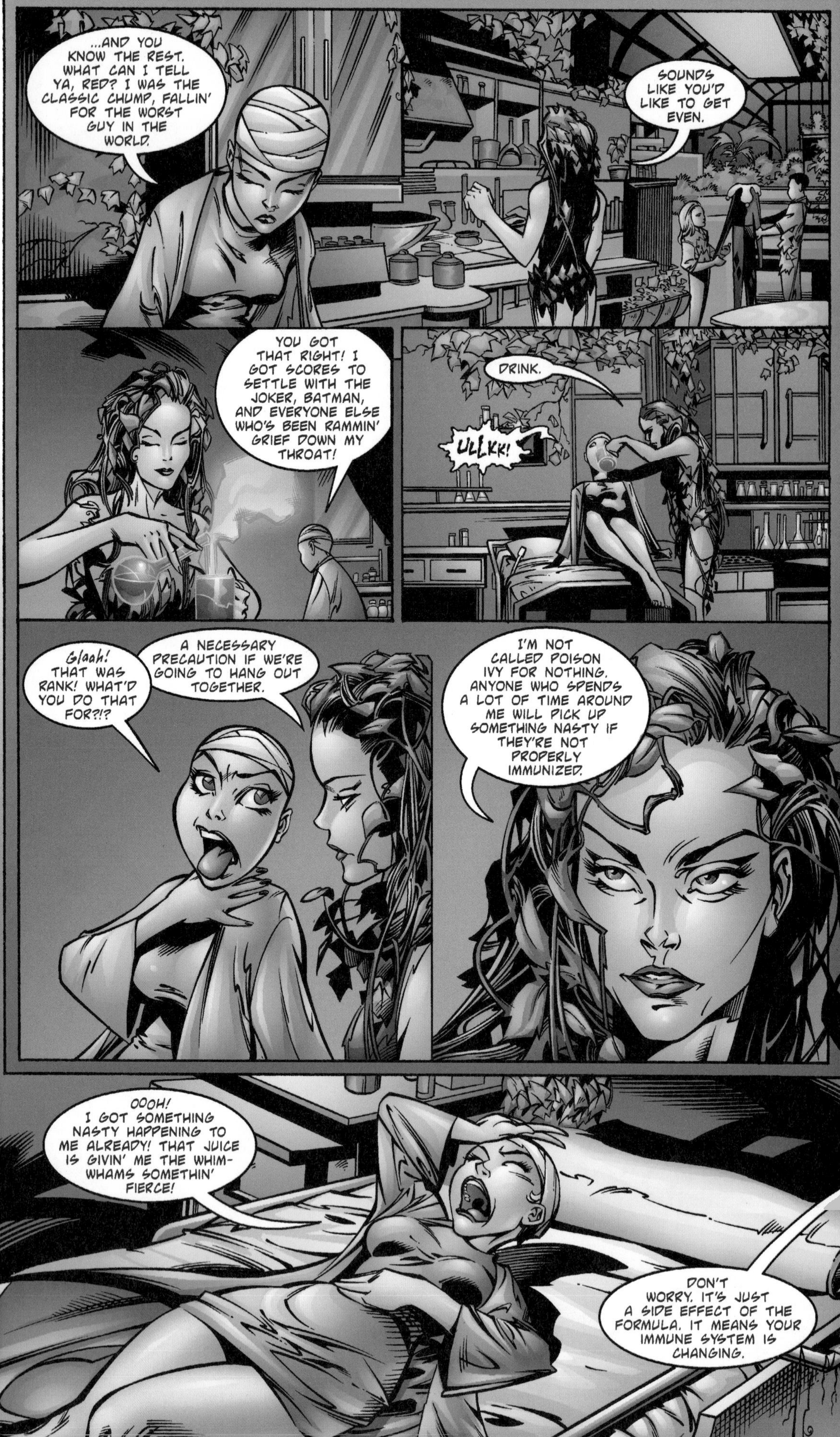
...AND YOU KNOW THE REST. WHAT CAN I TELL YA, RED? I WAS THE CLASSIC CHUMP, FALLIN' FOR THE WORST GUY IN THE WORLD.
SOUNDS LIKE YOU'D LIKE TO GET EVEN.
YOU GOT THAT RIGHT! I GOT SCORES TO SETTLE WITH THE JOKER, BATMAN, AND EVERYONE ELSE WHO'S BEEN RAMMIN' GRIEF DOWN MY THROAT!
DRINK.
ULLKK!
Glaah! THAT WAS RANK! WHAT'D YOU DO THAT FOR?!?
A NECESSARY PRECAUTION IF WE'RE GOING TO HANG OUT TOGETHER.
I'M NOT CALLED POISON IVY FOR NOTHING. ANYONE WHO SPENDS A LOT OF TIME AROUND ME WILL PICK UP SOMETHING NASTY IF THEY'RE NOT PROPERLY IMMUNIZED.
OOOH! I GOT SOMETHING NASTY HAPPENING TO ME ALREADY! THAT JUICE IS GIVIN' ME THE WHIM-WHAMS SOMETHIN' FIERCE!
DON'T WORRY. IT'S JUST A SIDE EFFECT OF THE FORMULA. IT MEANS YOUR IMMUNE SYSTEM IS CHANGING.

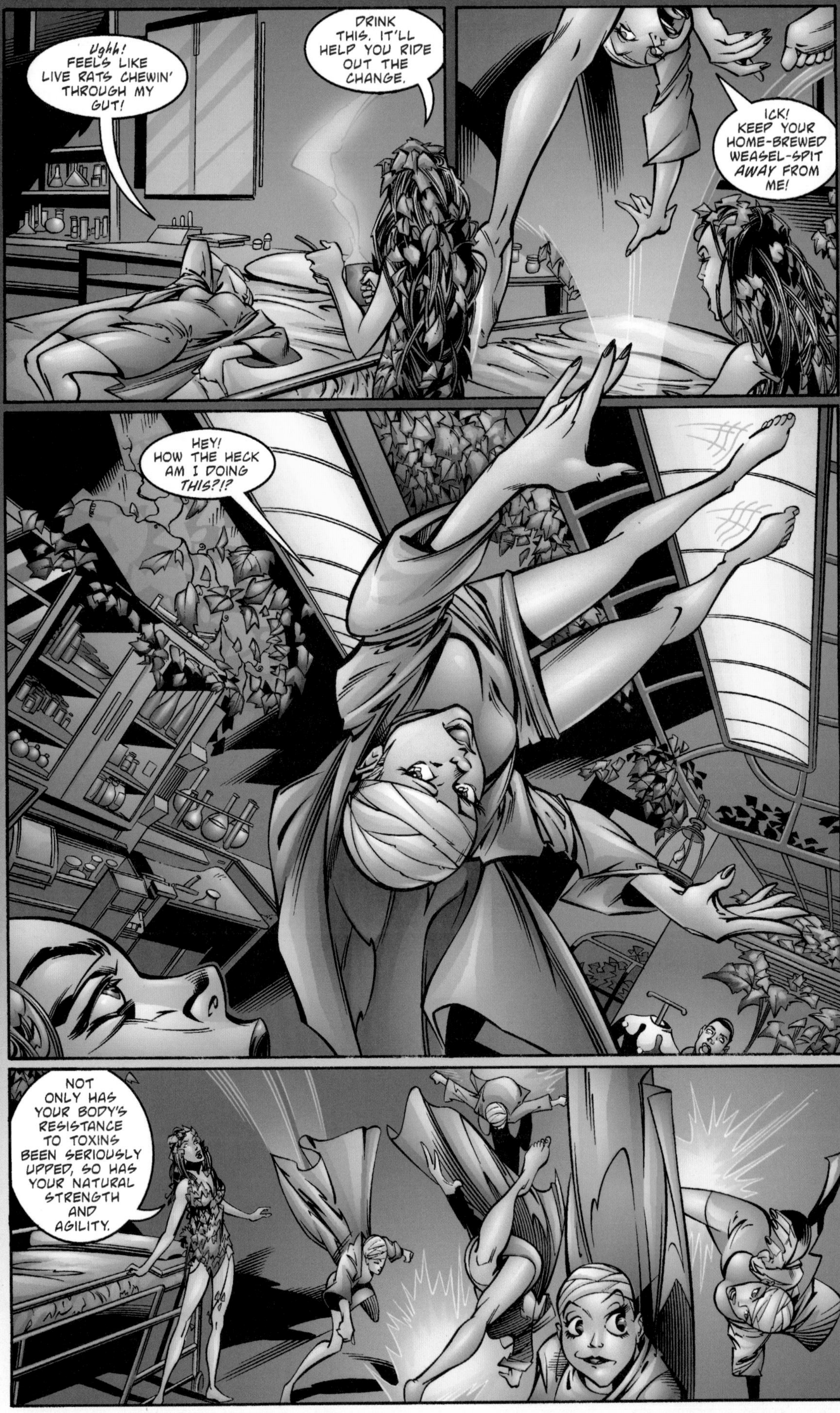
Ughh! Feels like live rats chewin' through my gut!
Drink this. It'll help you ride out the change.
Ick! Keep your home-brewed weasel-spit away from me!
Hey! How the heck am I doing this?!?
Not only has your body's resistance to toxins been seriously upped, so has your natural strength and agility.

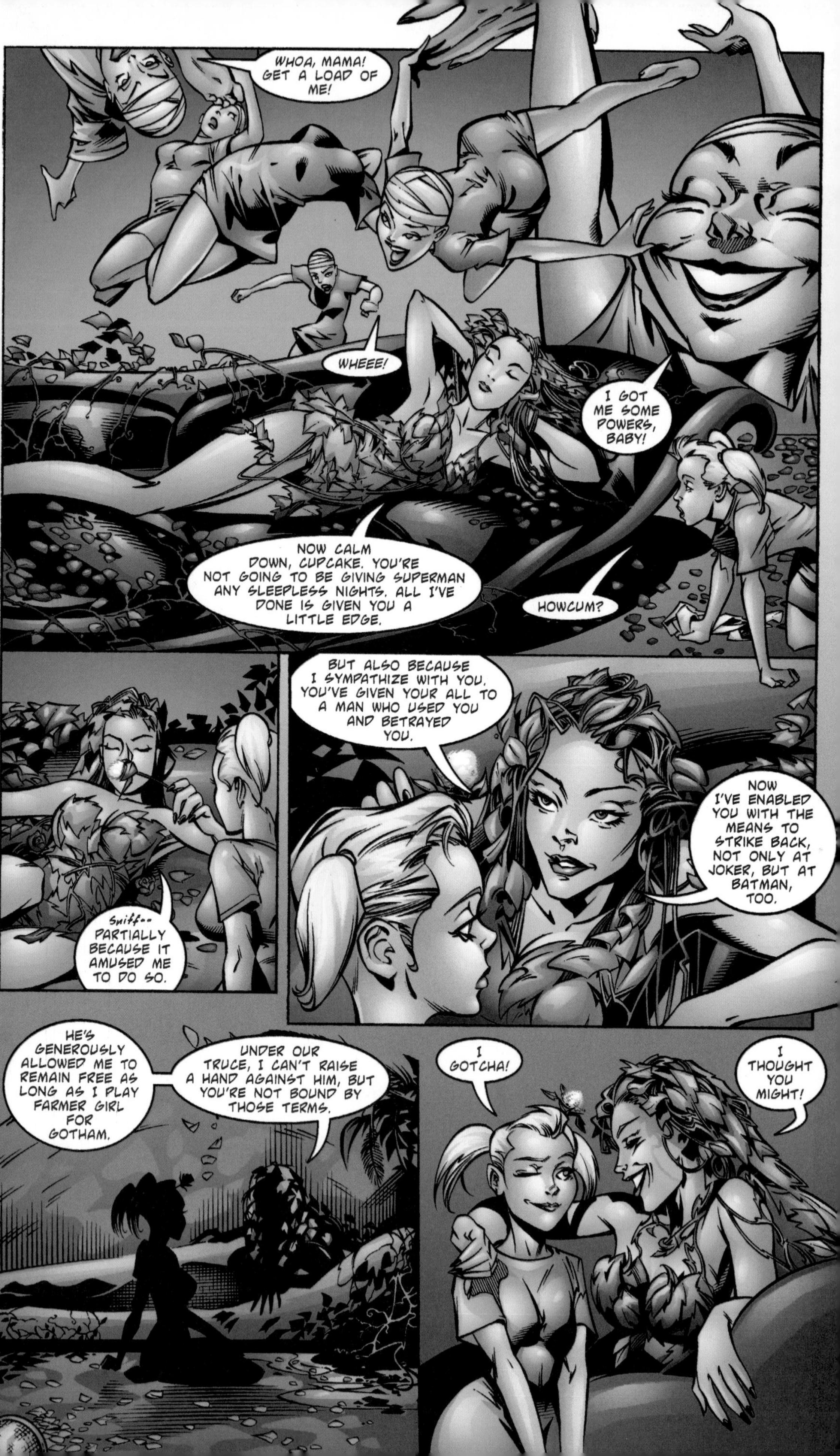
WHOA, MAMA! GET A LOAD OF ME!
WHEEE!
I GOT ME SOME POWERS, BABY!
NOW CALM DOWN, CUPCAKE. YOU'RE NOT GOING TO BE GIVING SUPERMAN ANY SLEEPLESS NIGHTS. ALL I'VE DONE IS GIVEN YOU A LITTLE EDGE.
HOWCUM?
Sniff... PARTIALLY BECAUSE IT AMUSED ME TO DO SO.
BUT ALSO BECAUSE I SYMPATHIZE WITH YOU. YOU'VE GIVEN YOUR ALL TO A MAN WHO USED YOU AND BETRAYED YOU.
NOW I'VE ENABLED YOU WITH THE MEANS TO STRIKE BACK, NOT ONLY AT JOKER, BUT AT BATMAN, TOO.
HE'S GENEROUSLY ALLOWED ME TO REMAIN FREE AS LONG AS I PLAY FARMER GIRL FOR GOTHAM.
UNDER OUR TRUCE, I CAN'T RAISE A HAND AGAINST HIM, BUT YOU'RE NOT BOUND BY THOSE TERMS.
I GOTCHA!
I THOUGHT YOU MIGHT!

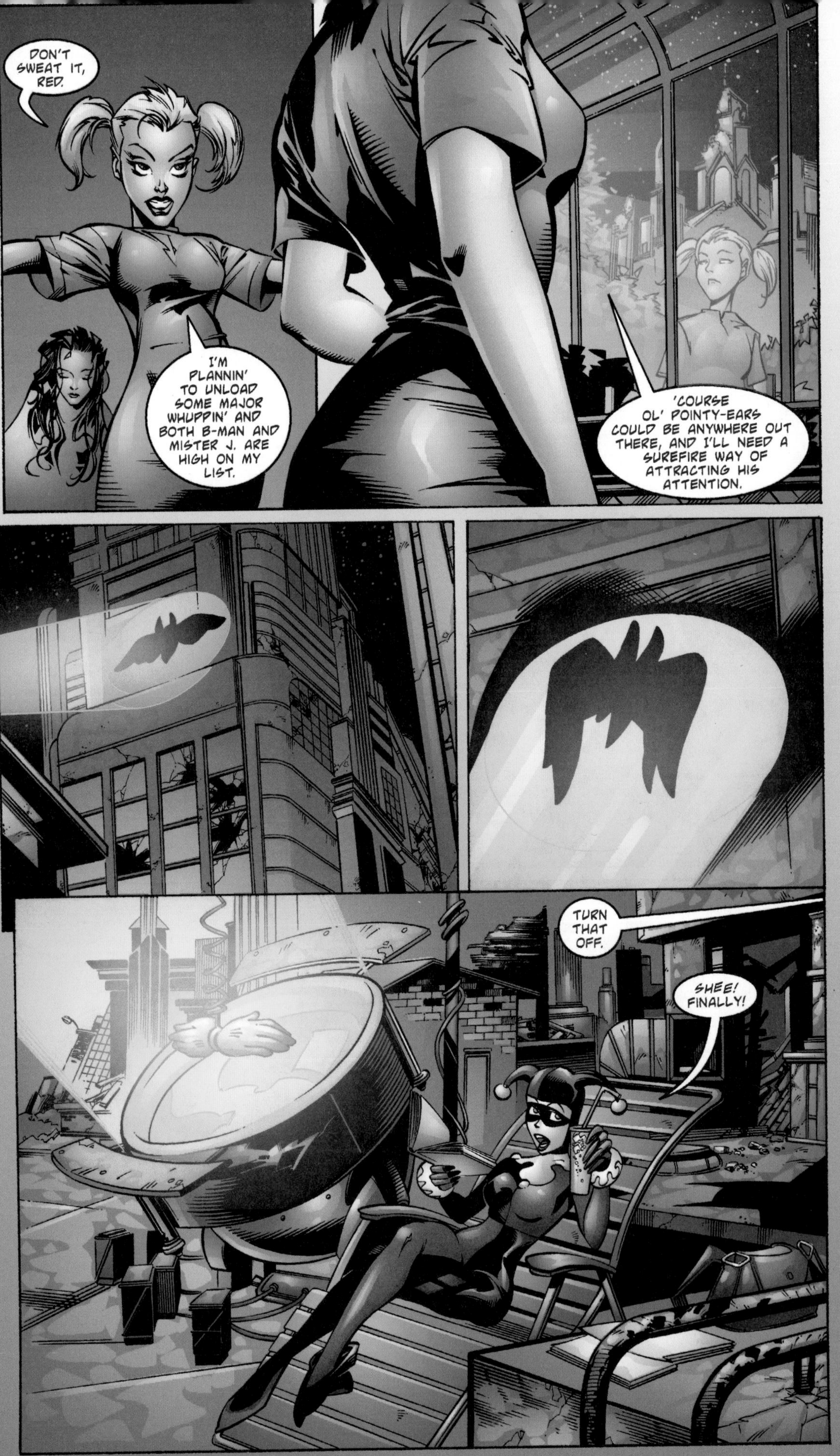
DON'T SWEAT IT, RED.
I'M PLANNIN' TO UNLOAD SOME MAJOR WHUPPIN' AND BOTH B-MAN AND MISTER J. ARE HIGH ON MY LIST.
'COURSE OL' POINTY-EARS COULD BE ANYWHERE OUT THERE, AND I'LL NEED A SUREFIRE WAY OF ATTRACTING HIS ATTENTION.
TURN THAT OFF.
SHEE! FINALLY!

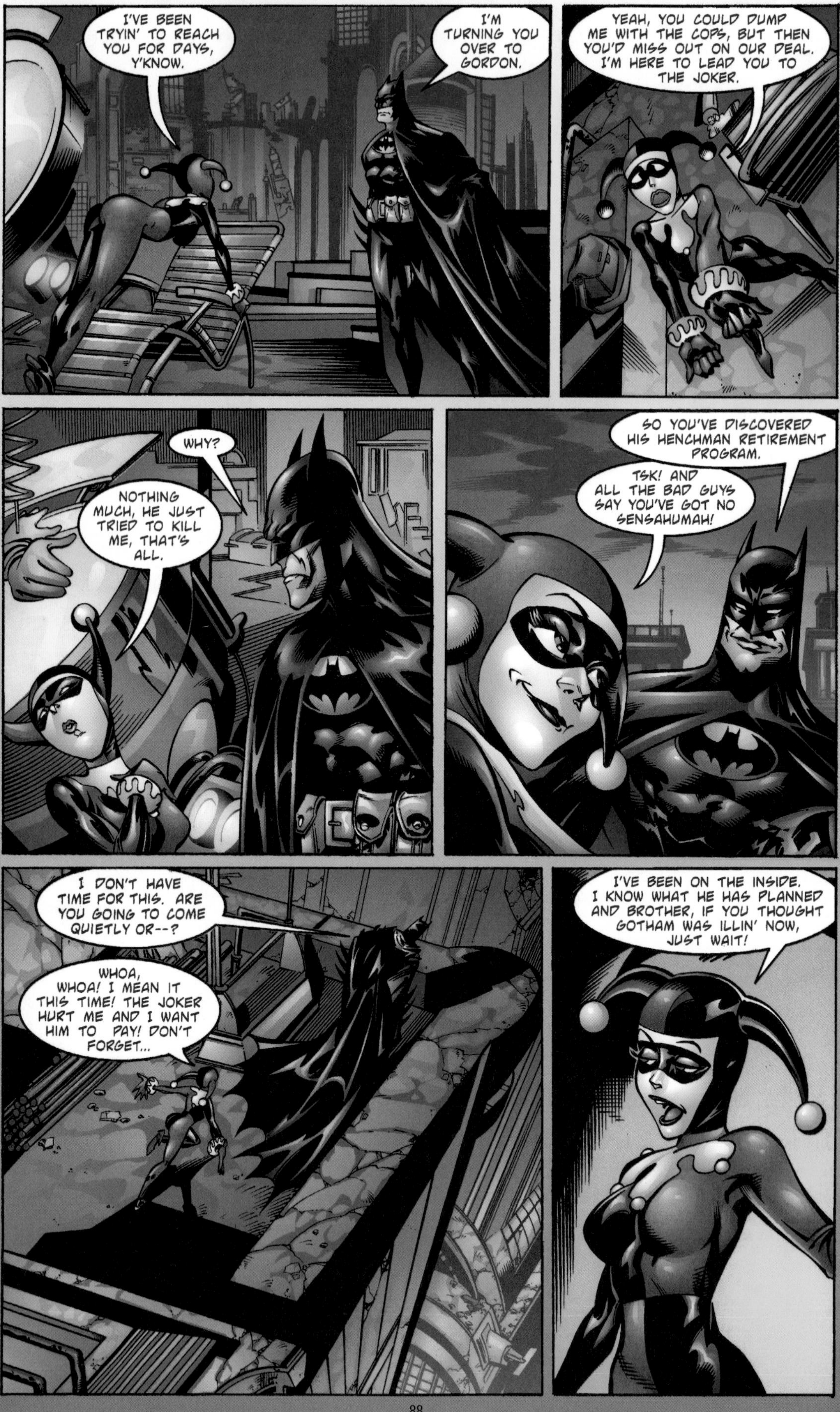

I'VE BEEN TRYIN' TO REACH YOU FOR DAYS, Y'KNOW.
I'M TURNING YOU OVER TO GORDON.
YEAH, YOU COULD DUMP ME WITH THE COPS, BUT THEN YOU'D MISS OUT ON OUR DEAL. I'M HERE TO LEAD YOU TO THE JOKER.
WHY?
NOTHING MUCH, HE JUST TRIED TO KILL ME, THAT'S ALL.
SO YOU'VE DISCOVERED HIS HENCHMAN RETIREMENT PROGRAM.
TSK! AND ALL THE BAD GUYS SAY YOU'VE GOT NO SENSAHUMAH!
I DON'T HAVE TIME FOR THIS. ARE YOU GOING TO COME QUIETLY OR--?
WHOA, WHOA! I MEAN IT THIS TIME! THE JOKER HURT ME AND I WANT HIM TO PAY! DON'T FORGET...
I'VE BEEN ON THE INSIDE. I KNOW WHAT HE HAS PLANNED AND BROTHER, IF YOU THOUGHT GOTHAM WAS ILLIN' NOW, JUST WAIT!

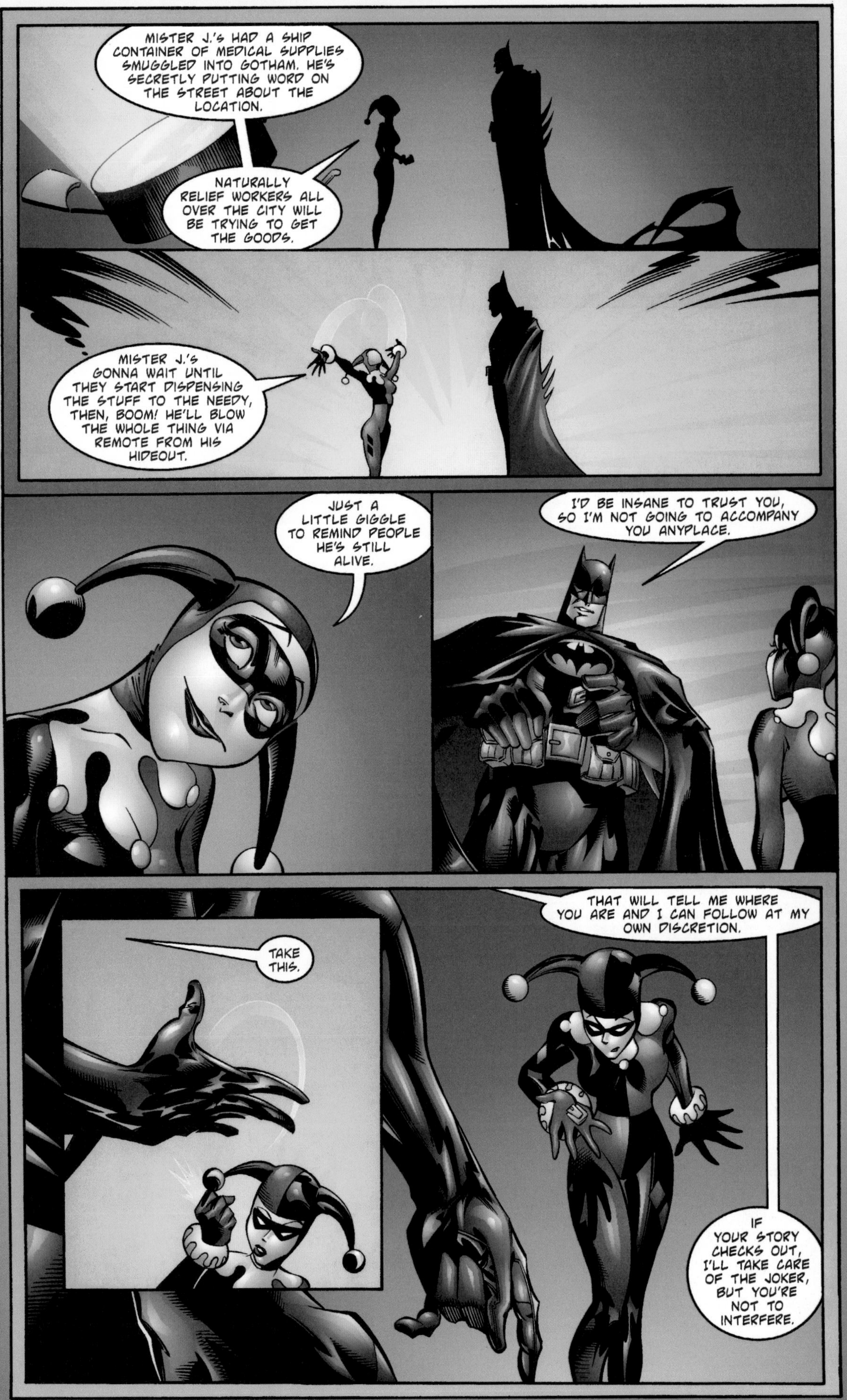

MISTER J.'S HAD A SHIP CONTAINER OF MEDICAL SUPPLIES SMUGGLED INTO GOTHAM. HE'S SECRETLY PUTTING WORD ON THE STREET ABOUT THE LOCATION.
NATURALLY RELIEF WORKERS ALL OVER THE CITY WILL BE TRYING TO GET THE GOODS.
MISTER J.'S GONNA WAIT UNTIL THEY START DISPENSING THE STUFF TO THE NEEDY, THEN, BOOM! HE'LL BLOW THE WHOLE THING VIA REMOTE FROM HIS HIDEOUT.
JUST A LITTLE GIGGLE TO REMIND PEOPLE HE'S STILL ALIVE.
I'D BE INSANE TO TRUST YOU, SO I'M NOT GOING TO ACCOMPANY YOU ANYPLACE.
TAKE THIS.
THAT WILL TELL ME WHERE YOU ARE AND I CAN FOLLOW AT MY OWN DISCRETION.
IF YOUR STORY CHECKS OUT, I'LL TAKE CARE OF THE JOKER, BUT YOU'RE NOT TO INTERFERE.

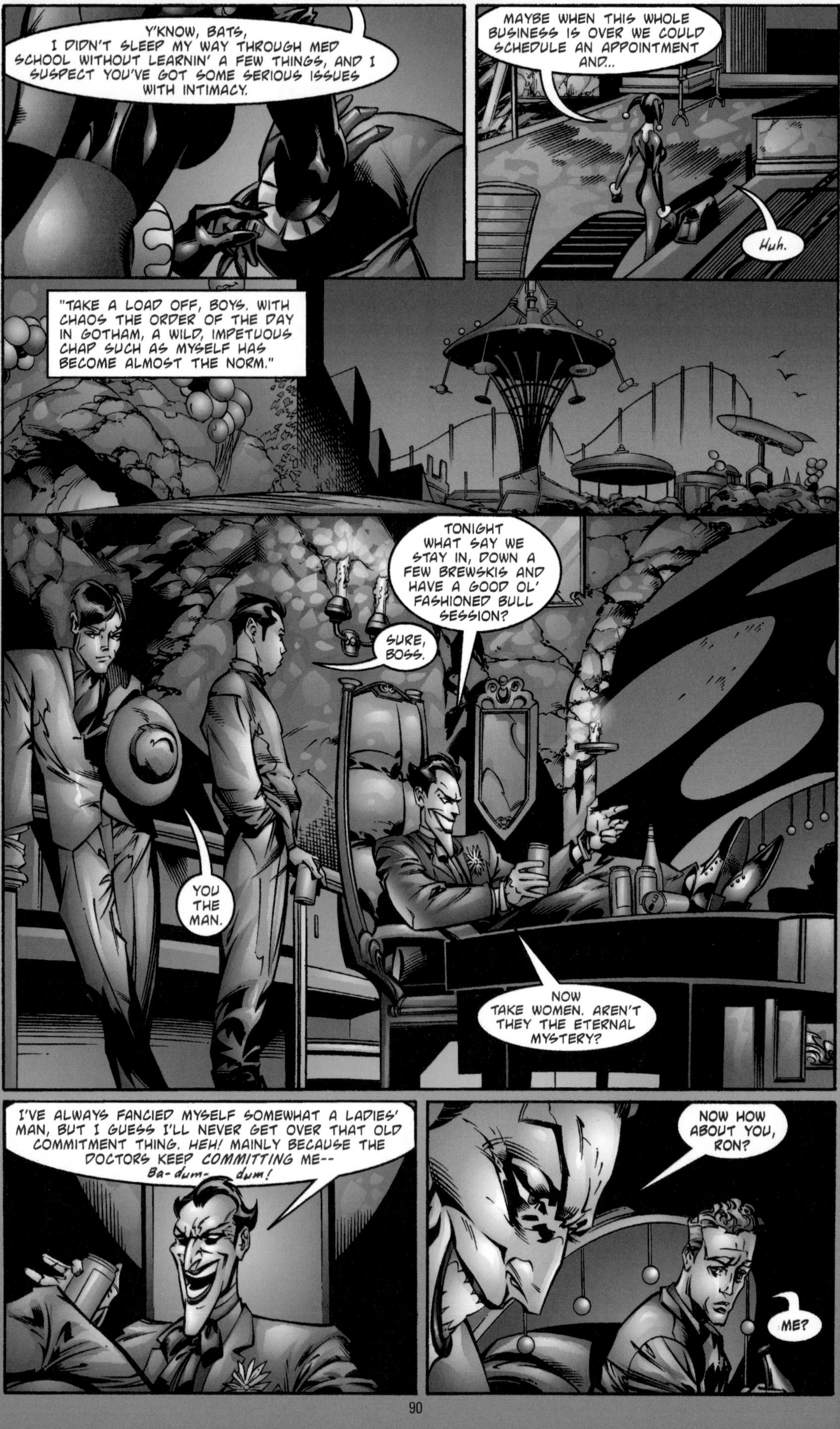
Y'KNOW, BATS, I DIDN'T SLEEP MY WAY THROUGH MED SCHOOL WITHOUT LEARNIN' A FEW THINGS, AND I SUSPECT YOU'VE GOT SOME SERIOUS ISSUES WITH INTIMACY.
MAYBE WHEN THIS WHOLE BUSINESS IS OVER WE COULD SCHEDULE AN APPOINTMENT AND...
Huh.
"TAKE A LOAD OFF, BOYS. WITH CHAOS THE ORDER OF THE DAY IN GOTHAM, A WILD, IMPETUOUS CHAP SUCH AS MYSELF HAS BECOME ALMOST THE NORM."
TONIGHT WHAT SAY WE STAY IN, DOWN A FEW BREWSKIS AND HAVE A GOOD OL' FASHIONED BULL SESSION?
SURE, BOSS.
YOU THE MAN.
NOW TAKE WOMEN. AREN'T THEY THE ETERNAL MYSTERY?
I'VE ALWAYS FANCIED MYSELF SOMEWHAT A LADIES' MAN, BUT I GUESS I'LL NEVER GET OVER THAT OLD COMMITMENT THING. HEH! MAINLY BECAUSE THE DOCTORS KEEP COMMITTING ME--
Ba-dum- dum!
NOW HOW ABOUT YOU, RON?
ME?

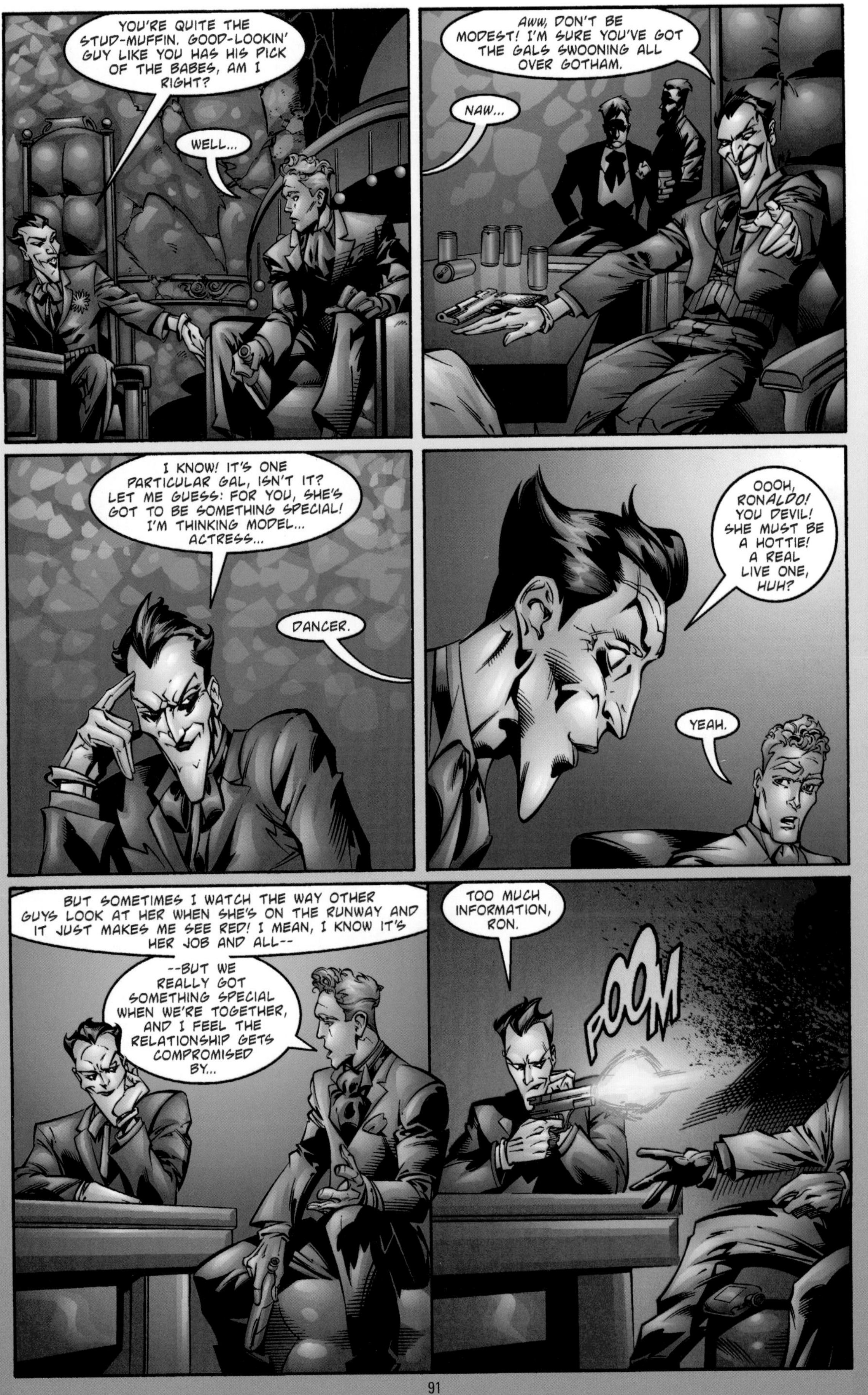
YOU'RE QUITE THE STUD-MUFFIN. GOOD-LOOKIN' GUY LIKE YOU HAS HIS PICK OF THE BABES, AM I RIGHT?
WELL...
AWW, DON'T BE MODEST! I'M SURE YOU'VE GOT THE GALS SWOONING ALL OVER GOTHAM.
NAW...
I KNOW! IT'S ONE PARTICULAR GAL, ISN'T IT? LET ME GUESS: FOR YOU, SHE'S GOT TO BE SOMETHING SPECIAL! I'M THINKING MODEL... ACTRESS...
DANCER.
OOOH, RONALDO! YOU DEVIL! SHE MUST BE A HOTTIE! A REAL LIVE ONE, HUH?
YEAH.
BUT SOMETIMES I WATCH THE WAY OTHER GUYS LOOK AT HER WHEN SHE'S ON THE RUNWAY AND IT JUST MAKES ME SEE RED! I MEAN, I KNOW IT'S HER JOB AND ALL--
--BUT WE REALLY GOT SOMETHING SPECIAL WHEN WE'RE TOGETHER, AND I FEEL THE RELATIONSHIP GETS COMPROMISED BY...
TOO MUCH INFORMATION, RON.
FOOM

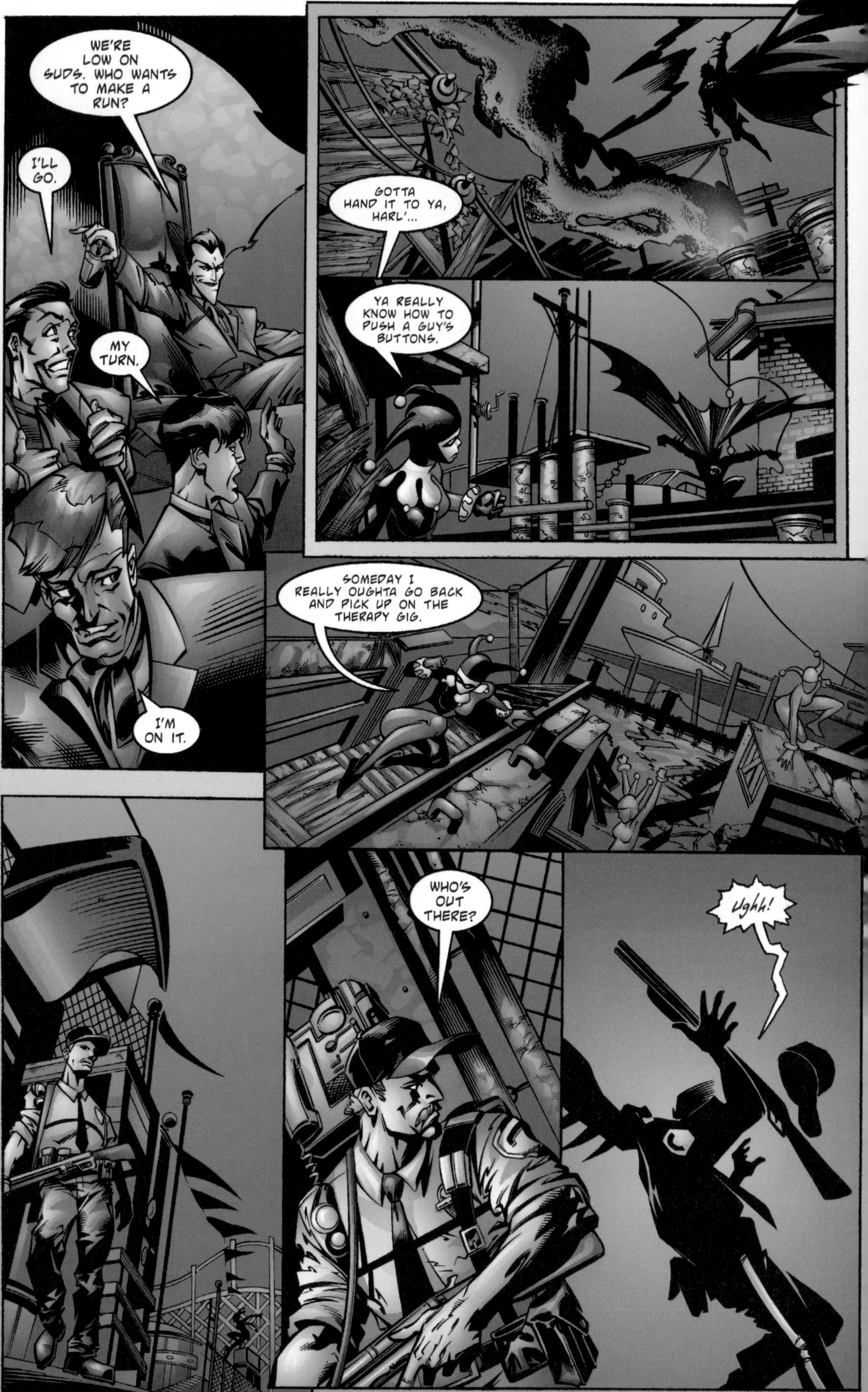

WE'RE LOW ON SUDS. WHO WANTS TO MAKE A RUN?
I'LL GO.
MY TURN.
I'M ON IT.
GOTTA HAND IT TO YA, HARL'...
YA REALLY KNOW HOW TO PUSH A GUY'S BUTTONS.
SOMEDAY I REALLY OUGHTA GO BACK AND PICK UP ON THE THERAPY GIG.
WHO'S OUT THERE?
Ughh!

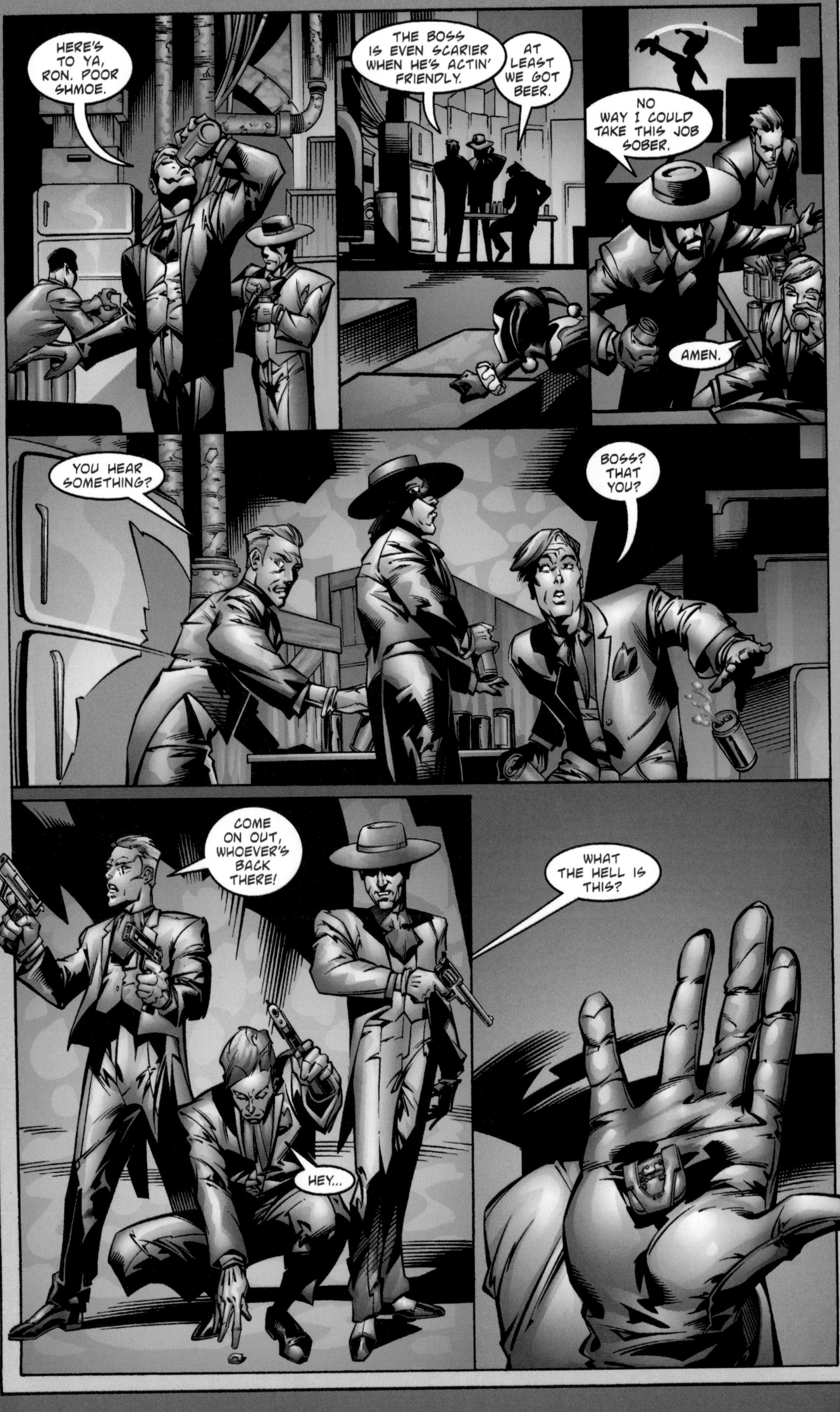
HERE'S TO YA, RON. POOR SHMOE.
THE BOSS IS EVEN SCARIER WHEN HE'S ACTIN' FRIENDLY.
AT LEAST WE GOT BEER.
NO WAY I COULD TAKE THIS JOB SOBER.
AMEN.
YOU HEAR SOMETHING?
BOSS? THAT YOU?
COME ON OUT, WHOEVER'S BACK THERE!
HEY...
WHAT THE HELL IS THIS?

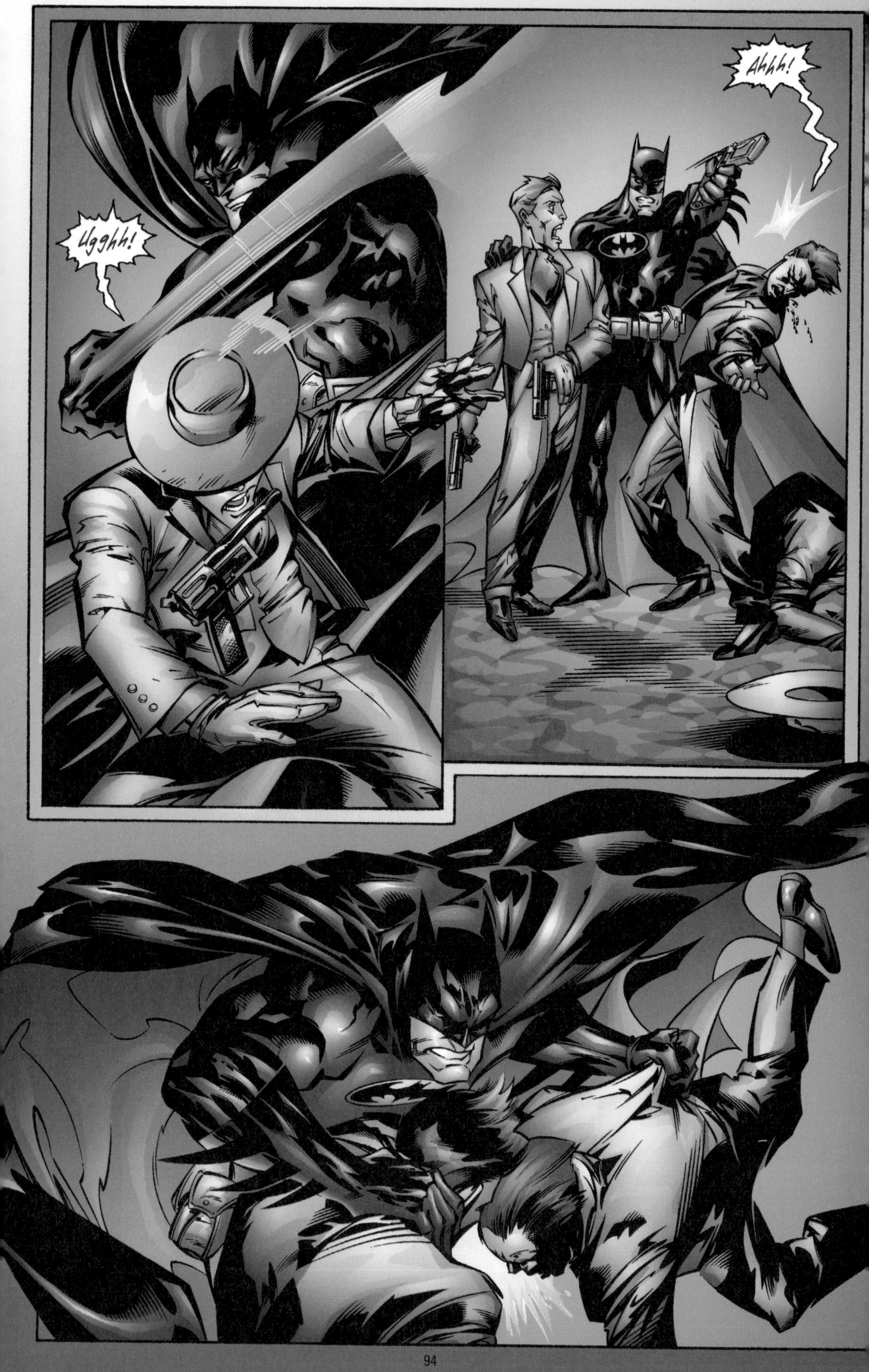
Ugghh!
Ahhh!

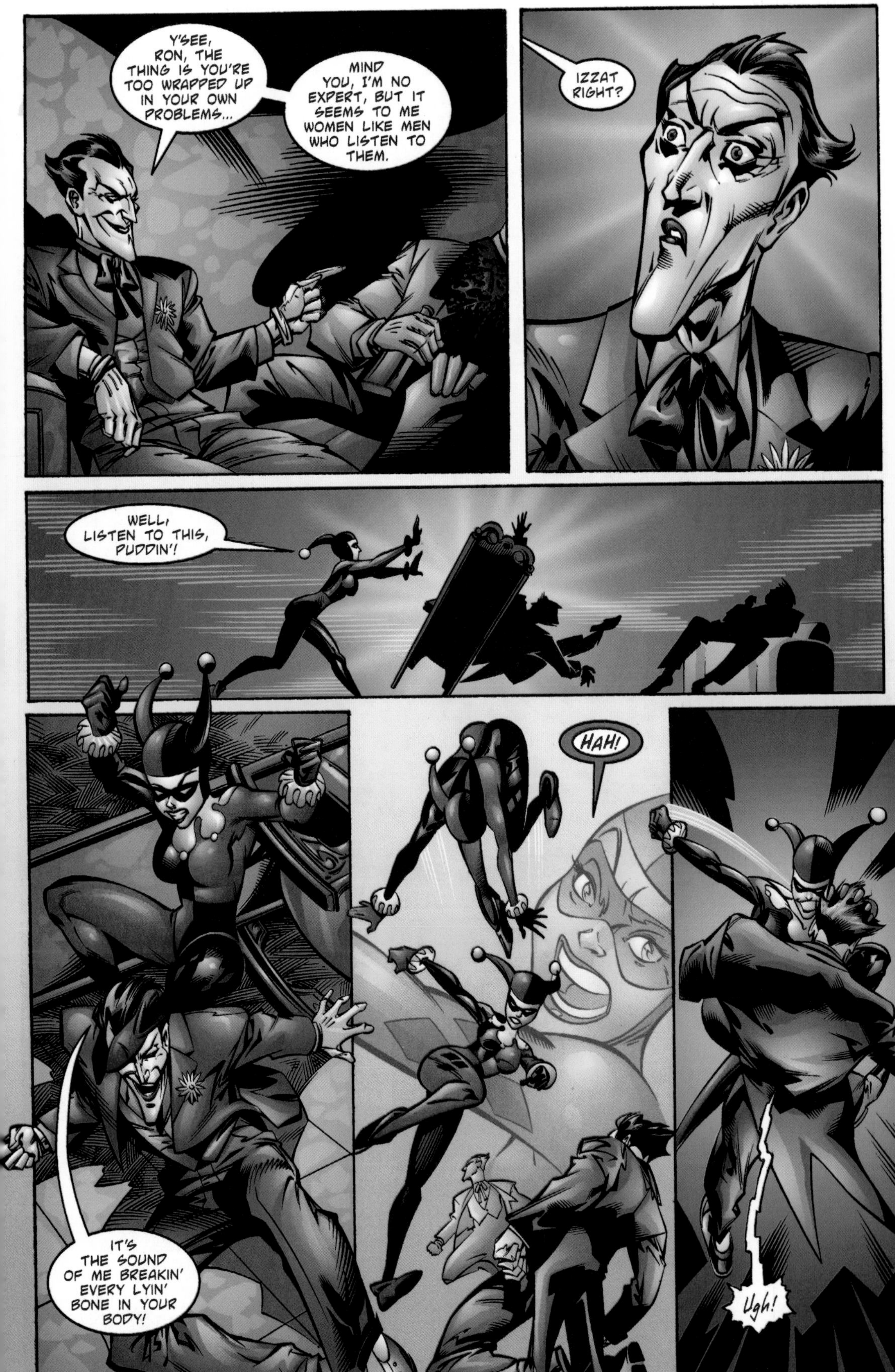
Y'SEE, RON, THE THING IS YOU'RE TOO WRAPPED UP IN YOUR OWN PROBLEMS...
MIND YOU, I'M NO EXPERT, BUT IT SEEMS TO ME WOMEN LIKE MEN WHO LISTEN TO THEM.
IZZAT RIGHT?
WELL, LISTEN TO THIS, PUDDIN'!
HAH!
IT'S THE SOUND OF ME BREAKIN' EVERY LYIN' BONE IN YOUR BODY!
Ugh!

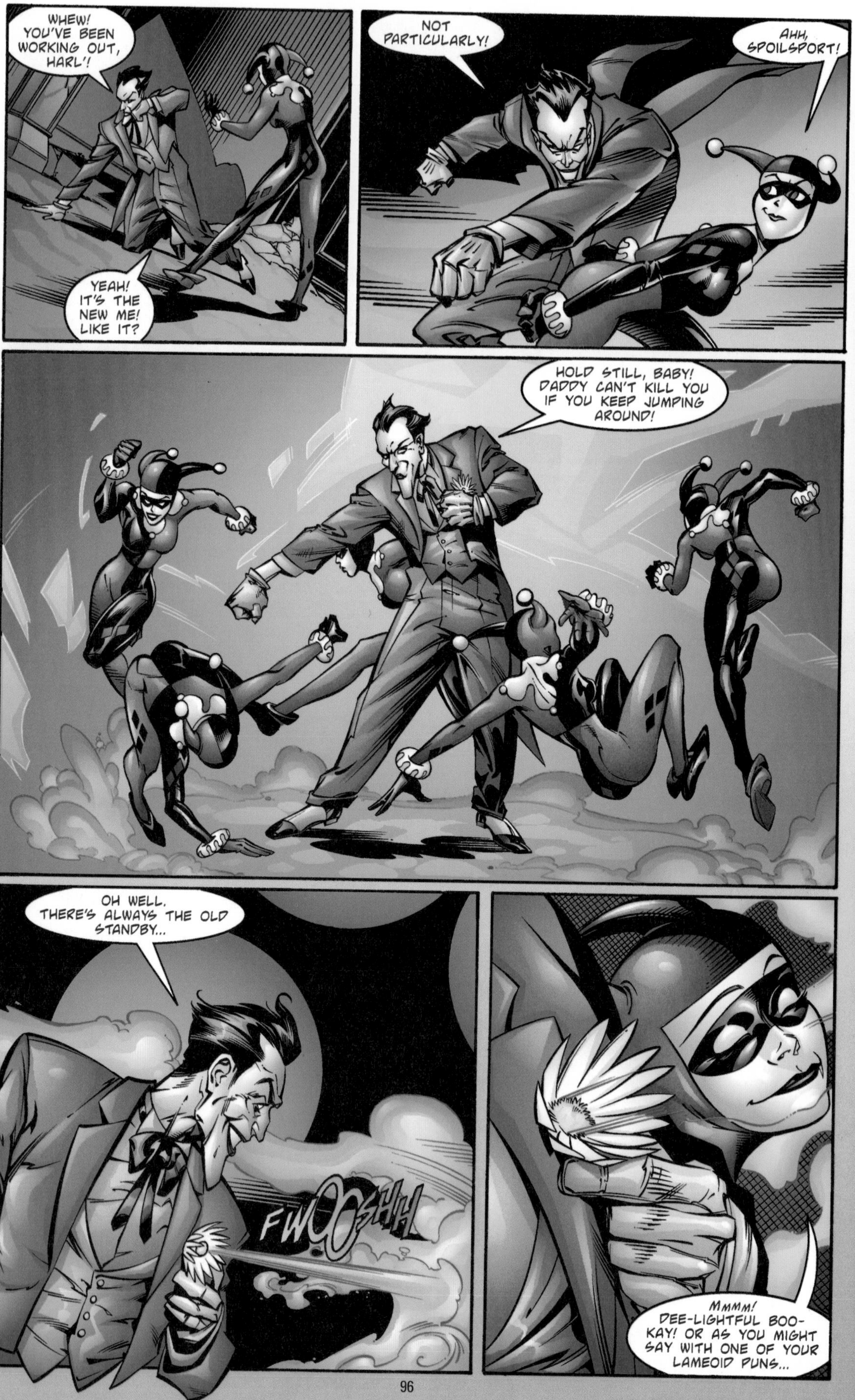
WHEW! YOU'VE BEEN WORKING OUT, HARL'!
YEAH! IT'S THE NEW ME! LIKE IT?
NOT PARTICULARLY!
AHH, SPOILSPORT!
HOLD STILL, BABY! DADDY CAN'T KILL YOU IF YOU KEEP JUMPING AROUND!
OH WELL. THERE'S ALWAYS THE OLD STANDBY...
FWOOSHH
MMMM! DEE-LIGHTFUL BOO-KAY! OR AS YOU MIGHT SAY WITH ONE OF YOUR LAMEOID PUNS...

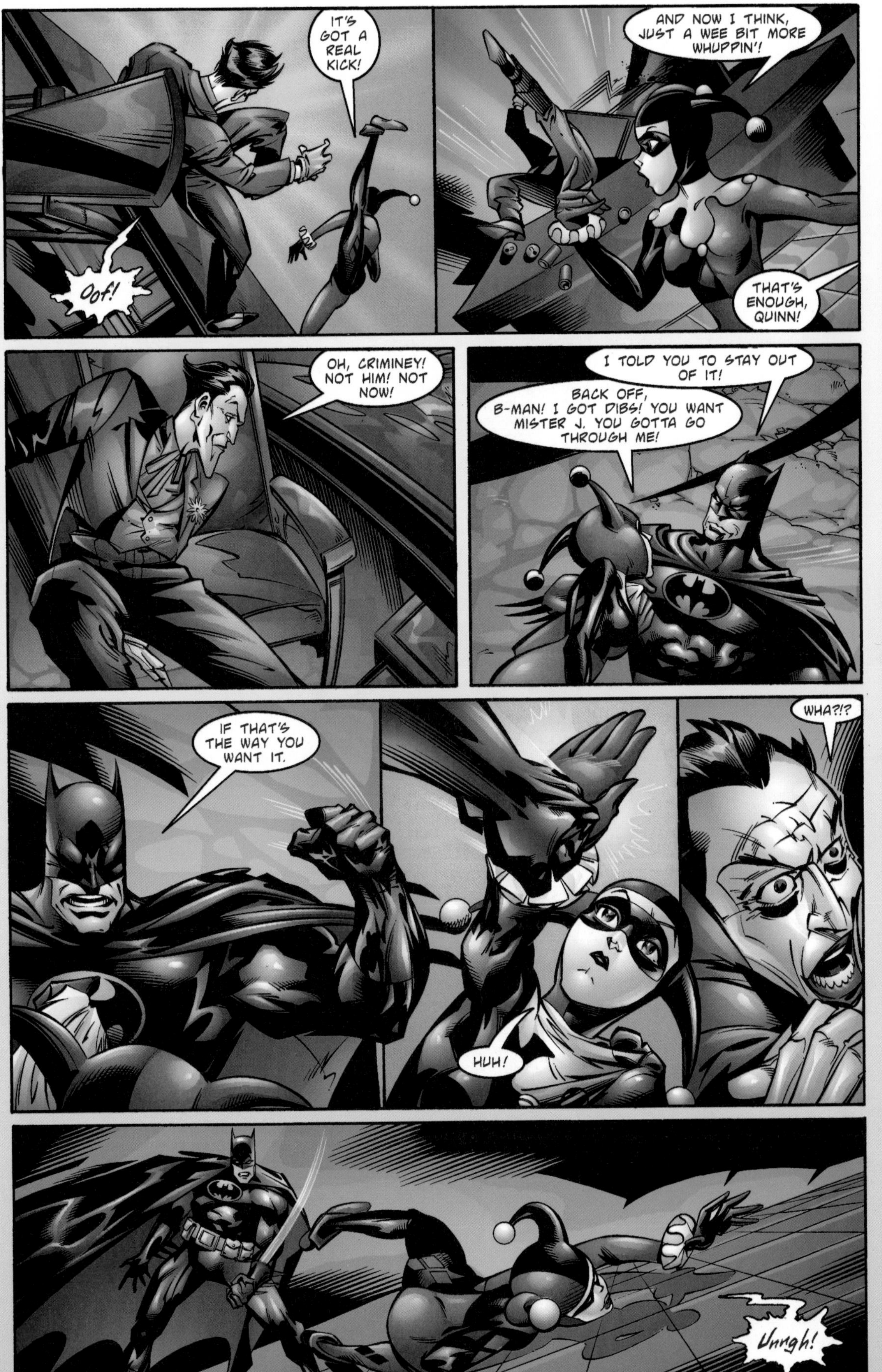

IT'S GOT A REAL KICK!
Oof!
AND NOW I THINK, JUST A WEE BIT MORE WHUPPIN'!
THAT'S ENOUGH, QUINN!
OH, CRIMINEY! NOT HIM! NOT NOW!
I TOLD YOU TO STAY OUT OF IT!
BACK OFF, B-MAN! I GOT DIBS! YOU WANT MISTER J. YOU GOTTA GO THROUGH ME!
IF THAT'S THE WAY YOU WANT IT.
HUH!
WHA?!?
Unngh!

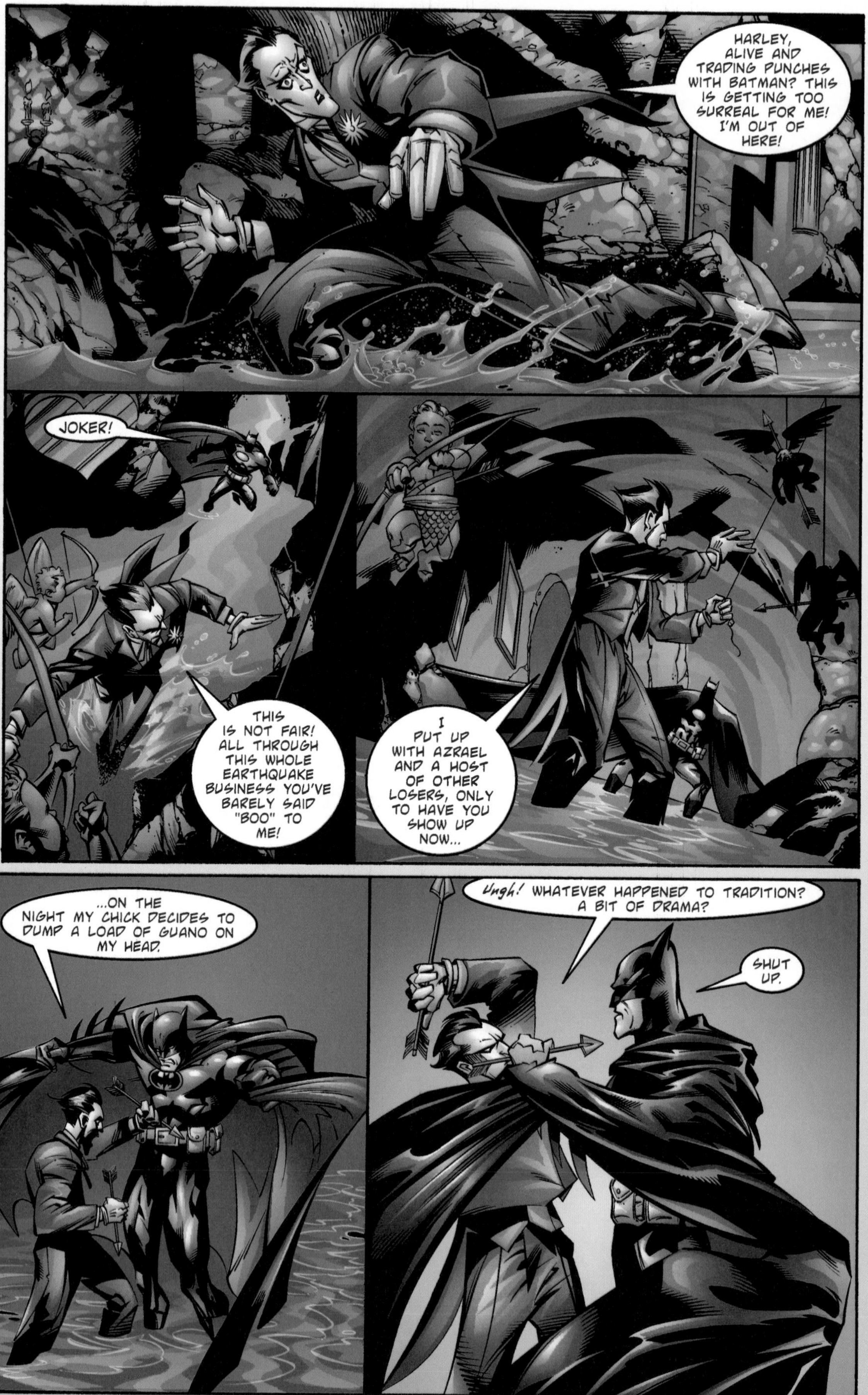
HARLEY, ALIVE AND TRADING PUNCHES WITH BATMAN? THIS IS GETTING TOO SURREAL FOR ME! I'M OUT OF HERE!
JOKER!
THIS IS NOT FAIR! ALL THROUGH THIS WHOLE EARTHQUAKE BUSINESS YOU'VE BARELY SAID "BOO" TO ME!
I PUT UP WITH AZRAEL AND A HOST OF OTHER LOSERS, ONLY TO HAVE YOU SHOW UP NOW...
...ON THE NIGHT MY CHICK DECIDES TO DUMP A LOAD OF GUANO ON MY HEAD.
Ungh! WHATEVER HAPPENED TO TRADITION? A BIT OF DRAMA?
SHUT UP.

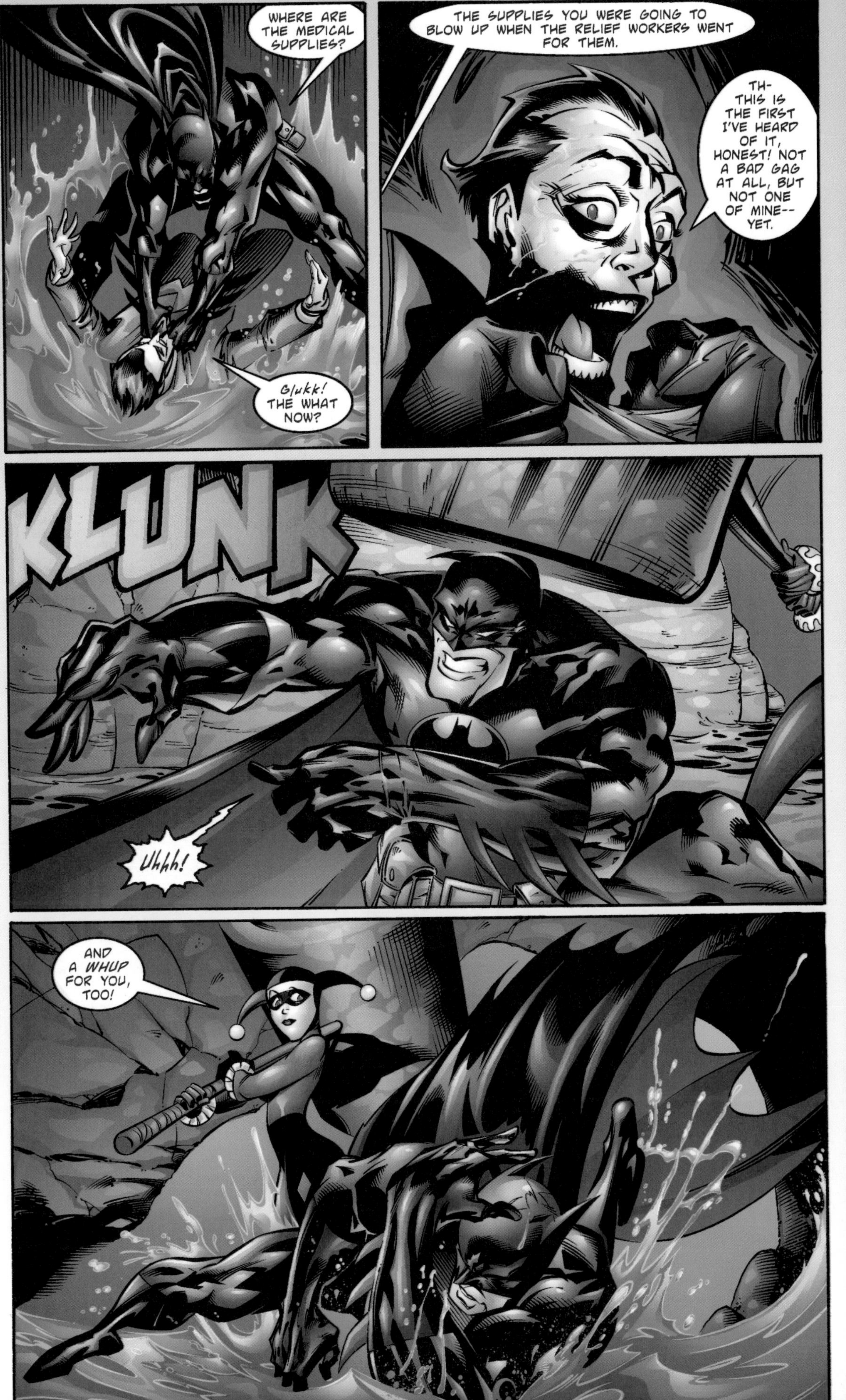
WHERE ARE THE MEDICAL SUPPLIES?
Glukk! THE WHAT NOW?
THE SUPPLIES YOU WERE GOING TO BLOW UP WHEN THE RELIEF WORKERS WENT FOR THEM.
TH-THIS IS THE FIRST I'VE HEARD OF IT, HONEST! NOT A BAD GAG AT ALL, BUT NOT ONE OF MINE--YET.
KLUNK
Uhhh!
AND A WHUP FOR YOU, TOO!

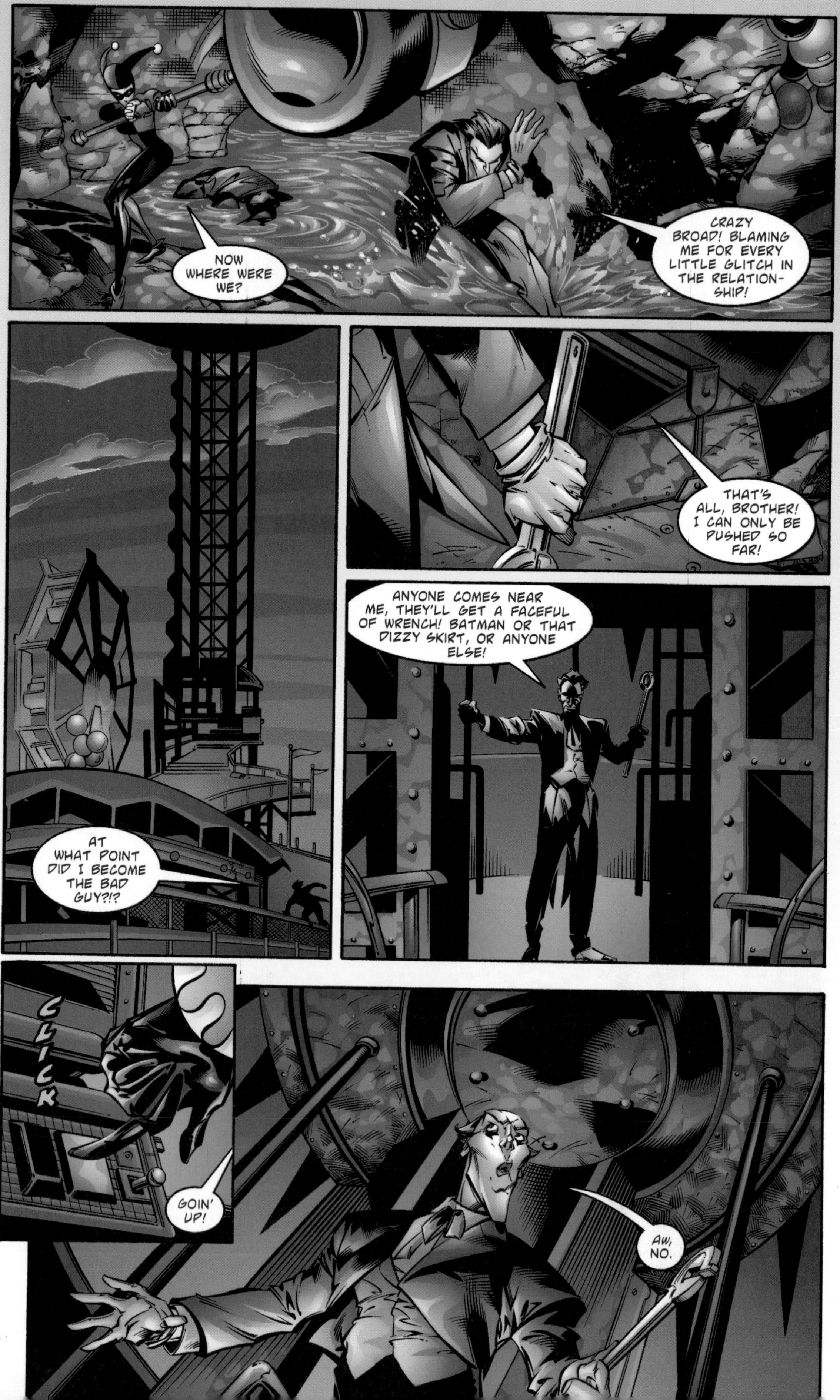
NOW WHERE WERE WE?
CRAZY BROAD! BLAMING ME FOR EVERY LITTLE GLITCH IN THE RELATION-SHIP!
AT WHAT POINT DID I BECOME THE BAD GUY?!?
THAT'S ALL, BROTHER! I CAN ONLY BE PUSHED SO FAR!
ANYONE COMES NEAR ME, THEY'LL GET A FACEFUL OF WRENCH! BATMAN OR THAT DIZZY SKIRT, OR ANYONE ELSE!
CLICK
GOIN' UP!
AW, NO.

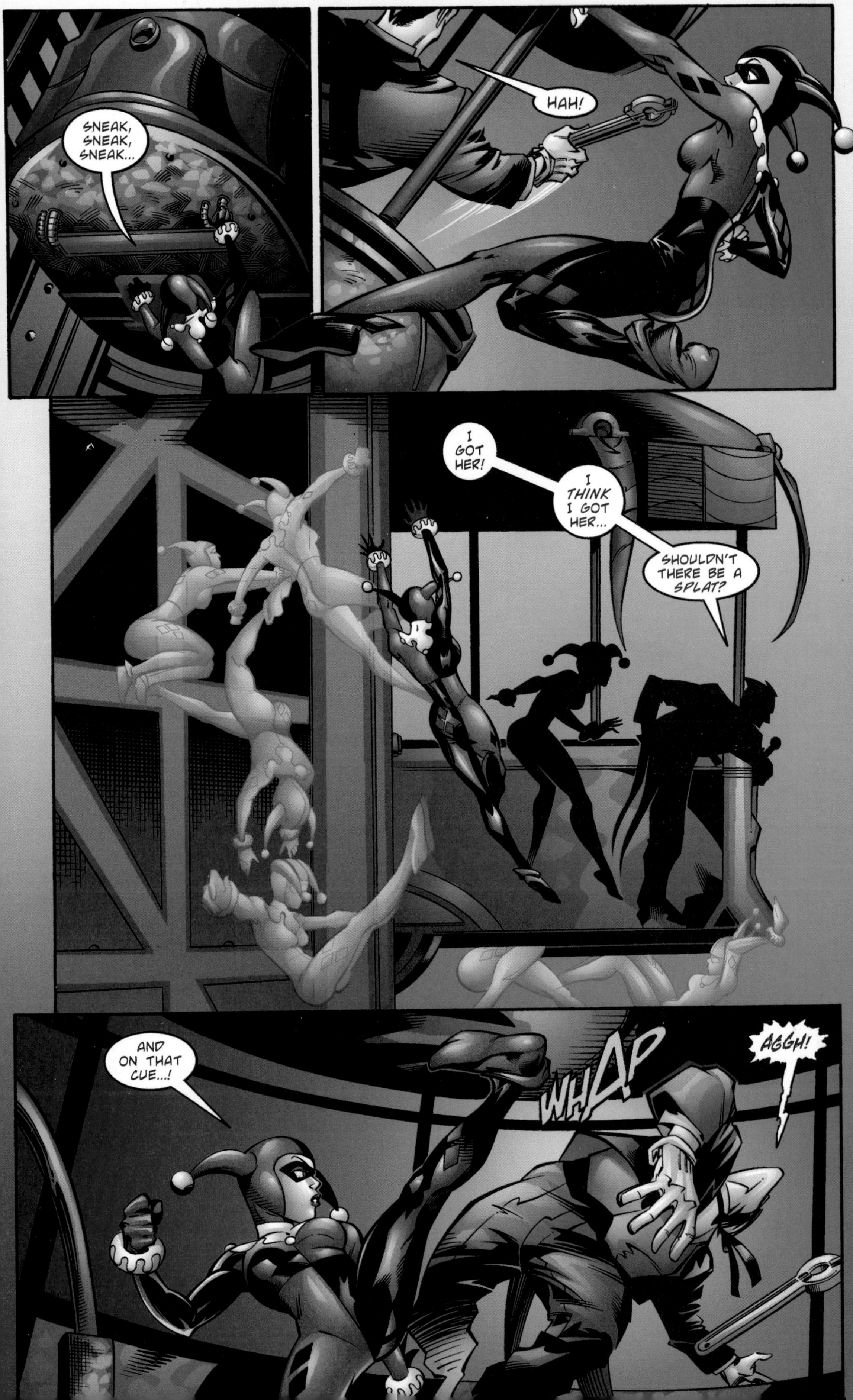
SNEAK, SNEAK, SNEAK...
HAH!
I GOT HER!
I THINK I GOT HER...
SHOULDN'T THERE BE A SPLAT?
AND ON THAT CUE...!
WHAP
AGGH!

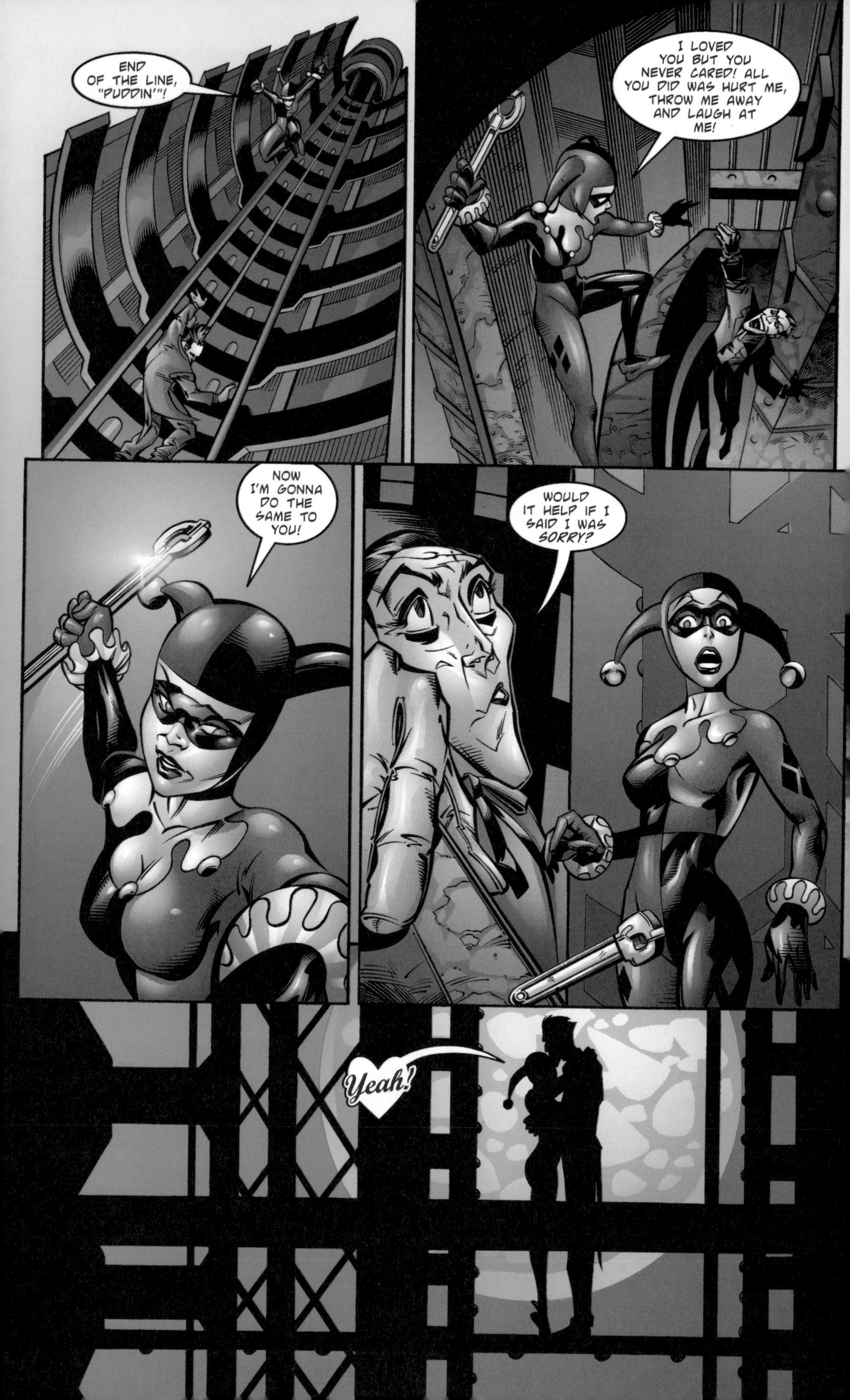
END OF THE LINE, "PUDDIN'"!
I LOVED YOU BUT YOU NEVER CARED! ALL YOU DID WAS HURT ME, THROW ME AWAY AND LAUGH AT ME!
NOW I'M GONNA DO THE SAME TO YOU!
WOULD IT HELP IF I SAID I WAS SORRY?
Yeah!

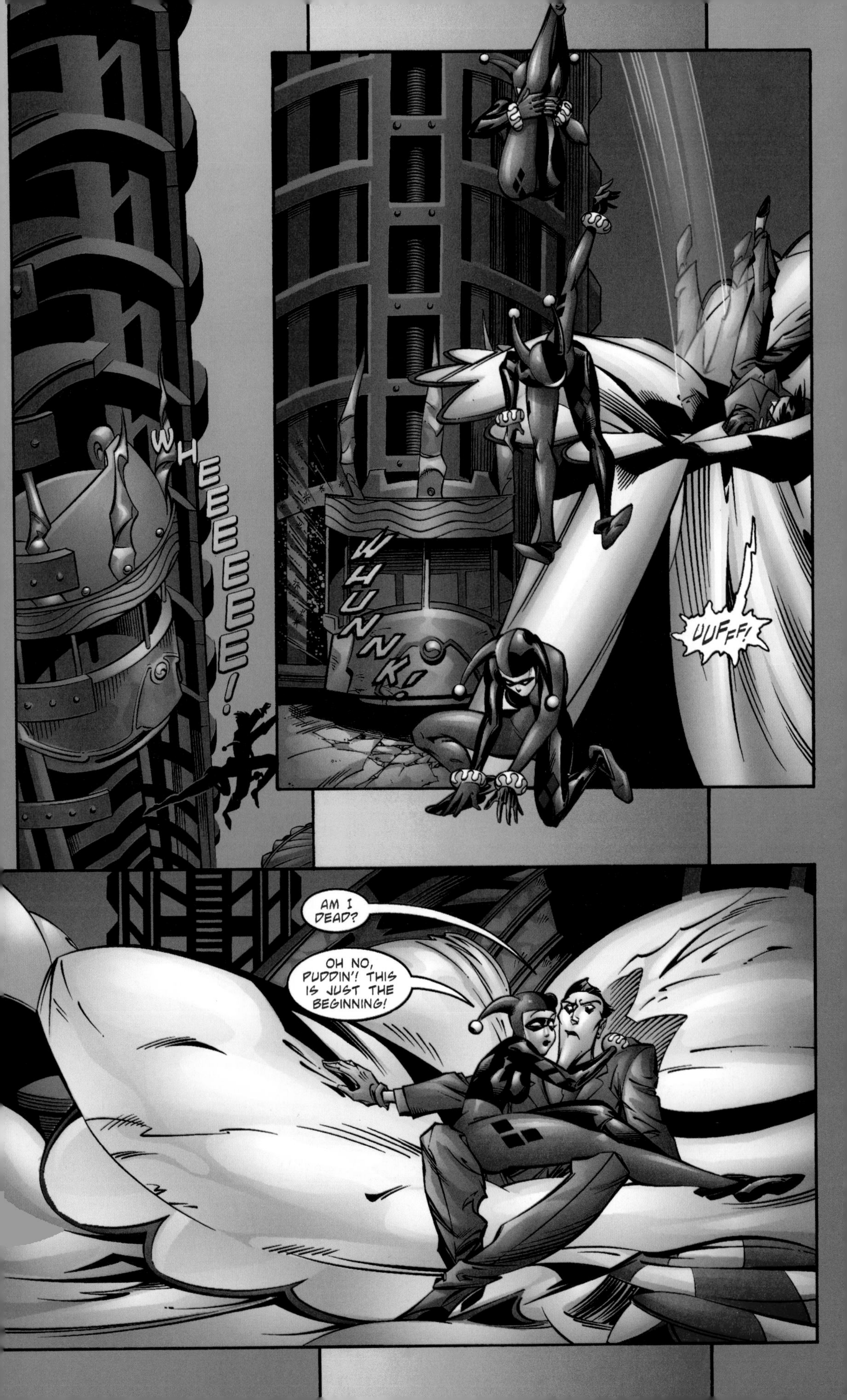
WHEEEEEEEE!
WHUNNK!
UUFFF!
AM I DEAD?
OH NO, PUDDIN'! THIS IS JUST THE BEGINNING!

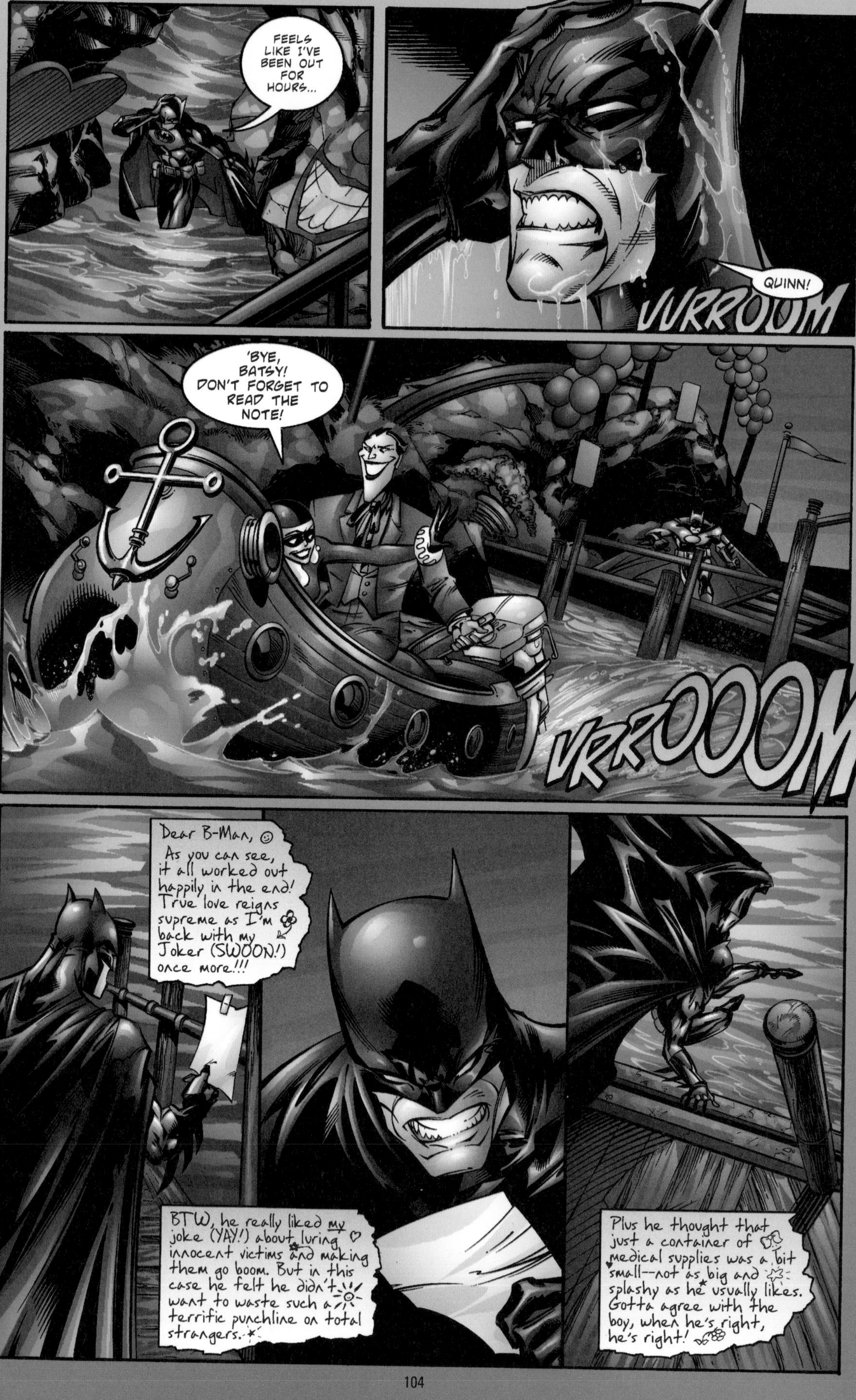

FEELS LIKE I'VE BEEN OUT FOR HOURS...
QUINN!
VURROOM
'BYE, BATSY! DON'T FORGET TO READ THE NOTE!
VRROOOM
Dear B-Man, ☺ As you can see, it all worked out happily in the end! True love reigns supreme as I'm back with my Joker (SWOON!) once more!!!
BTW, he really liked my joke (YAY!) about luring innocent victims and making them go boom. But in this case he felt he didn't want to waste such a terrific punchline on total strangers.
Plus he thought that just a container of medical supplies was a bit small--not as big and splashy as he usually likes. Gotta agree with the boy, when he's right, he's right!

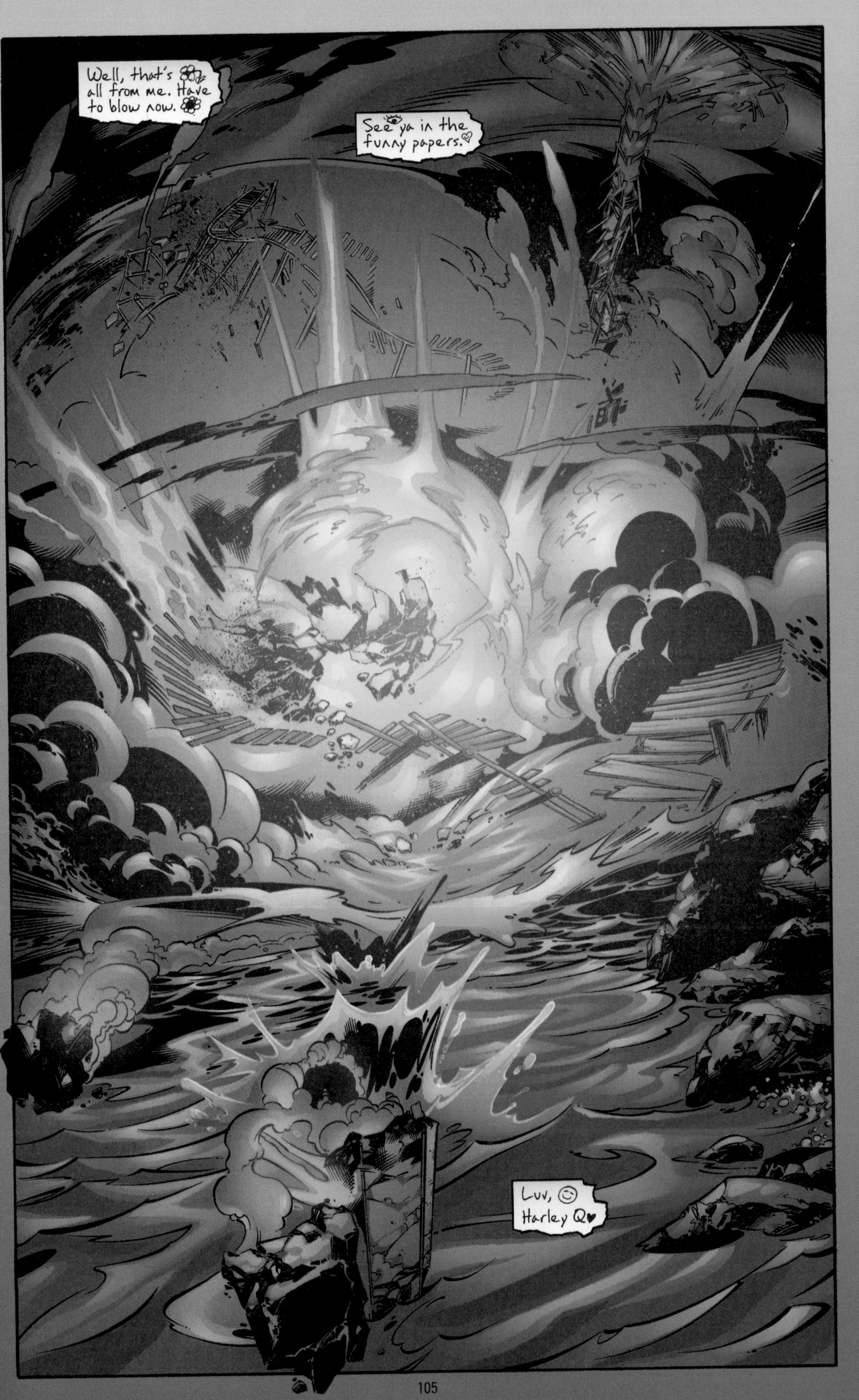

Well, that's all from me. Have to blow now.
See ya in the funny papers.
Luv, Harley Q

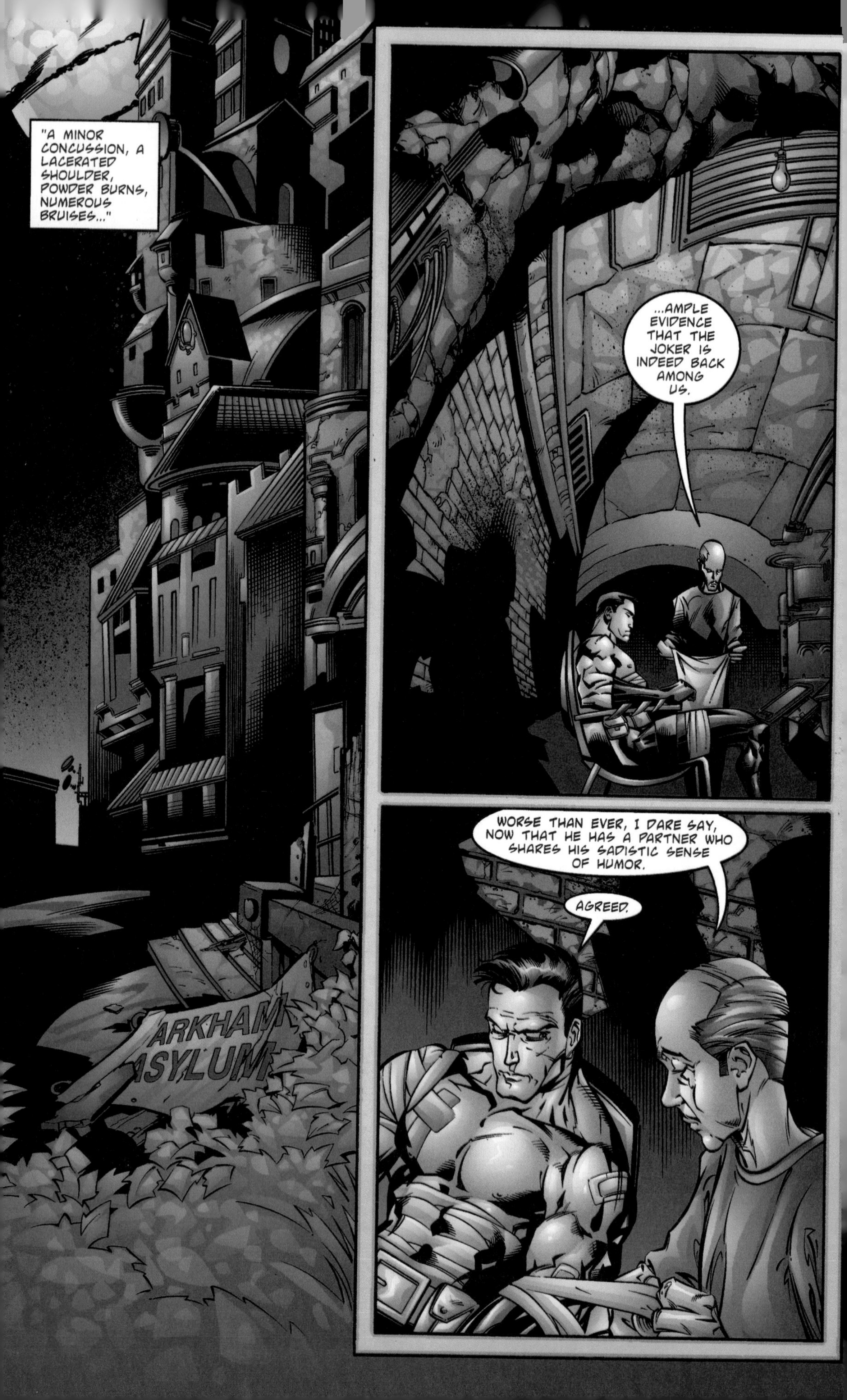
"A MINOR CONCUSSION, A LACERATED SHOULDER, POWDER BURNS, NUMEROUS BRUISES..."
ARKHAM ASYLUM
...AMPLE EVIDENCE THAT THE JOKER IS INDEED BACK AMONG US.
WORSE THAN EVER, I DARE SAY, NOW THAT HE HAS A PARTNER WHO SHARES HIS SADISTIC SENSE OF HUMOR.
AGREED.

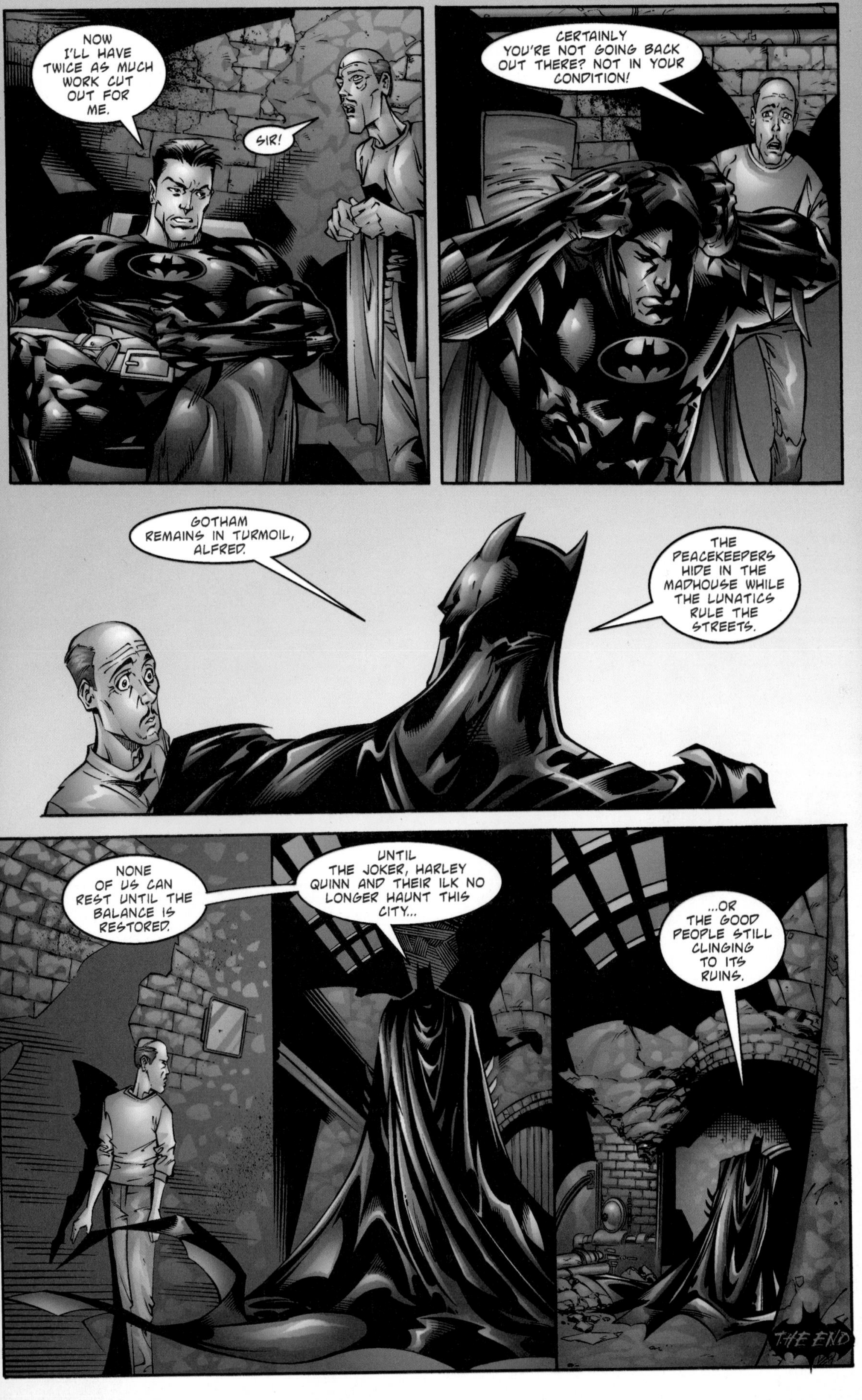
NOW I'LL HAVE TWICE AS MUCH WORK CUT OUT FOR ME.
SIR!
CERTAINLY YOU'RE NOT GOING BACK OUT THERE? NOT IN YOUR CONDITION!
GOTHAM REMAINS IN TURMOIL, ALFRED.
THE PEACEKEEPERS HIDE IN THE MADHOUSE WHILE THE LUNATICS RULE THE STREETS.
NONE OF US CAN REST UNTIL THE BALANCE IS RESTORED.
UNTIL THE JOKER, HARLEY QUINN AND THEIR ILK NO LONGER HAUNT THIS CITY...
...OR THE GOOD PEOPLE STILL CLINGING TO ITS RUINS.
THE END

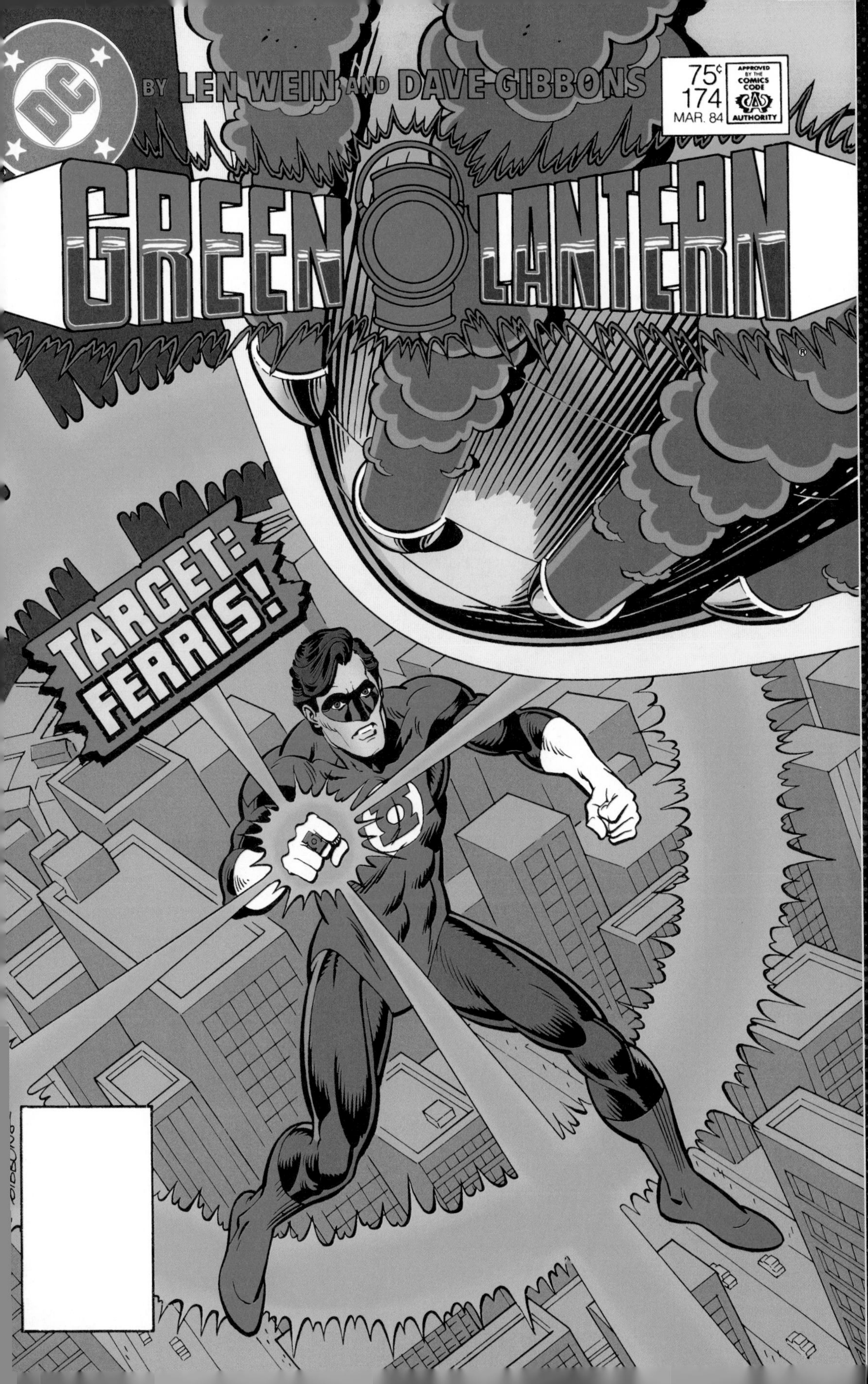
BY LEN WEIN AND DAVE GIBBONS
75¢
174
MAR. 84
APPROVED BY THE COMICS CODE AUTHORITY
GREEN LANTERN
TARGET: FERRIS!

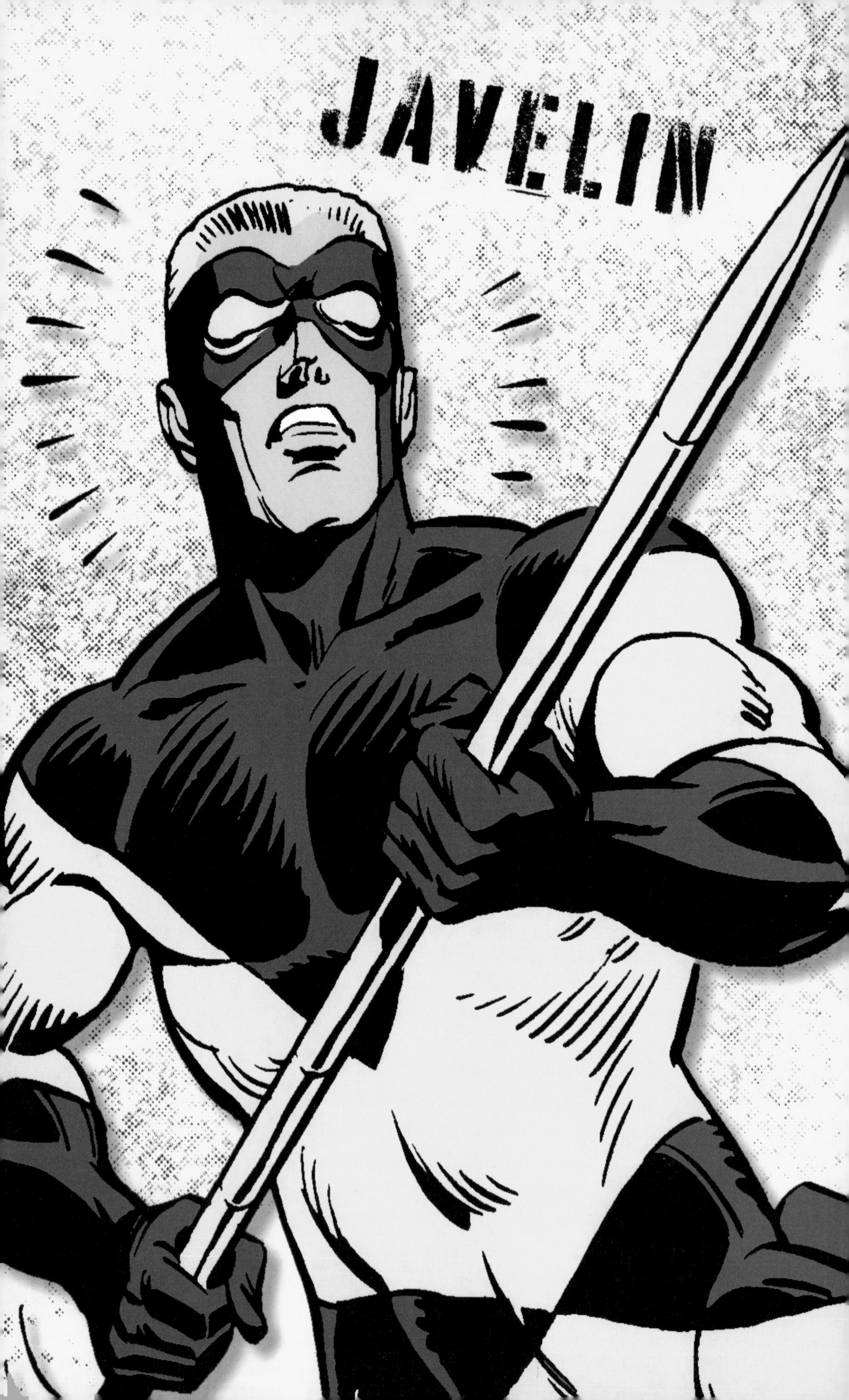
JAVELIN

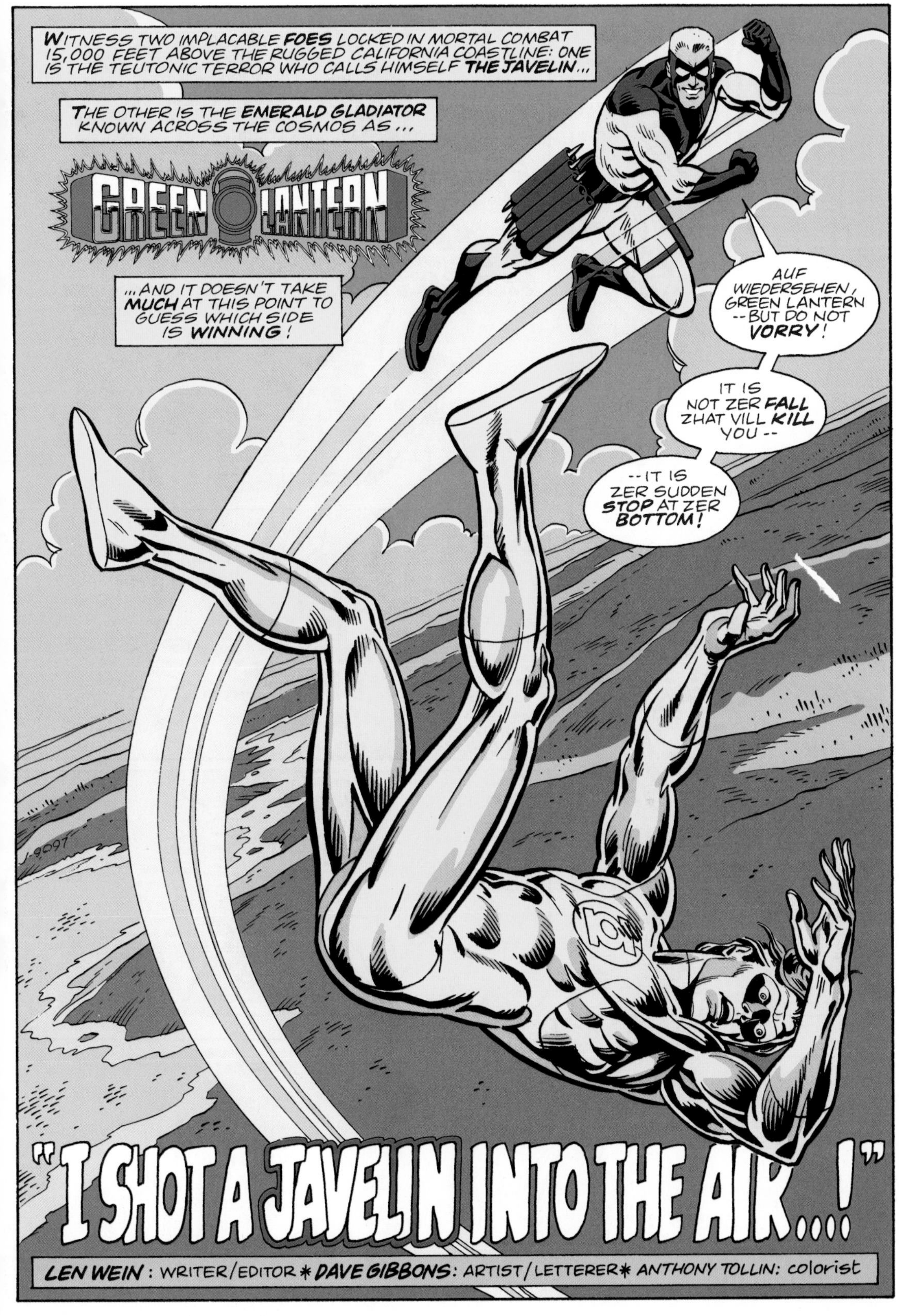
WITNESS TWO IMPLACABLE FOES LOCKED IN MORTAL COMBAT 15,000 FEET ABOVE THE RUGGED CALIFORNIA COASTLINE: ONE IS THE TEUTONIC TERROR WHO CALLS HIMSELF THE JAVELIN...
THE OTHER IS THE EMERALD GLADIATOR KNOWN ACROSS THE COSMOS AS...
GREEN LANTERN
...AND IT DOESN'T TAKE MUCH AT THIS POINT TO GUESS WHICH SIDE IS WINNING!
AUF WIEDERSEHEN, GREEN LANTERN --BUT DO NOT VORRY!
IT IS NOT ZER FALL ZHAT VILL KILL YOU --
--IT IS ZER SUDDEN STOP AT ZER BOTTOM!
"I SHOT A JAVELIN INTO THE AIR...!"
LEN WEIN: WRITER/EDITOR * DAVE GIBBONS: ARTIST/LETTERER * ANTHONY TOLLIN: colorist

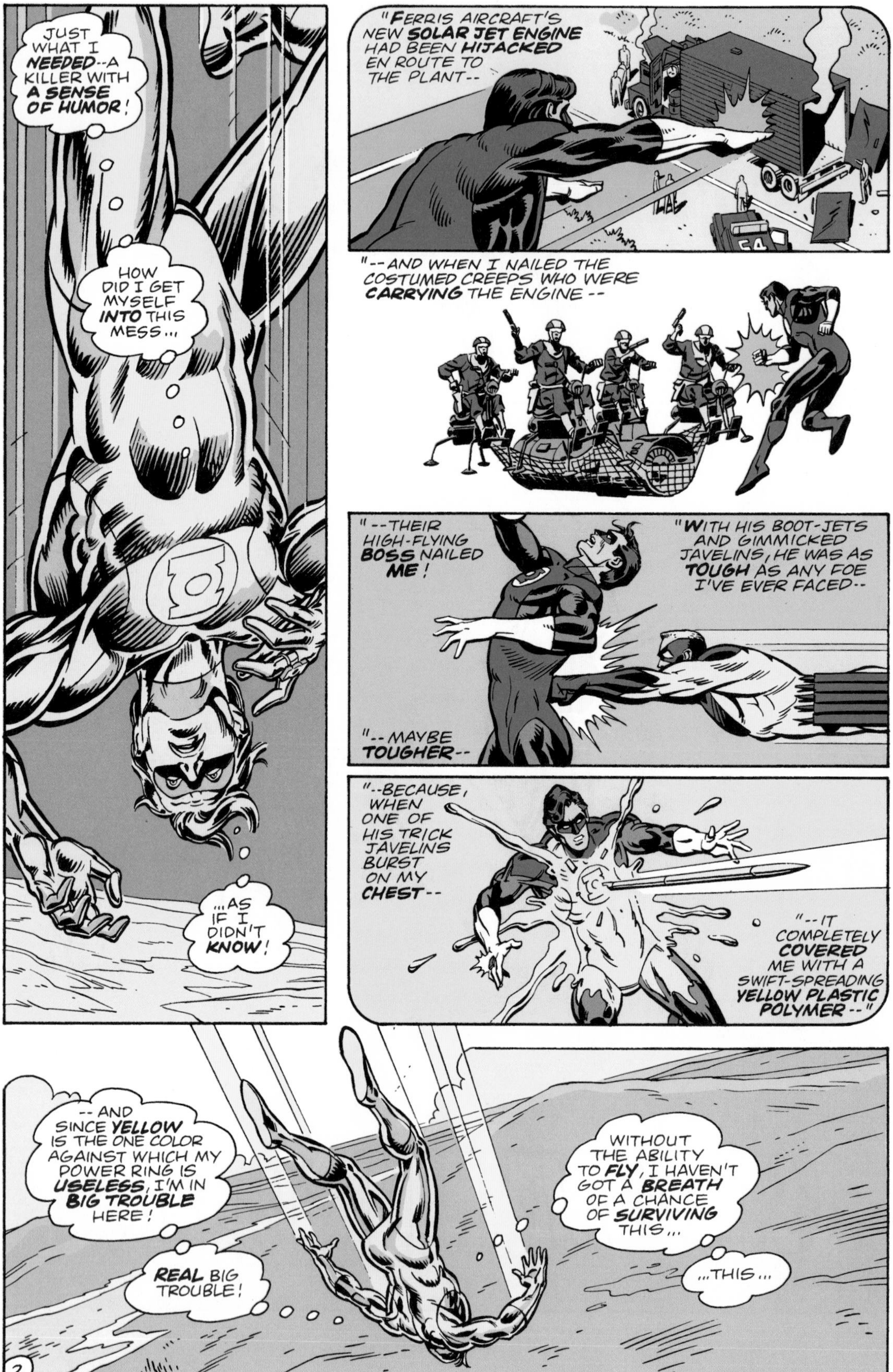

JUST WHAT I NEEDED--A KILLER WITH A SENSE OF HUMOR!
HOW DID I GET MYSELF INTO THIS MESS...
...AS IF I DIDN'T KNOW!
"FERRIS AIRCRAFT'S NEW SOLAR JET ENGINE HAD BEEN HIJACKED EN ROUTE TO THE PLANT--
"--AND WHEN I NAILED THE COSTUMED CREEPS WHO WERE CARRYING THE ENGINE--
"--THEIR HIGH-FLYING BOSS NAILED ME!
"WITH HIS BOOT-JETS AND GIMMICKED JAVELINS, HE WAS AS TOUGH AS ANY FOE I'VE EVER FACED--
"--MAYBE TOUGHER--
"--BECAUSE, WHEN ONE OF HIS TRICK JAVELINS BURST ON MY CHEST--
"--IT COMPLETELY COVERED ME WITH A SWIFT-SPREADING YELLOW PLASTIC POLYMER--"
--AND SINCE YELLOW IS THE ONE COLOR AGAINST WHICH MY POWER RING IS USELESS, I'M IN BIG TROUBLE HERE!
REAL BIG TROUBLE!
WITHOUT THE ABILITY TO FLY, I HAVEN'T GOT A BREATH OF A CHANCE OF SURVIVING THIS...
...THIS...
2

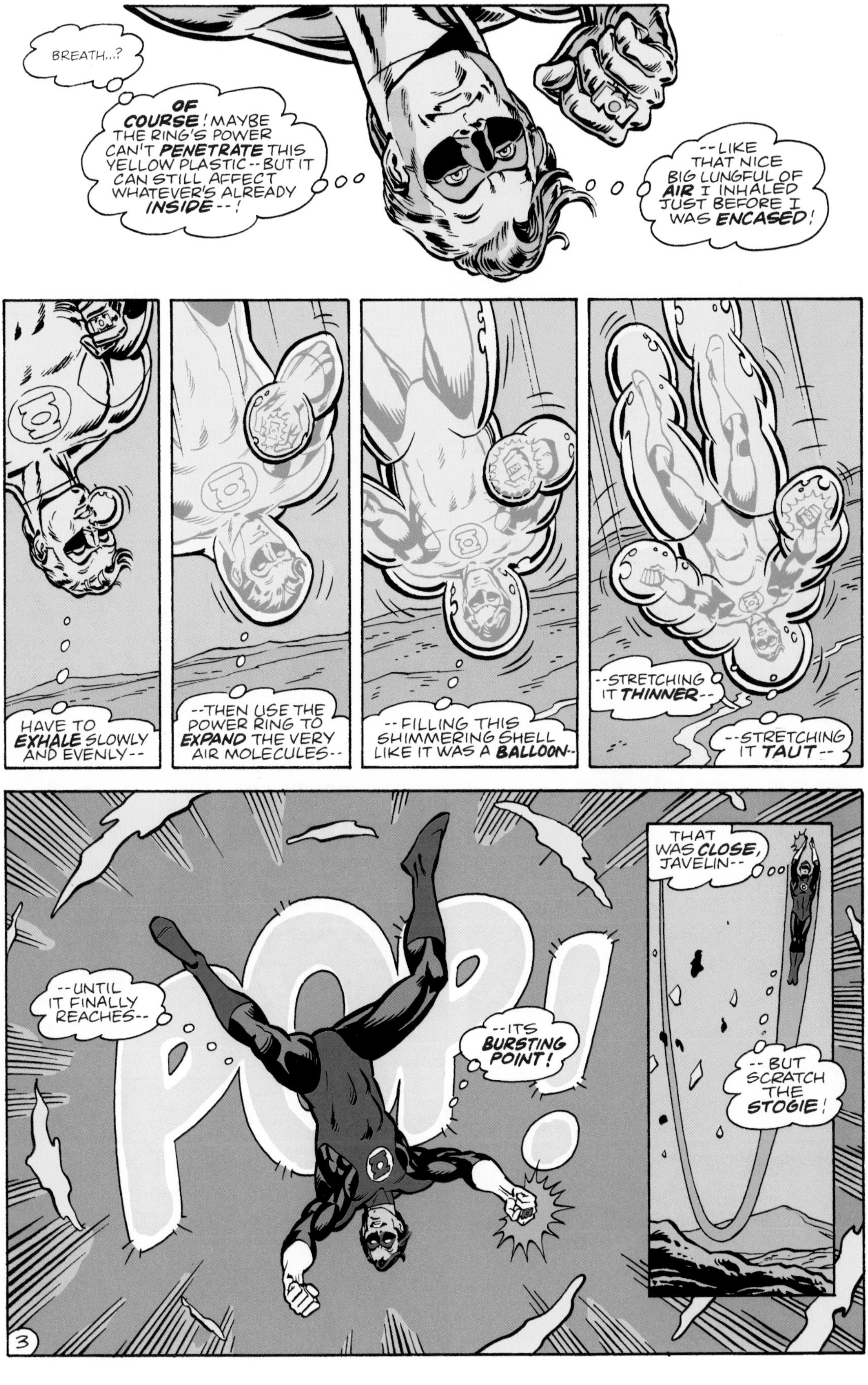
BREATH...?
OF COURSE! MAYBE THE RING'S POWER CAN'T PENETRATE THIS YELLOW PLASTIC--BUT IT CAN STILL AFFECT WHATEVER'S ALREADY INSIDE--!
--LIKE THAT NICE BIG LUNGFUL OF AIR I INHALED JUST BEFORE I WAS ENCASED!
HAVE TO EXHALE SLOWLY AND EVENLY--
--THEN USE THE POWER RING TO EXPAND THE VERY AIR MOLECULES--
--FILLING THIS SHIMMERING SHELL LIKE IT WAS A BALLOON--
--STRETCHING IT THINNER--
--STRETCHING IT TAUT--
--UNTIL IT FINALLY REACHES--
POP!
--ITS BURSTING POINT!
THAT WAS CLOSE, JAVELIN--
--BUT SCRATCH THE STOGIE!
3

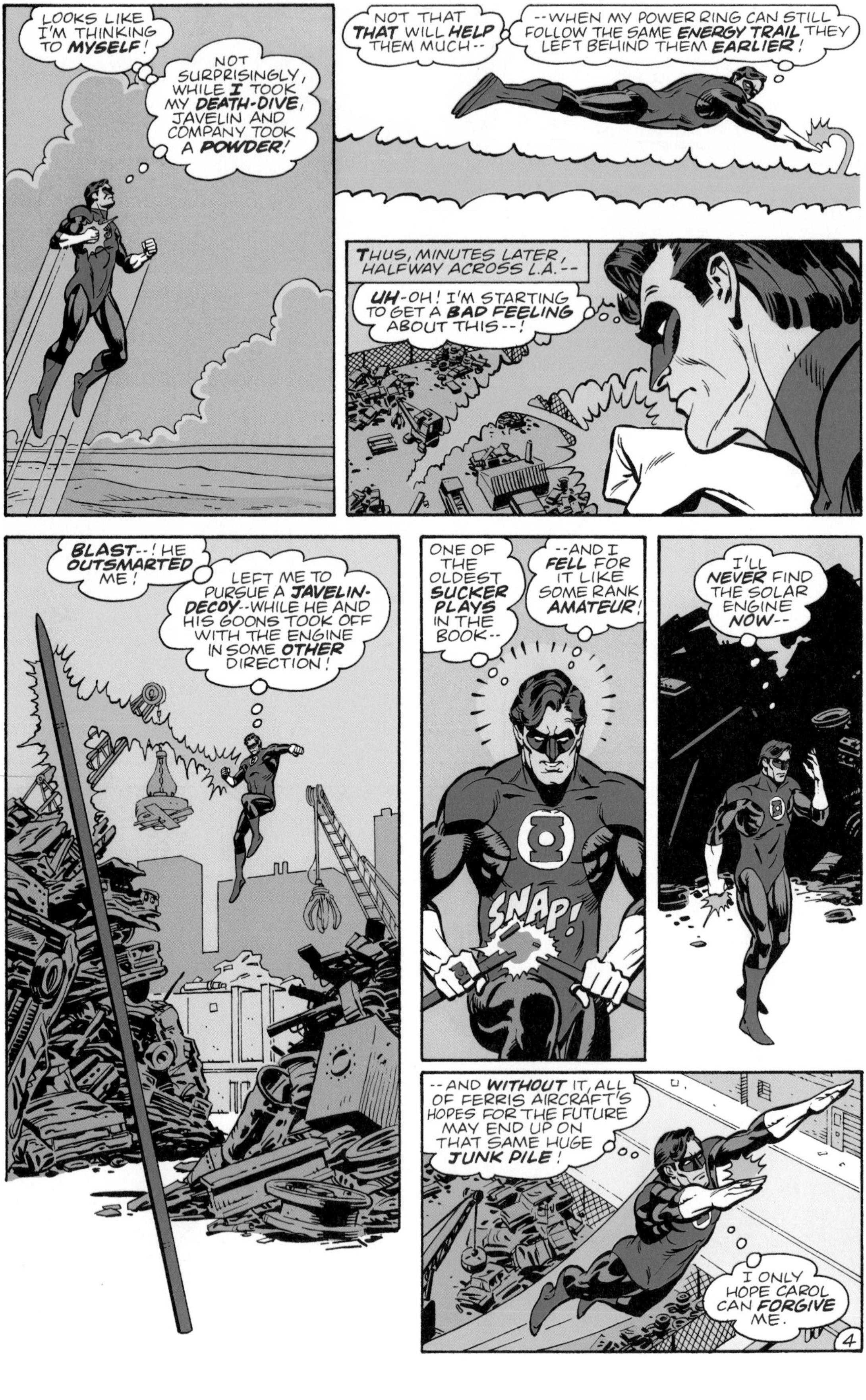
LOOKS LIKE I'M THINKING TO MYSELF!
NOT SURPRISINGLY, WHILE I TOOK MY DEATH-DIVE, JAVELIN AND COMPANY TOOK A POWDER!
NOT THAT THAT WILL HELP THEM MUCH--
--WHEN MY POWER RING CAN STILL FOLLOW THE SAME ENERGY TRAIL THEY LEFT BEHIND THEM EARLIER!
THUS, MINUTES LATER, HALFWAY ACROSS L.A.--
UH-OH! I'M STARTING TO GET A BAD FEELING ABOUT THIS--!
BLAST--! HE OUTSMARTED ME!
LEFT ME TO PURSUE A JAVELIN-DECOY--WHILE HE AND HIS GOONS TOOK OFF WITH THE ENGINE IN SOME OTHER DIRECTION!
ONE OF THE OLDEST SUCKER PLAYS IN THE BOOK--
--AND I FELL FOR IT LIKE SOME RANK AMATEUR!
SNAP!
I'LL NEVER FIND THE SOLAR ENGINE NOW--
--AND WITHOUT IT, ALL OF FERRIS AIRCRAFT'S HOPES FOR THE FUTURE MAY END UP ON THAT SAME HUGE JUNK PILE!
I ONLY HOPE CAROL CAN FORGIVE ME.
4

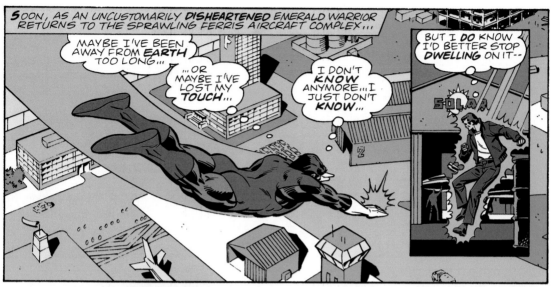

SOON, AS AN UNCUSTOMARILY **DISHEARTENED** EMERALD WARRIOR RETURNS TO THE SPRAWLING FERRIS AIRCRAFT COMPLEX...

MAYBE I'VE BEEN AWAY FROM **EARTH** TOO LONG...

...OR MAYBE I'VE LOST MY **TOUCH**...

I DON'T **KNOW** ANYMORE...I JUST DON'T **KNOW**...

BUT I **DO** KNOW I'D BETTER STOP **DWELLING** ON IT--

--BEFORE **HAL JORDAN** DEVELOPS A PERMANENT **TWITCH**!

HELLO, **TOM**.

HAL, YOU'RE **BACK**! I WAS STARTING TO **WORRY** ABOUT YOU.

ANY **LUCK** WITH THE **SOLAR ENGINE**?

PLENTY...ALL **BAD**!

I LOST THE ENGINE **AND** THE GOONS WHO **STOLE** IT!

SWELL! HIS LORD-SHIP WON'T BE HAPPY TO **HEAR** THAT!

BUT THEN, **CARL FERRIS** ISN'T HAPPY ABOUT MUCH OF **ANY-THING** THESE DAYS!

IS **CAROL** AROUND?

NOPE. SHE'S OVER AT THE **EMERGENCY MEETING** HER DAD JUST CALLED--

--WHICH IS WHERE **YOU** SHOULD PROBABLY BE, IF YOU WANT TO KEEP YOUR **JOB**!

I'M ON MY **WAY**!

SEE YOU **LATER**, MR. KALMAKU.

IF THERE **IS** A LATER, HAL.

BUT THE WAY THINGS HAVE BEEN **GOING** AROUND HERE LATELY, I WOULDN'T WANT TO **BET** ON IT!

⑤

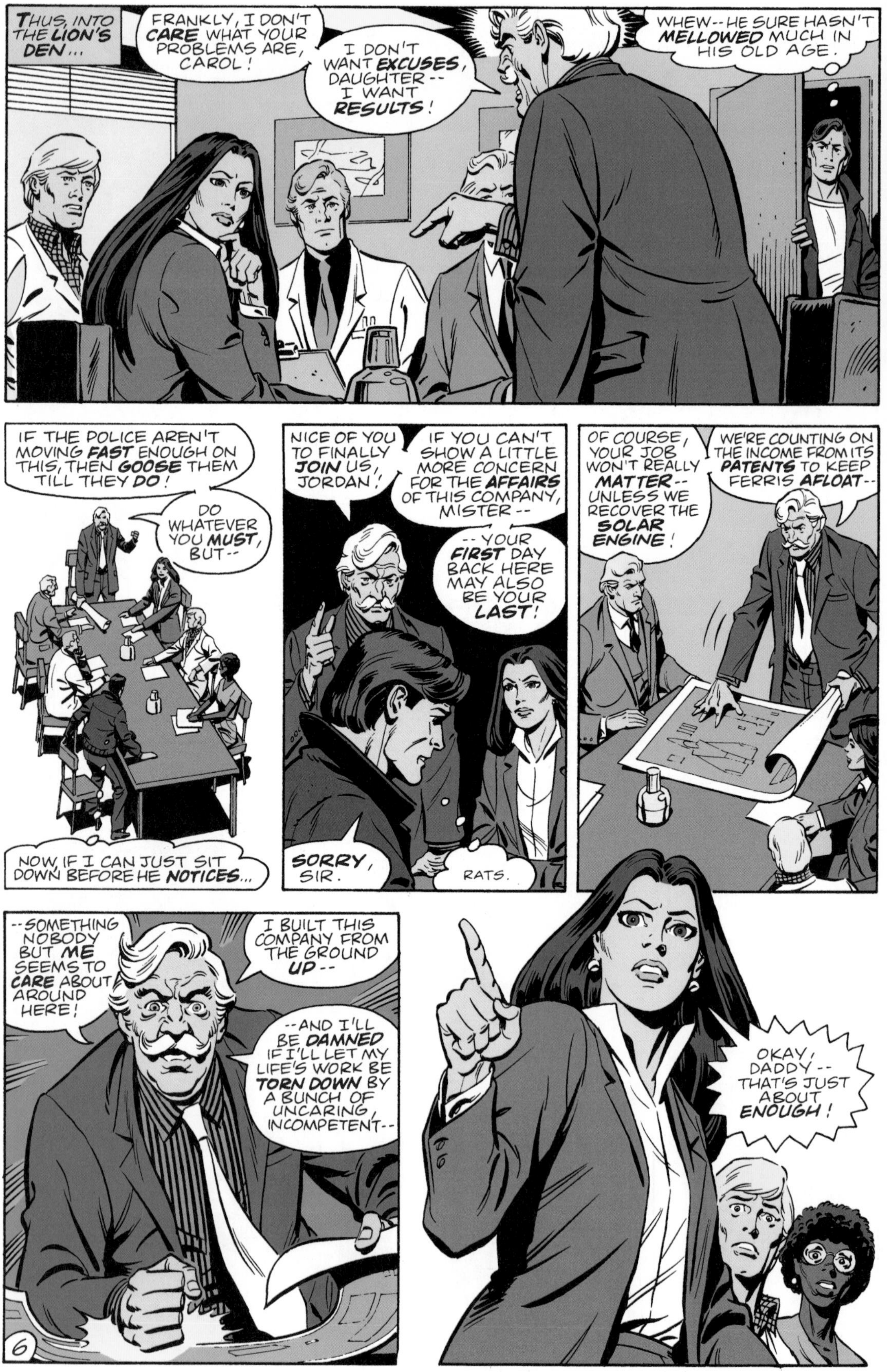
THUS, INTO THE LION'S DEN...
FRANKLY, I DON'T CARE WHAT YOUR PROBLEMS ARE, CAROL!
I DON'T WANT EXCUSES, DAUGHTER -- I WANT RESULTS!
WHEW--HE SURE HASN'T MELLOWED MUCH IN HIS OLD AGE.
IF THE POLICE AREN'T MOVING FAST ENOUGH ON THIS, THEN GOOSE THEM TILL THEY DO!
DO WHATEVER YOU MUST, BUT--
NOW, IF I CAN JUST SIT DOWN BEFORE HE NOTICES...
NICE OF YOU TO FINALLY JOIN US, JORDAN!
IF YOU CAN'T SHOW A LITTLE MORE CONCERN FOR THE AFFAIRS OF THIS COMPANY, MISTER --
-- YOUR FIRST DAY BACK HERE MAY ALSO BE YOUR LAST!
SORRY, SIR.
RATS.
OF COURSE, YOUR JOB WON'T REALLY MATTER -- UNLESS WE RECOVER THE SOLAR ENGINE!
WE'RE COUNTING ON THE INCOME FROM ITS PATENTS TO KEEP FERRIS AFLOAT--
--SOMETHING NOBODY BUT ME SEEMS TO CARE ABOUT AROUND HERE!
I BUILT THIS COMPANY FROM THE GROUND UP--
--AND I'LL BE DAMNED IF I'LL LET MY LIFE'S WORK BE TORN DOWN BY A BUNCH OF UNCARING, INCOMPETENT--
6
OKAY, DADDY -- THAT'S JUST ABOUT ENOUGH!

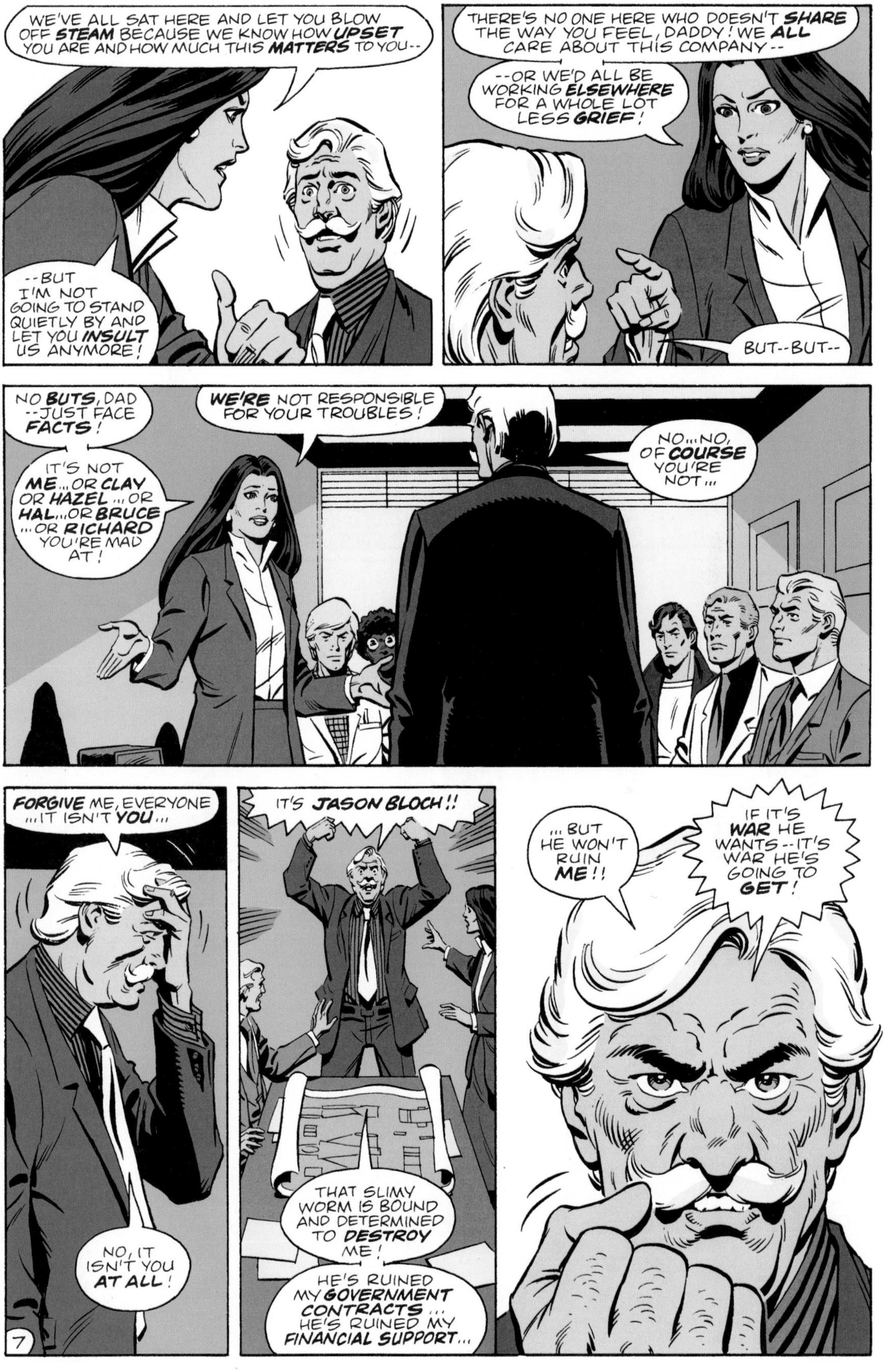
WE'VE ALL SAT HERE AND LET YOU BLOW OFF STEAM BECAUSE WE KNOW HOW UPSET YOU ARE AND HOW MUCH THIS MATTERS TO YOU--
--BUT I'M NOT GOING TO STAND QUIETLY BY AND LET YOU INSULT US ANYMORE!
THERE'S NO ONE HERE WHO DOESN'T SHARE THE WAY YOU FEEL, DADDY! WE ALL CARE ABOUT THIS COMPANY--
--OR WE'D ALL BE WORKING ELSEWHERE FOR A WHOLE LOT LESS GRIEF!
BUT--BUT--
NO BUTS, DAD --JUST FACE FACTS!
IT'S NOT ME...OR CLAY OR HAZEL...OR HAL...OR BRUCE ...OR RICHARD YOU'RE MAD AT!
WE'RE NOT RESPONSIBLE FOR YOUR TROUBLES!
NO...NO, OF COURSE YOU'RE NOT...
FORGIVE ME, EVERYONE ...IT ISN'T YOU...
NO, IT ISN'T YOU AT ALL!
7
IT'S JASON BLOCH!!
THAT SLIMY WORM IS BOUND AND DETERMINED TO DESTROY ME!
HE'S RUINED MY GOVERNMENT CONTRACTS... HE'S RUINED MY FINANCIAL SUPPORT...
...BUT HE WON'T RUIN ME!!
IF IT'S WAR HE WANTS--IT'S WAR HE'S GOING TO GET!

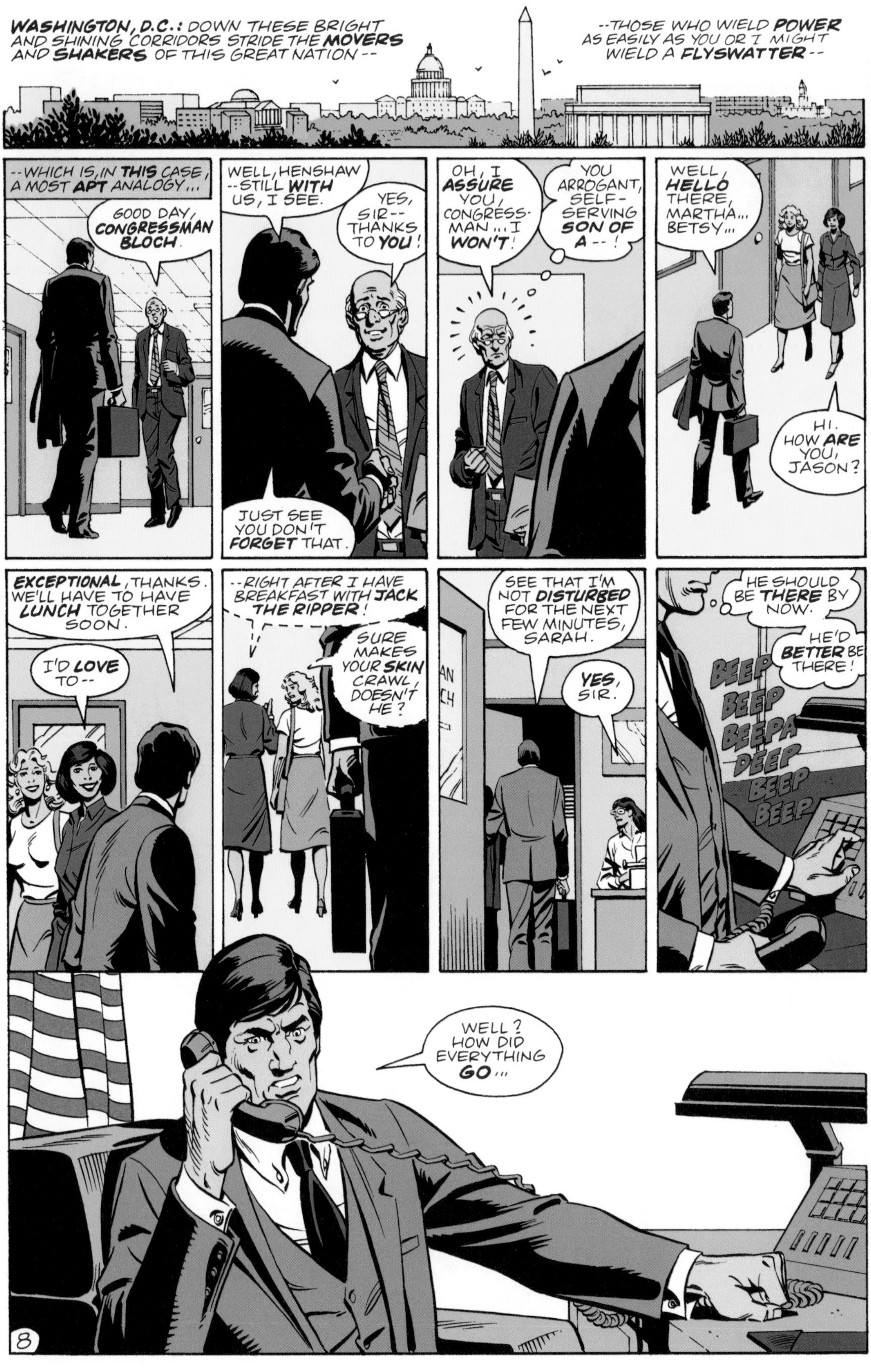
WASHINGTON, D.C.: DOWN THESE BRIGHT AND SHINING CORRIDORS STRIDE THE MOVERS AND SHAKERS OF THIS GREAT NATION --
--THOSE WHO WIELD POWER AS EASILY AS YOU OR I MIGHT WIELD A FLYSWATTER --
--WHICH IS, IN THIS CASE, A MOST APT ANALOGY...
GOOD DAY, CONGRESSMAN BLOCH.
WELL, HENSHAW --STILL WITH US, I SEE.
YES, SIR-- THANKS TO YOU!
JUST SEE YOU DON'T FORGET THAT.
OH, I ASSURE YOU, CONGRESSMAN... I WON'T!
YOU ARROGANT, SELF-SERVING SON OF A --!
WELL, HELLO THERE, MARTHA... BETSY...
HI. HOW ARE YOU, JASON?
EXCEPTIONAL, THANKS. WE'LL HAVE TO HAVE LUNCH TOGETHER SOON.
I'D LOVE TO--
--RIGHT AFTER I HAVE BREAKFAST WITH JACK THE RIPPER!
SURE MAKES YOUR SKIN CRAWL, DOESN'T HE?
SEE THAT I'M NOT DISTURBED FOR THE NEXT FEW MINUTES, SARAH.
YES, SIR.
HE SHOULD BE THERE BY NOW.
HE'D BETTER BE THERE!
BEEP BEEP BEEPA DEEP BEEP BEEP
WELL? HOW DID EVERYTHING GO...
8

"...JAVELIN!"

ZHERE IS NO REASON TO **CONCERN** YOURSELF, HERR CONGRESS-MAN--

--I HAFF TAKEN CARE OF **EFERYTZING!**

EXCELLENT... **EXCELLENT!**

THEN YOU'VE **DESTROYED** FERRIS'S BLASTED **SOLAR ENGINE?**

ACTUALLY, MEIN HERR--I HAFF **NOT!**

I DECIDED IT VOULD BE A SHAME TO **VASTE** SUCH A MARVELOUS MECHANISM!

WHAT--?!?

WHEN **THE MONITOR** PUT ME IN **TOUCH** WITH YOU, MISTER--HE SAID YOU WERE A MAN WHO GOT THE **JOB** DONE!

I INTEND TO **DESTROY** FERRIS AIRCRAFT FOR DESTROYING MY **FATHER**--AND IF YOU **CROSS** ME, JAVELIN...

...I'LL DESTROY YOU, **TOO!!**

TEMPER, HERR BLOCH --**TEMPER!**

IF YOU VANT ME TO **ELIMINATE** FERRIS AIRCRAFT FOR YOU, IT VILL BE MY **PLEASURE!**

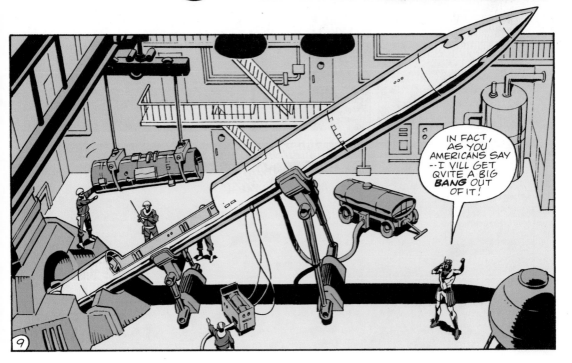

IN FACT, AS YOU AMERICANS SAY --I VILL GET QVITE A BIG **BANG** OUT OF IT!

9

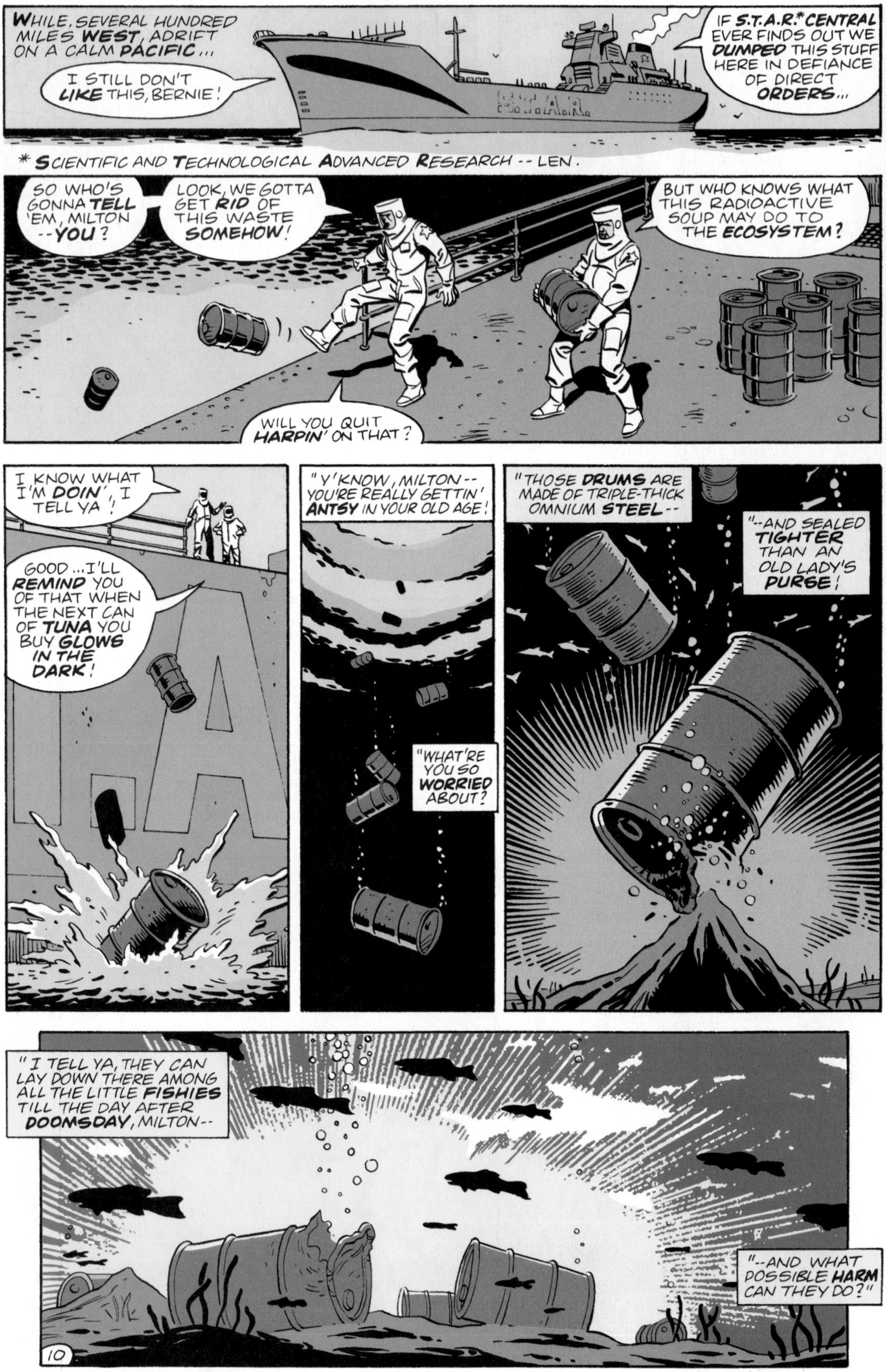

WHILE, SEVERAL HUNDRED MILES WEST, ADRIFT ON A CALM PACIFIC...
I STILL DON'T LIKE THIS, BERNIE!
IF S.T.A.R.* CENTRAL EVER FINDS OUT WE DUMPED THIS STUFF HERE IN DEFIANCE OF DIRECT ORDERS...
* SCIENTIFIC AND TECHNOLOGICAL ADVANCED RESEARCH -- LEN.
SO WHO'S GONNA TELL 'EM, MILTON --YOU?
LOOK, WE GOTTA GET RID OF THIS WASTE SOMEHOW!
BUT WHO KNOWS WHAT THIS RADIOACTIVE SOUP MAY DO TO THE ECOSYSTEM?
WILL YOU QUIT HARPIN' ON THAT?
I KNOW WHAT I'M DOIN', I TELL YA!
GOOD...I'LL REMIND YOU OF THAT WHEN THE NEXT CAN OF TUNA YOU BUY GLOWS IN THE DARK!
"Y'KNOW, MILTON -- YOU'RE REALLY GETTIN' ANTSY IN YOUR OLD AGE!
"WHAT'RE YOU SO WORRIED ABOUT?
"THOSE DRUMS ARE MADE OF TRIPLE-THICK OMNIUM STEEL--
"--AND SEALED TIGHTER THAN AN OLD LADY'S PURSE!
"I TELL YA, THEY CAN LAY DOWN THERE AMONG ALL THE LITTLE FISHIES TILL THE DAY AFTER DOOMSDAY, MILTON--
"--AND WHAT POSSIBLE HARM CAN THEY DO?"
10

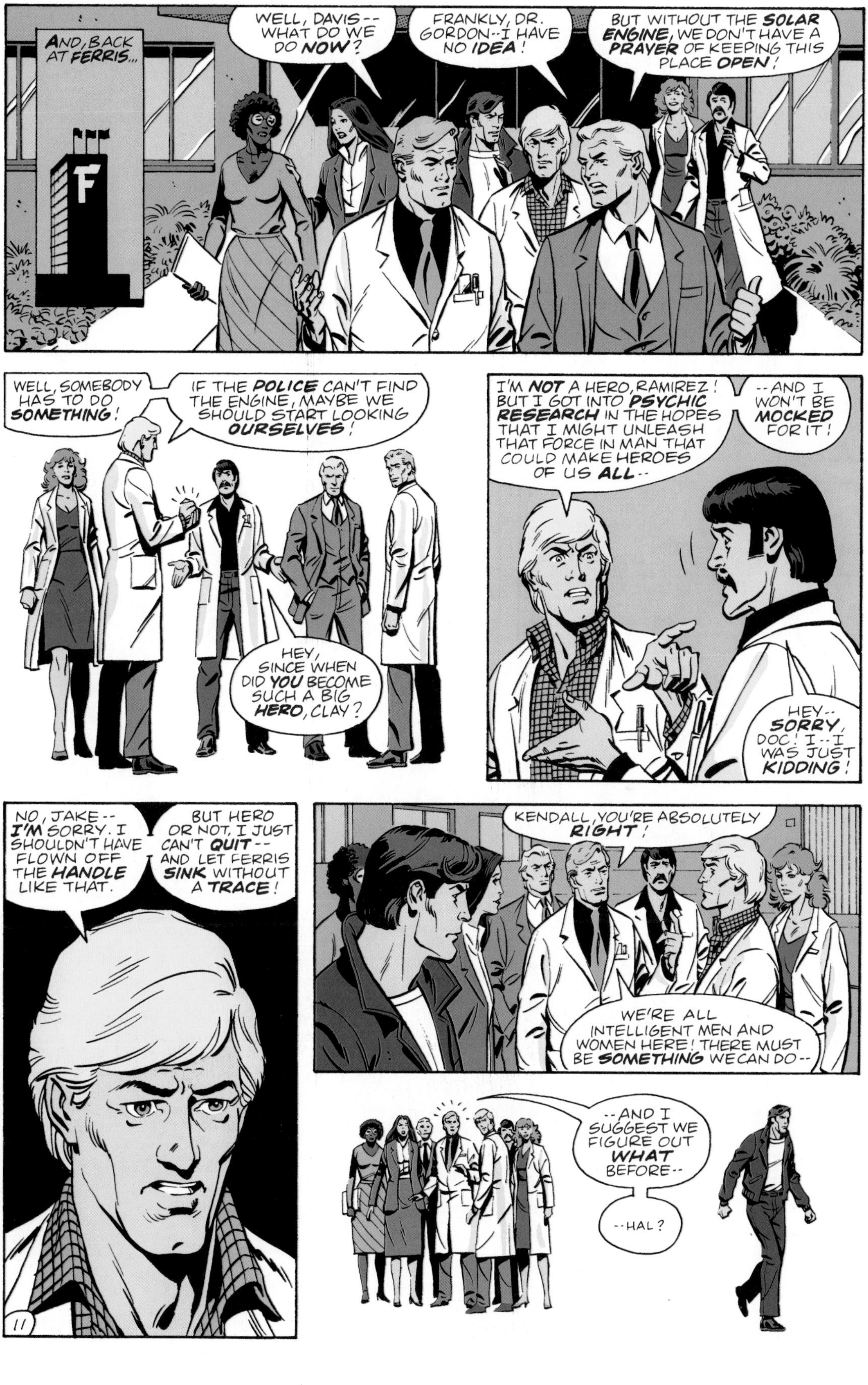
AND, BACK AT FERRIS...
WELL, DAVIS -- WHAT DO WE DO NOW?
FRANKLY, DR. GORDON -- I HAVE NO IDEA!
BUT WITHOUT THE SOLAR ENGINE, WE DON'T HAVE A PRAYER OF KEEPING THIS PLACE OPEN!
WELL, SOMEBODY HAS TO DO SOMETHING!
IF THE POLICE CAN'T FIND THE ENGINE, MAYBE WE SHOULD START LOOKING OURSELVES!
HEY, SINCE WHEN DID YOU BECOME SUCH A BIG HERO, CLAY?
I'M NOT A HERO, RAMIREZ! BUT I GOT INTO PSYCHIC RESEARCH IN THE HOPES THAT I MIGHT UNLEASH THAT FORCE IN MAN THAT COULD MAKE HEROES OF US ALL --
-- AND I WON'T BE MOCKED FOR IT!
HEY -- SORRY, DOC! I -- I WAS JUST KIDDING!
NO, JAKE -- I'M SORRY. I SHOULDN'T HAVE FLOWN OFF THE HANDLE LIKE THAT.
BUT HERO OR NOT, I JUST CAN'T QUIT -- AND LET FERRIS SINK WITHOUT A TRACE!
11
KENDALL, YOU'RE ABSOLUTELY RIGHT!
WE'RE ALL INTELLIGENT MEN AND WOMEN HERE! THERE MUST BE SOMETHING WE CAN DO --
-- AND I SUGGEST WE FIGURE OUT WHAT BEFORE --
-- HAL?

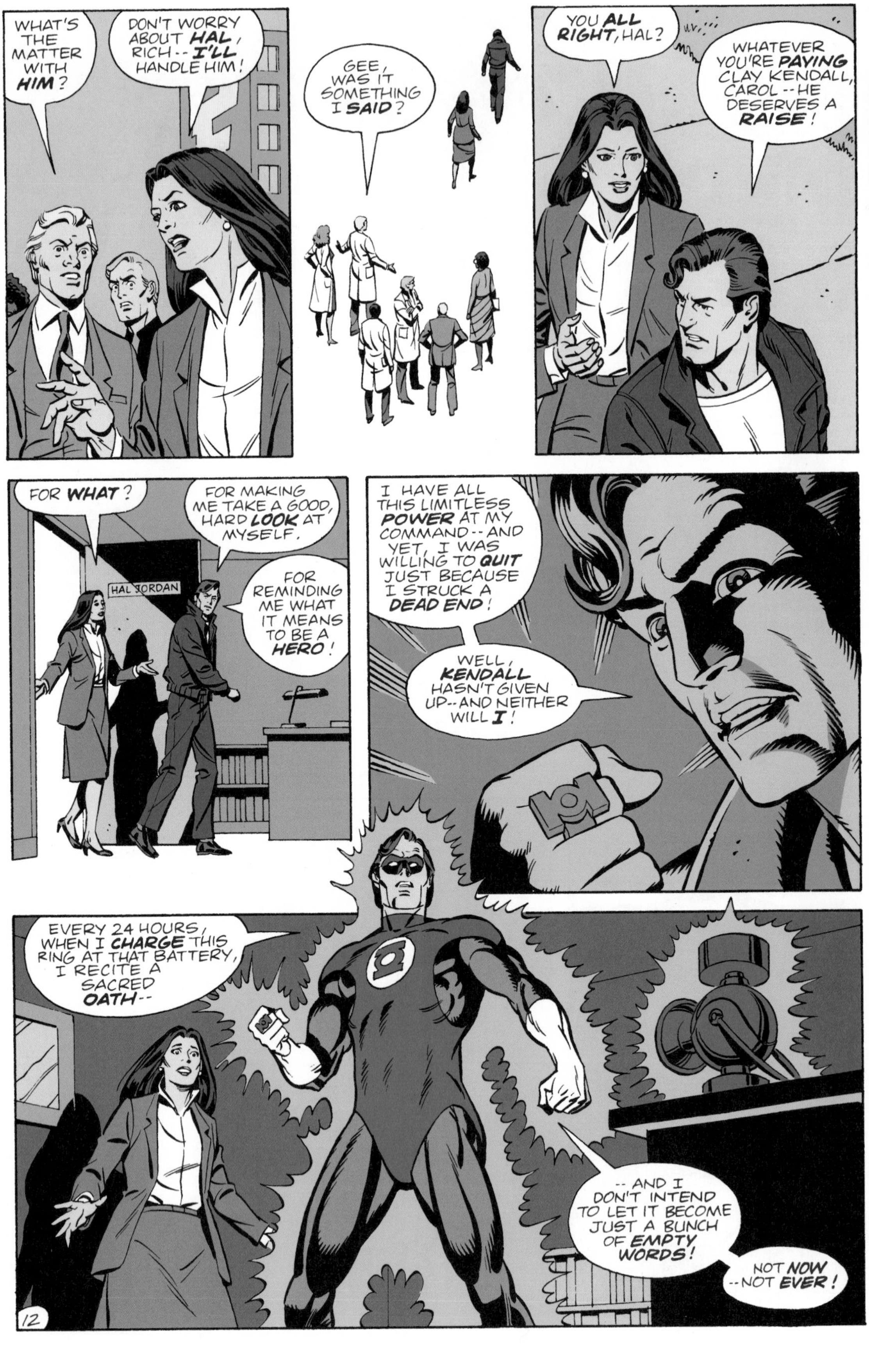
WHAT'S THE MATTER WITH HIM?
DON'T WORRY ABOUT HAL, RICH -- I'LL HANDLE HIM!
GEE, WAS IT SOMETHING I SAID?
YOU ALL RIGHT, HAL?
WHATEVER YOU'RE PAYING CLAY KENDALL, CAROL -- HE DESERVES A RAISE!
FOR WHAT?
FOR MAKING ME TAKE A GOOD, HARD LOOK AT MYSELF.
FOR REMINDING ME WHAT IT MEANS TO BE A HERO!
HAL JORDAN
I HAVE ALL THIS LIMITLESS POWER AT MY COMMAND -- AND YET, I WAS WILLING TO QUIT JUST BECAUSE I STRUCK A DEAD END!
WELL, KENDALL HASN'T GIVEN UP -- AND NEITHER WILL I!
EVERY 24 HOURS, WHEN I CHARGE THIS RING AT THAT BATTERY, I RECITE A SACRED OATH --
-- AND I DON'T INTEND TO LET IT BECOME JUST A BUNCH OF EMPTY WORDS!
NOT NOW -- NOT EVER!
12

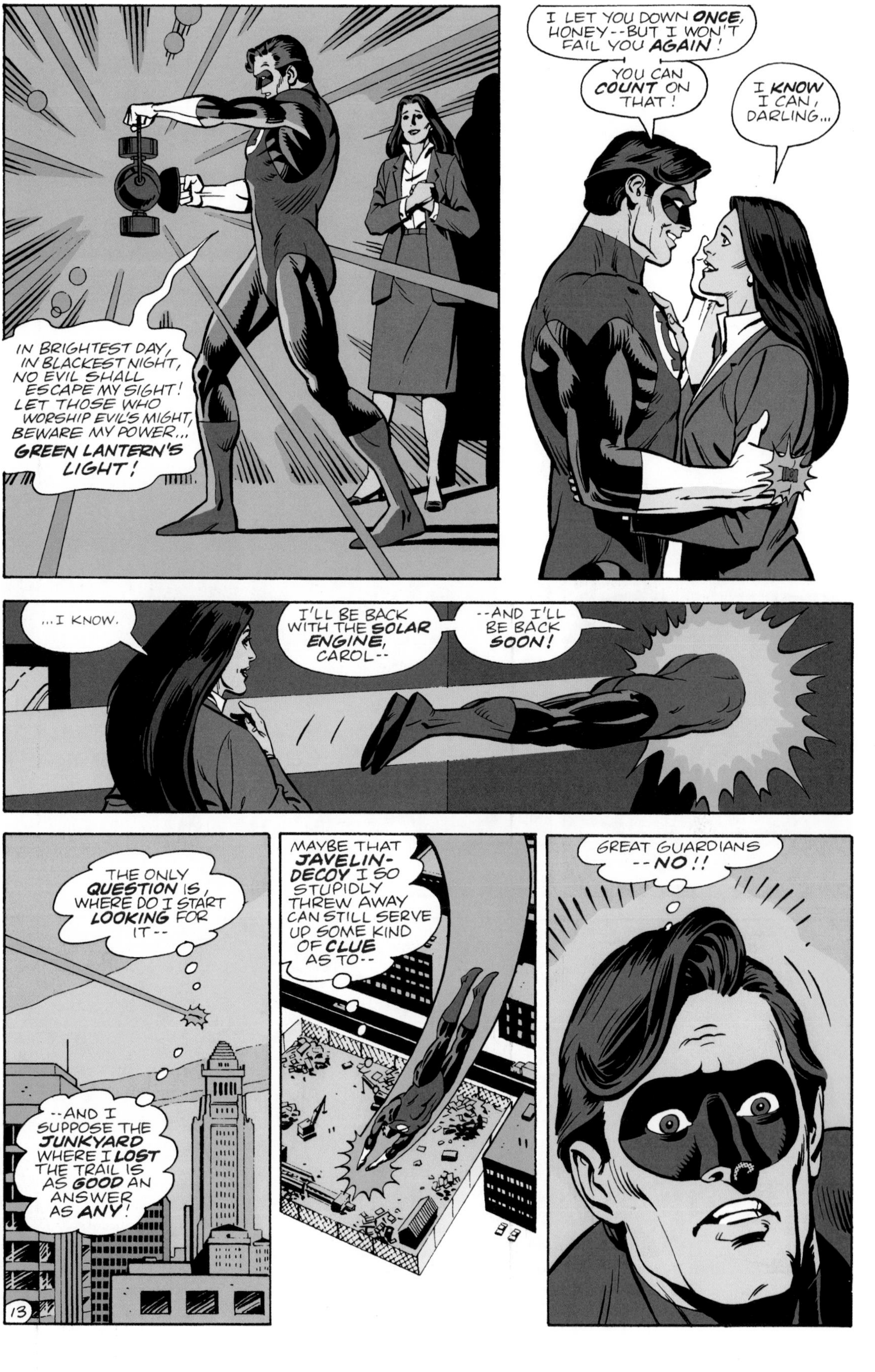
IN BRIGHTEST DAY, IN BLACKEST NIGHT, NO EVIL SHALL ESCAPE MY SIGHT! LET THOSE WHO WORSHIP EVIL'S MIGHT, BEWARE MY POWER... GREEN LANTERN'S LIGHT!
I LET YOU DOWN ONCE, HONEY--BUT I WON'T FAIL YOU AGAIN!
YOU CAN COUNT ON THAT!
I KNOW I CAN, DARLING...
...I KNOW.
I'LL BE BACK WITH THE SOLAR ENGINE, CAROL--
--AND I'LL BE BACK SOON!
THE ONLY QUESTION IS, WHERE DO I START LOOKING FOR IT--
--AND I SUPPOSE THE JUNKYARD WHERE I LOST THE TRAIL IS AS GOOD AN ANSWER AS ANY!
13
MAYBE THAT JAVELIN-DECOY I SO STUPIDLY THREW AWAY CAN STILL SERVE UP SOME KIND OF CLUE AS TO--
GREAT GUARDIANS --NO!!

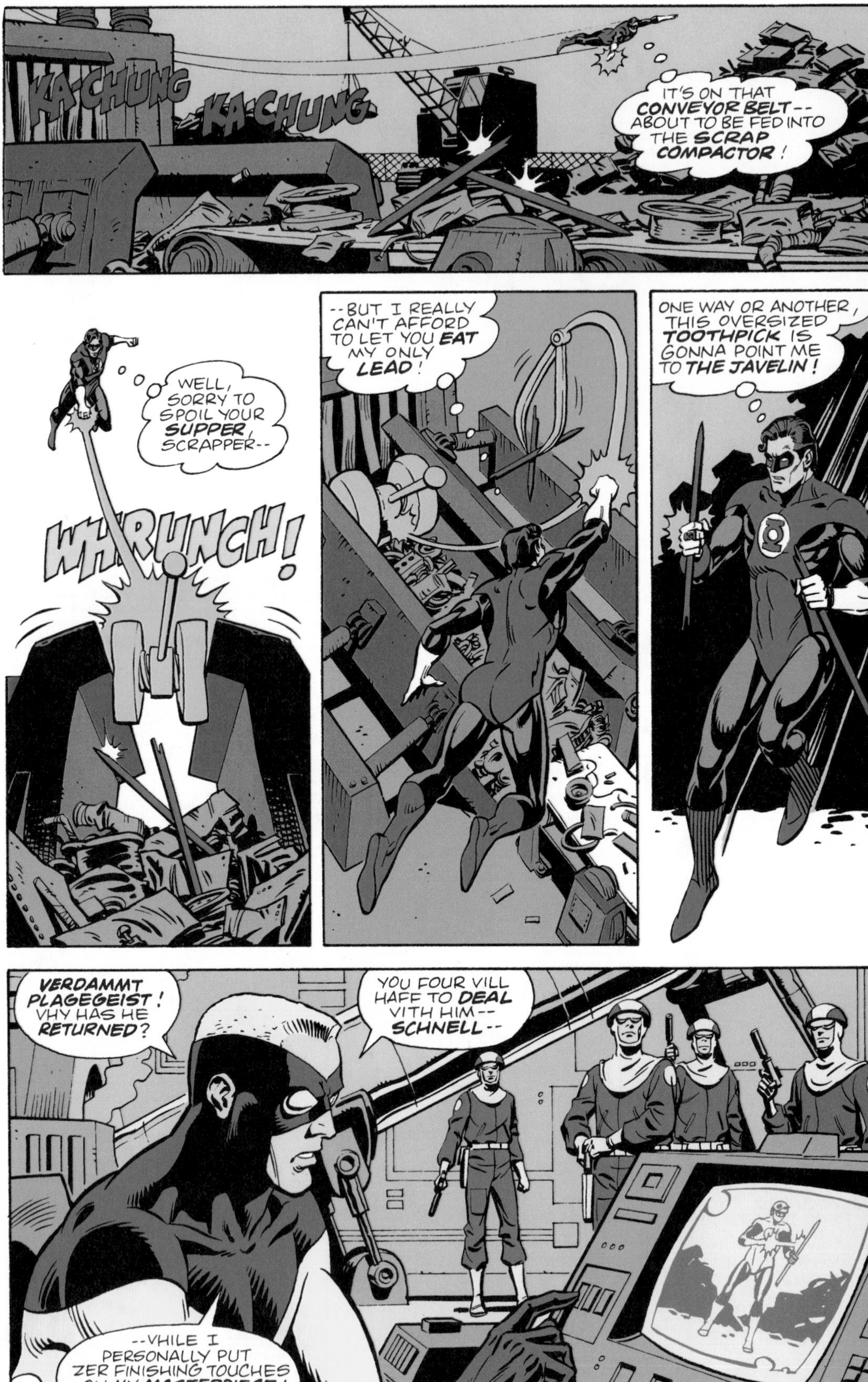
KA-CHUNG
KA-CHUNG
IT'S ON THAT CONVEYOR BELT-- ABOUT TO BE FED INTO THE SCRAP COMPACTOR!
WELL, SORRY TO SPOIL YOUR SUPPER, SCRAPPER--
WHRUNCH!
--BUT I REALLY CAN'T AFFORD TO LET YOU EAT MY ONLY LEAD!
ONE WAY OR ANOTHER, THIS OVERSIZED TOOTHPICK IS GONNA POINT ME TO THE JAVELIN!
VERDAMMT PLAGEGEIST! VHY HAS HE RETURNED?
YOU FOUR VILL HAFF TO DEAL VITH HIM-- SCHNELL--
--VHILE I PERSONALLY PUT ZER FINISHING TOUCHES ON MY MASTERPIECE!
14

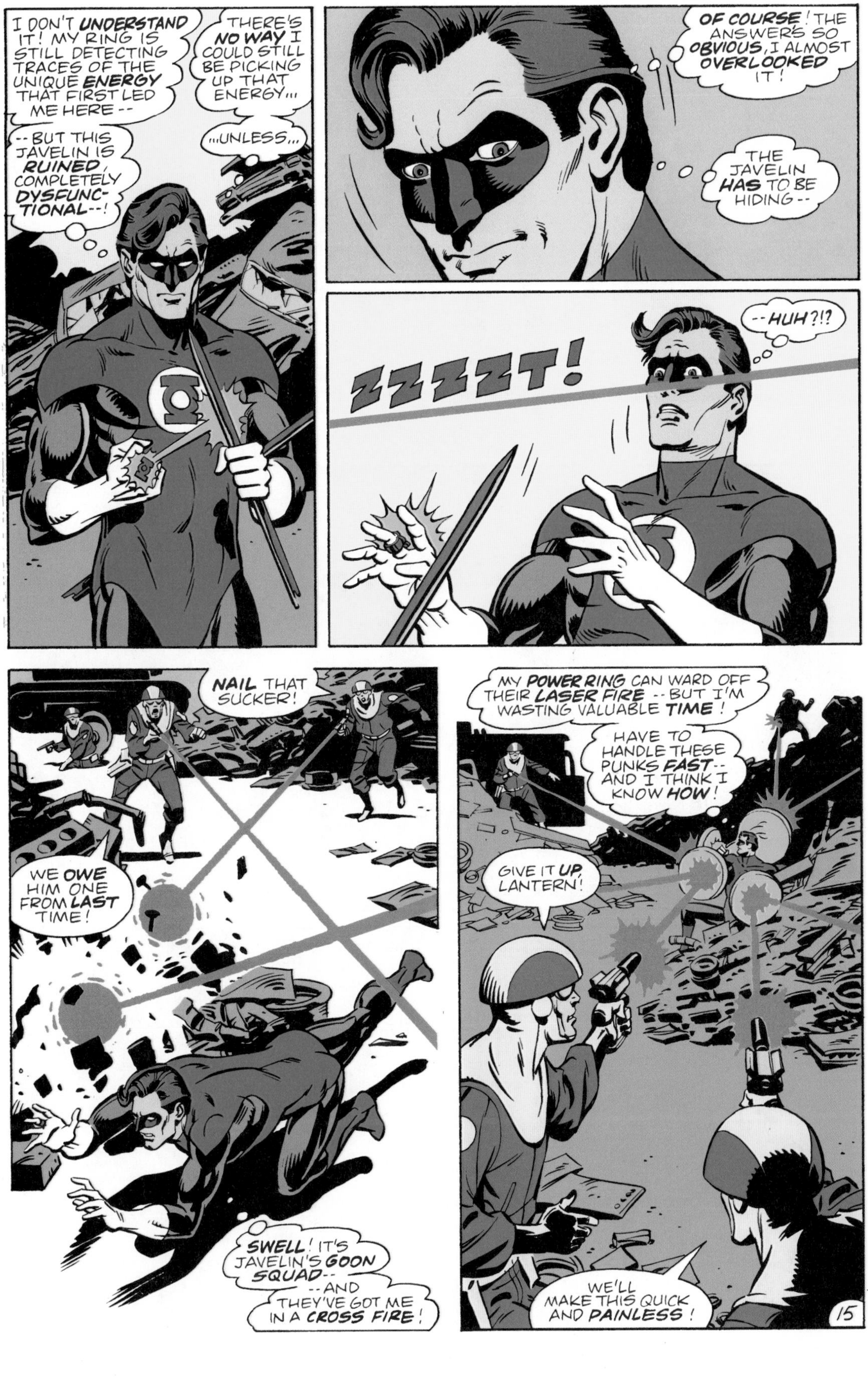
I DON'T UNDERSTAND IT! MY RING IS STILL DETECTING TRACES OF THE UNIQUE ENERGY THAT FIRST LED ME HERE --
-- BUT THIS JAVELIN IS RUINED, COMPLETELY DYSFUNCTIONAL--!
THERE'S NO WAY I COULD STILL BE PICKING UP THAT ENERGY...
...UNLESS...
OF COURSE! THE ANSWER'S SO OBVIOUS, I ALMOST OVERLOOKED IT!
THE JAVELIN HAS TO BE HIDING --
ZZZZT!
-- HUH?!?
NAIL THAT SUCKER!
WE OWE HIM ONE FROM LAST TIME!
SWELL! IT'S JAVELIN'S GOON SQUAD--
--AND THEY'VE GOT ME IN A CROSS FIRE!
MY POWER RING CAN WARD OFF THEIR LASER FIRE -- BUT I'M WASTING VALUABLE TIME!
HAVE TO HANDLE THESE PUNKS FAST-- AND I THINK I KNOW HOW!
GIVE IT UP, LANTERN!
WE'LL MAKE THIS QUICK AND PAINLESS!
15

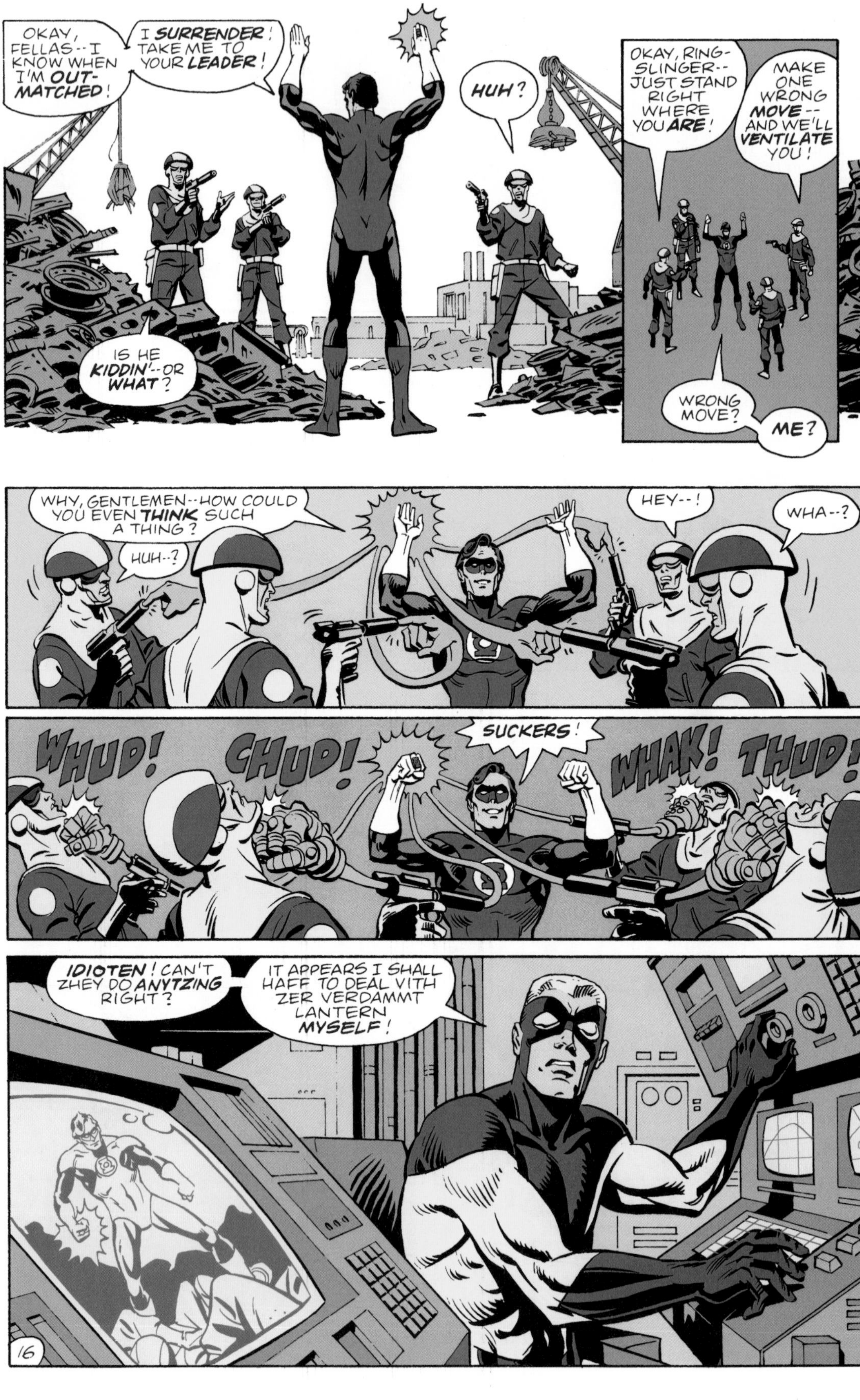

OKAY, FELLAS--I KNOW WHEN I'M OUT-MATCHED!
I SURRENDER! TAKE ME TO YOUR LEADER!
HUH?
IS HE KIDDIN'--OR WHAT?
OKAY, RING-SLINGER--JUST STAND RIGHT WHERE YOU ARE!
MAKE ONE WRONG MOVE--AND WE'LL VENTILATE YOU!
WRONG MOVE?
ME?
WHY, GENTLEMEN--HOW COULD YOU EVEN THINK SUCH A THING?
HUH--?
HEY--!
WHA--?
WHUD!
CHUD!
SUCKERS!
WHAK!
THUD!
IDIOTEN! CAN'T ZHEY DO ANYTZING RIGHT?
IT APPEARS I SHALL HAFF TO DEAL VITH ZER VERDAMMT LANTERN MYSELF!
16

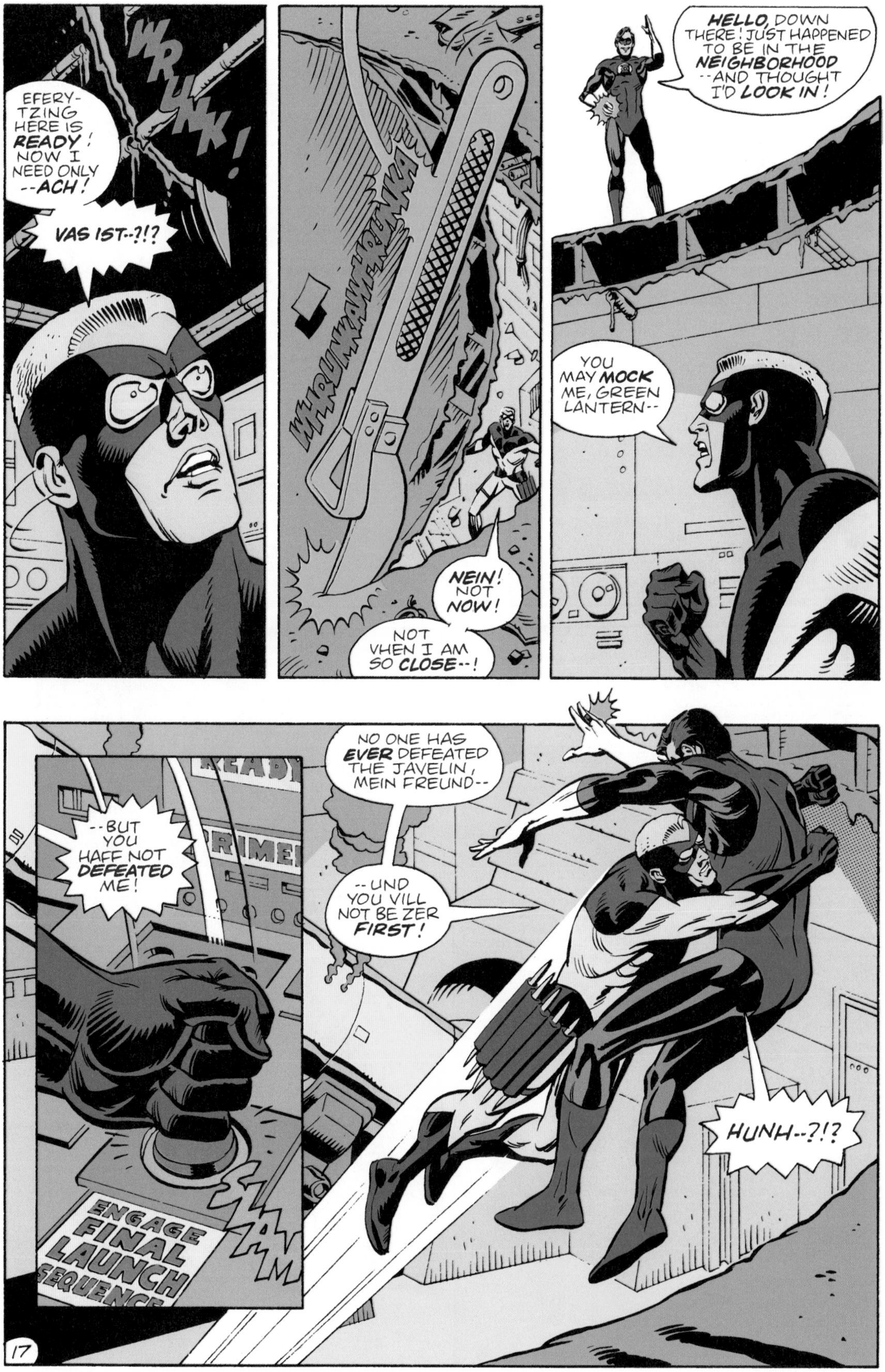
WRUNK!
EFERYTZING HERE IS READY! NOW I NEED ONLY --ACH!
VAS IST--?!?
WHRUNKAWHRUNKA
NEIN! NOT NOW!
NOT VHEN I AM SO CLOSE--!
HELLO, DOWN THERE! JUST HAPPENED TO BE IN THE NEIGHBORHOOD --AND THOUGHT I'D LOOK IN!
YOU MAY MOCK ME, GREEN LANTERN--
--BUT YOU HAFF NOT DEFEATED ME!
ENGAGE FINAL LAUNCH SEQUENCE
NO ONE HAS EVER DEFEATED THE JAVELIN, MEIN FREUND--
--UND YOU VILL NOT BE ZER FIRST!
HUNH--?!?
17

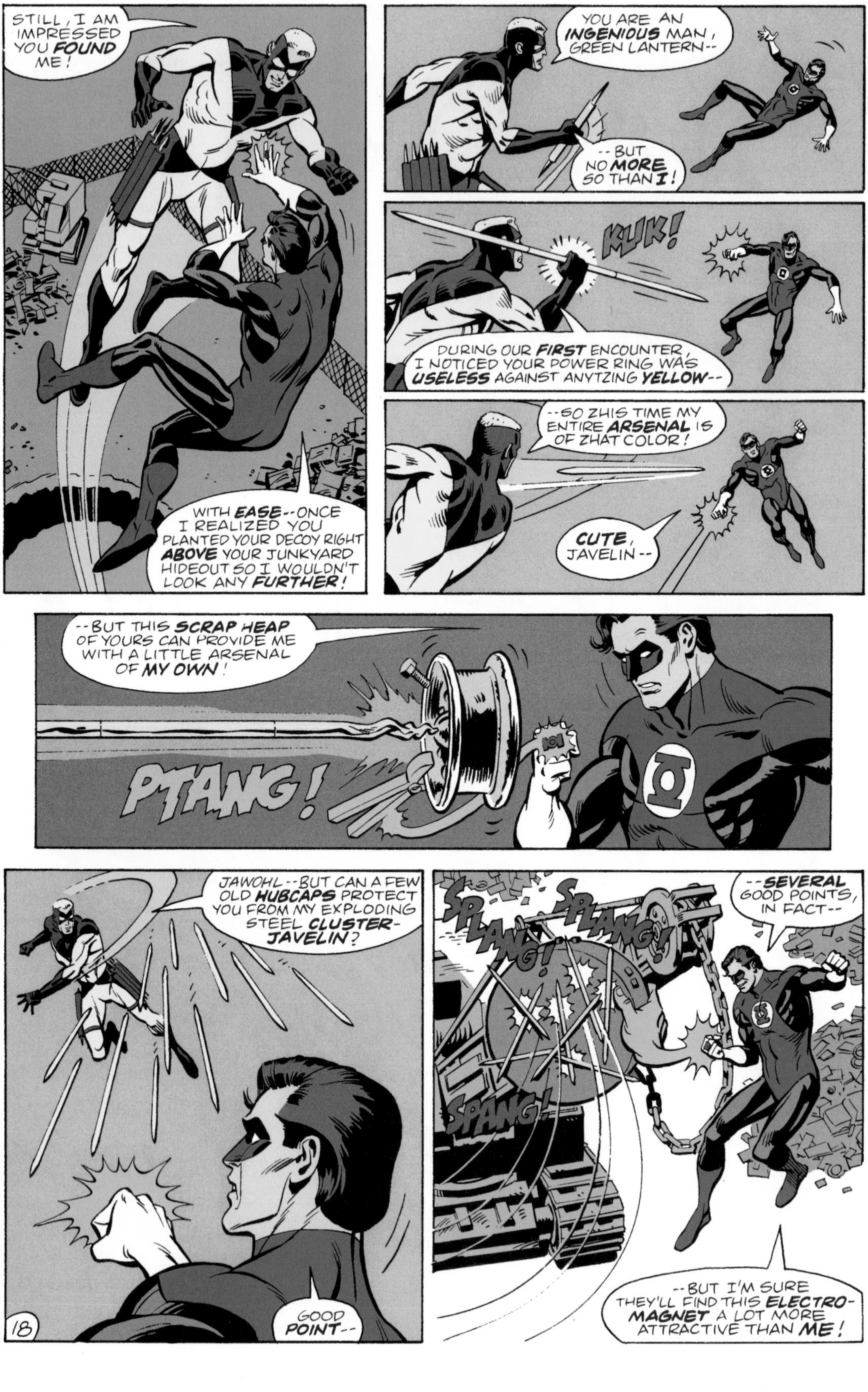
STILL, I AM IMPRESSED YOU FOUND ME!
YOU ARE AN INGENIOUS MAN, GREEN LANTERN--
--BUT NO MORE SO THAN I!
WITH EASE--ONCE I REALIZED YOU PLANTED YOUR DECOY RIGHT ABOVE YOUR JUNKYARD HIDEOUT SO I WOULDN'T LOOK ANY FURTHER!
KUK!
DURING OUR FIRST ENCOUNTER, I NOTICED YOUR POWER RING WAS USELESS AGAINST ANYTZING YELLOW--
--SO ZHIS TIME MY ENTIRE ARSENAL IS OF ZHAT COLOR!
CUTE, JAVELIN--
--BUT THIS SCRAP HEAP OF YOURS CAN PROVIDE ME WITH A LITTLE ARSENAL OF MY OWN!
PTANG!
JAWOHL--BUT CAN A FEW OLD HUBCAPS PROTECT YOU FROM MY EXPLODING STEEL CLUSTER-JAVELIN?
18
GOOD POINT--
SPLANG!
SPLANG!
SPANG!
--SEVERAL GOOD POINTS, IN FACT--
--BUT I'M SURE THEY'LL FIND THIS ELECTRO-MAGNET A LOT MORE ATTRACTIVE THAN ME!

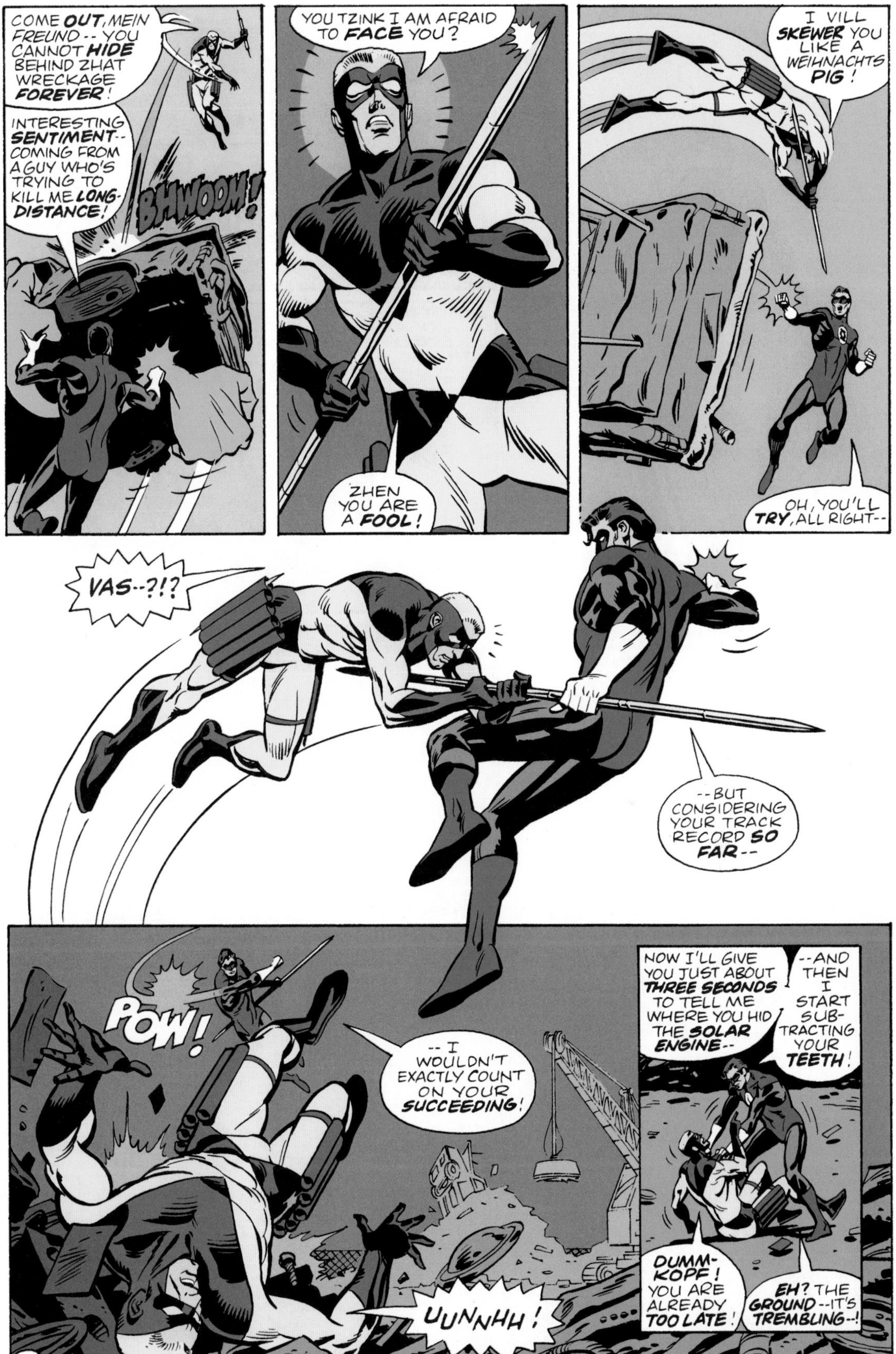

COME OUT, MEIN FREUND -- YOU CANNOT HIDE BEHIND ZHAT WRECKAGE FOREVER!
INTERESTING SENTIMENT-- COMING FROM A GUY WHO'S TRYING TO KILL ME LONG-DISTANCE!
BHWOOM!
YOU TZINK I AM AFRAID TO FACE YOU?
ZHEN YOU ARE A FOOL!
I VILL SKEWER YOU LIKE A WEIHNACHTS PIG!
OH, YOU'LL TRY, ALL RIGHT--
VAS--?!?
--BUT CONSIDERING YOUR TRACK RECORD SO FAR--
POW!
-- I WOULDN'T EXACTLY COUNT ON YOUR SUCCEEDING!
UUNNHH!
NOW I'LL GIVE YOU JUST ABOUT THREE SECONDS TO TELL ME WHERE YOU HID THE SOLAR ENGINE--
--AND THEN I START SUB-TRACTING YOUR TEETH!
DUMM-KOPF! YOU ARE ALREADY TOO LATE!
EH? THE GROUND --IT'S TREMBLING--!
19

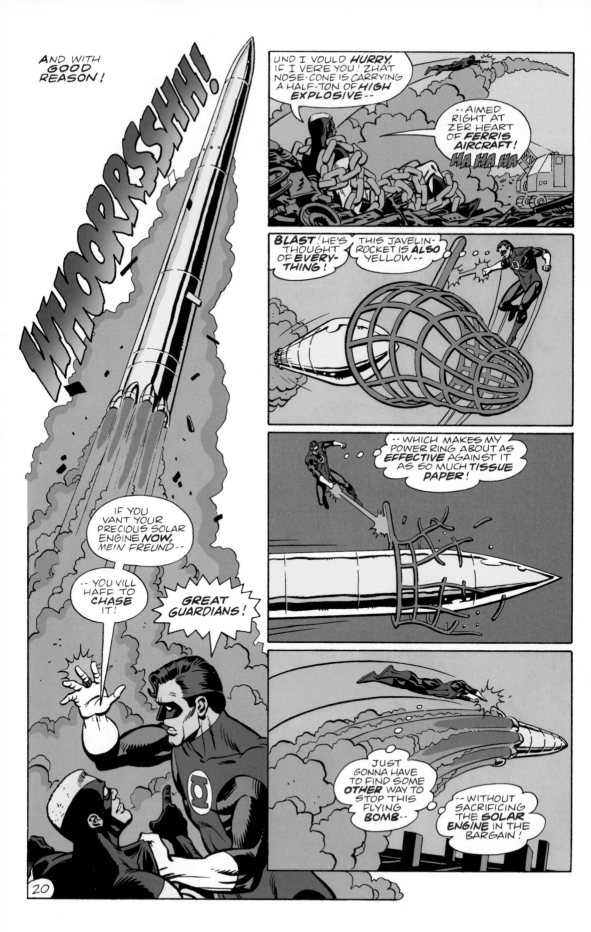

AND WITH GOOD REASON!

WHOORRSSHH!

UND I VOULD *HURRY*, IF I VERE YOU! ZHAT NOSE-CONE IS CARRYING A HALF-TON OF *HIGH* EXPLOSIVE--

--AIMED RIGHT AT ZER HEART OF *FERRIS AIRCRAFT!* HA HA HA

BLAST! HE'S THOUGHT OF *EVERY-THING!*

THIS *JAVELIN-ROCKET* IS *ALSO* YELLOW--

--WHICH MAKES MY *POWER RING* ABOUT AS *EFFECTIVE* AGAINST IT AS SO MUCH *TISSUE PAPER!*

IF YOU VANT YOUR PRECIOUS SOLAR ENGINE *NOW*, MEIN FREUND--

--YOU VILL HAFF TO *CHASE* IT!

GREAT GUARDIANS!

JUST GONNA HAVE TO FIND SOME *OTHER* WAY TO STOP THIS FLYING *BOMB*--

--WITHOUT SACRIFICING THE *SOLAR ENGINE* IN THE BARGAIN!

20

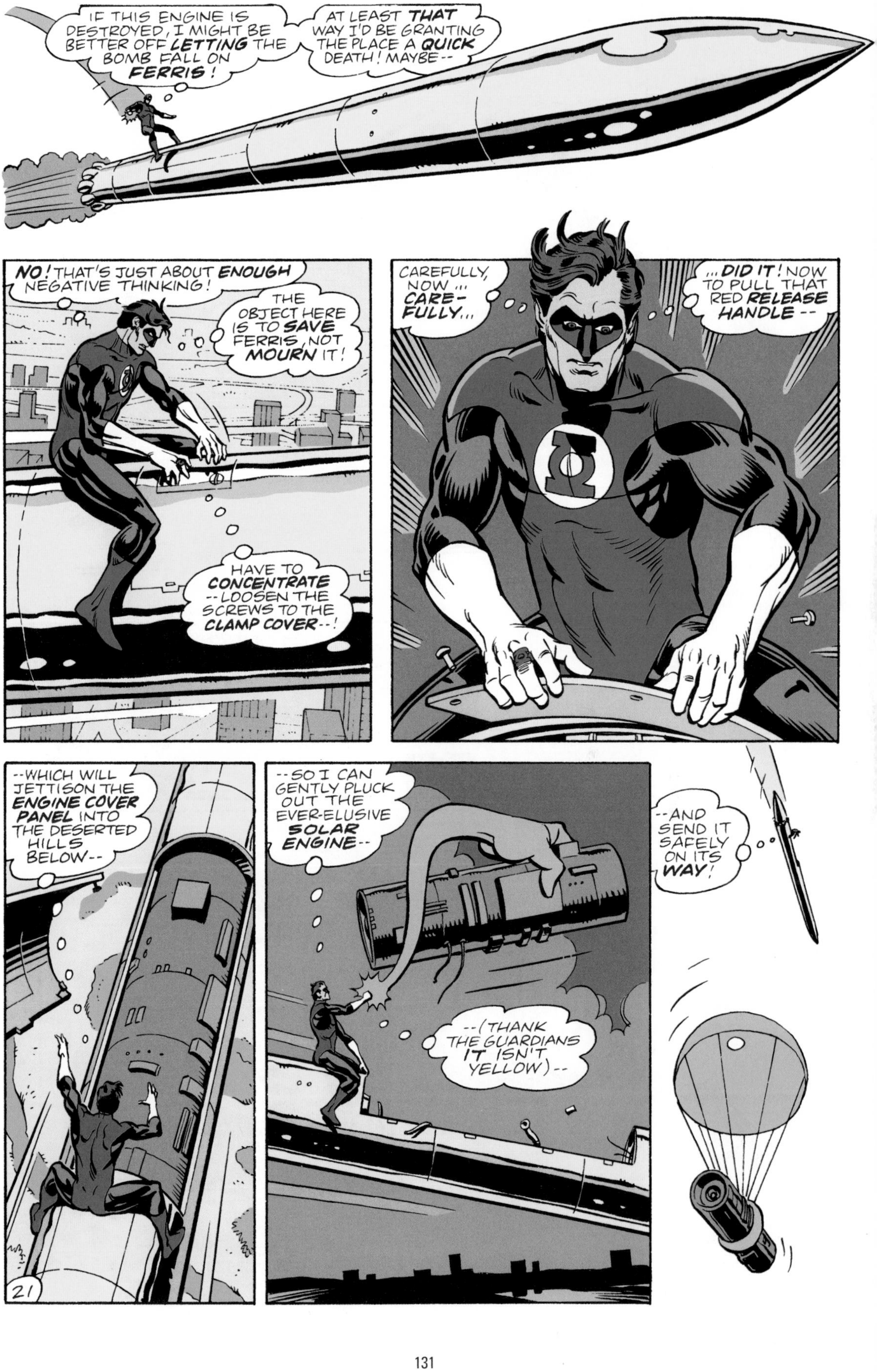
IF THIS ENGINE IS DESTROYED, I MIGHT BE BETTER OFF LETTING THE BOMB FALL ON FERRIS!
AT LEAST THAT WAY I'D BE GRANTING THE PLACE A QUICK DEATH! MAYBE--
NO! THAT'S JUST ABOUT ENOUGH NEGATIVE THINKING!
THE OBJECT HERE IS TO SAVE FERRIS, NOT MOURN IT!
HAVE TO CONCENTRATE --LOOSEN THE SCREWS TO THE CLAMP COVER--!
CAREFULLY, NOW... CARE-FULLY...
...DID IT! NOW TO PULL THAT RED RELEASE HANDLE --
--WHICH WILL JETTISON THE ENGINE COVER PANEL INTO THE DESERTED HILLS BELOW--
--SO I CAN GENTLY PLUCK OUT THE EVER-ELUSIVE SOLAR ENGINE--
--(THANK THE GUARDIANS IT ISN'T YELLOW)--
--AND SEND IT SAFELY ON ITS WAY!
21

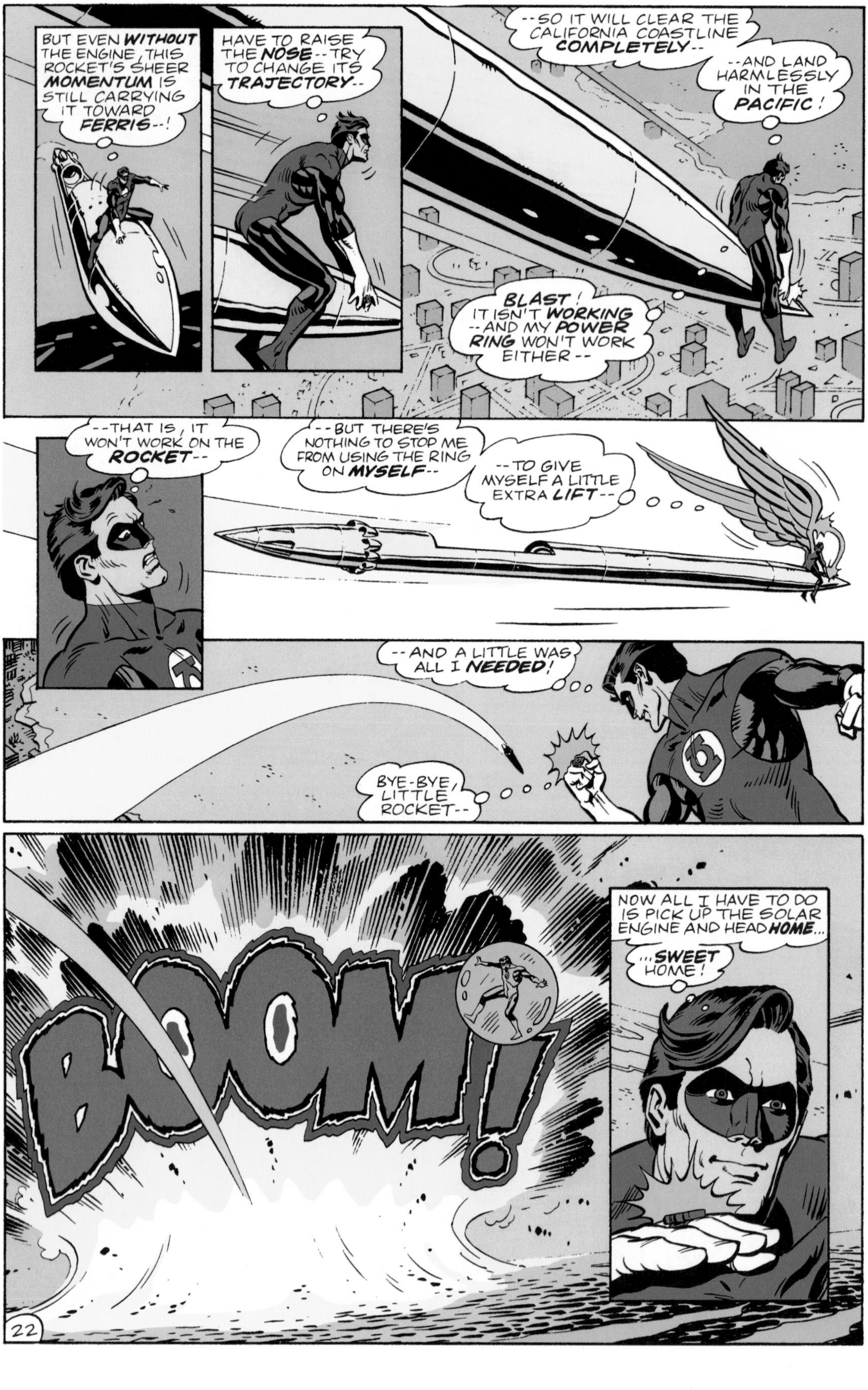
BUT EVEN WITHOUT THE ENGINE, THIS ROCKET'S SHEER MOMENTUM IS STILL CARRYING IT TOWARD FERRIS--!
HAVE TO RAISE THE NOSE--TRY TO CHANGE ITS TRAJECTORY--
--SO IT WILL CLEAR THE CALIFORNIA COASTLINE COMPLETELY--
--AND LAND HARMLESSLY IN THE PACIFIC!
BLAST! IT ISN'T WORKING --AND MY POWER RING WON'T WORK EITHER--
--THAT IS, IT WON'T WORK ON THE ROCKET--
--BUT THERE'S NOTHING TO STOP ME FROM USING THE RING ON MYSELF--
--TO GIVE MYSELF A LITTLE EXTRA LIFT--
--AND A LITTLE WAS ALL I NEEDED!
BYE-BYE, LITTLE ROCKET--
BOOOM!
NOW ALL I HAVE TO DO IS PICK UP THE SOLAR ENGINE AND HEAD HOME...
...SWEET HOME!
22

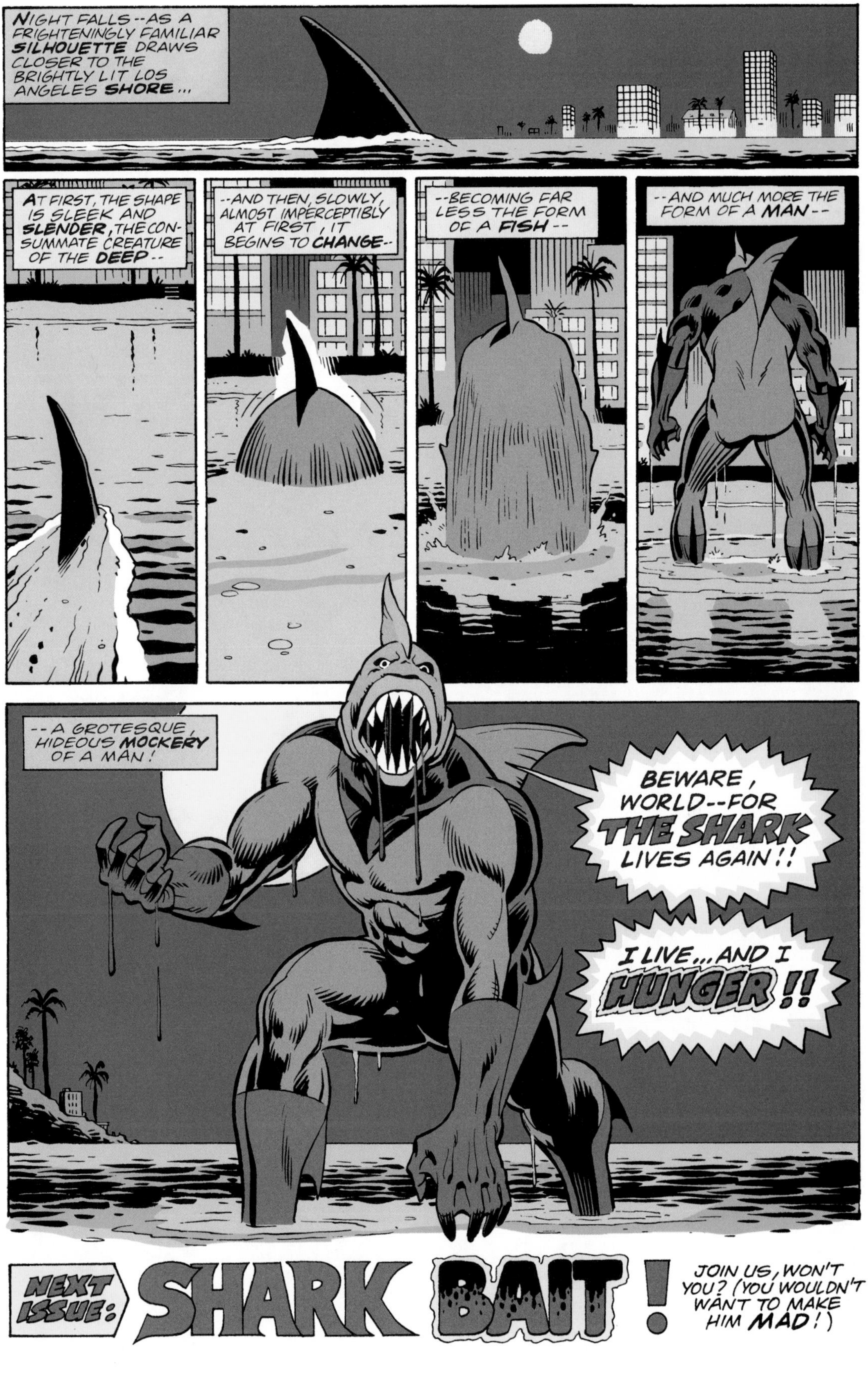

NIGHT FALLS--AS A FRIGHTENINGLY FAMILIAR SILHOUETTE DRAWS CLOSER TO THE BRIGHTLY LIT LOS ANGELES SHORE...
AT FIRST, THE SHAPE IS SLEEK AND SLENDER, THE CONSUMMATE CREATURE OF THE DEEP--
--AND THEN, SLOWLY, ALMOST IMPERCEPTIBLY AT FIRST, IT BEGINS TO CHANGE--
--BECOMING FAR LESS THE FORM OF A FISH--
--AND MUCH MORE THE FORM OF A MAN--
--A GROTESQUE, HIDEOUS MOCKERY OF A MAN!
BEWARE, WORLD--FOR THE SHARK LIVES AGAIN!!
I LIVE...AND I HUNGER!!
NEXT ISSUE: SHARK BAIT!
JOIN US, WON'T YOU? (YOU WOULDN'T WANT TO MAKE HIM MAD!)

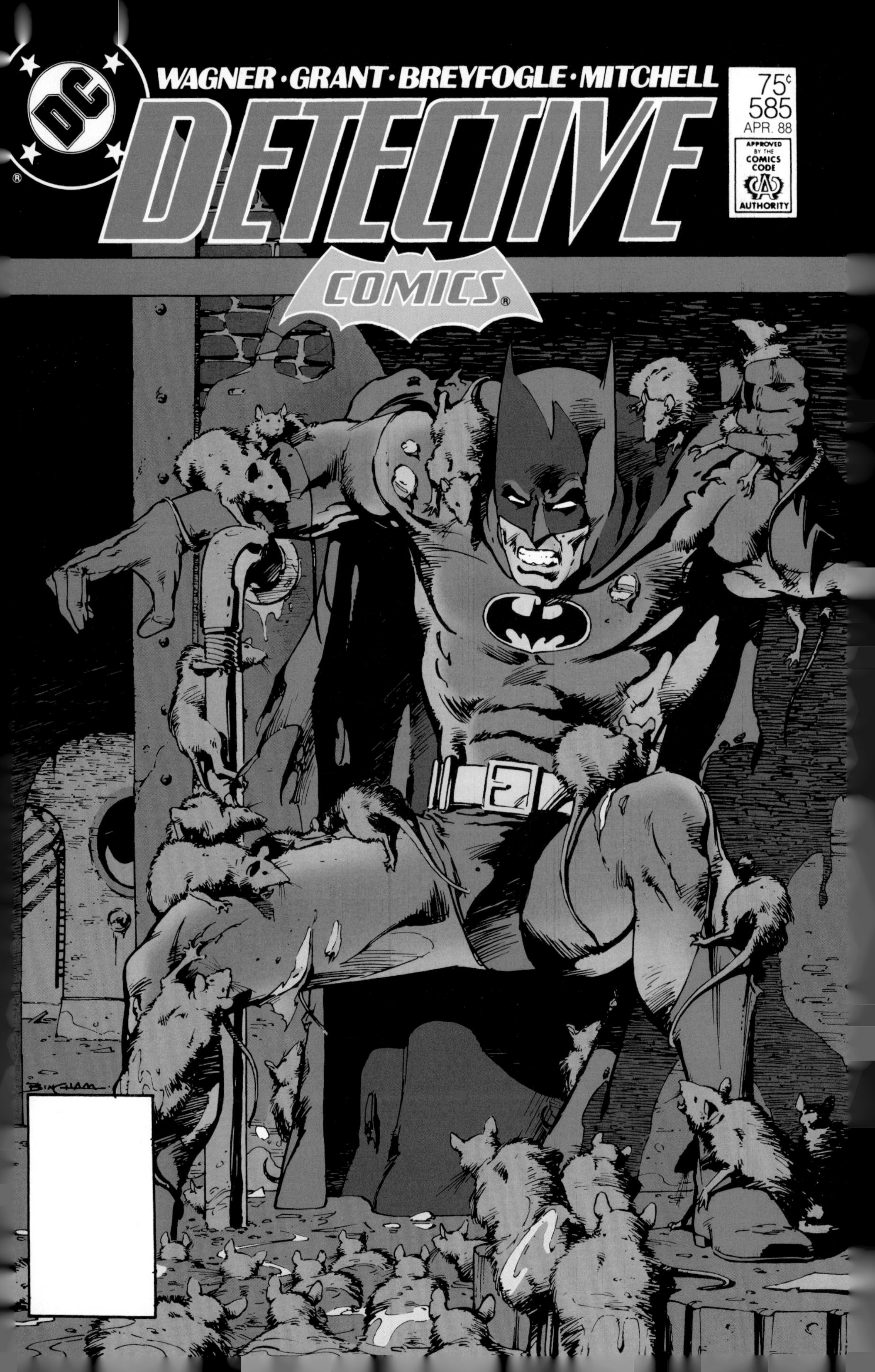
WAGNER·GRANT·BREYFOGLE·MITCHELL
DETECTIVE
COMICS
75¢
585
APR. 88
APPROVED BY THE COMICS CODE AUTHORITY

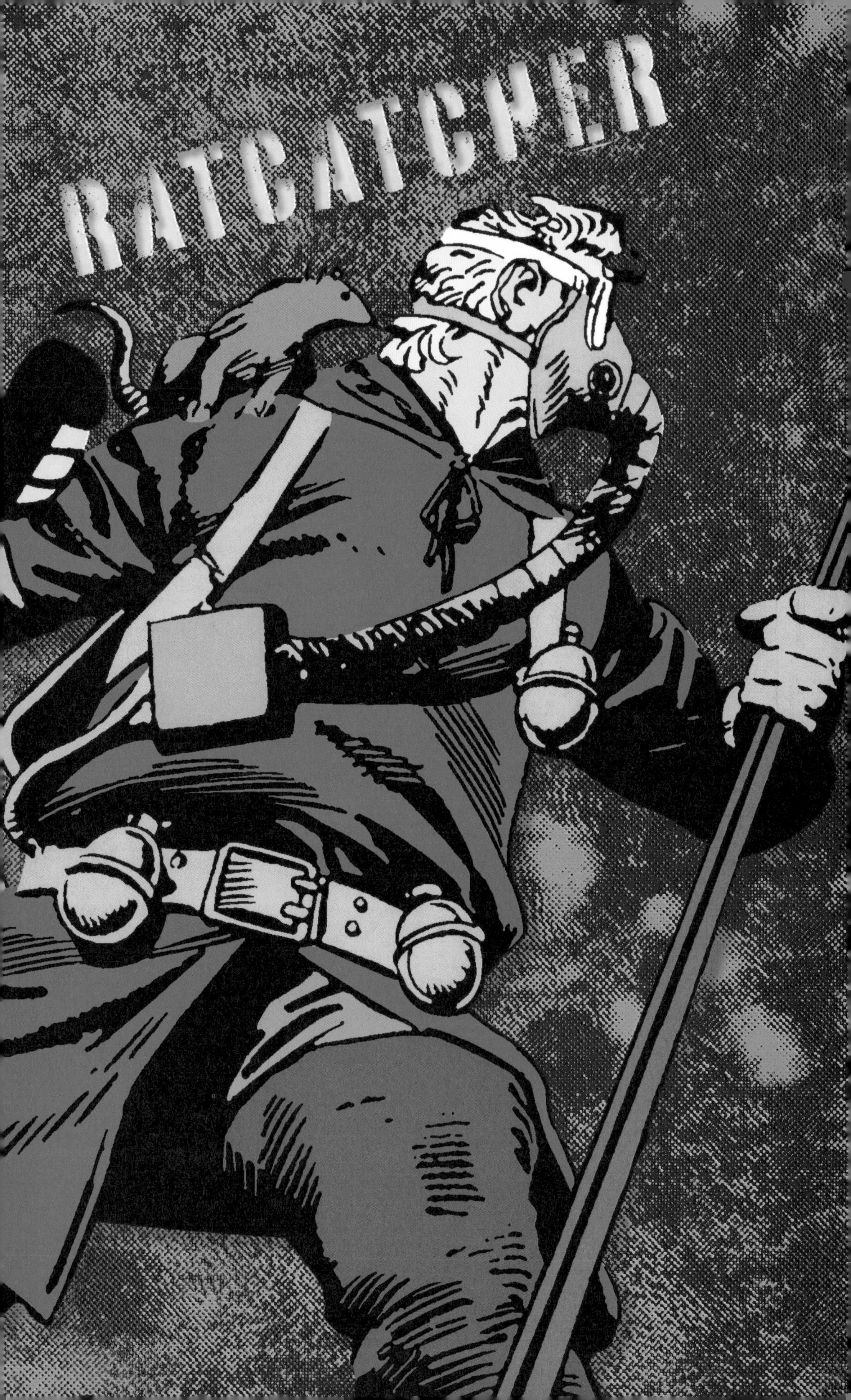
RATCATCHER

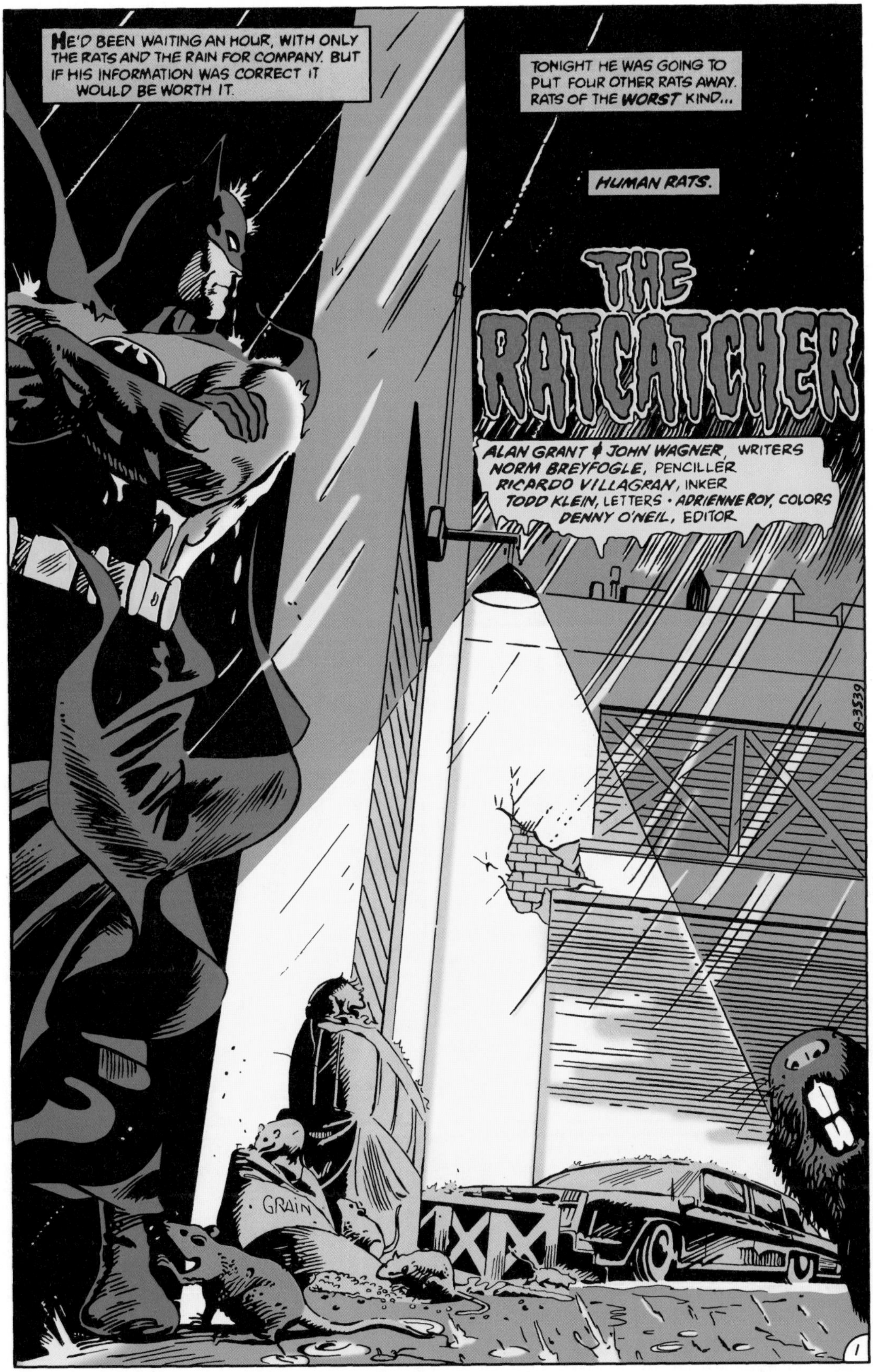
HE'D BEEN WAITING AN HOUR, WITH ONLY THE RATS AND THE RAIN FOR COMPANY. BUT IF HIS INFORMATION WAS CORRECT IT WOULD BE WORTH IT.
TONIGHT HE WAS GOING TO PUT FOUR OTHER RATS AWAY. RATS OF THE WORST KIND...
HUMAN RATS.
THE RATCATCHER
ALAN GRANT & JOHN WAGNER, WRITERS
NORM BREYFOGLE, PENCILLER
RICARDO VILLAGRAN, INKER
TODD KLEIN, LETTERS • ADRIENNE ROY, COLORS
DENNY O'NEIL, EDITOR
GRAIN
1

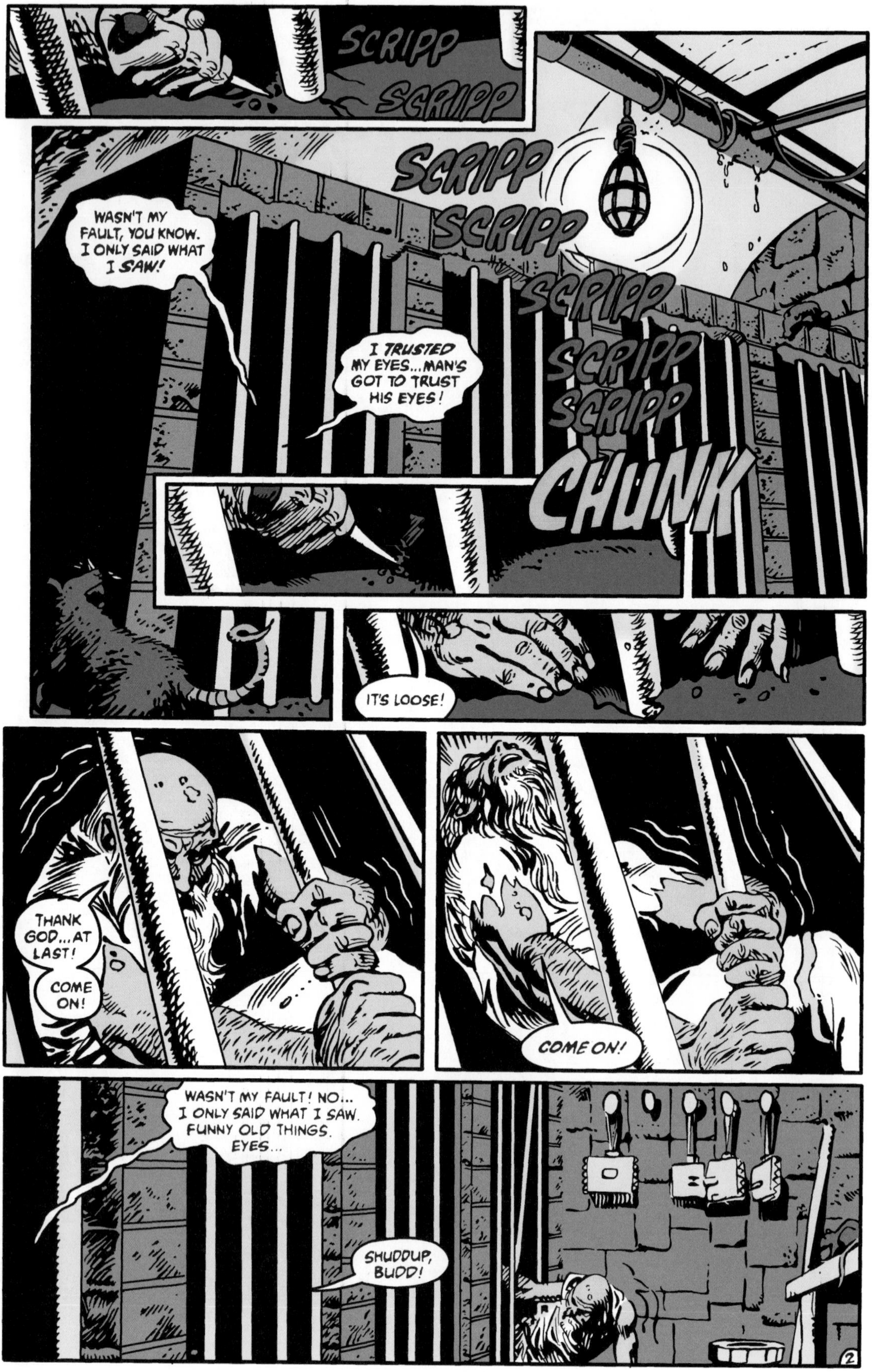
SCRIPP
SCRIPP
SCRIPP
SCRIPP
SCRIPP
SCRIPP
SCRIPP
WASN'T MY FAULT, YOU KNOW. I ONLY SAID WHAT I SAW!
I TRUSTED MY EYES...MAN'S GOT TO TRUST HIS EYES!
CHUNK
IT'S LOOSE!
THANK GOD...AT LAST!
COME ON!
COME ON!
WASN'T MY FAULT! NO... I ONLY SAID WHAT I SAW. FUNNY OLD THINGS. EYES...
SHUDDUP, BUDD!
2

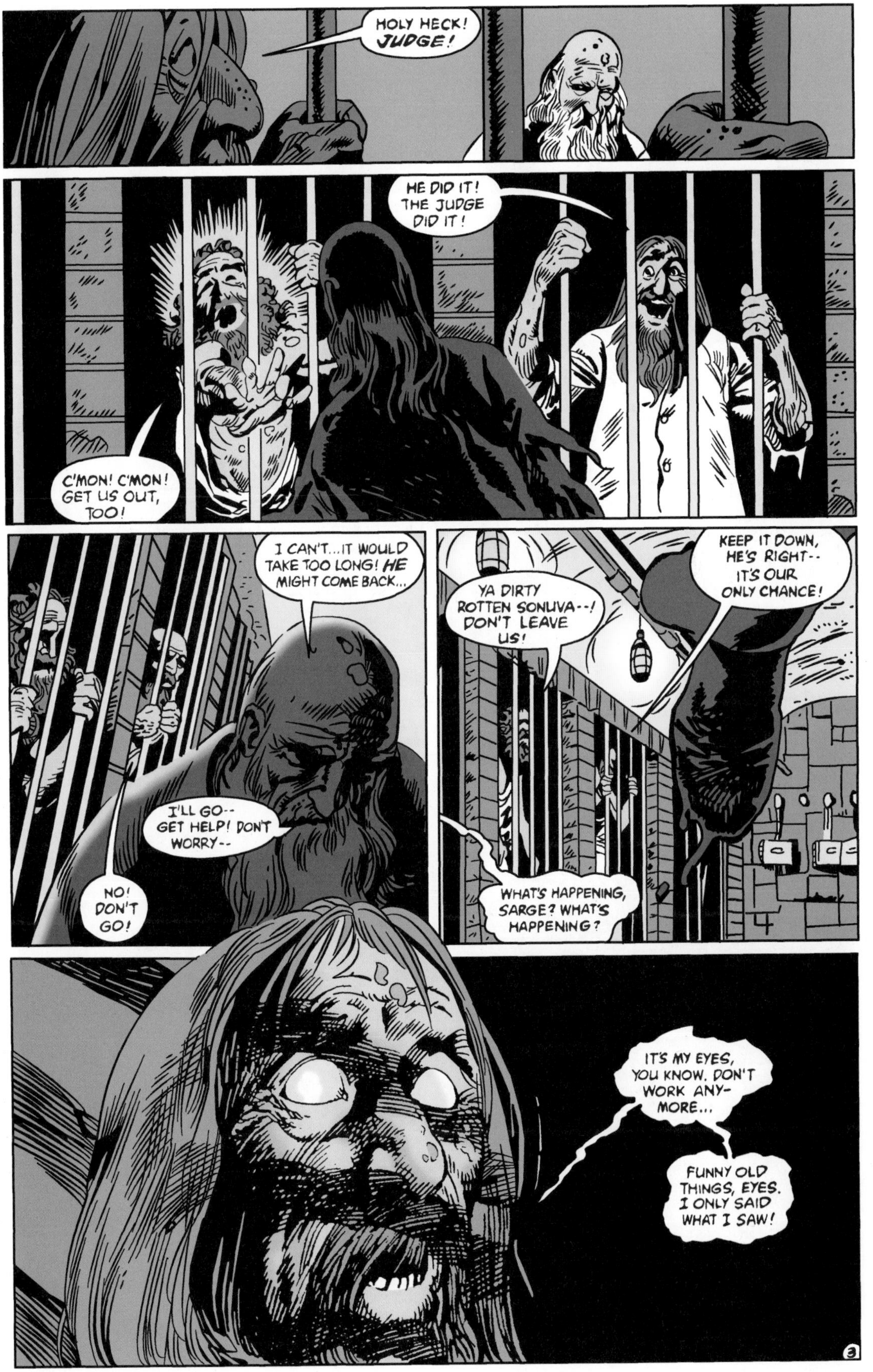
HOLY HECK! JUDGE!
HE DID IT! THE JUDGE DID IT!
C'MON! C'MON! GET US OUT, TOO!
I CAN'T...IT WOULD TAKE TOO LONG! HE MIGHT COME BACK...
I'LL GO-- GET HELP! DON'T WORRY--
NO! DON'T GO!
KEEP IT DOWN, HE'S RIGHT-- IT'S OUR ONLY CHANCE!
YA DIRTY ROTTEN SONUVA--! DON'T LEAVE US!
WHAT'S HAPPENING, SARGE? WHAT'S HAPPENING?
IT'S MY EYES, YOU KNOW. DON'T WORK ANY-MORE...
FUNNY OLD THINGS, EYES. I ONLY SAID WHAT I SAW!
3

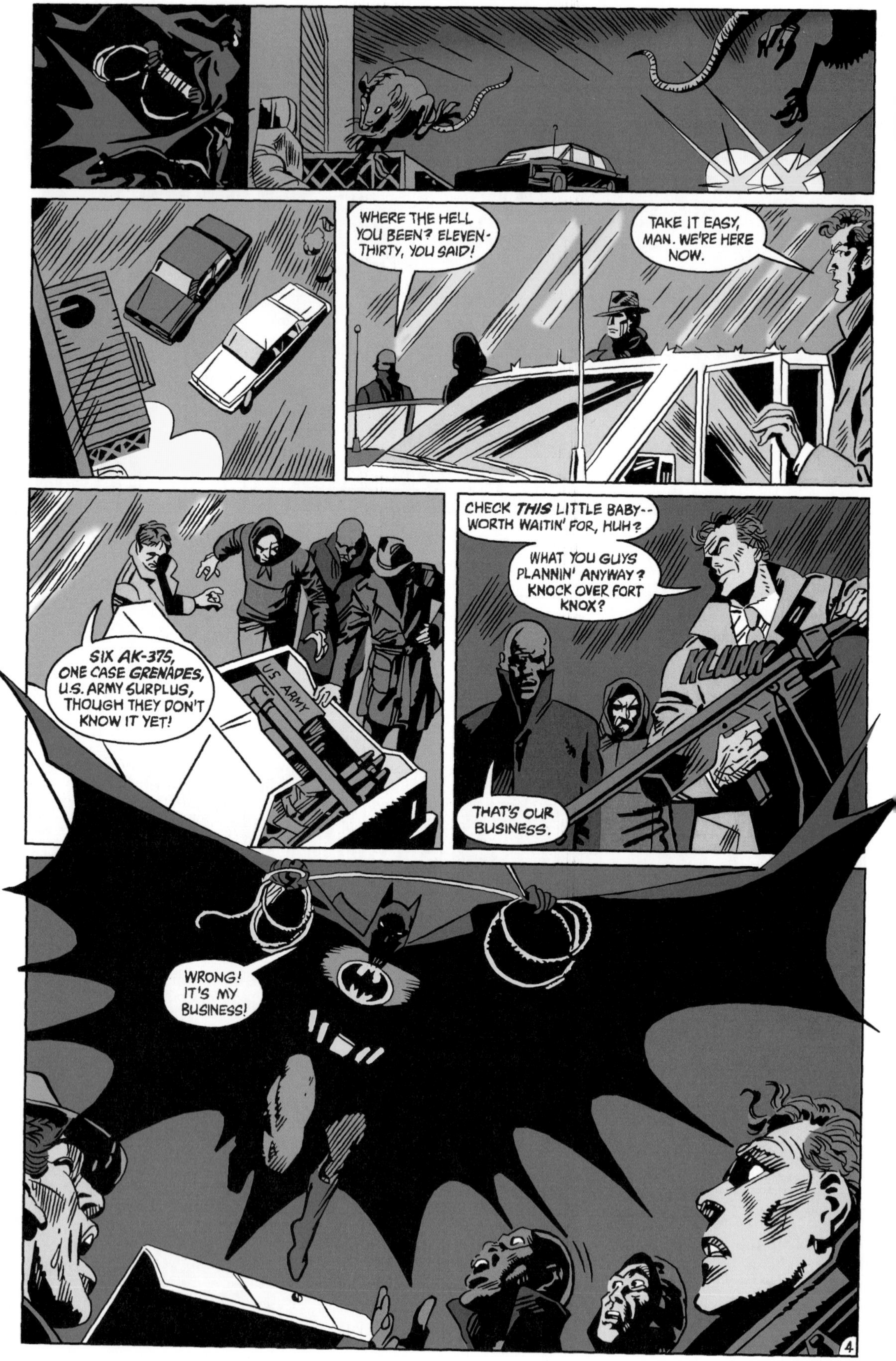
WHERE THE HELL YOU BEEN? ELEVEN-THIRTY, YOU SAID!
TAKE IT EASY, MAN. WE'RE HERE NOW.
SIX AK-375, ONE CASE GRENADES, U.S. ARMY SURPLUS, THOUGH THEY DON'T KNOW IT YET!
U.S. ARMY
CHECK THIS LITTLE BABY-- WORTH WAITIN' FOR, HUH?
WHAT YOU GUYS PLANNIN' ANYWAY? KNOCK OVER FORT KNOX?
KLUNK
THAT'S OUR BUSINESS.
WRONG! IT'S MY BUSINESS!
4

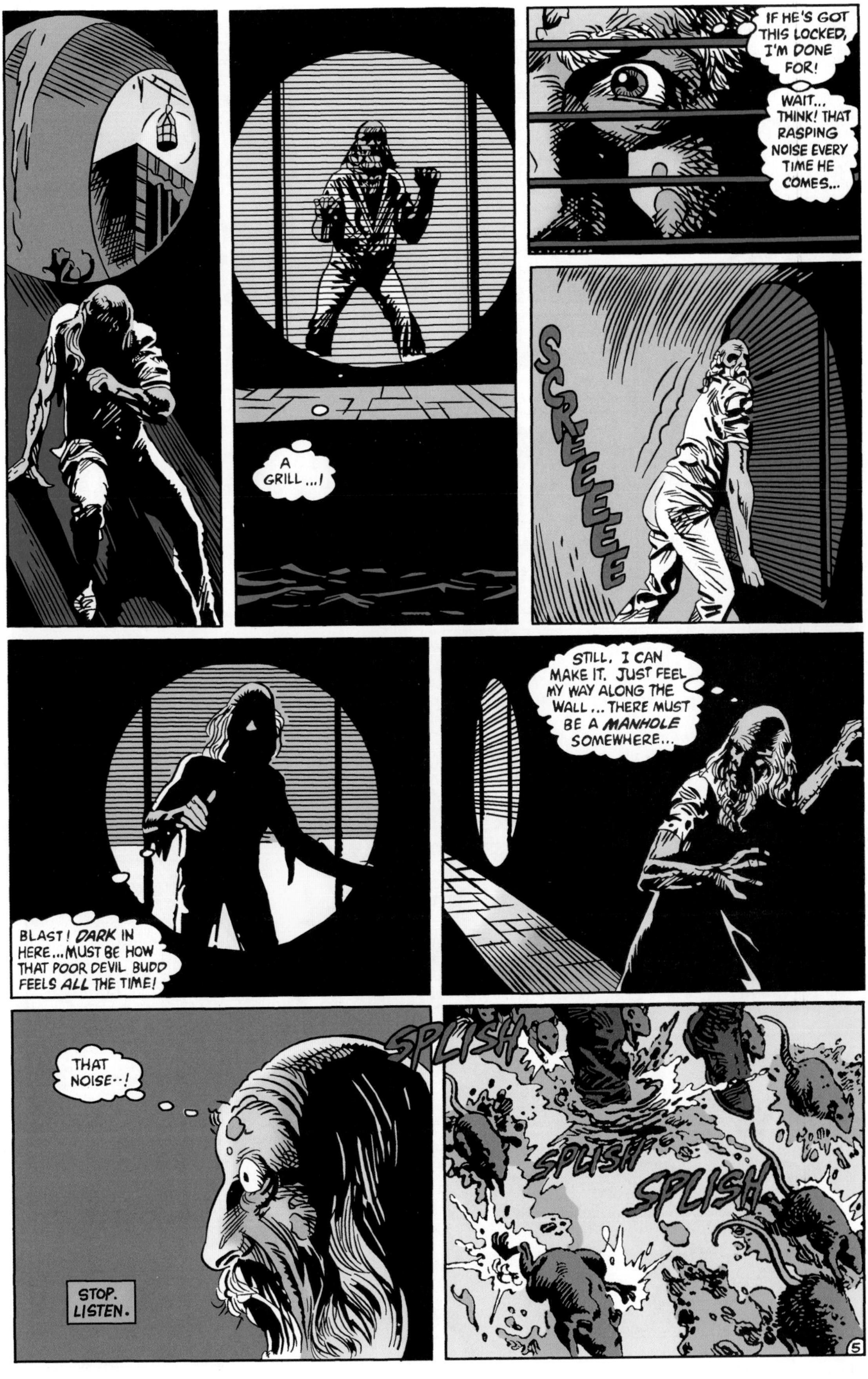
IF HE'S GOT THIS LOCKED, I'M DONE FOR!
WAIT... THINK! THAT RASPING NOISE EVERY TIME HE COMES...
A GRILL...!
SCREEEEEE
STILL, I CAN MAKE IT. JUST FEEL MY WAY ALONG THE WALL... THERE MUST BE A MANHOLE SOMEWHERE...
BLAST! DARK IN HERE... MUST BE HOW THAT POOR DEVIL BUDD FEELS ALL THE TIME!
THAT NOISE--!
STOP. LISTEN.
SPLISH
SPLISH
SPLISH
5

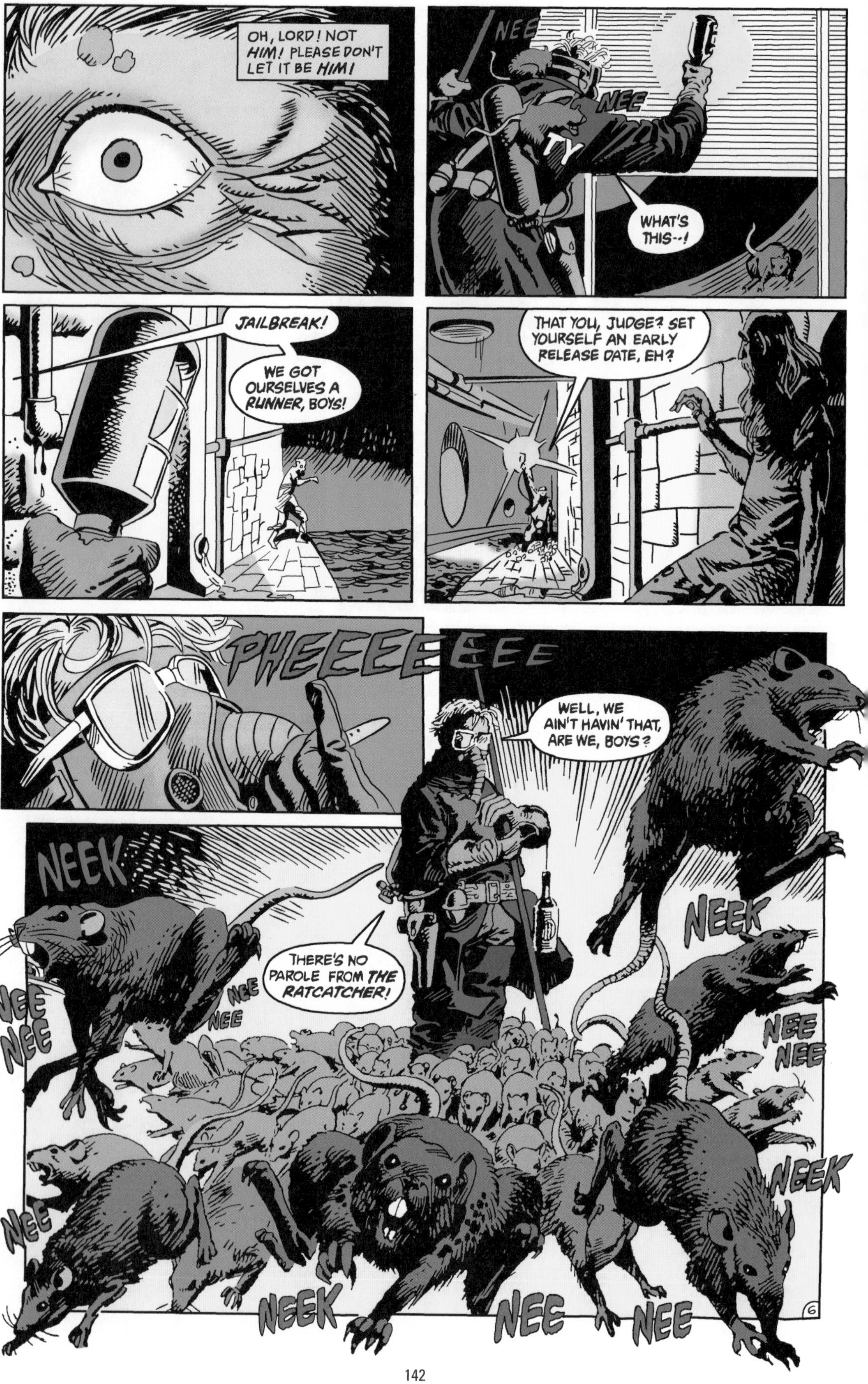
OH, LORD! NOT HIM! PLEASE DON'T LET IT BE HIM!
NEE
NEE
TY
WHAT'S THIS--!
JAILBREAK!
WE GOT OURSELVES A RUNNER, BOYS!
THAT YOU, JUDGE? SET YOURSELF AN EARLY RELEASE DATE, EH?
PHEEEEEEEE
WELL, WE AIN'T HAVIN' THAT, ARE WE, BOYS?
NEEK
THERE'S NO PAROLE FROM THE RATCATCHER!
NEE NEE
NEE NEE
NEEK
NEE NEE
NEEK
NEE
NEEK
NEE
NEE
6

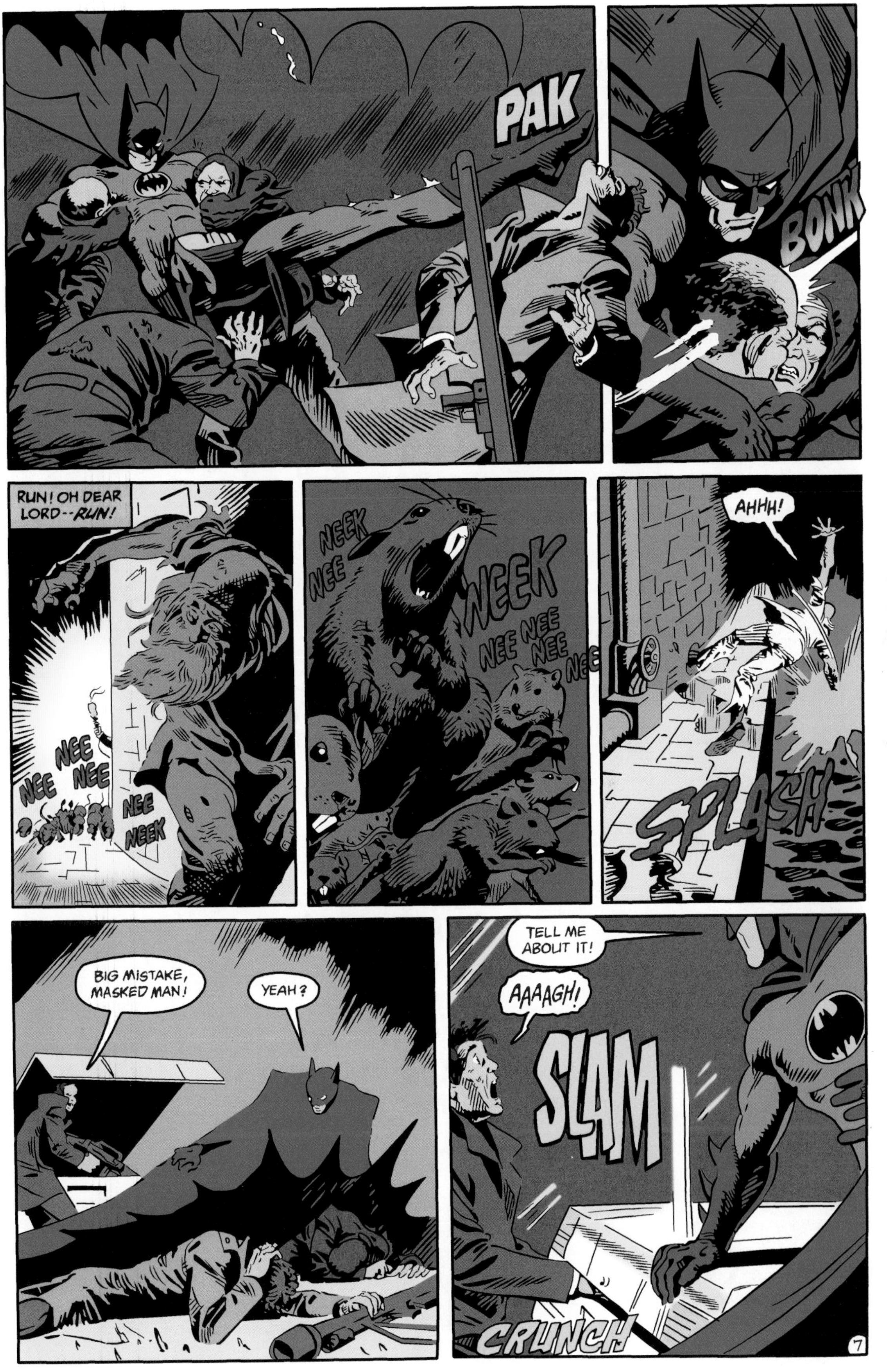
PAK
BONK
RUN! OH DEAR LORD--RUN!
NEE NEE NEE NEE NEEK
NEEK NEE
NEEK NEE NEE NEE NEE
AHHH!
SPLASH
BIG MISTAKE, MASKED MAN!
YEAH?
TELL ME ABOUT IT!
AAAAGH!
SLAM
CRUNCH
7

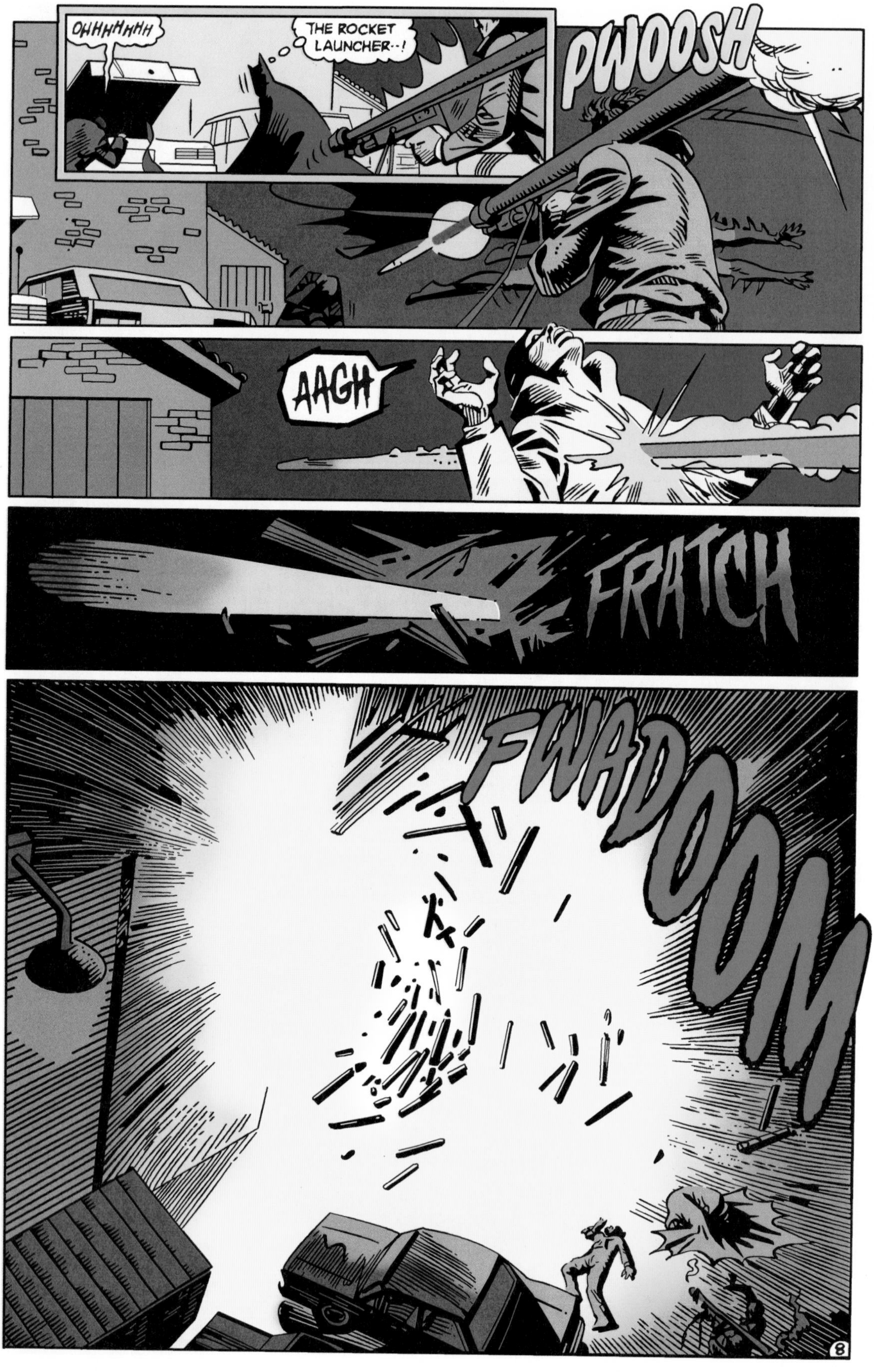
OHHHHHHH
THE ROCKET LAUNCHER--!
PWOOSH
AAGH
FRATCH
FWADOOOM
8

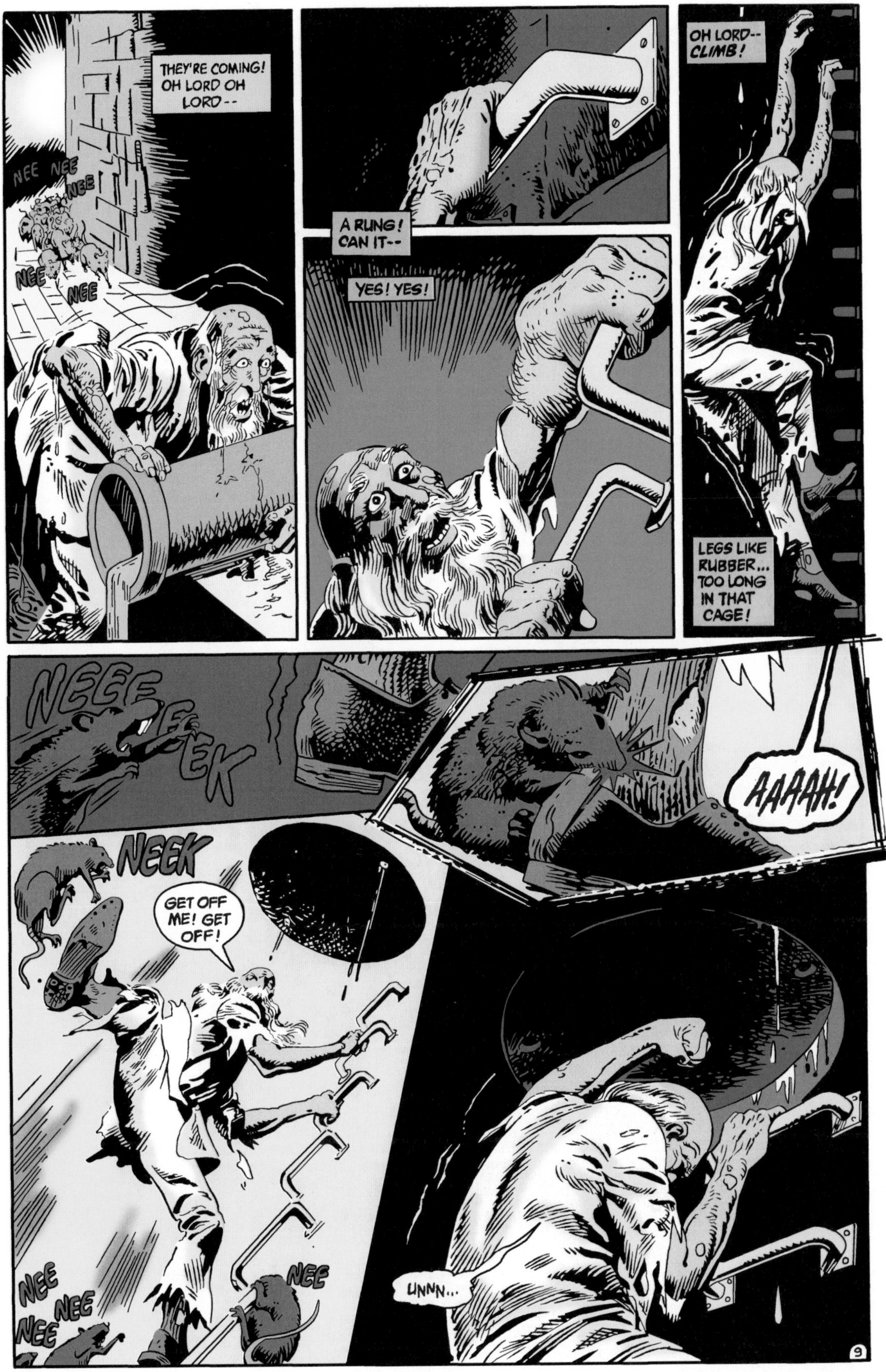
THEY'RE COMING! OH LORD OH LORD--
NEE NEE NEE
NEE NEE
A RUNG! CAN IT--
YES! YES!
OH LORD-- CLIMB!
LEGS LIKE RUBBER... TOO LONG IN THAT CAGE!
NEEE EEEK
AAAAH!
NEEK
GET OFF ME! GET OFF!
NEE NEE NEE
NEE
UNNN...
9

FRESH AIR! PRAISE BE!

OFF!

NEEK

NEE

NEE NEE

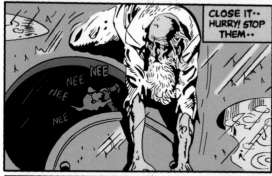

CLOSE IT·· HURRY! STOP THEM··

NEE NEE

NEE NEE

NEE

OHDEARLORRRR-!

NEEK

NEE

NEE

NEE

HE'S A TRIER-- WE GOT TO GIVE HIM THAT, BOYS! BUT HE'S GONE TOO FAR NOW. HE'S GOT TO BE *SILENCED!*

UNDERSTAND ME, BOYS?

NEE NEE

NEE NEE

NEE

NEE NEE

NEE

NEE

NEE

NEE NEE

NEE NEE

NEEK

NEE

LIGHT AHEAD! A FIRE ...PEOPLE!

RUN!

NEE NEE

NEE

NEE

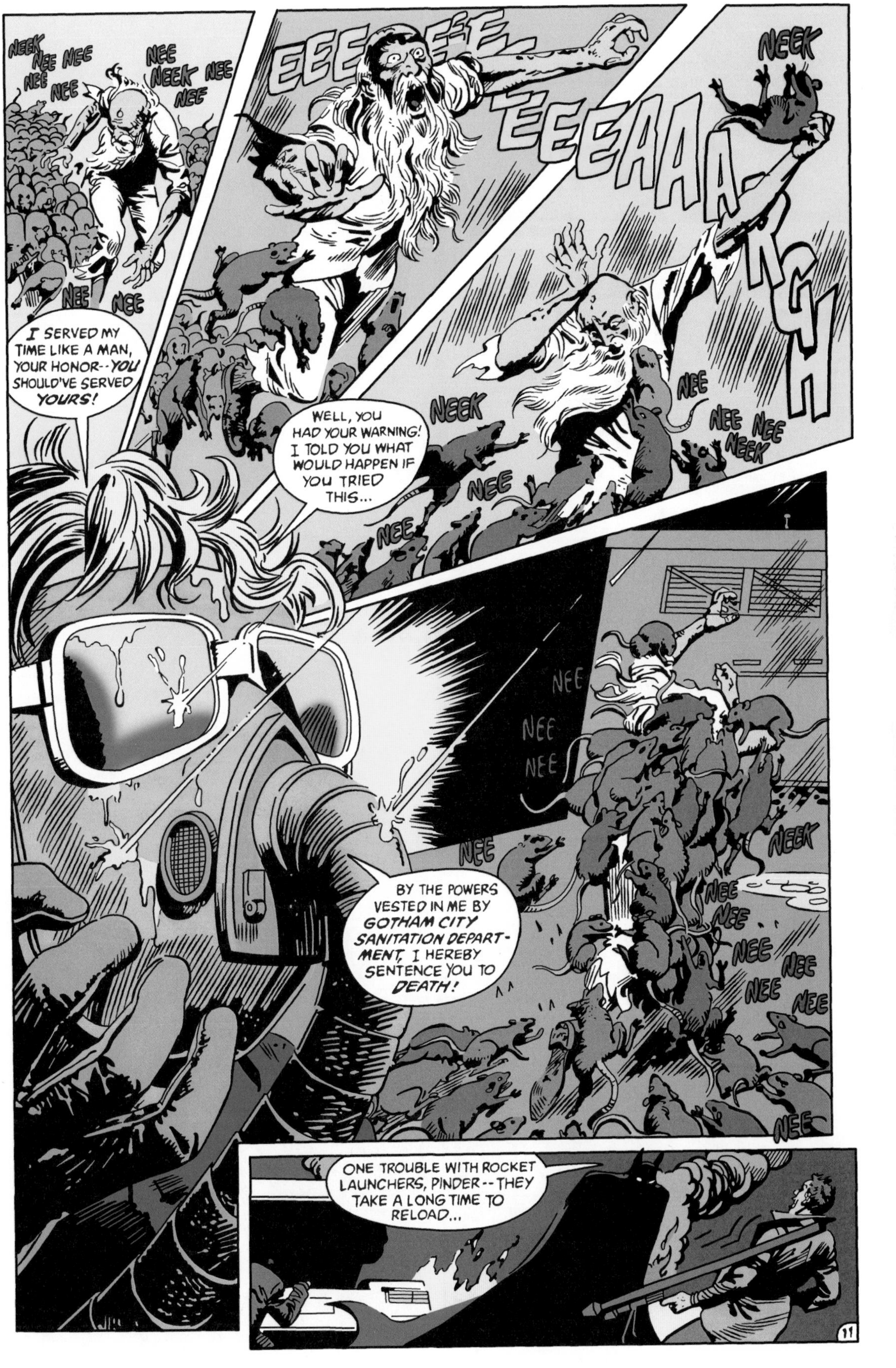
NEEK NEE NEE NEE NEE NEE NEEK NEE NEE
EEEEEEE-
NEE NEE
I SERVED MY TIME LIKE A MAN, YOUR HONOR--YOU SHOULD'VE SERVED YOURS!
EEEAAA-RGH
NEEK
WELL, YOU HAD YOUR WARNING! I TOLD YOU WHAT WOULD HAPPEN IF YOU TRIED THIS...
NEEK
NEE NEE NEE NEEK
NEE
NEE
NEE NEE NEE
NEE
BY THE POWERS VESTED IN ME BY GOTHAM CITY SANITATION DEPARTMENT, I HEREBY SENTENCE YOU TO DEATH!
NEEK
NEE NEE NEE NEE NEE NEE
ONE TROUBLE WITH ROCKET LAUNCHERS, PINDER--THEY TAKE A LONG TIME TO RELOAD...
11

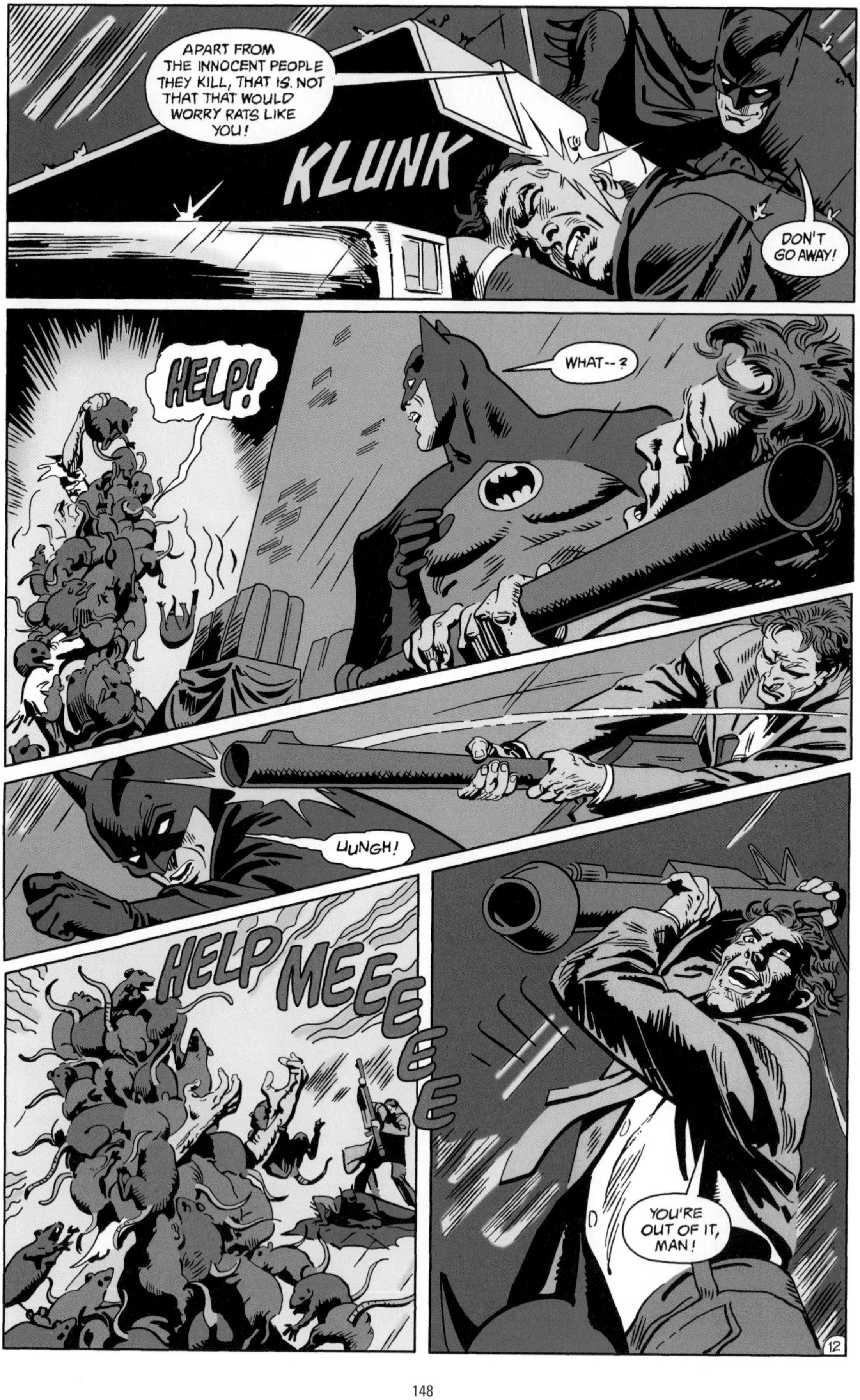
APART FROM THE INNOCENT PEOPLE THEY KILL, THAT IS. NOT THAT THAT WOULD WORRY RATS LIKE YOU!
KLUNK
DON'T GO AWAY!
HELP!
WHAT--?
UUNGH!
HELP MEEEEEE
YOU'RE OUT OF IT, MAN!
12

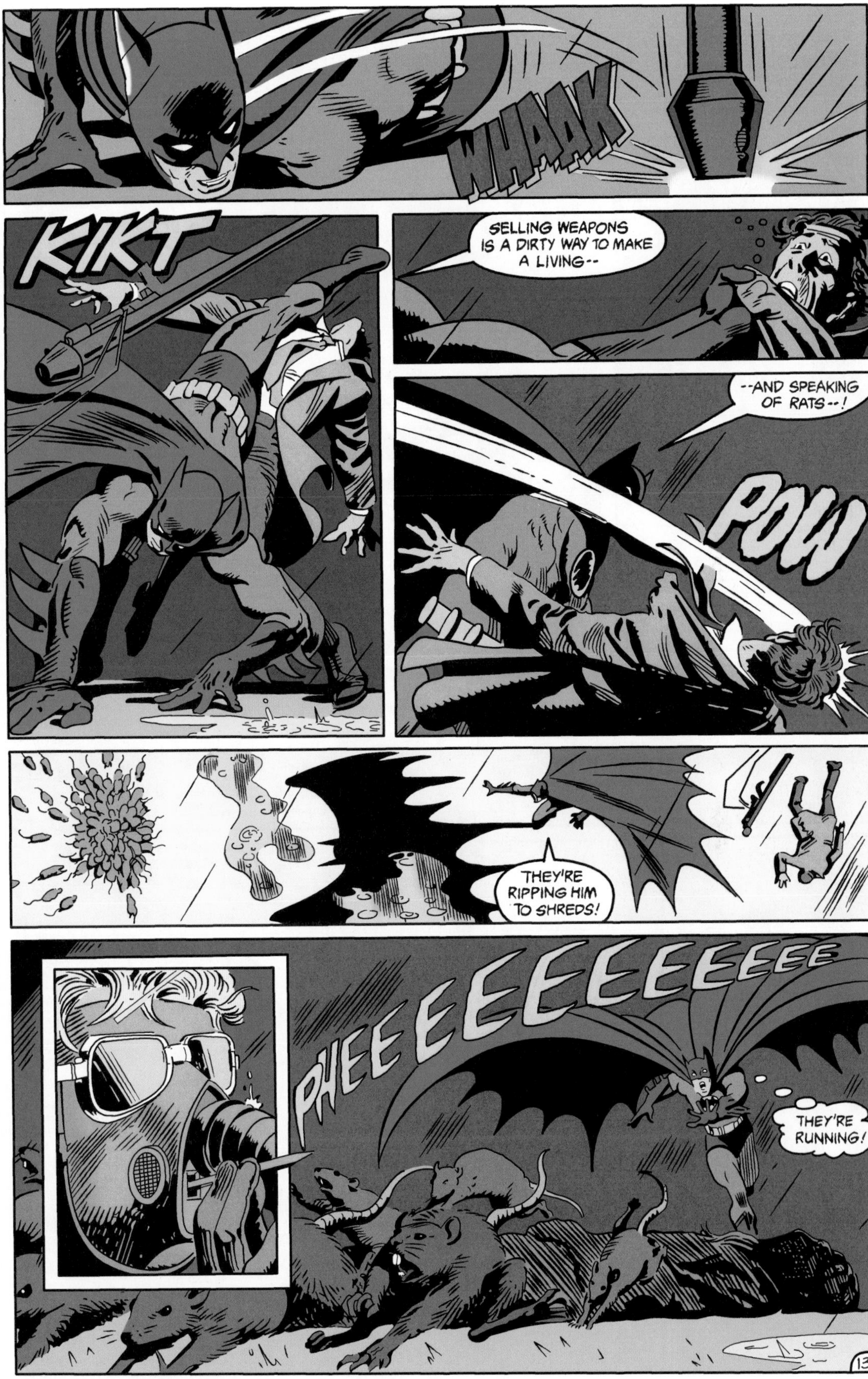
WHAAK
KIKT
SELLING WEAPONS IS A DIRTY WAY TO MAKE A LIVING--
--AND SPEAKING OF RATS--!
POW
THEY'RE RIPPING HIM TO SHREDS!
PHEEEEEEEEEEEEEE
THEY'RE RUNNING!
13

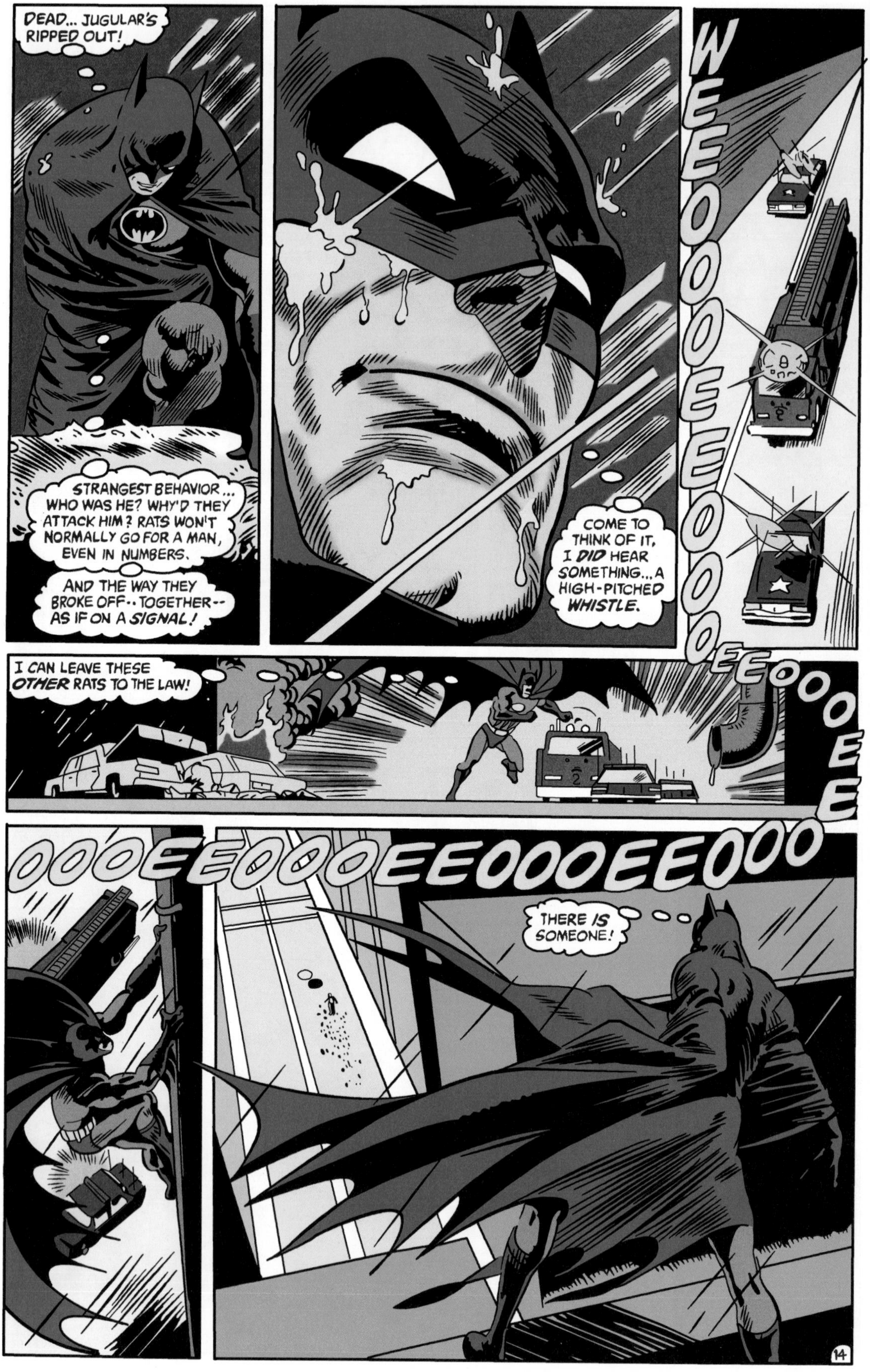
DEAD... JUGULAR'S RIPPED OUT!
STRANGEST BEHAVIOR... WHO WAS HE? WHY'D THEY ATTACK HIM? RATS WON'T NORMALLY GO FOR A MAN, EVEN IN NUMBERS.
AND THE WAY THEY BROKE OFF-- TOGETHER-- AS IF ON A SIGNAL!
COME TO THINK OF IT, I DID HEAR SOMETHING... A HIGH-PITCHED WHISTLE.
WEEEOOOOEEEEOOOOEEOOOOEEE
I CAN LEAVE THESE OTHER RATS TO THE LAW!
OOOEEOOOOEEOOOEEOOO
THERE IS SOMEONE!
14

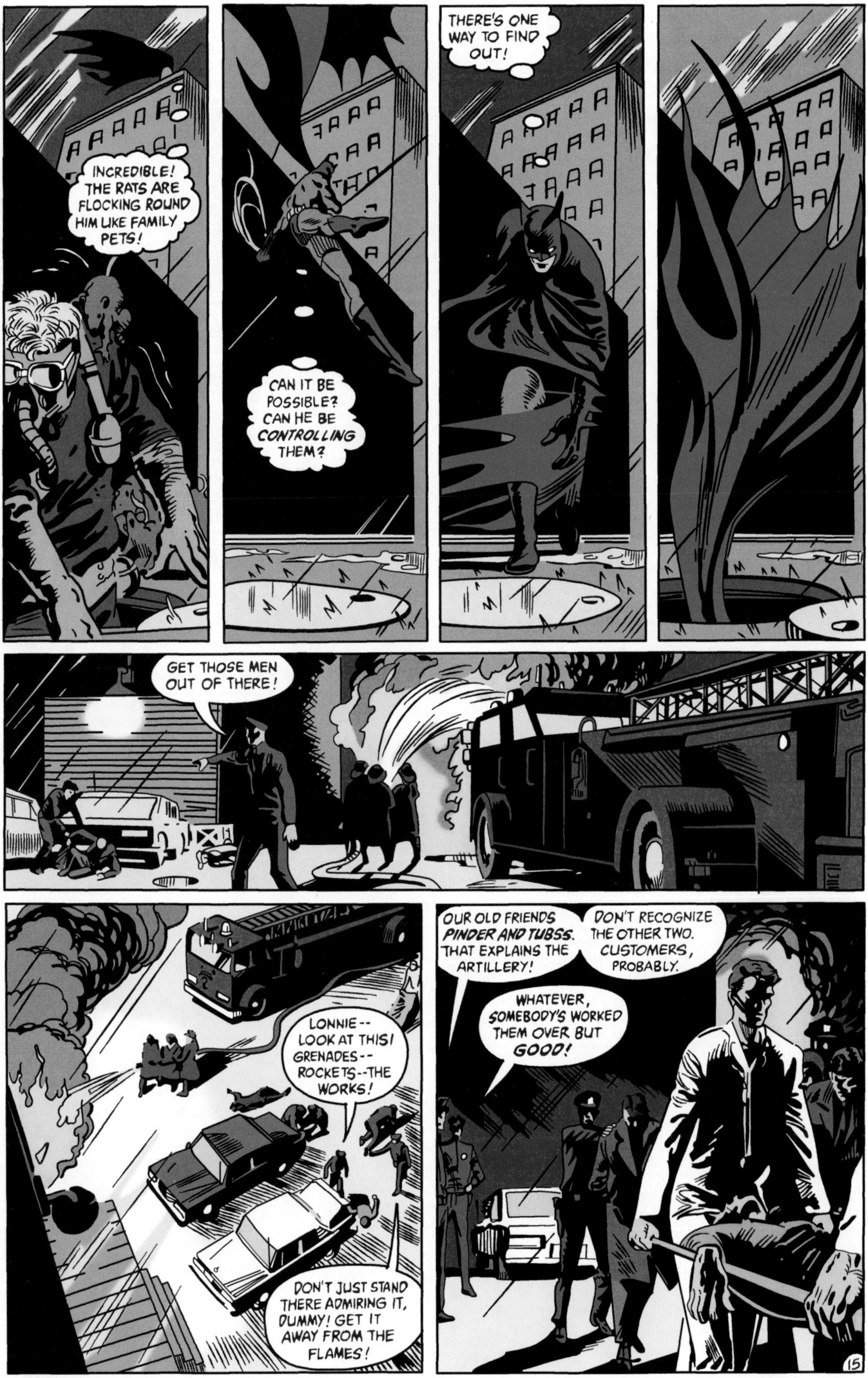
INCREDIBLE! THE RATS ARE FLOCKING ROUND HIM LIKE FAMILY PETS!
CAN IT BE POSSIBLE? CAN HE BE CONTROLLING THEM?
THERE'S ONE WAY TO FIND OUT!
GET THOSE MEN OUT OF THERE!
LONNIE-- LOOK AT THIS! GRENADES-- ROCKETS--THE WORKS!
DON'T JUST STAND THERE ADMIRING IT, DUMMY! GET IT AWAY FROM THE FLAMES!
OUR OLD FRIENDS PINDER AND TUBSS. THAT EXPLAINS THE ARTILLERY!
DON'T RECOGNIZE THE OTHER TWO. CUSTOMERS, PROBABLY.
WHATEVER, SOMEBODY'S WORKED THEM OVER BUT GOOD!
15

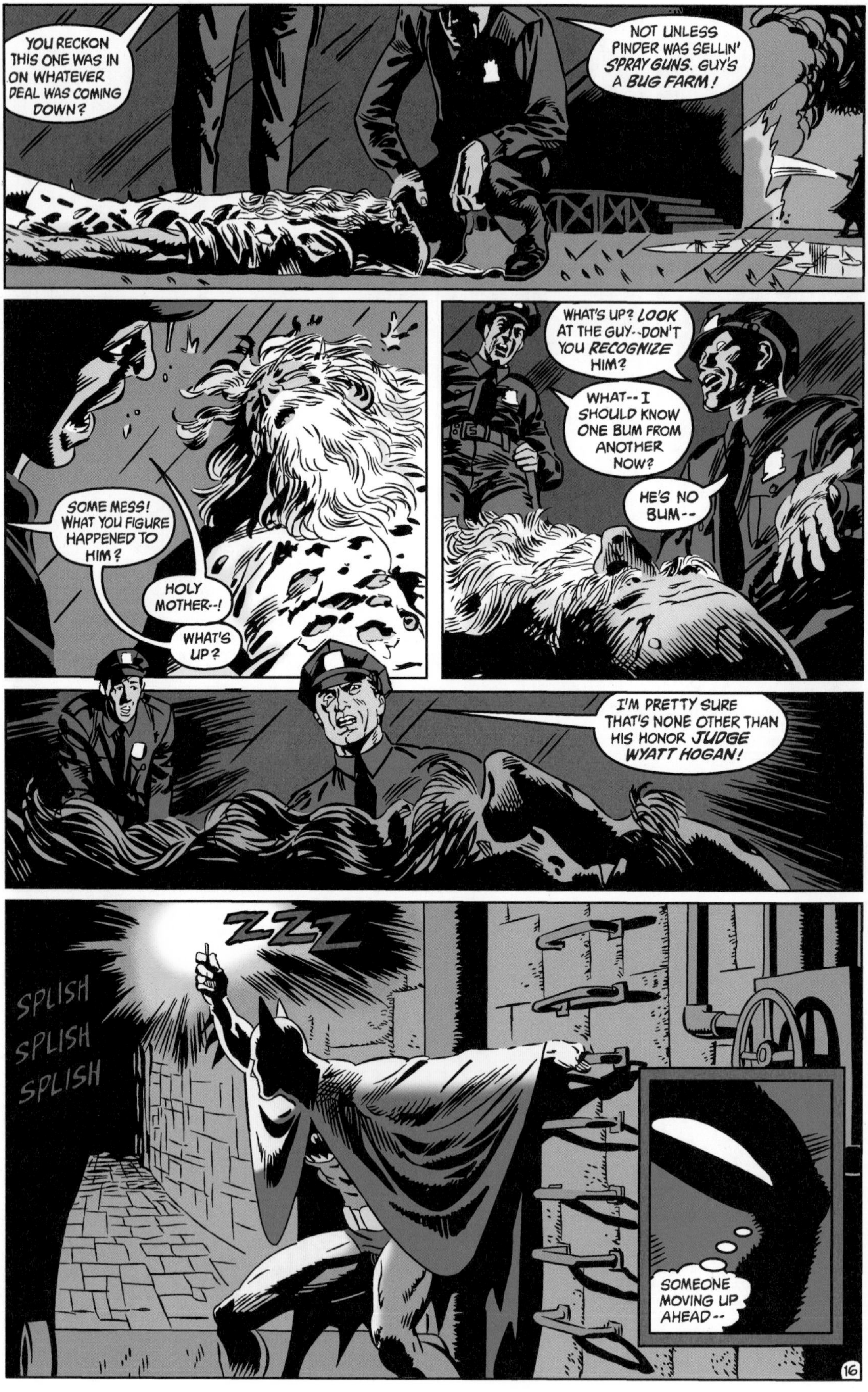
YOU RECKON THIS ONE WAS IN ON WHATEVER DEAL WAS COMING DOWN?
NOT UNLESS PINDER WAS SELLIN' SPRAY GUNS. GUY'S A BUG FARM!
SOME MESS! WHAT YOU FIGURE HAPPENED TO HIM?
HOLY MOTHER--!
WHAT'S UP?
WHAT'S UP? LOOK AT THE GUY--DON'T YOU RECOGNIZE HIM?
WHAT-- I SHOULD KNOW ONE BUM FROM ANOTHER NOW?
HE'S NO BUM--
I'M PRETTY SURE THAT'S NONE OTHER THAN HIS HONOR JUDGE WYATT HOGAN!
ZZZ
SPLISH
SPLISH
SPLISH
SOMEONE MOVING UP AHEAD--
16

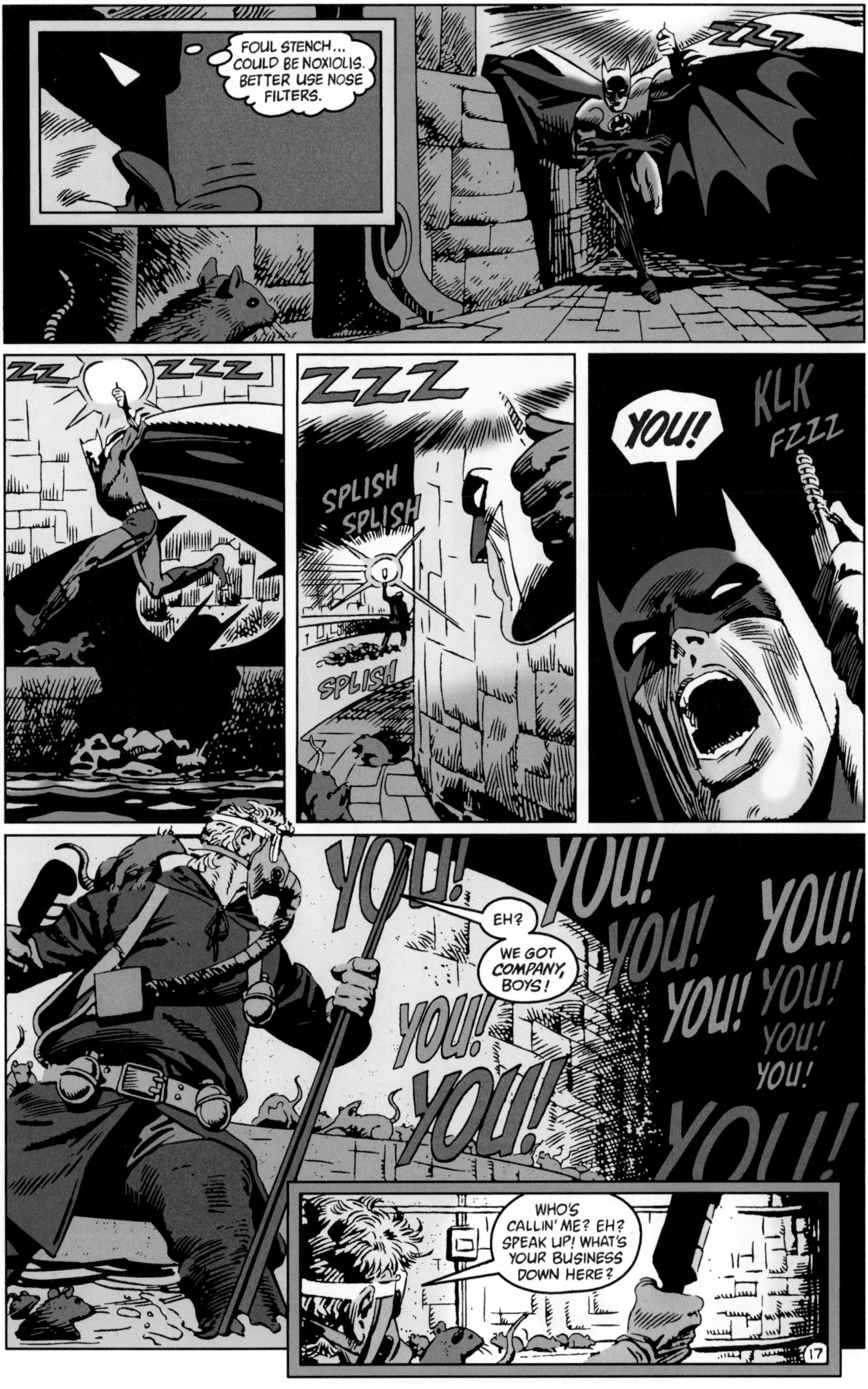
FOUL STENCH... COULD BE NOXIOLIS. BETTER USE NOSE FILTERS.
ZZZ
ZZ ZZZ
ZZZ
SPLISH SPLISH
SPLISH
YOU!
KLK FZZZ
YOU! YOU! YOU! YOU! YOU! YOU!
EH?
WE GOT COMPANY, BOYS!
YOU! YOU! YOU! YOU! YOU! YOU!!
WHO'S CALLIN' ME? EH? SPEAK UP! WHAT'S YOUR BUSINESS DOWN HERE?
17

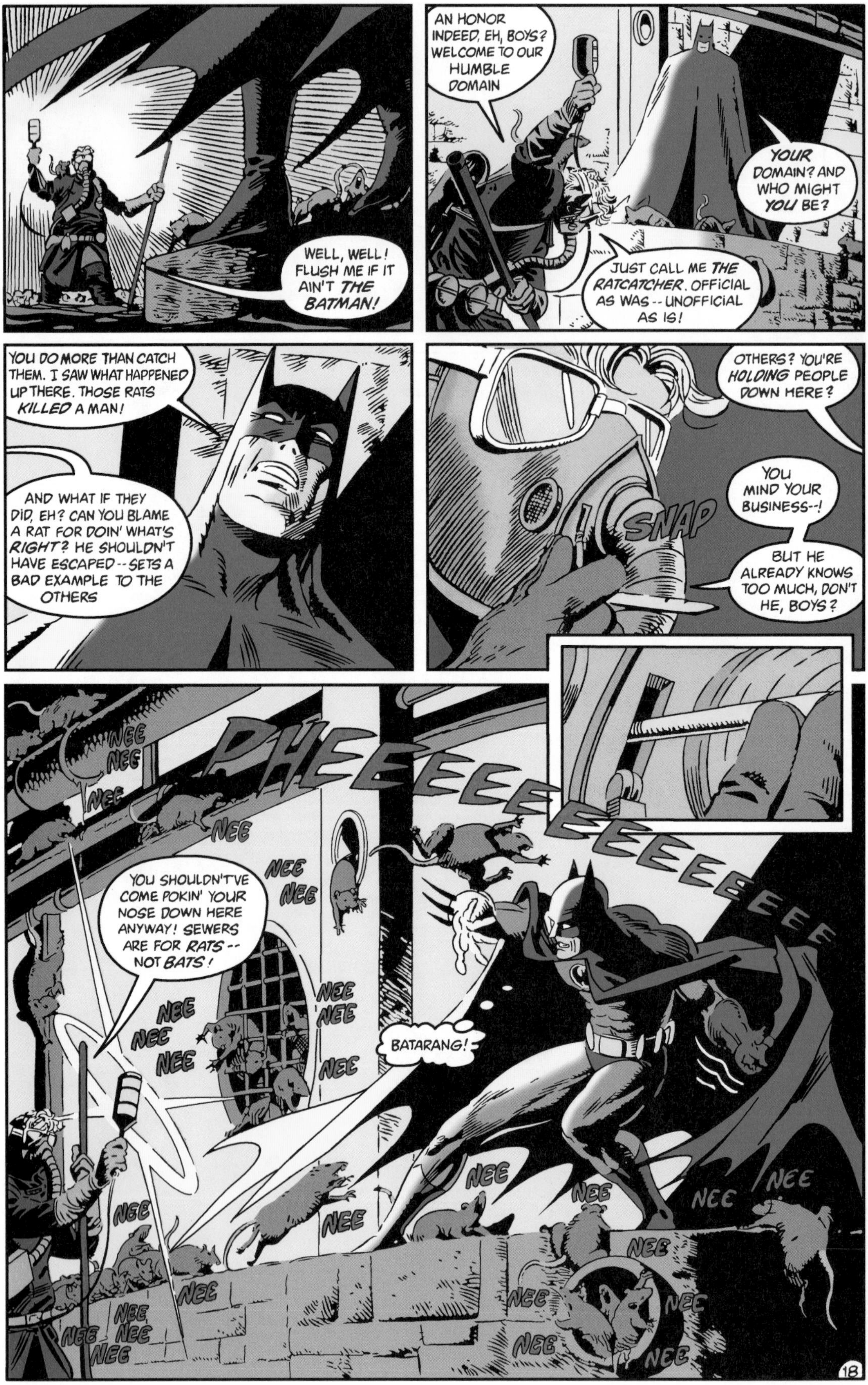
WELL, WELL! FLUSH ME IF IT AIN'T THE BATMAN!
AN HONOR INDEED, EH, BOYS? WELCOME TO OUR HUMBLE DOMAIN
YOUR DOMAIN? AND WHO MIGHT YOU BE?
JUST CALL ME THE RATCATCHER. OFFICIAL AS WAS -- UNOFFICIAL AS IS!
YOU DO MORE THAN CATCH THEM. I SAW WHAT HAPPENED UP THERE. THOSE RATS KILLED A MAN!
AND WHAT IF THEY DID, EH? CAN YOU BLAME A RAT FOR DOIN' WHAT'S RIGHT? HE SHOULDN'T HAVE ESCAPED -- SETS A BAD EXAMPLE TO THE OTHERS
OTHERS? YOU'RE HOLDING PEOPLE DOWN HERE?
SNAP
YOU MIND YOUR BUSINESS--!
BUT HE ALREADY KNOWS TOO MUCH, DON'T HE, BOYS?
PHEEEEEEEEEEEEEEEE
NEE NEE NEE NEE
NEE NEE
YOU SHOULDN'T'VE COME POKIN' YOUR NOSE DOWN HERE ANYWAY! SEWERS ARE FOR RATS -- NOT BATS!
NEE NEE NEE
NEE NEE NEE
BATARANG!
NEE NEE NEE NEE NEE NEE
NEE NEE NEE NEE NEE NEE NEE NEE
18

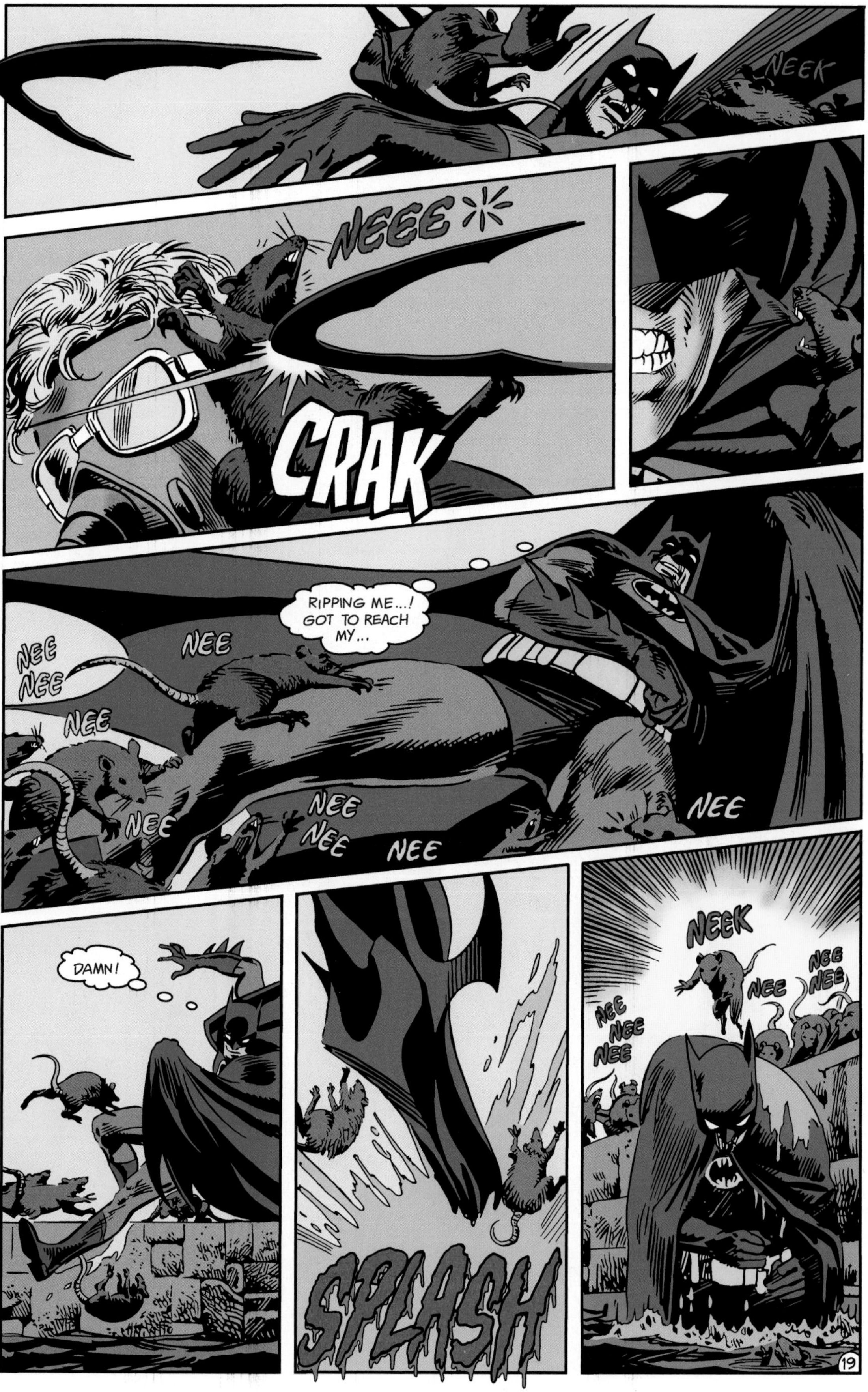
NEEK
NEEE
CRAK
RIPPING ME...! GOT TO REACH MY...
NEE NEE
NEE
NEE
NEE
NEE NEE
NEE
NEE
DAMN!
SPLASH
NEEK
NEE
NEE NEE
NEE NEE NEE
19

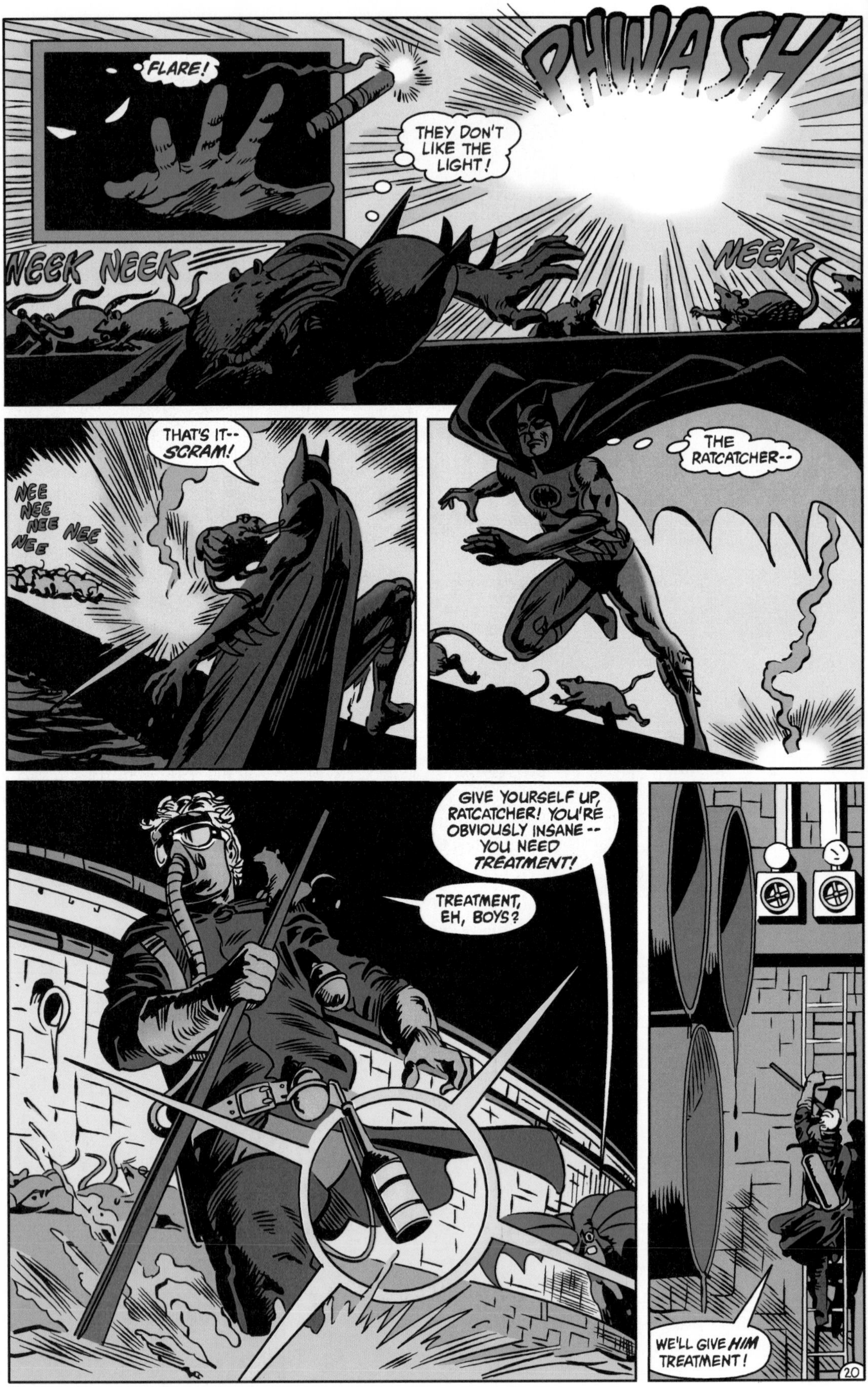
FLARE!
THEY DON'T LIKE THE LIGHT!
PHWASH
NEEK NEEK
NEEK
THAT'S IT-- SCRAM!
NEE NEE NEE NEE NEE
THE RATCATCHER--
GIVE YOURSELF UP, RATCATCHER! YOU'RE OBVIOUSLY INSANE -- YOU NEED TREATMENT!
TREATMENT, EH, BOYS?
WE'LL GIVE HIM TREATMENT!
20

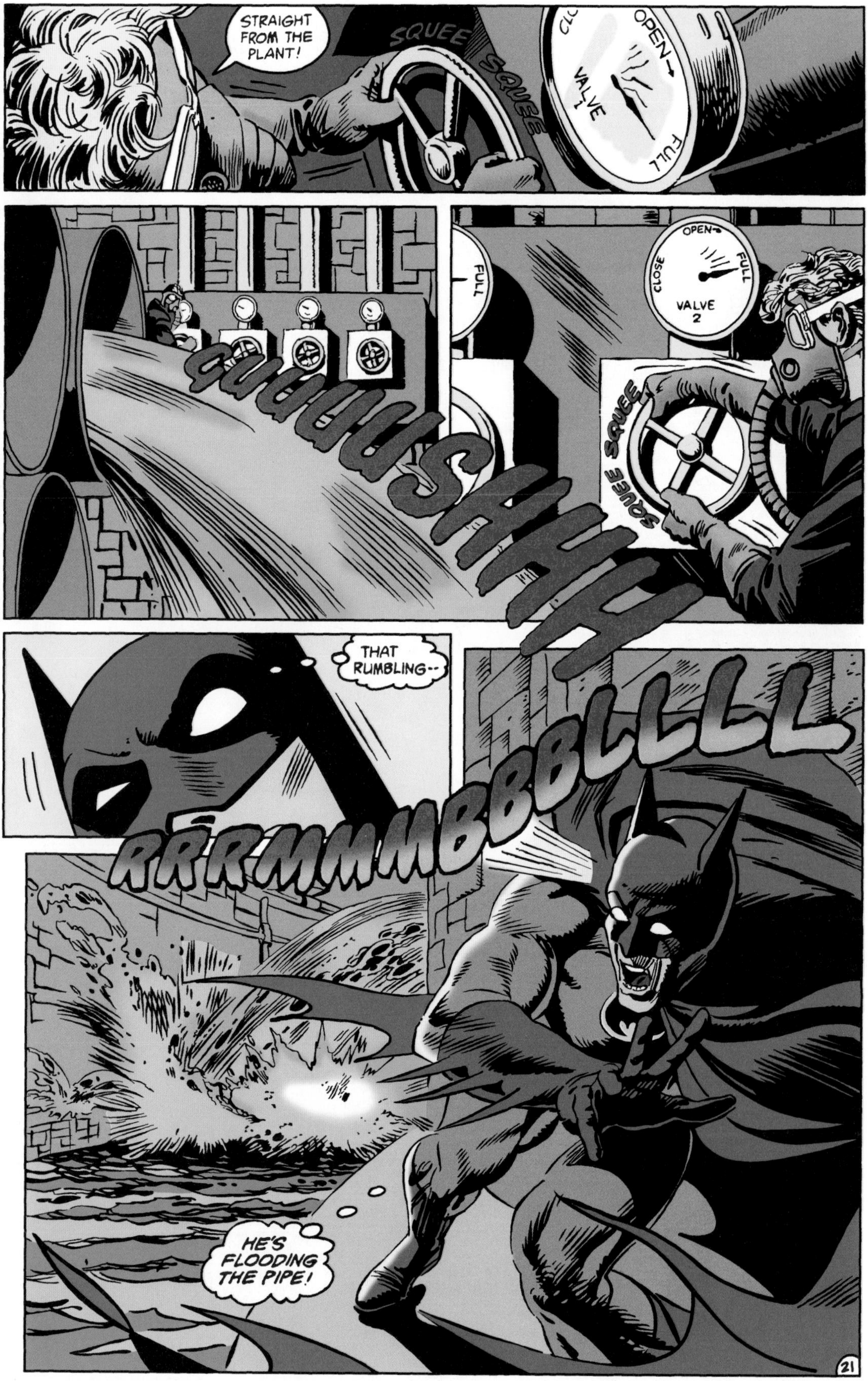
STRAIGHT FROM THE PLANT!
SQUEE
SQUEE
OPEN
CLO
VALVE 1
FULL
OPEN
FULL
CLOSE
VALVE 2
FULL
GUUUUSHHHH
SQUEE SQUEE
THAT RUMBLING--
RRRMMMMBBBLLLLL
HE'S FLOODING THE PIPE!
21

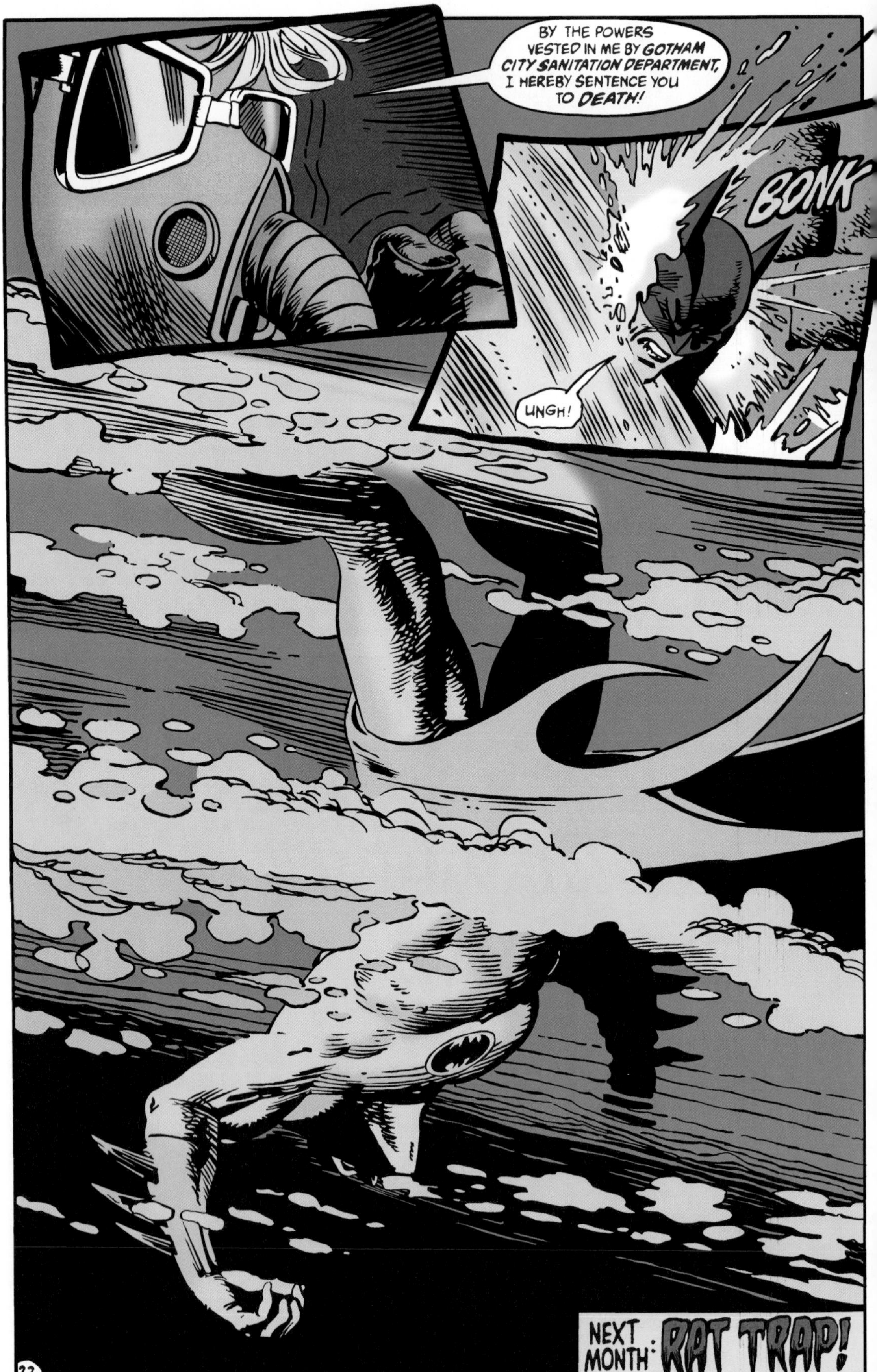
BY THE POWERS VESTED IN ME BY GOTHAM CITY SANITATION DEPARTMENT, I HEREBY SENTENCE YOU TO DEATH!
BONK
UNGH!
22
NEXT MONTH: RAT TRAP!

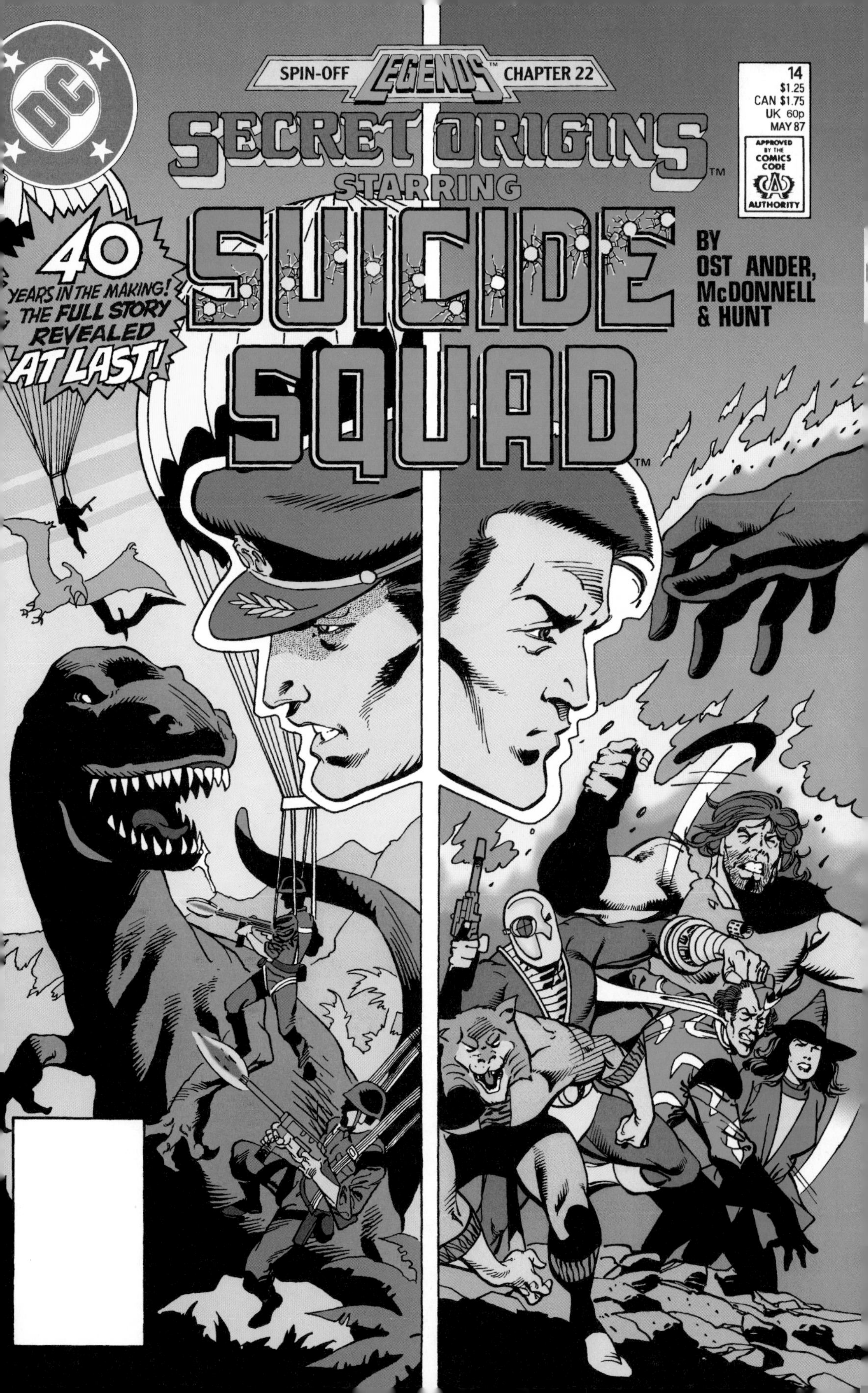

SPIN-OFF LEGENDS™ CHAPTER 22
SECRET ORIGINS™
STARRING
SUICIDE SQUAD™
14
$1.25
CAN $1.75
UK 60p
MAY 87
APPROVED BY THE COMICS CODE AUTHORITY
40 YEARS IN THE MAKING! THE FULL STORY REVEALED AT LAST!
BY
OST ANDER,
McDONNELL
& HUNT

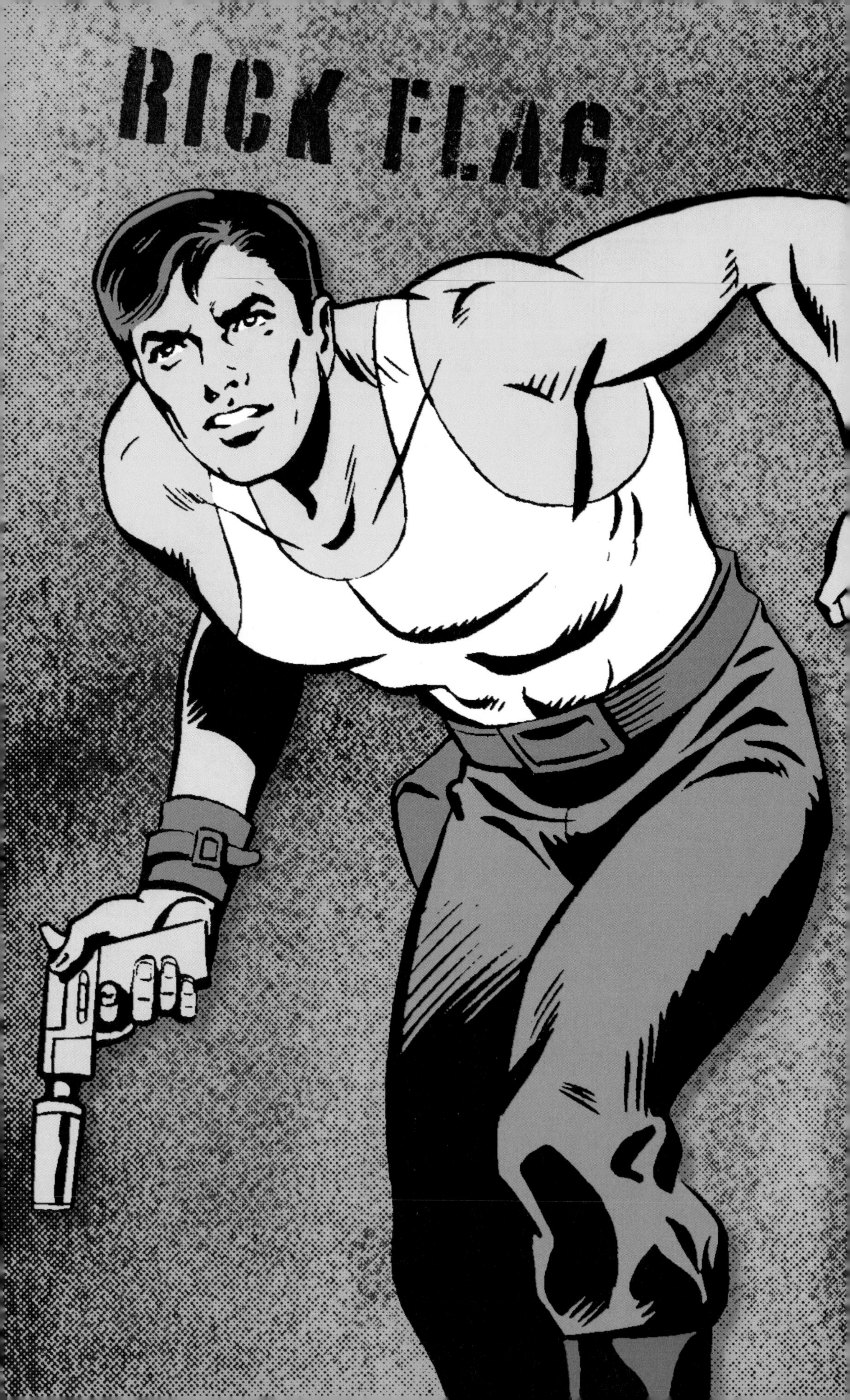
RICK FLAG

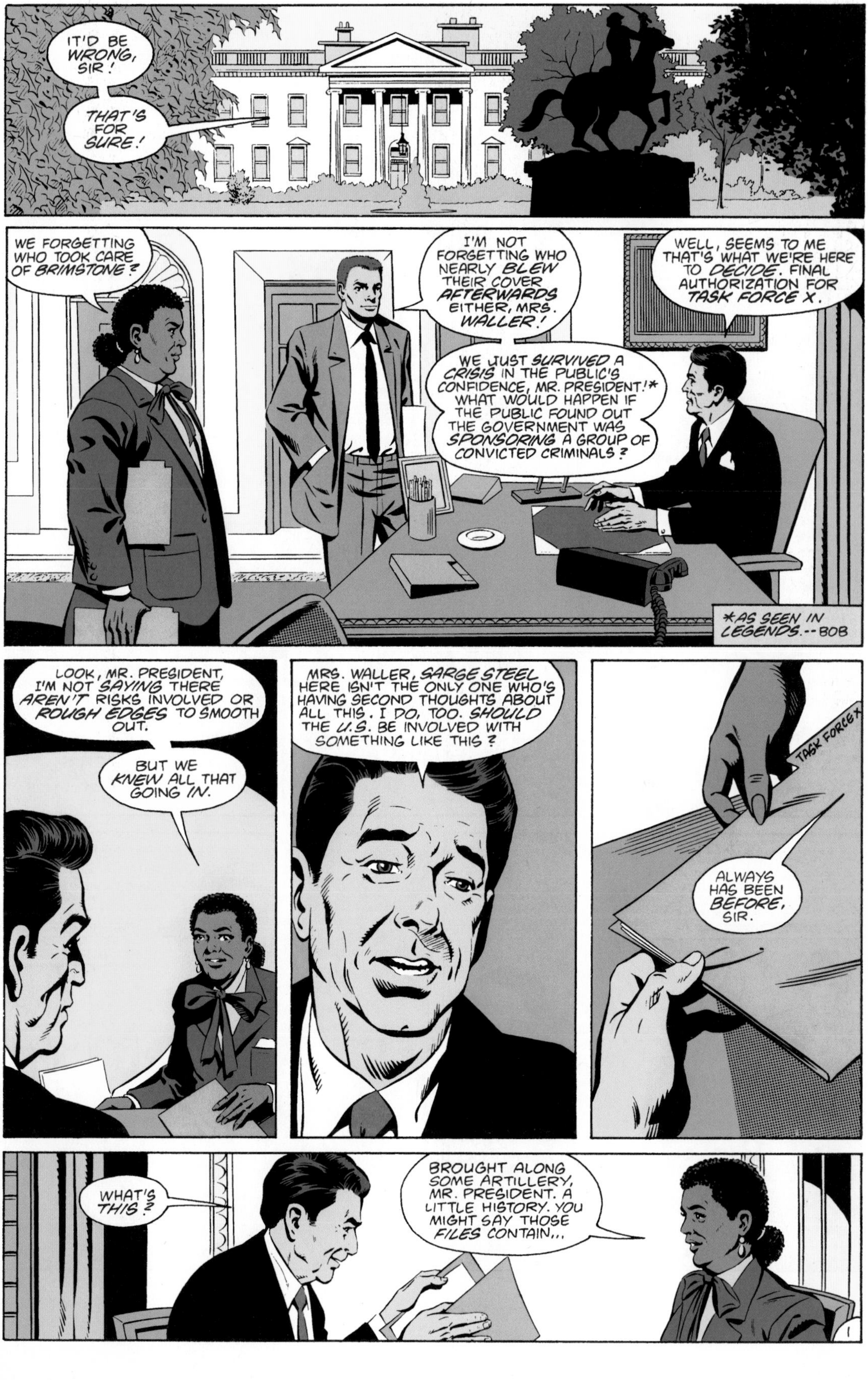
IT'D BE WRONG, SIR!
THAT'S FOR SURE!
WE FORGETTING WHO TOOK CARE OF BRIMSTONE?
I'M NOT FORGETTING WHO NEARLY BLEW THEIR COVER AFTERWARDS EITHER, MRS. WALLER!
WE JUST SURVIVED A CRISIS IN THE PUBLIC'S CONFIDENCE, MR. PRESIDENT!* WHAT WOULD HAPPEN IF THE PUBLIC FOUND OUT THE GOVERNMENT WAS SPONSORING A GROUP OF CONVICTED CRIMINALS?
WELL, SEEMS TO ME THAT'S WHAT WE'RE HERE TO DECIDE. FINAL AUTHORIZATION FOR TASK FORCE X.
*AS SEEN IN LEGENDS.--BOB
LOOK, MR. PRESIDENT, I'M NOT SAYING THERE AREN'T RISKS INVOLVED OR ROUGH EDGES TO SMOOTH OUT.
BUT WE KNEW ALL THAT GOING IN.
MRS. WALLER, SARGE STEEL HERE ISN'T THE ONLY ONE WHO'S HAVING SECOND THOUGHTS ABOUT ALL THIS. I DO, TOO. SHOULD THE U.S. BE INVOLVED WITH SOMETHING LIKE THIS?
TASK FORCE X
ALWAYS HAS BEEN BEFORE, SIR.
WHAT'S THIS?
BROUGHT ALONG SOME ARTILLERY, MR. PRESIDENT. A LITTLE HISTORY. YOU MIGHT SAY THOSE FILES CONTAIN...
1

JOHN OSTRANDER
WRITER
LUKE McDONNELL
PENCILLER
DAVE HUNT
INKER
ALBERT DE GUZMAN
LETTERER
CARL GAFFORD
COLORIST
ROBERT GREENBERGER
EDITOR

the secret origin of the SUICIDE SQUAD™

"GOT TO START BACK IN WORLD WAR II, ON DINOSAUR ISLAND, AND AN ACTION CODE-NAMED 'THE WAR THAT TIME FORGOT!' A RAG-TAG GROUP LABELED SQUADRON S IS ASSIGNED AND THEY SOON CALL THEMSELVES THE SUICIDE SQUADRON, BECAUSE BEING ASSIGNED TO IT WAS CONSIDERED GROUNDS FOR SUICIDE!

"THIS IS WHERE THEY SENT THE BROKEN MEN -- THE ALIENATED, THE DISAFFECTED, THE BORDERLINE WHACKOS-- ALL THE MOST EXPENDABLE SORTS. AND THEY KNEW THEY WERE EXPENDABLE.

"CASULTIES WERE HIGH. MORALE AND DISCIPLINE WERE LOW. THE MEN SEEMED READIER TO FIGHT EACH OTHER THAN THE ENEMY. BRASS HAD TO DO SOMETHING."

2

GOOD, BAD, INDIFFERENT-- THEY'RE STILL *OUR* MEN. WE'VE GOT TO GIVE THEM A FIGHTING CHANCE TO SURVIVE.

THEY NEED A C.O., TOUGH, MEAN, AND COMMITTED, WHO'LL MAKE THEM WORK *TOGETHER!*

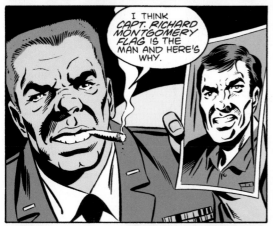

I THINK CAPT. RICHARD MONTGOMERY FLAG IS THE MAN AND HERE'S WHY.

"AS A ROOKIE FLYER, HE WAS OUT WITH HIS SQUADRON OF TBFs WHEN THEY CAME UPON A JAP FLAT-TOP."

LET'S GET THAT FLAT-TOP, GANG! USE ATTACK PLAN THREE! RICK, YOU COME IN LAST! WE'LL PAVE THE WAY!

THEY'RE TAKING ALL THE RISKS, SO THERE'LL BE LESS TO CLOBBER ME WHEN I MAKE MY RUN!

LOOK AT THAT FLAK!

BOOM!

BUH-BOOM!

THEY'VE ALL BEEN HIT!

NO ONE LEFT NOW... BUT ME...!

"THEN, OUT OF NOWHERE, HE HEARD A FAINT VOICE ON THE INTERCOM."

...UP TO YOU NOW... RICK... CARRY ON... FOR US--!

3

163

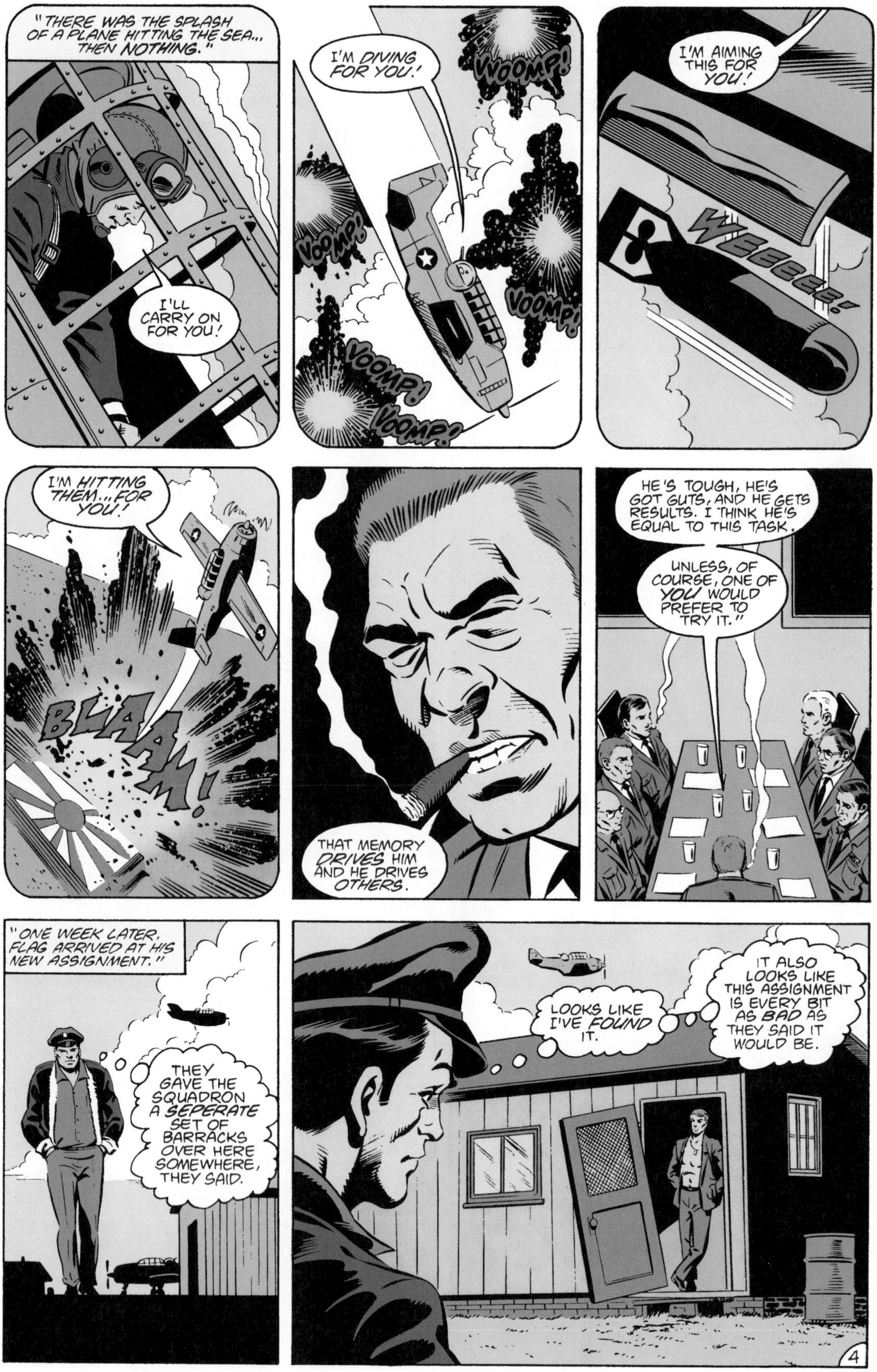
"THERE WAS THE SPLASH OF A PLANE HITTING THE SEA... THEN NOTHING."
I'LL CARRY ON FOR YOU!
I'M DIVING FOR YOU!
WOOMP!
VOOMP!
VOOMP!
VOOMP!
VOOMP!
I'M AIMING THIS FOR YOU!
WEEEEE!
I'M HITTING THEM... FOR YOU!
BLAAM!
THAT MEMORY DRIVES HIM AND HE DRIVES OTHERS.
HE'S TOUGH, HE'S GOT GUTS, AND HE GETS RESULTS. I THINK HE'S EQUAL TO THIS TASK.
UNLESS, OF COURSE, ONE OF YOU WOULD PREFER TO TRY IT."
"ONE WEEK LATER, FLAG ARRIVED AT HIS NEW ASSIGNMENT."
THEY GAVE THE SQUADRON A SEPERATE SET OF BARRACKS OVER HERE SOMEWHERE, THEY SAID.
LOOKS LIKE I'VE FOUND IT.
IT ALSO LOOKS LIKE THIS ASSIGNMENT IS EVERY BIT AS BAD AS THEY SAID IT WOULD BE.
4

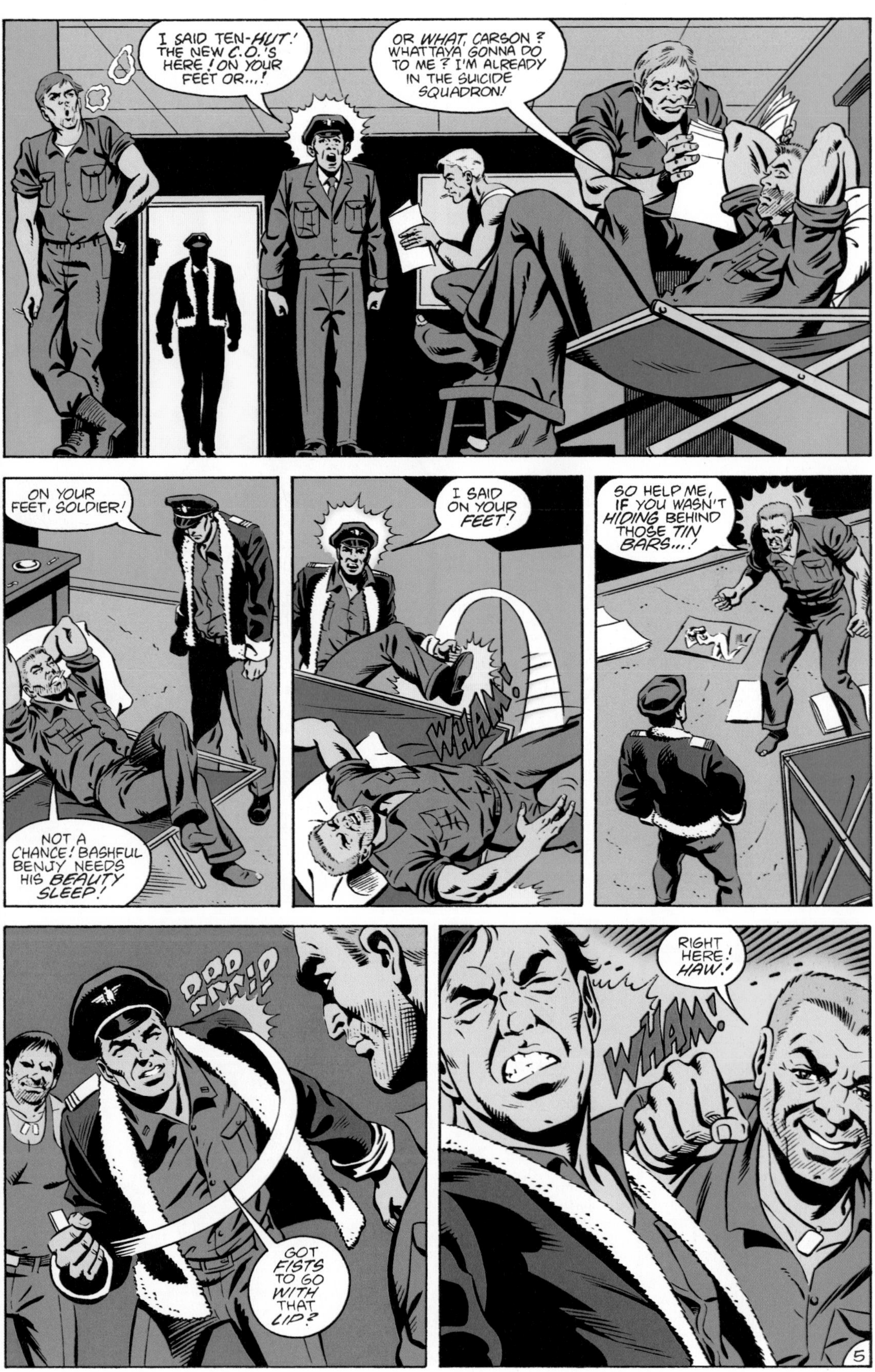
I SAID TEN-HUT! THE NEW C.O.'S HERE! ON YOUR FEET OR...!
OR WHAT, CARSON? WHATTAYA GONNA DO TO ME? I'M ALREADY IN THE SUICIDE SQUADRON!
ON YOUR FEET, SOLDIER!
NOT A CHANCE! BASHFUL BENJY NEEDS HIS BEAUTY SLEEP!
I SAID ON YOUR FEET!
WHAM!
SO HELP ME, IF YOU WASN'T HIDING BEHIND THOSE TIN BARS...!
GOT FISTS TO GO WITH THAT LIP?
RIGHT HERE! HAW!
WHAM!
5

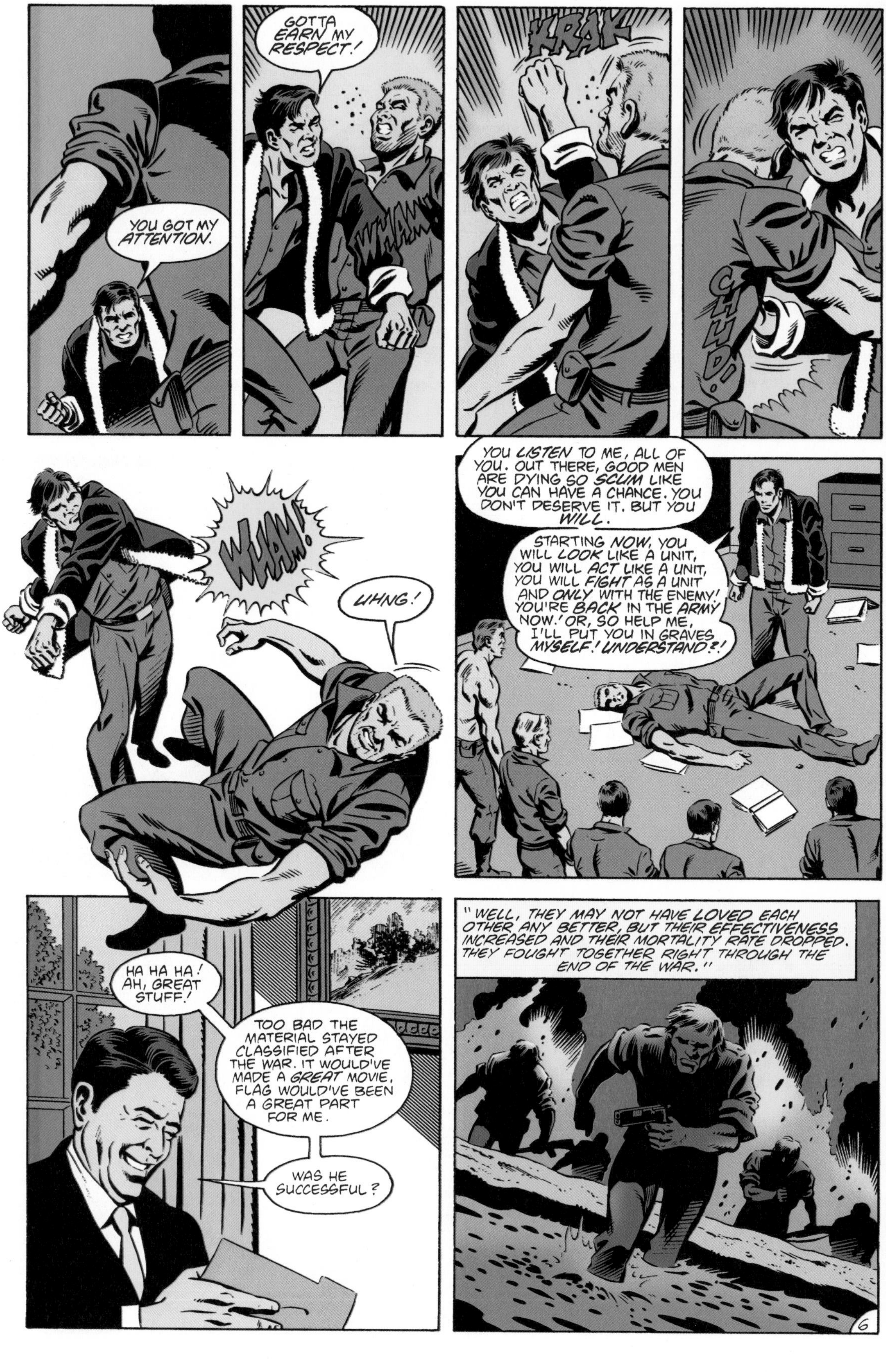
YOU GOT MY ATTENTION.
GOTTA EARN MY RESPECT!
WHAM
KRAK
CHUD!
WHAM!
UHNG!
YOU LISTEN TO ME, ALL OF YOU. OUT THERE, GOOD MEN ARE DYING SO SCUM LIKE YOU CAN HAVE A CHANCE. YOU DON'T DESERVE IT. BUT YOU WILL.
STARTING NOW, YOU WILL LOOK LIKE A UNIT, YOU WILL ACT LIKE A UNIT, YOU WILL FIGHT AS A UNIT AND ONLY WITH THE ENEMY! YOU'RE BACK IN THE ARMY NOW! OR, SO HELP ME, I'LL PUT YOU IN GRAVES MYSELF! UNDERSTAND?!
HA HA HA! AH, GREAT STUFF!
TOO BAD THE MATERIAL STAYED CLASSIFIED AFTER THE WAR. IT WOULD'VE MADE A GREAT MOVIE. FLAG WOULD'VE BEEN A GREAT PART FOR ME.
WAS HE SUCCESSFUL?
"WELL, THEY MAY NOT HAVE LOVED EACH OTHER ANY BETTER, BUT THEIR EFFECTIVENESS INCREASED AND THEIR MORTALITY RATE DROPPED. THEY FOUGHT TOGETHER RIGHT THROUGH THE END OF THE WAR."
6

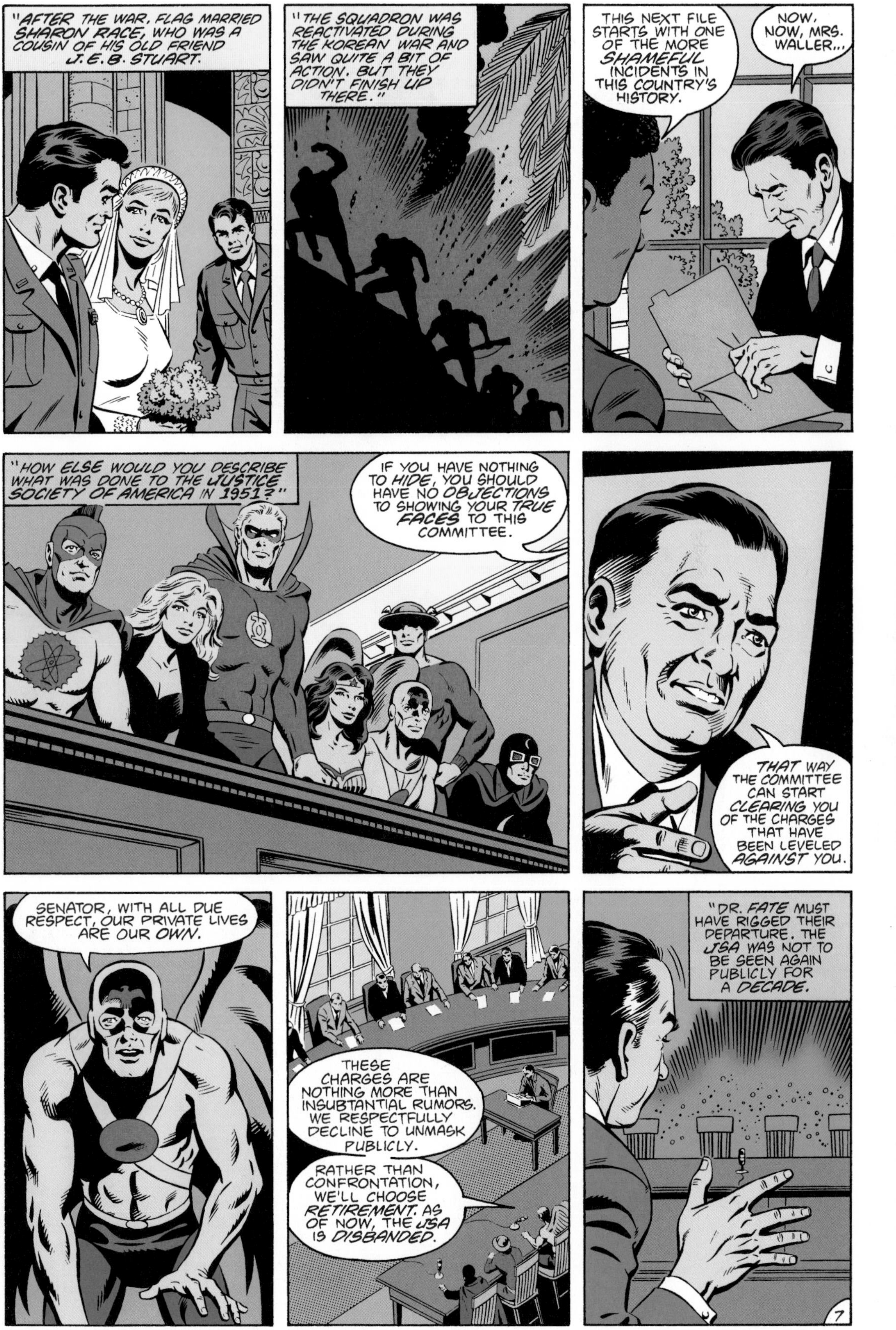
"AFTER THE WAR, FLAG MARRIED SHARON RACE, WHO WAS A COUSIN OF HIS OLD FRIEND J.E.B. STUART.
"THE SQUADRON WAS REACTIVATED DURING THE KOREAN WAR AND SAW QUITE A BIT OF ACTION. BUT THEY DIDN'T FINISH UP THERE."
THIS NEXT FILE STARTS WITH ONE OF THE MORE SHAMEFUL INCIDENTS IN THIS COUNTRY'S HISTORY.
NOW, NOW, MRS. WALLER...
"HOW ELSE WOULD YOU DESCRIBE WHAT WAS DONE TO THE JUSTICE SOCIETY OF AMERICA IN 1951?"
IF YOU HAVE NOTHING TO HIDE, YOU SHOULD HAVE NO OBJECTIONS TO SHOWING YOUR TRUE FACES TO THIS COMMITTEE.
THAT WAY THE COMMITTEE CAN START CLEARING YOU OF THE CHARGES THAT HAVE BEEN LEVELED AGAINST YOU.
SENATOR, WITH ALL DUE RESPECT, OUR PRIVATE LIVES ARE OUR OWN.
THESE CHARGES ARE NOTHING MORE THAN INSUBSTANTIAL RUMORS. WE RESPECTFULLY DECLINE TO UNMASK PUBLICLY.
RATHER THAN CONFRONTATION, WE'LL CHOOSE RETIREMENT. AS OF NOW, THE JSA IS DISBANDED.
"DR. FATE MUST HAVE RIGGED THEIR DEPARTURE. THE JSA WAS NOT TO BE SEEN AGAIN PUBLICLY FOR A DECADE.
7

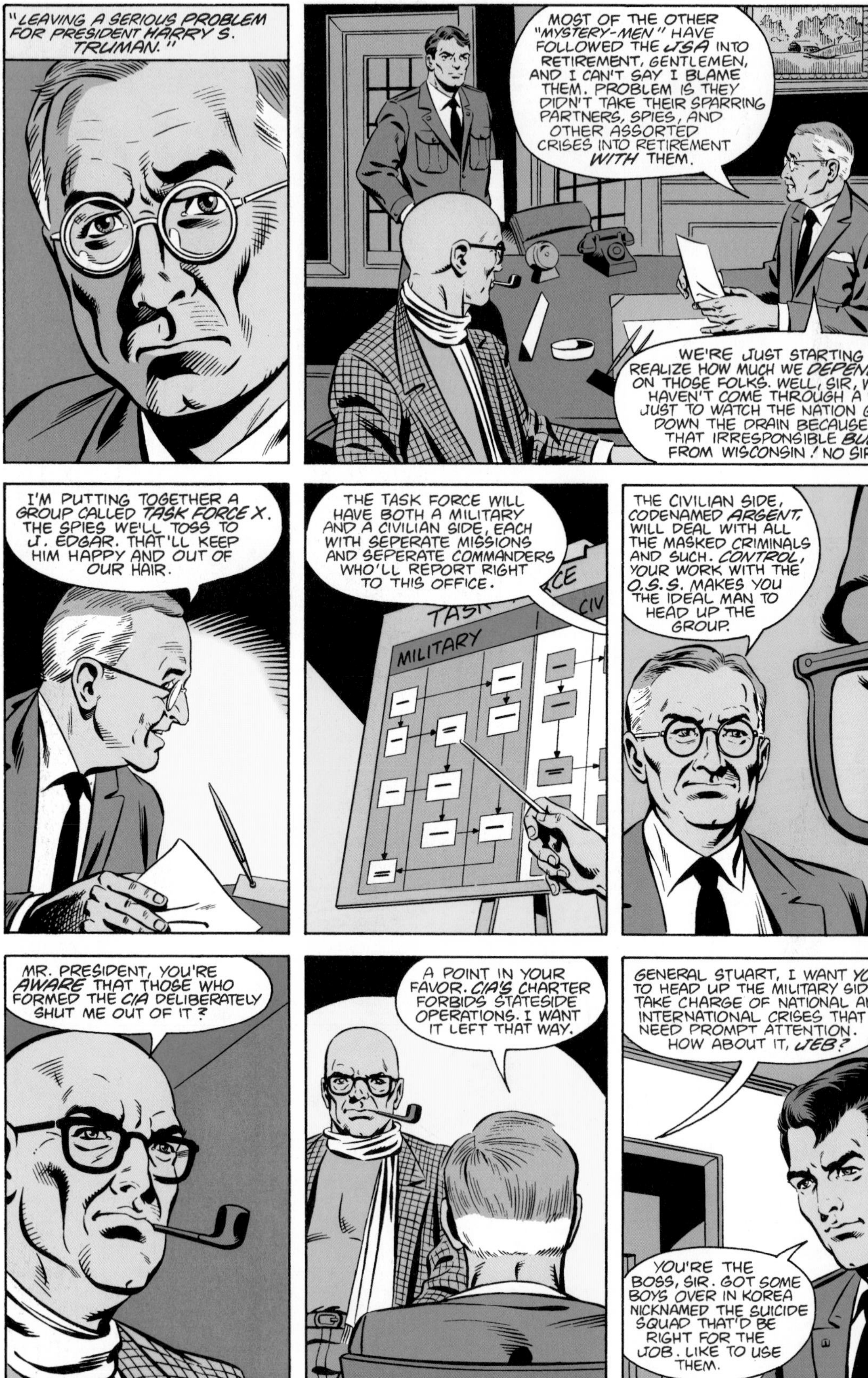
"LEAVING A SERIOUS PROBLEM FOR PRESIDENT HARRY S. TRUMAN."
MOST OF THE OTHER "MYSTERY-MEN" HAVE FOLLOWED THE JSA INTO RETIREMENT, GENTLEMEN, AND I CAN'T SAY I BLAME THEM. PROBLEM IS THEY DIDN'T TAKE THEIR SPARRING PARTNERS, SPIES, AND OTHER ASSORTED CRISES INTO RETIREMENT WITH THEM.
WE'RE JUST STARTING TO REALIZE HOW MUCH WE DEPENDED ON THOSE FOLKS. WELL, SIR, WE HAVEN'T COME THROUGH A WAR JUST TO WATCH THE NATION GO DOWN THE DRAIN BECAUSE OF THAT IRRESPONSIBLE BULLY FROM WISCONSIN! NO SIR!
I'M PUTTING TOGETHER A GROUP CALLED TASK FORCE X. THE SPIES WE'LL TOSS TO J. EDGAR. THAT'LL KEEP HIM HAPPY AND OUT OF OUR HAIR.
THE TASK FORCE WILL HAVE BOTH A MILITARY AND A CIVILIAN SIDE, EACH WITH SEPERATE MISSIONS AND SEPERATE COMMANDERS WHO'LL REPORT RIGHT TO THIS OFFICE.
MILITARY
THE CIVILIAN SIDE, CODENAMED ARGENT, WILL DEAL WITH ALL THE MASKED CRIMINALS AND SUCH. CONTROL, YOUR WORK WITH THE O.S.S. MAKES YOU THE IDEAL MAN TO HEAD UP THE GROUP.
MR. PRESIDENT, YOU'RE AWARE THAT THOSE WHO FORMED THE CIA DELIBERATELY SHUT ME OUT OF IT?
A POINT IN YOUR FAVOR. CIA'S CHARTER FORBIDS STATESIDE OPERATIONS. I WANT IT LEFT THAT WAY.
GENERAL STUART, I WANT YOU TO HEAD UP THE MILITARY SIDE. TAKE CHARGE OF NATIONAL AND INTERNATIONAL CRISES THAT NEED PROMPT ATTENTION. HOW ABOUT IT, JEB?
YOU'RE THE BOSS, SIR. GOT SOME BOYS OVER IN KOREA NICKNAMED THE SUICIDE SQUAD THAT'D BE RIGHT FOR THE JOB. LIKE TO USE THEM.
8

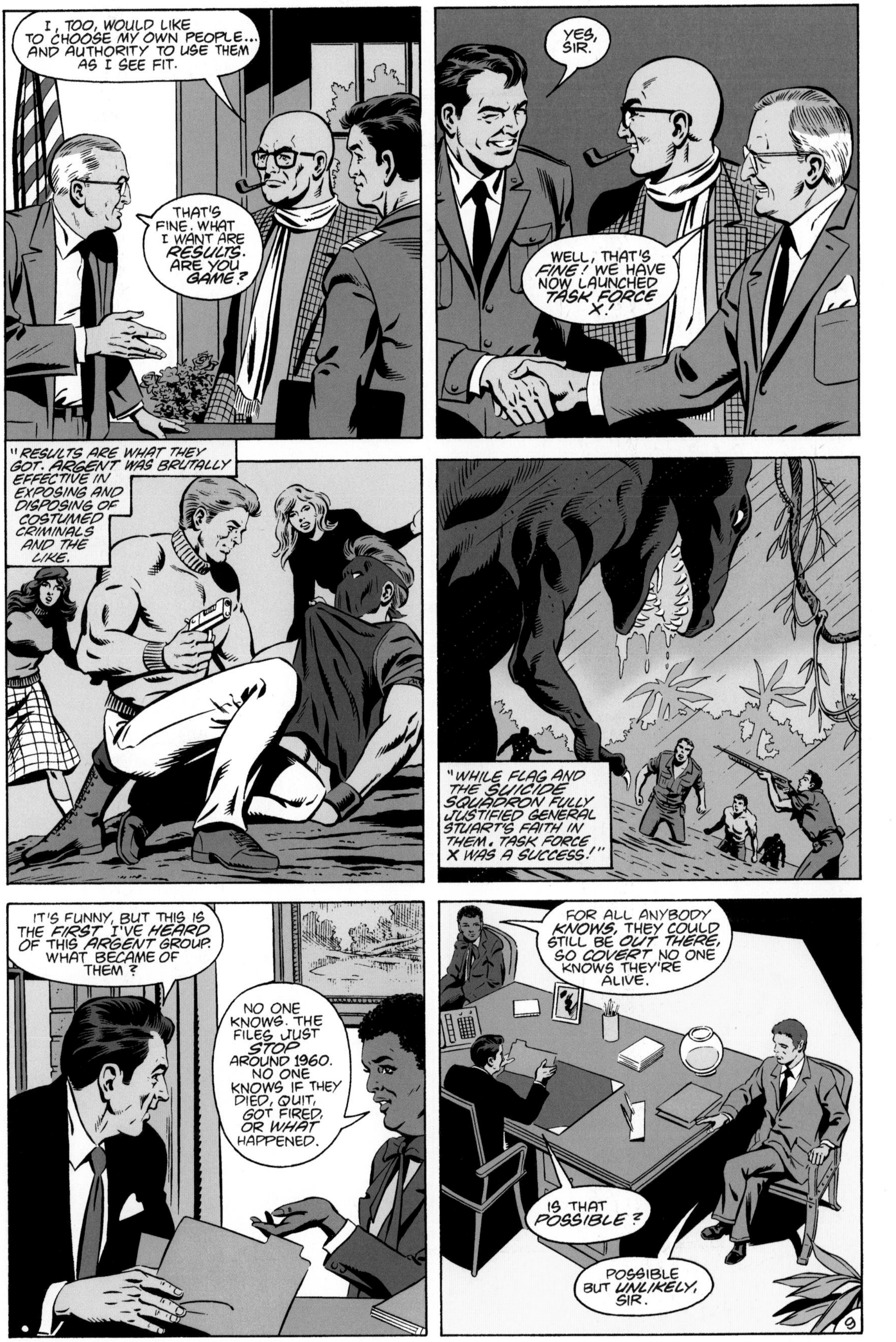
I, TOO, WOULD LIKE TO CHOOSE MY OWN PEOPLE... AND AUTHORITY TO USE THEM AS I SEE FIT.
THAT'S FINE. WHAT I WANT ARE RESULTS. ARE YOU GAME?
YES, SIR.
WELL, THAT'S FINE! WE HAVE NOW LAUNCHED TASK FORCE X!
"RESULTS ARE WHAT THEY GOT. ARGENT WAS BRUTALLY EFFECTIVE IN EXPOSING AND DISPOSING OF COSTUMED CRIMINALS AND THE LIKE.
"WHILE FLAG AND THE SUICIDE SQUADRON FULLY JUSTIFIED GENERAL STUART'S FAITH IN THEM, TASK FORCE X WAS A SUCCESS!"
IT'S FUNNY, BUT THIS IS THE FIRST I'VE HEARD OF THIS ARGENT GROUP. WHAT BECAME OF THEM?
NO ONE KNOWS. THE FILES JUST STOP AROUND 1960. NO ONE KNOWS IF THEY DIED, QUIT, GOT FIRED, OR WHAT HAPPENED.
FOR ALL ANYBODY KNOWS, THEY COULD STILL BE OUT THERE, SO COVERT NO ONE KNOWS THEY'RE ALIVE.
IS THAT POSSIBLE?
POSSIBLE BUT UNLIKELY, SIR.
9

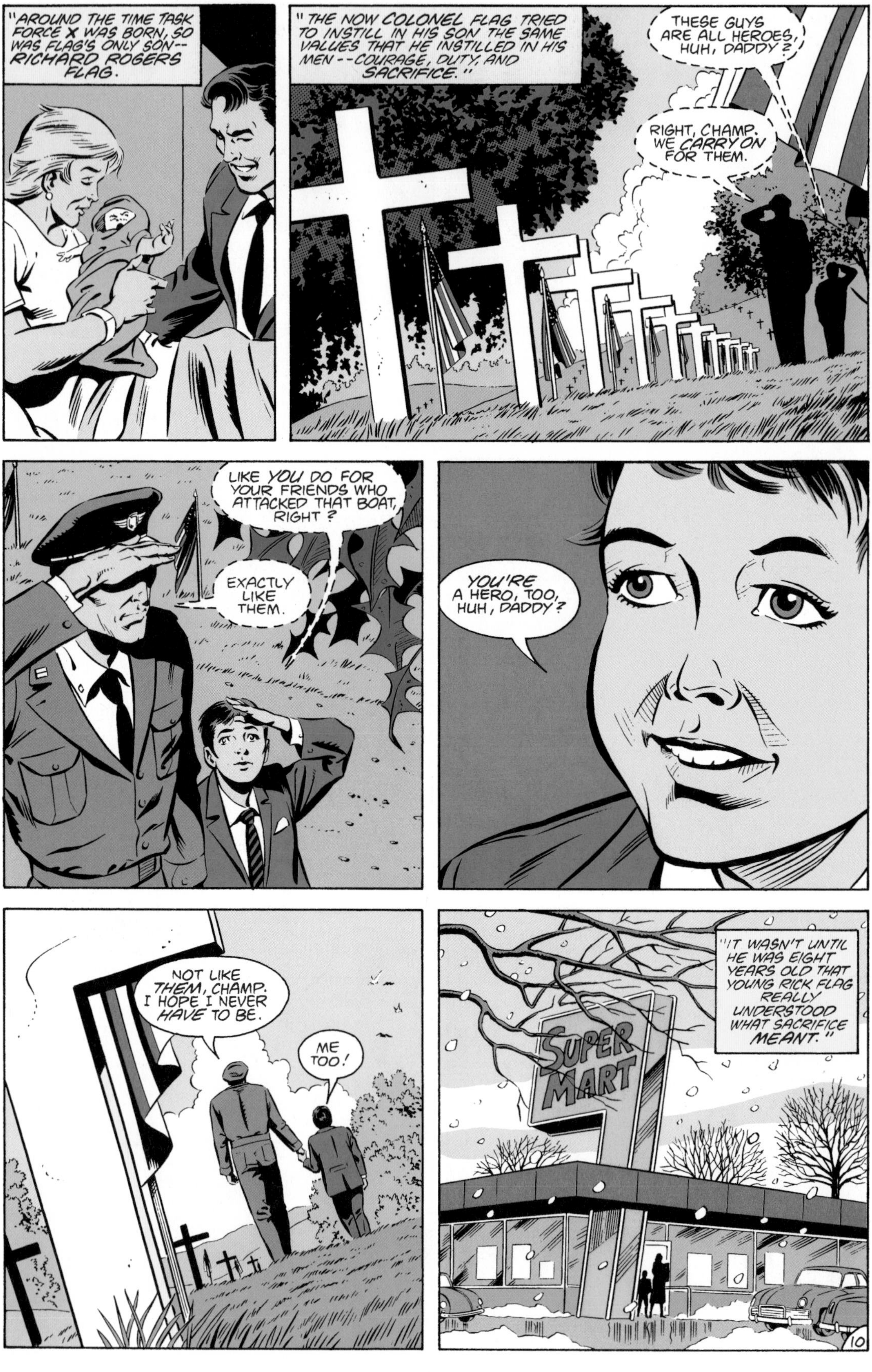
"AROUND THE TIME TASK FORCE X WAS BORN, SO WAS FLAG'S ONLY SON--RICHARD ROGERS FLAG.
"THE NOW COLONEL FLAG TRIED TO INSTILL IN HIS SON THE SAME VALUES THAT HE INSTILLED IN HIS MEN--COURAGE, DUTY, AND SACRIFICE."
THESE GUYS ARE ALL HEROES, HUH, DADDY?
RIGHT, CHAMP. WE CARRY ON FOR THEM.
LIKE YOU DO FOR YOUR FRIENDS WHO ATTACKED THAT BOAT, RIGHT?
EXACTLY LIKE THEM.
YOU'RE A HERO, TOO, HUH, DADDY?
NOT LIKE THEM, CHAMP. I HOPE I NEVER HAVE TO BE.
ME TOO!
"IT WASN'T UNTIL HE WAS EIGHT YEARS OLD THAT YOUNG RICK FLAG REALLY UNDERSTOOD WHAT SACRIFICE MEANT."
SUPER MART
10

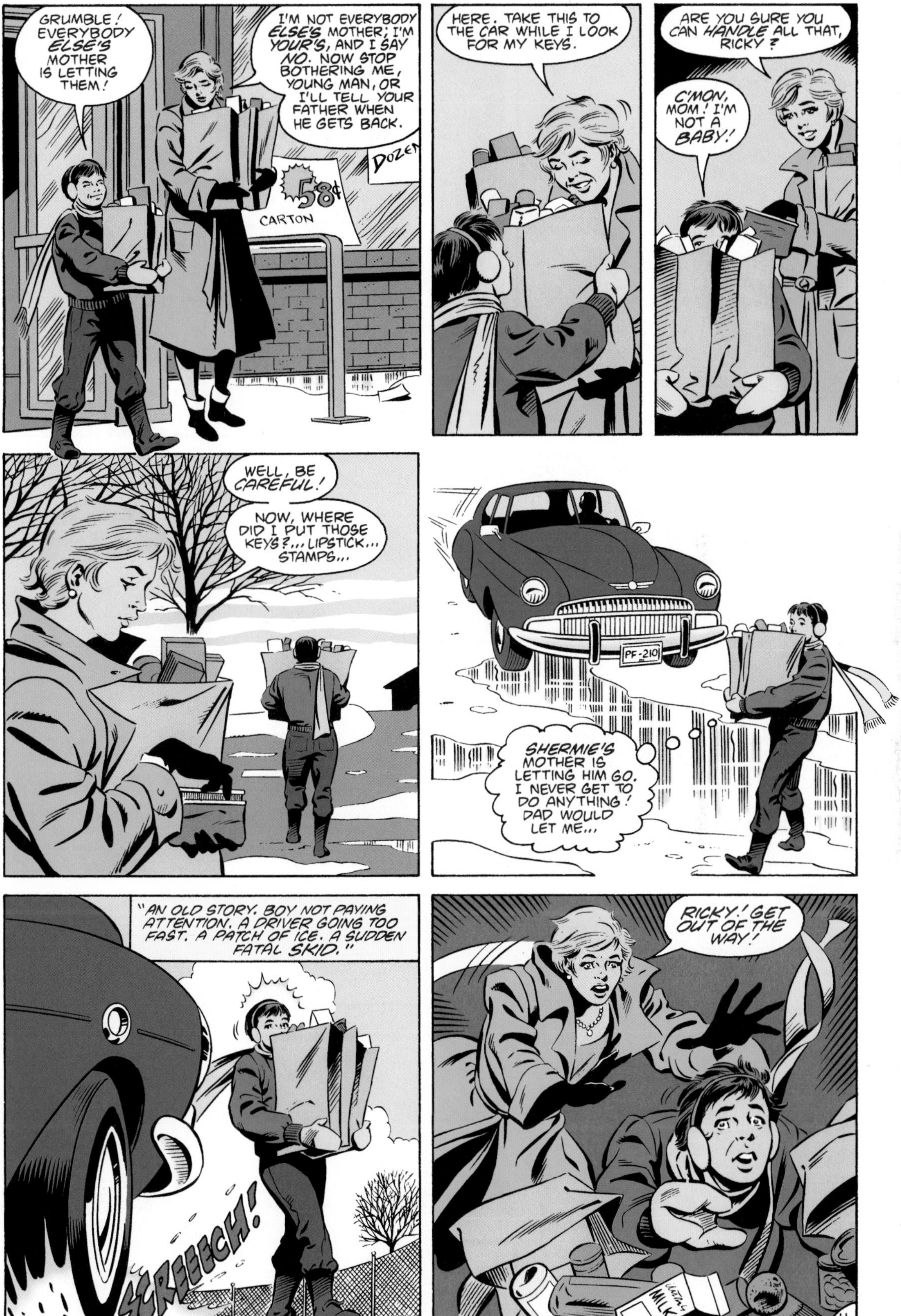
GRUMBLE! EVERYBODY ELSE'S MOTHER IS LETTING THEM!
I'M NOT EVERYBODY ELSE'S MOTHER; I'M YOUR'S, AND I SAY NO. NOW STOP BOTHERING ME, YOUNG MAN, OR I'LL TELL YOUR FATHER WHEN HE GETS BACK.
DOZEN
58¢
CARTON
HERE. TAKE THIS TO THE CAR WHILE I LOOK FOR MY KEYS.
ARE YOU SURE YOU CAN HANDLE ALL THAT, RICKY?
C'MON, MOM! I'M NOT A BABY!
WELL, BE CAREFUL!
NOW, WHERE DID I PUT THOSE KEYS?... LIPSTICK... STAMPS...
PF-210
SHERMIE'S MOTHER IS LETTING HIM GO. I NEVER GET TO DO ANYTHING! DAD WOULD LET ME...
"AN OLD STORY. BOY NOT PAYING ATTENTION. A DRIVER GOING TOO FAST. A PATCH OF ICE. A SUDDEN FATAL SKID."
SCREEECH!
RICKY! GET OUT OF THE WAY!
MILK
11

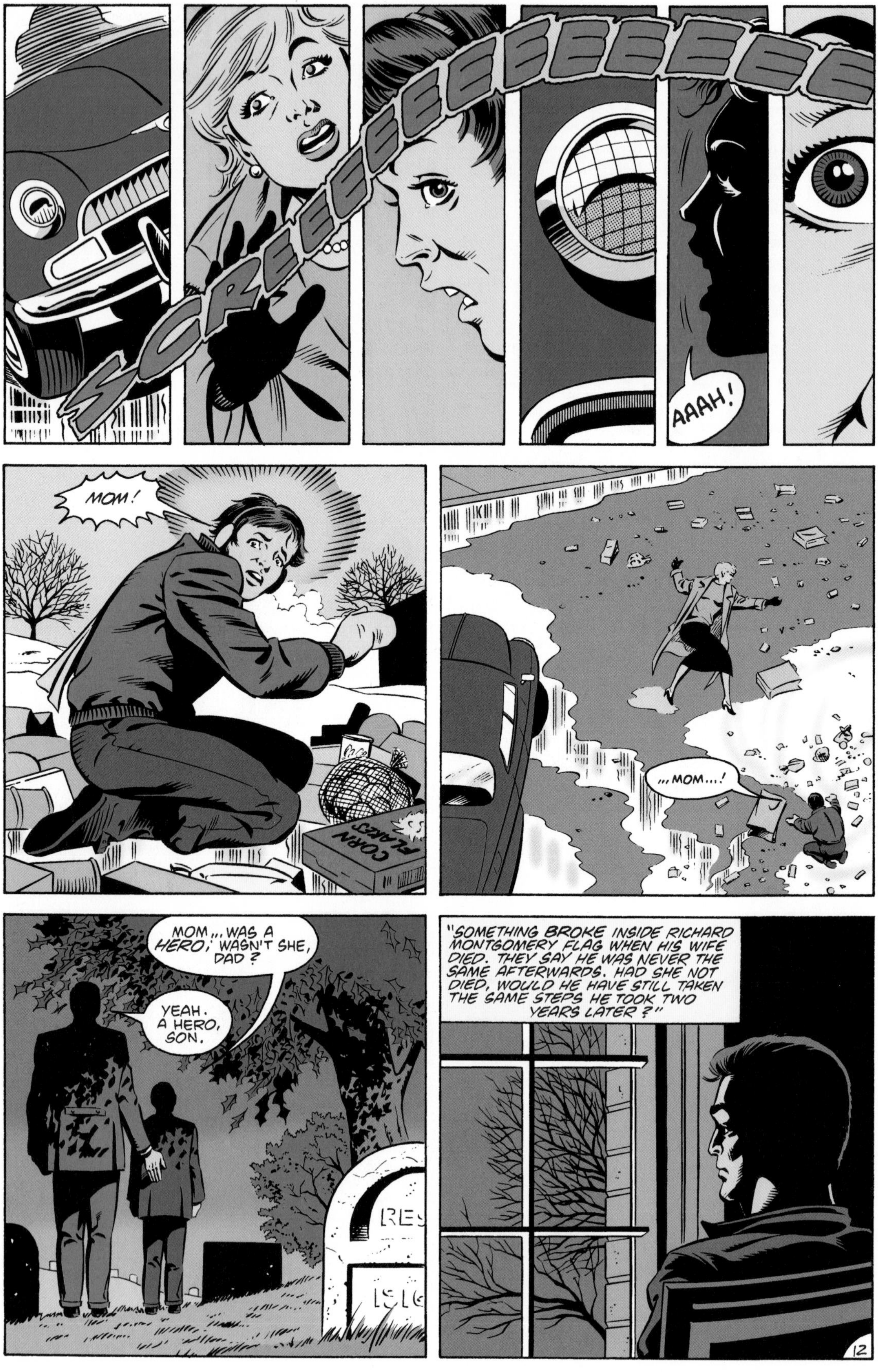
SCREEEEEEEEEEEEEEEE
AAAH!
MOM!
CORN FLAKES
...MOM...!
MOM... WAS A HERO, WASN'T SHE, DAD?
YEAH. A HERO, SON.
"SOMETHING BROKE INSIDE RICHARD MONTGOMERY FLAG WHEN HIS WIFE DIED. THEY SAY HE WAS NEVER THE SAME AFTERWARDS. HAD SHE NOT DIED, WOULD HE HAVE STILL TAKEN THE SAME STEPS HE TOOK TWO YEARS LATER?"
12

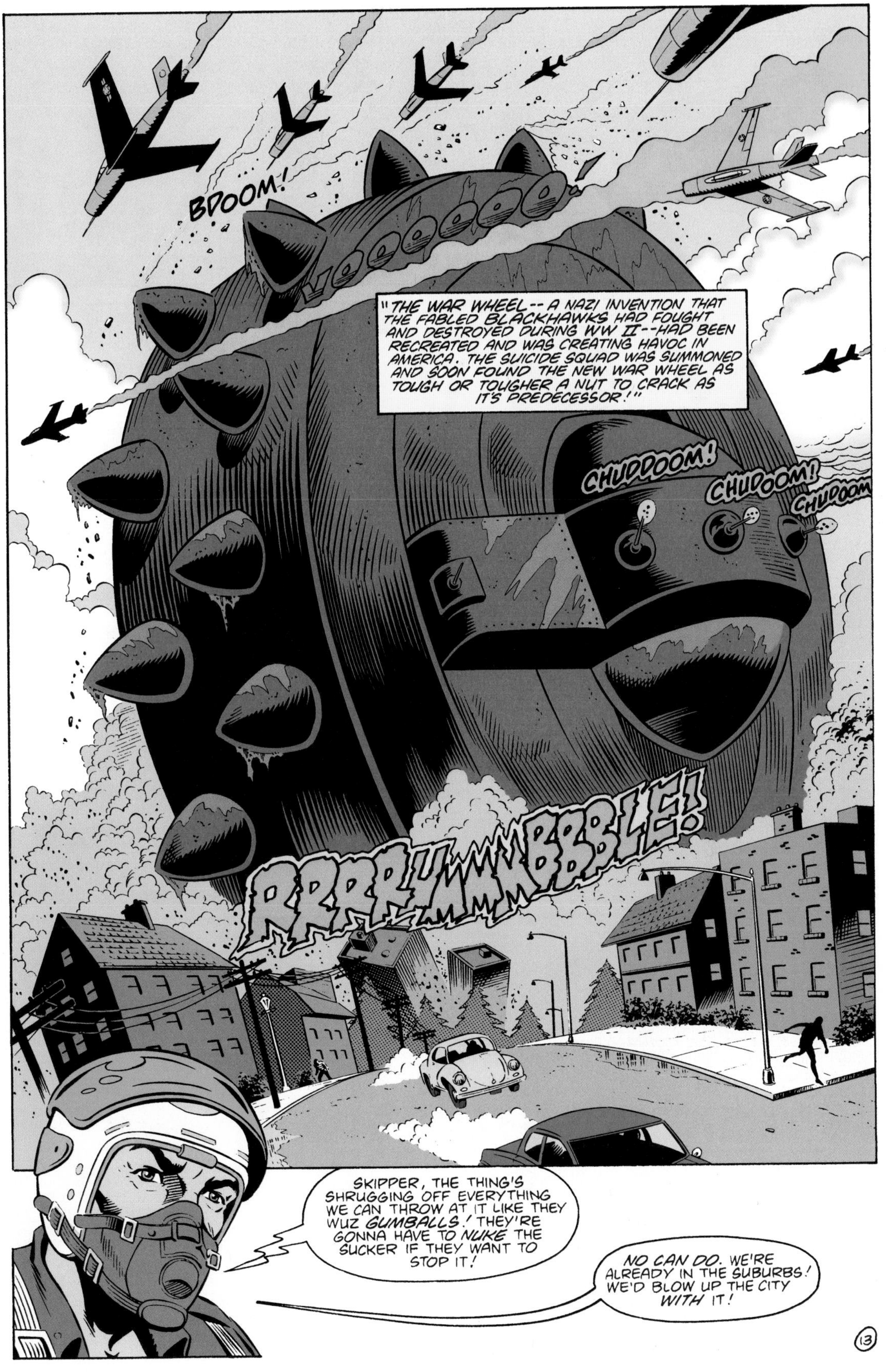
BDOOM!
VOOOOOOOO
"THE WAR WHEEL-- A NAZI INVENTION THAT THE FABLED BLACKHAWKS HAD FOUGHT AND DESTROYED DURING WW II--HAD BEEN RECREATED AND WAS CREATING HAVOC IN AMERICA. THE SUICIDE SQUAD WAS SUMMONED AND SOON FOUND THE NEW WAR WHEEL AS TOUGH OR TOUGHER A NUT TO CRACK AS IT'S PREDECESSOR!"
CHUDDOOM!
CHUDOOM!
RRRRUMMMBBBLE!
SKIPPER, THE THING'S SHRUGGING OFF EVERYTHING WE CAN THROW AT IT LIKE THEY WUZ GUMBALLS! THEY'RE GONNA HAVE TO NUKE THE SUCKER IF THEY WANT TO STOP IT!
NO CAN DO. WE'RE ALREADY IN THE SUBURBS! WE'D BLOW UP THE CITY WITH IT!
13

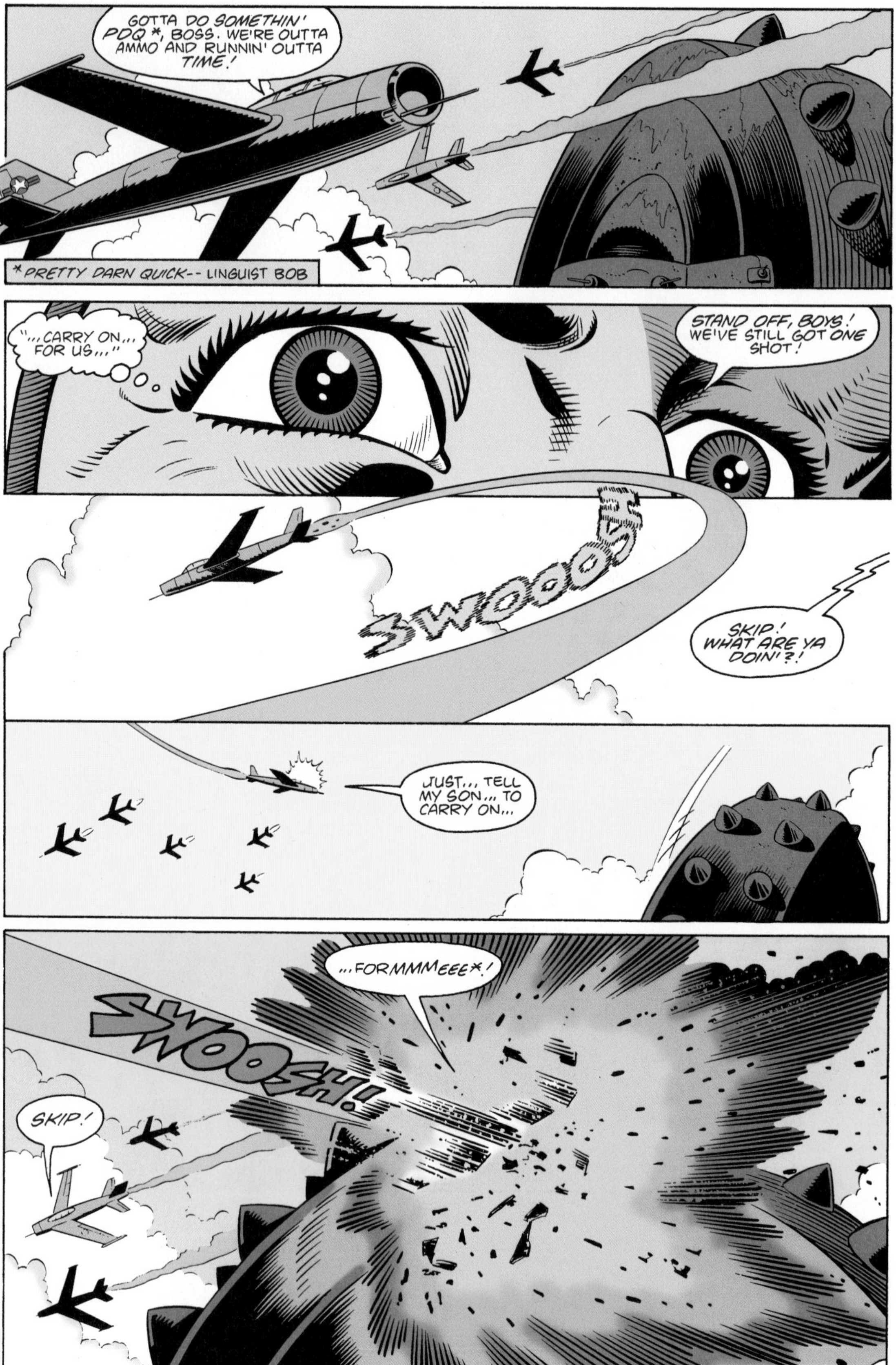
GOTTA DO SOMETHIN' PDQ *, BOSS. WE'RE OUTTA AMMO AND RUNNIN' OUTTA TIME!
*PRETTY DARN QUICK-- LINGUIST BOB
"...CARRY ON... FOR US..."
STAND OFF, BOYS! WE'VE STILL GOT ONE SHOT!
SWOOOSH
SKIP! WHAT ARE YA DOIN'?!
JUST... TELL MY SON... TO CARRY ON...
...FORMMMEEE*!
SWOOSH!
SKIP!
14

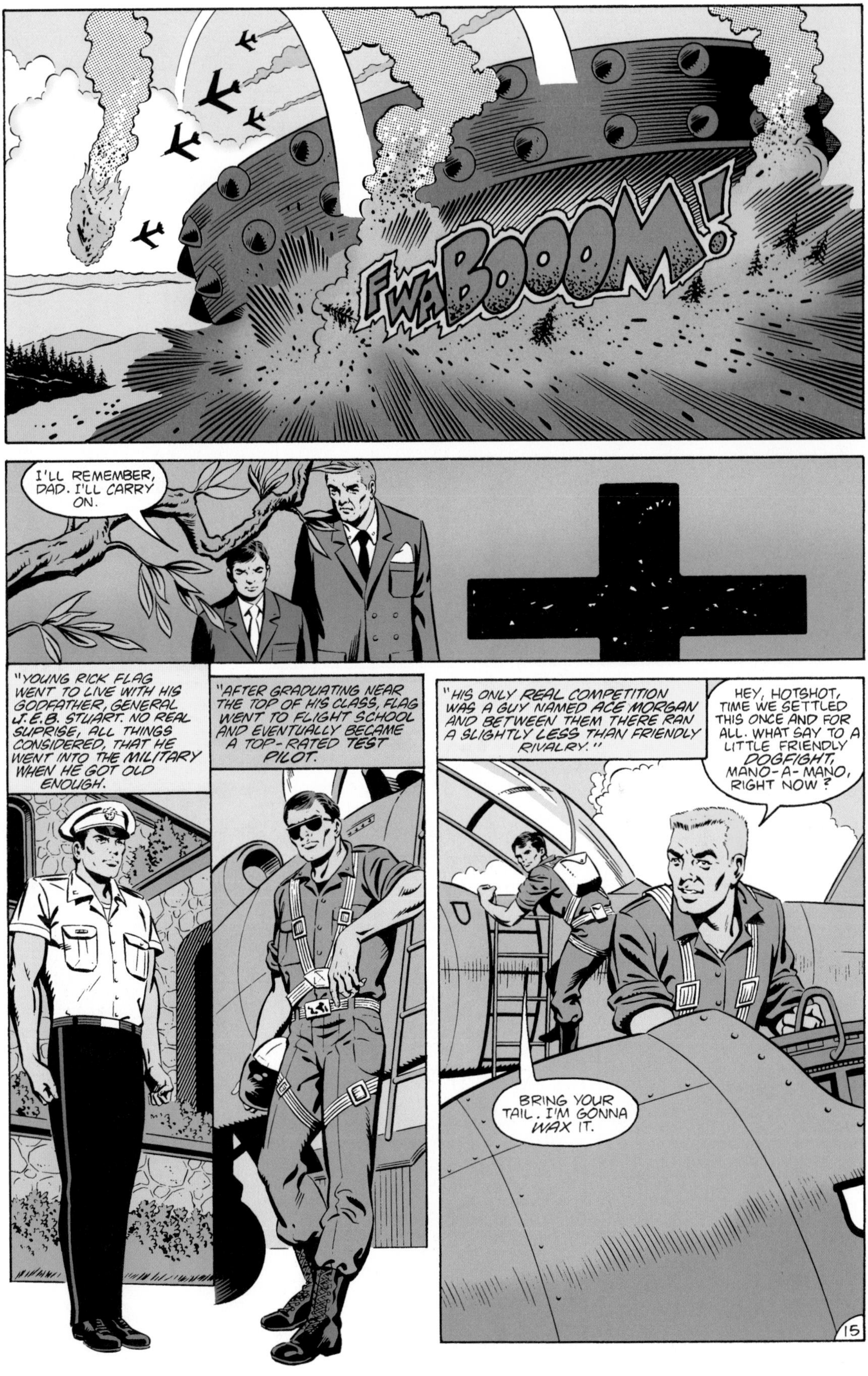
FWABOOOM!
I'LL REMEMBER, DAD. I'LL CARRY ON.
"YOUNG RICK FLAG WENT TO LIVE WITH HIS GODFATHER, GENERAL J.E.B. STUART. NO REAL SUPRISE, ALL THINGS CONSIDERED, THAT HE WENT INTO THE MILITARY WHEN HE GOT OLD ENOUGH.
"AFTER GRADUATING NEAR THE TOP OF HIS CLASS, FLAG WENT TO FLIGHT SCHOOL AND EVENTUALLY BECAME A TOP-RATED TEST PILOT.
"HIS ONLY REAL COMPETITION WAS A GUY NAMED ACE MORGAN AND BETWEEN THEM THERE RAN A SLIGHTLY LESS THAN FRIENDLY RIVALRY."
HEY, HOTSHOT, TIME WE SETTLED THIS ONCE AND FOR ALL. WHAT SAY TO A LITTLE FRIENDLY DOGFIGHT, MANO-A-MANO, RIGHT NOW?
BRING YOUR TAIL. I'M GONNA WAX IT.
15

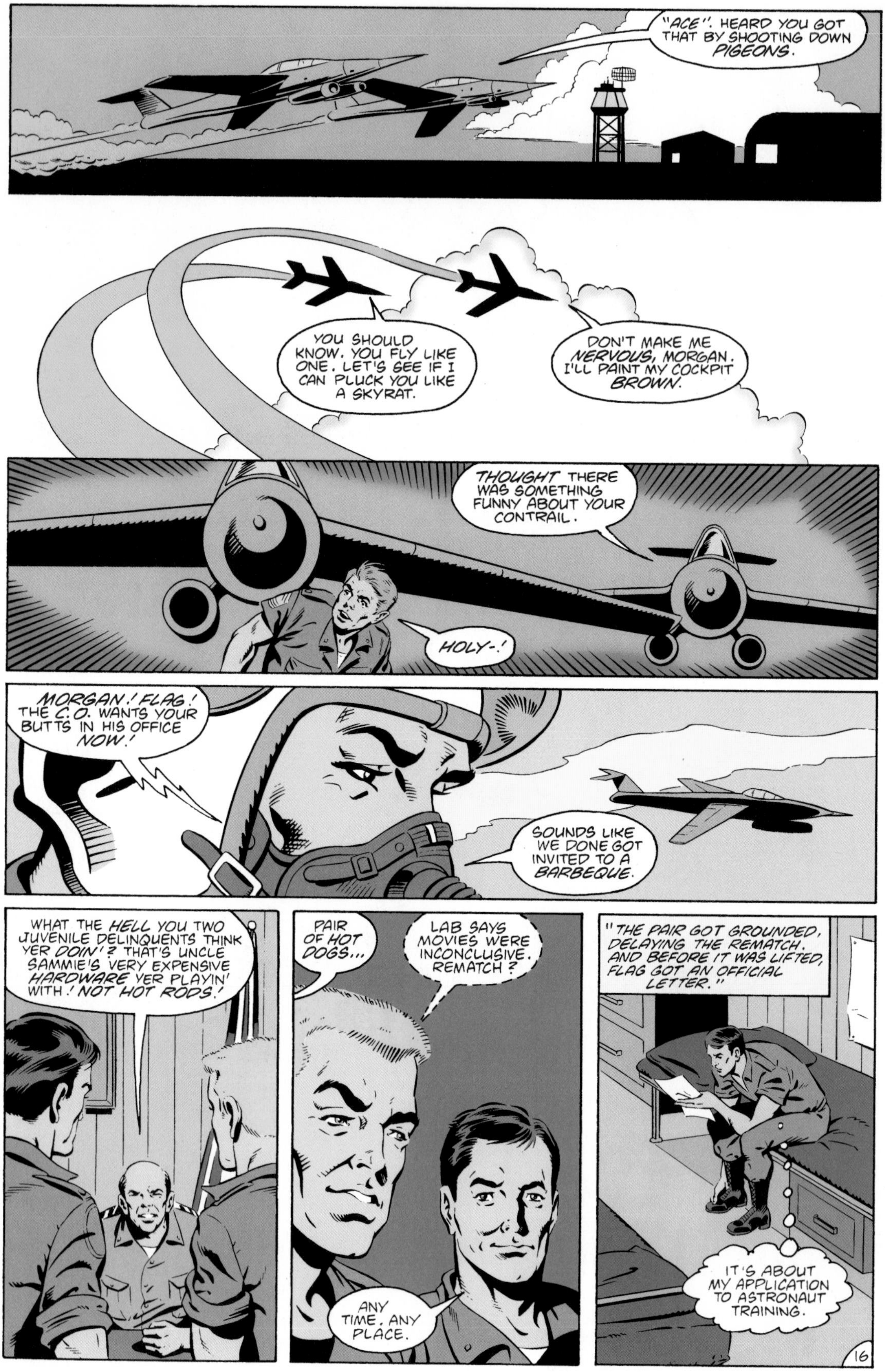
"ACE". HEARD YOU GOT THAT BY SHOOTING DOWN PIGEONS.
YOU SHOULD KNOW. YOU FLY LIKE ONE. LET'S SEE IF I CAN PLUCK YOU LIKE A SKYRAT.
DON'T MAKE ME NERVOUS, MORGAN. I'LL PAINT MY COCKPIT BROWN.
THOUGHT THERE WAS SOMETHING FUNNY ABOUT YOUR CONTRAIL.
HOLY-!
MORGAN! FLAG! THE C.O. WANTS YOUR BUTTS IN HIS OFFICE NOW!
SOUNDS LIKE WE DONE GOT INVITED TO A BARBEQUE.
WHAT THE HELL YOU TWO JUVENILE DELINQUENTS THINK YER DOIN'? THAT'S UNCLE SAMMIE'S VERY EXPENSIVE HARDWARE YER PLAYIN' WITH! NOT HOT RODS!
PAIR OF HOT DOGS...
LAB SAYS MOVIES WERE INCONCLUSIVE. REMATCH?
ANY TIME. ANY PLACE.
"THE PAIR GOT GROUNDED, DELAYING THE REMATCH. AND BEFORE IT WAS LIFTED, FLAG GOT AN OFFICIAL LETTER."
IT'S ABOUT MY APPLICATION TO ASTRONAUT TRAINING.
16

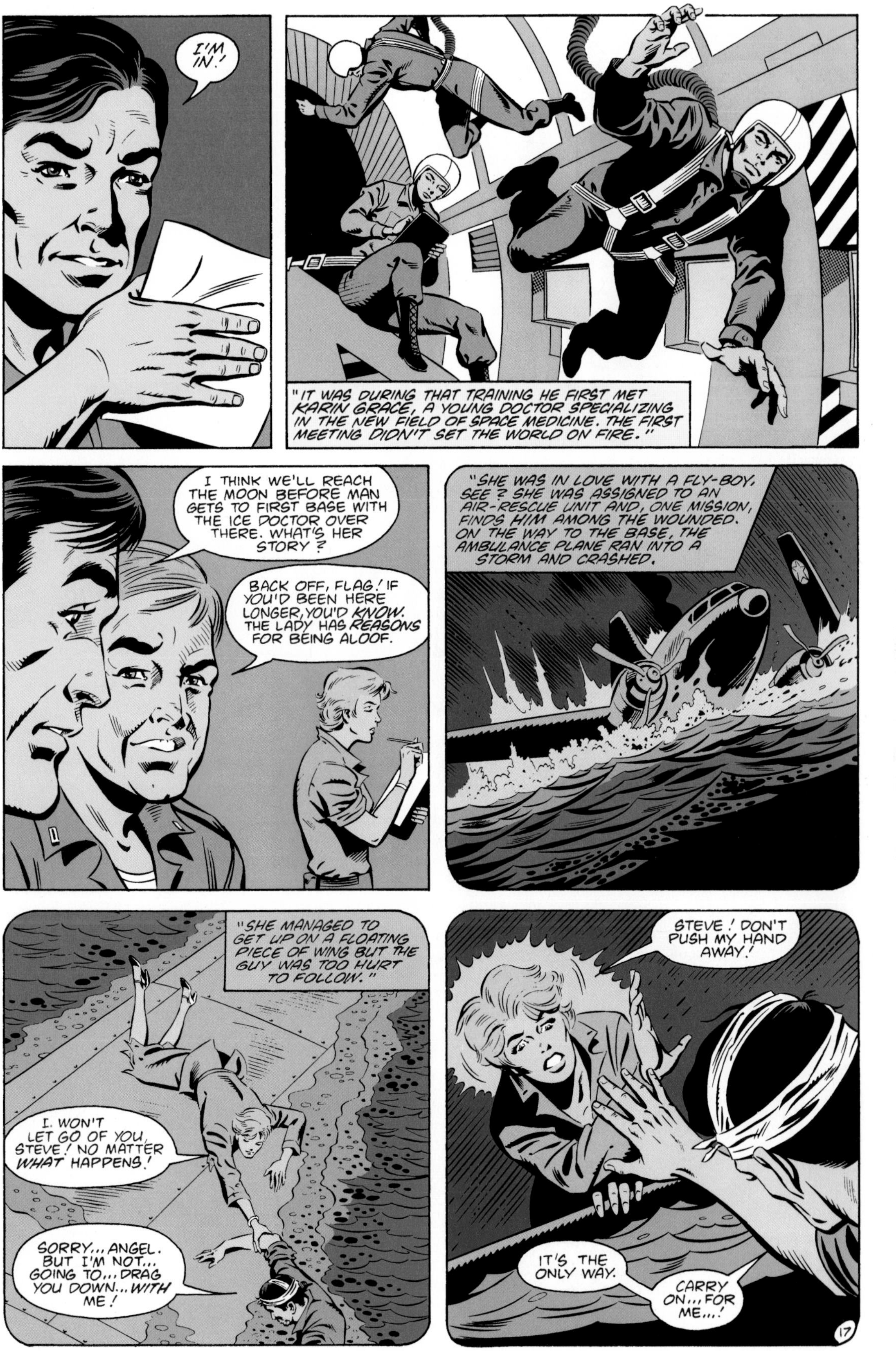

I'M IN!
"IT WAS DURING THAT TRAINING HE FIRST MET KARIN GRACE, A YOUNG DOCTOR SPECIALIZING IN THE NEW FIELD OF SPACE MEDICINE. THE FIRST MEETING DIDN'T SET THE WORLD ON FIRE."
I THINK WE'LL REACH THE MOON BEFORE MAN GETS TO FIRST BASE WITH THE ICE DOCTOR OVER THERE. WHAT'S HER STORY?
BACK OFF, FLAG! IF YOU'D BEEN HERE LONGER, YOU'D KNOW. THE LADY HAS REASONS FOR BEING ALOOF.
"SHE WAS IN LOVE WITH A FLY-BOY, SEE? SHE WAS ASSIGNED TO AN AIR-RESCUE UNIT AND, ONE MISSION, FINDS HIM AMONG THE WOUNDED. ON THE WAY TO THE BASE, THE AMBULANCE PLANE RAN INTO A STORM AND CRASHED.
"SHE MANAGED TO GET UP ON A FLOATING PIECE OF WING BUT THE GUY WAS TOO HURT TO FOLLOW."
I. WON'T LET GO OF YOU, STEVE! NO MATTER WHAT HAPPENS!
SORRY... ANGEL. BUT I'M NOT... GOING TO... DRAG YOU DOWN... WITH ME!
STEVE! DON'T PUSH MY HAND AWAY!
IT'S THE ONLY WAY.
CARRY ON... FOR ME...!
17

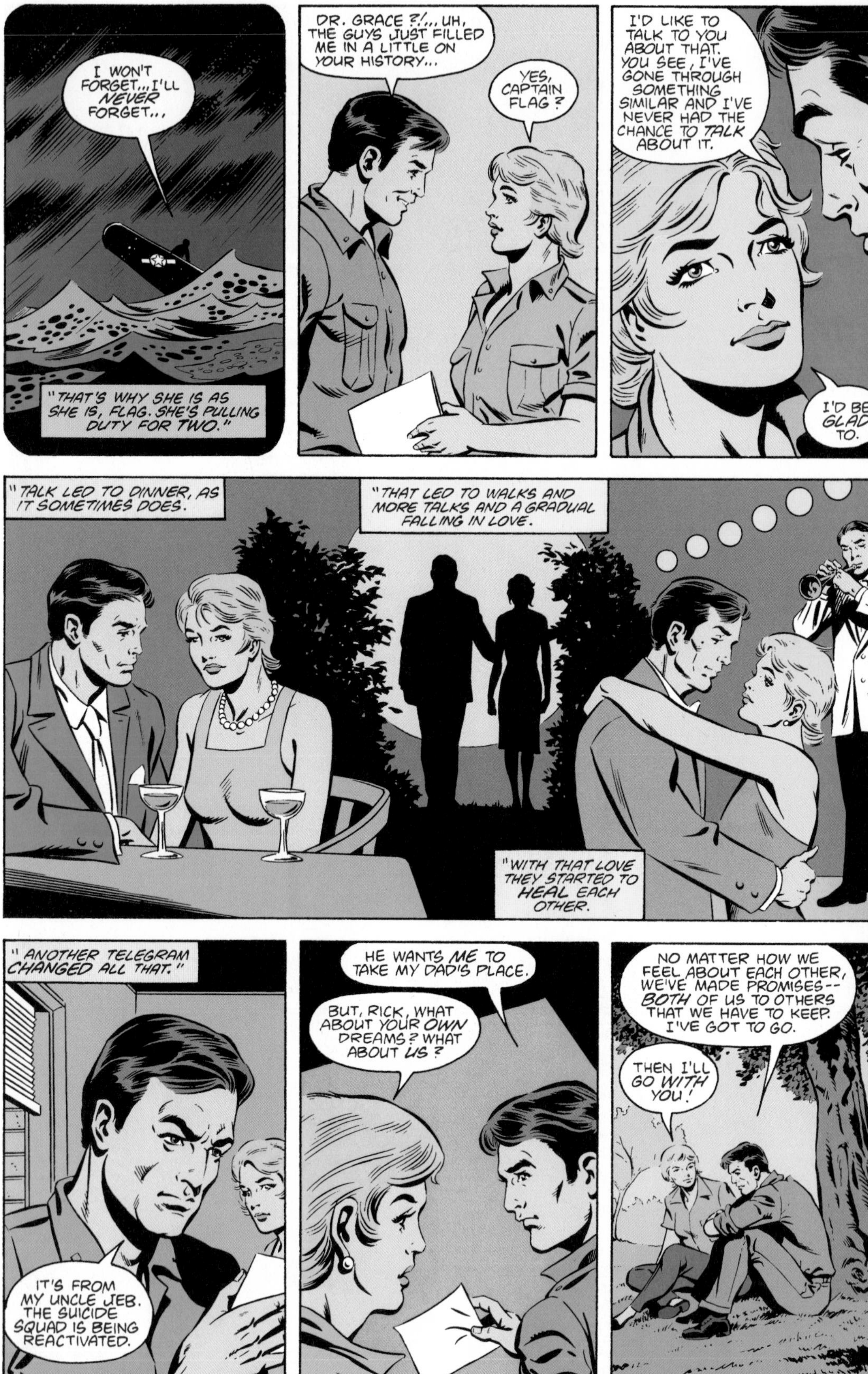

I WON'T FORGET... I'LL NEVER FORGET...
"THAT'S WHY SHE IS AS SHE IS, FLAG. SHE'S PULLING DUTY FOR TWO."
DR. GRACE ?!... UH, THE GUYS JUST FILLED ME IN A LITTLE ON YOUR HISTORY...
YES, CAPTAIN FLAG ?
I'D LIKE TO TALK TO YOU ABOUT THAT. YOU SEE, I'VE GONE THROUGH SOMETHING SIMILAR AND I'VE NEVER HAD THE CHANCE TO TALK ABOUT IT.
I'D BE GLAD TO.
"TALK LED TO DINNER, AS IT SOMETIMES DOES.
"THAT LED TO WALKS AND MORE TALKS AND A GRADUAL FALLING IN LOVE.
"WITH THAT LOVE THEY STARTED TO HEAL EACH OTHER.
"ANOTHER TELEGRAM CHANGED ALL THAT."
IT'S FROM MY UNCLE JEB. THE SUICIDE SQUAD IS BEING REACTIVATED.
HE WANTS ME TO TAKE MY DAD'S PLACE.
BUT, RICK, WHAT ABOUT YOUR OWN DREAMS? WHAT ABOUT US ?
NO MATTER HOW WE FEEL ABOUT EACH OTHER, WE'VE MADE PROMISES-- BOTH OF US TO OTHERS THAT WE HAVE TO KEEP. I'VE GOT TO GO.
THEN I'LL GO WITH YOU!
18

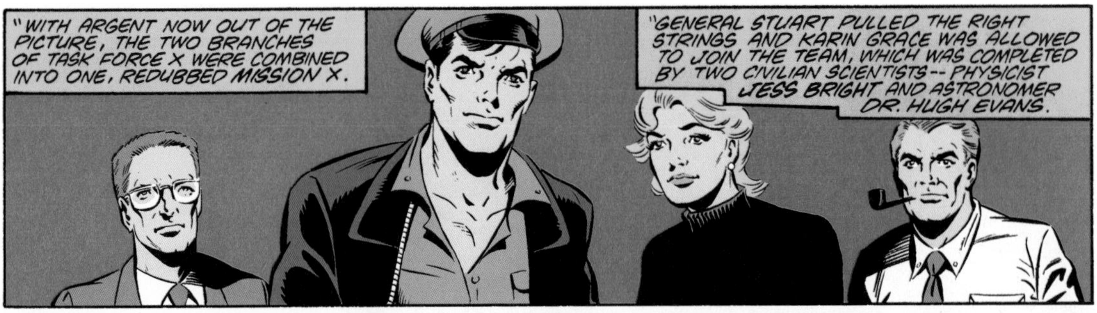
"WITH ARGENT NOW OUT OF THE PICTURE, THE TWO BRANCHES OF TASK FORCE X WERE COMBINED INTO ONE, REDUBBED MISSION X.
"GENERAL STUART PULLED THE RIGHT STRINGS AND KARIN GRACE WAS ALLOWED TO JOIN THE TEAM, WHICH WAS COMPLETED BY TWO CIVILIAN SCIENTISTS-- PHYSICIST JESS BRIGHT AND ASTRONOMER DR. HUGH EVANS.

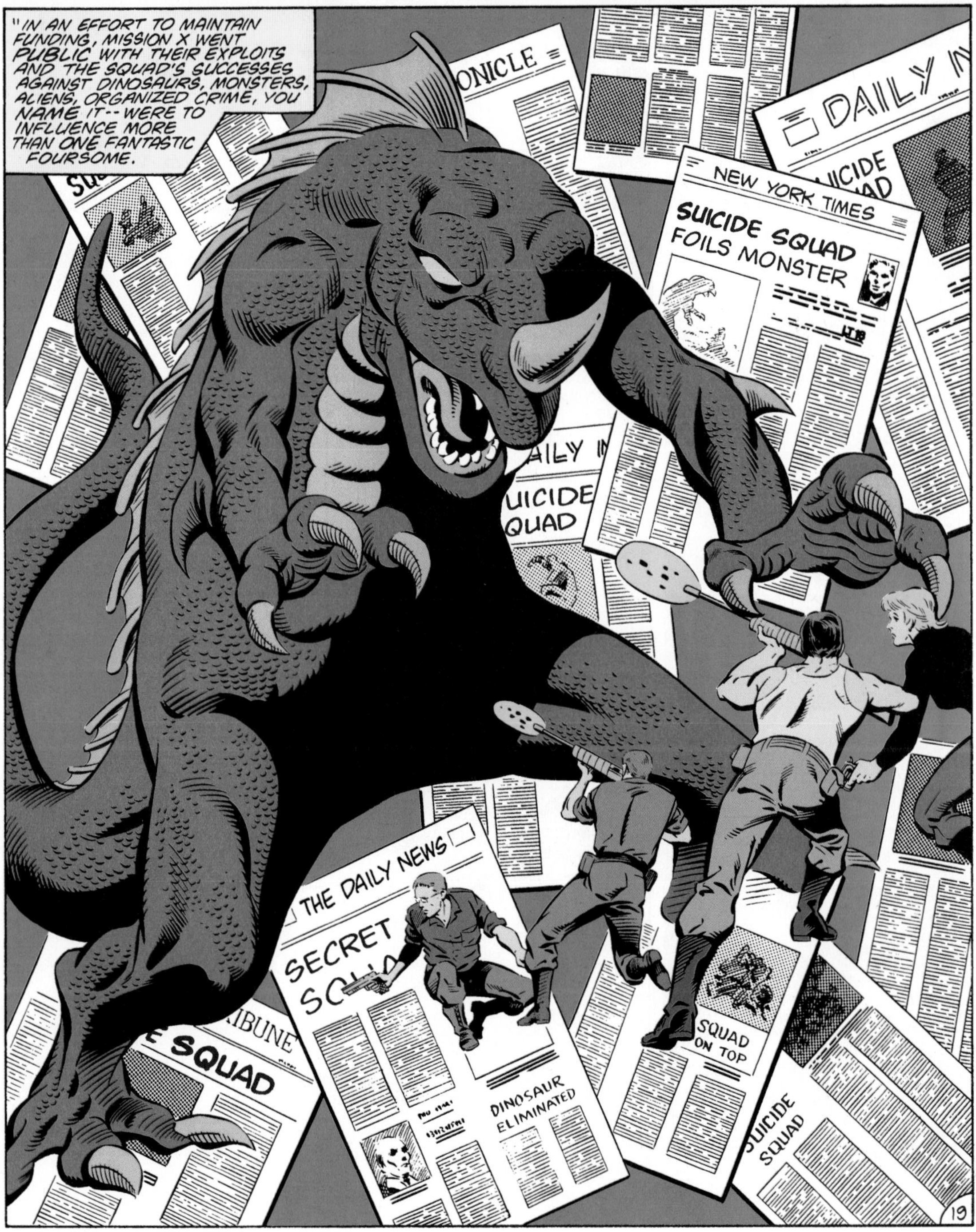
"IN AN EFFORT TO MAINTAIN FUNDING, MISSION X WENT PUBLIC WITH THEIR EXPLOITS AND THE SQUAD'S SUCCESSES AGAINST DINOSAURS, MONSTERS, ALIENS, ORGANIZED CRIME, YOU NAME IT--WERE TO INFLUENCE MORE THAN ONE FANTASTIC FOURSOME.
NEW YORK TIMES
SUICIDE SQUAD FOILS MONSTER
THE DAILY NEWS
SECRET
DINOSAUR ELIMINATED
SQUAD ON TOP
SQUAD
19

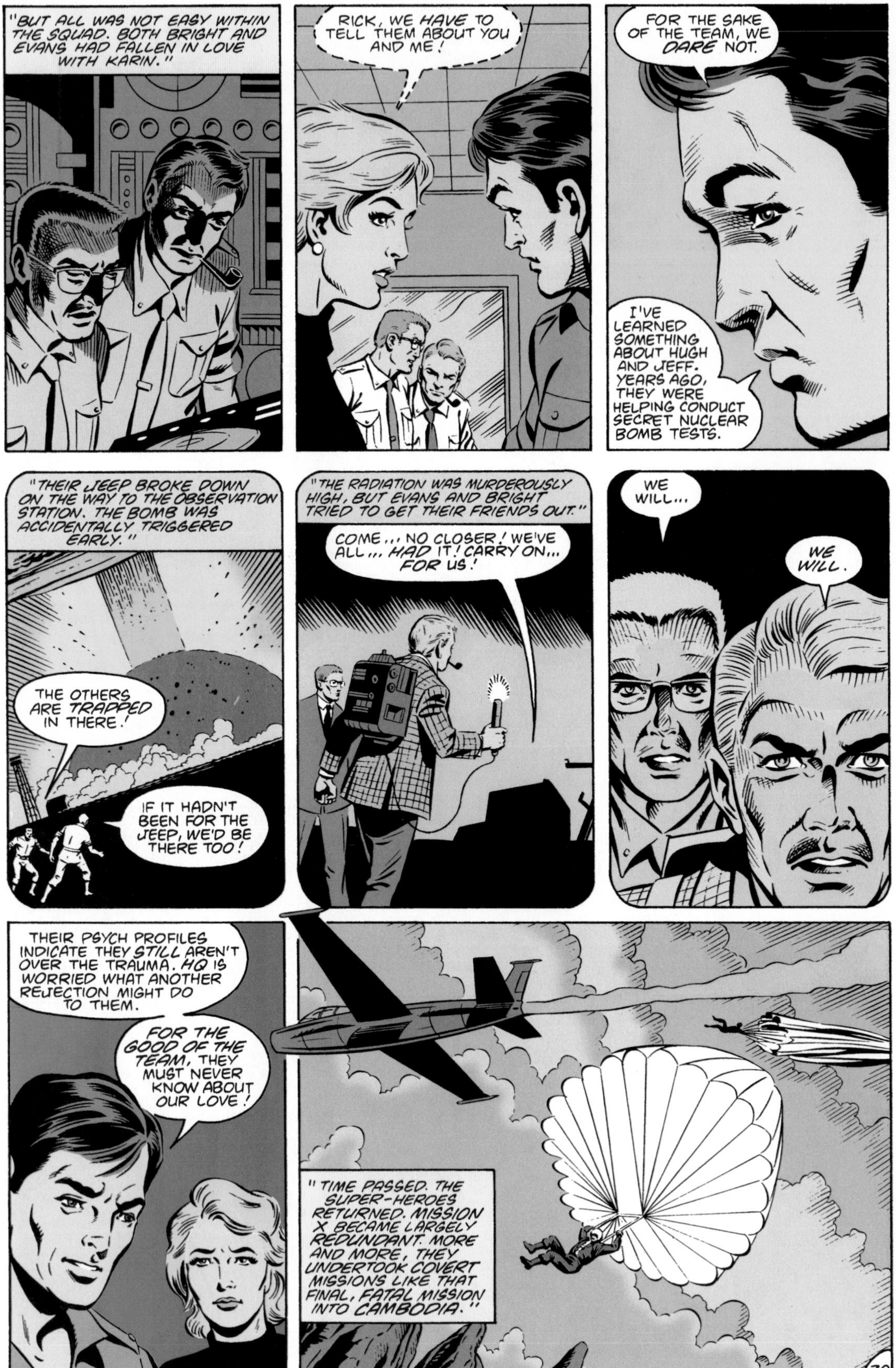
"BUT ALL WAS NOT EASY WITHIN THE SQUAD. BOTH BRIGHT AND EVANS HAD FALLEN IN LOVE WITH KARIN."
RICK, WE HAVE TO TELL THEM ABOUT YOU AND ME!
FOR THE SAKE OF THE TEAM, WE DARE NOT.
I'VE LEARNED SOMETHING ABOUT HUGH AND JEFF. YEARS AGO, THEY WERE HELPING CONDUCT SECRET NUCLEAR BOMB TESTS.
"THEIR JEEP BROKE DOWN ON THE WAY TO THE OBSERVATION STATION. THE BOMB WAS ACCIDENTALLY TRIGGERED EARLY."
THE OTHERS ARE TRAPPED IN THERE!
IF IT HADN'T BEEN FOR THE JEEP, WE'D BE THERE TOO!
"THE RADIATION WAS MURDEROUSLY HIGH, BUT EVANS AND BRIGHT TRIED TO GET THEIR FRIENDS OUT."
COME... NO CLOSER! WE'VE ALL... HAD IT! CARRY ON... FOR US!
WE WILL...
WE WILL.
THEIR PSYCH PROFILES INDICATE THEY STILL AREN'T OVER THE TRAUMA. HQ IS WORRIED WHAT ANOTHER REJECTION MIGHT DO TO THEM.
FOR THE GOOD OF THE TEAM, THEY MUST NEVER KNOW ABOUT OUR LOVE!
"TIME PASSED. THE SUPER-HEROES RETURNED. MISSION X BECAME LARGELY REDUNDANT. MORE AND MORE, THEY UNDERTOOK COVERT MISSIONS LIKE THAT FINAL, FATAL MISSION INTO CAMBODIA."
20

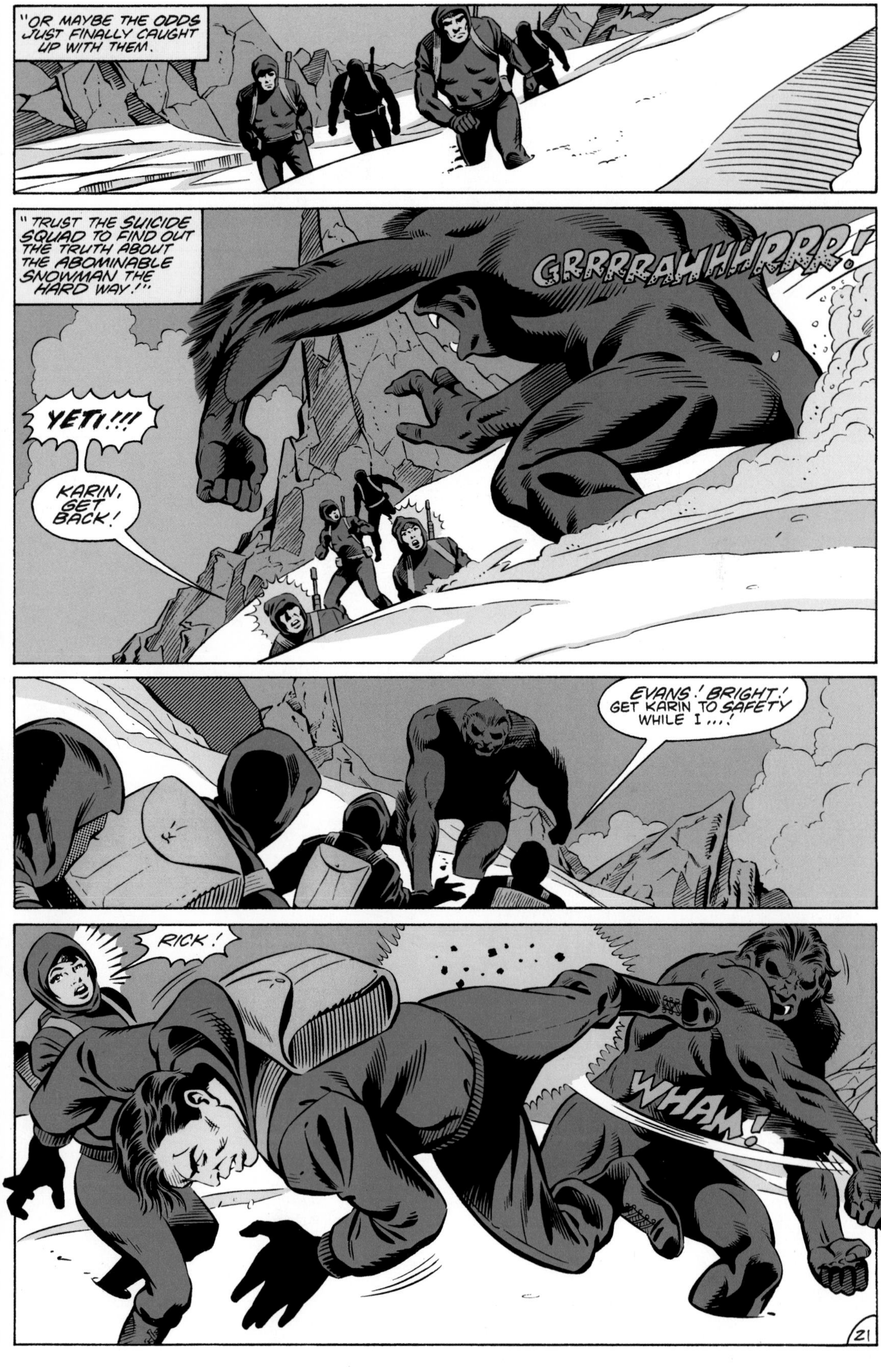

"OR MAYBE THE ODDS JUST FINALLY CAUGHT UP WITH THEM.
"TRUST THE SUICIDE SQUAD TO FIND OUT THE TRUTH ABOUT THE ABOMINABLE SNOWMAN THE HARD WAY!"
GRRRRAHHHRRR!
YETI!!!
KARIN, GET BACK!
EVANS! BRIGHT! GET KARIN TO SAFETY WHILE I...!
RICK!
WHAM!
21

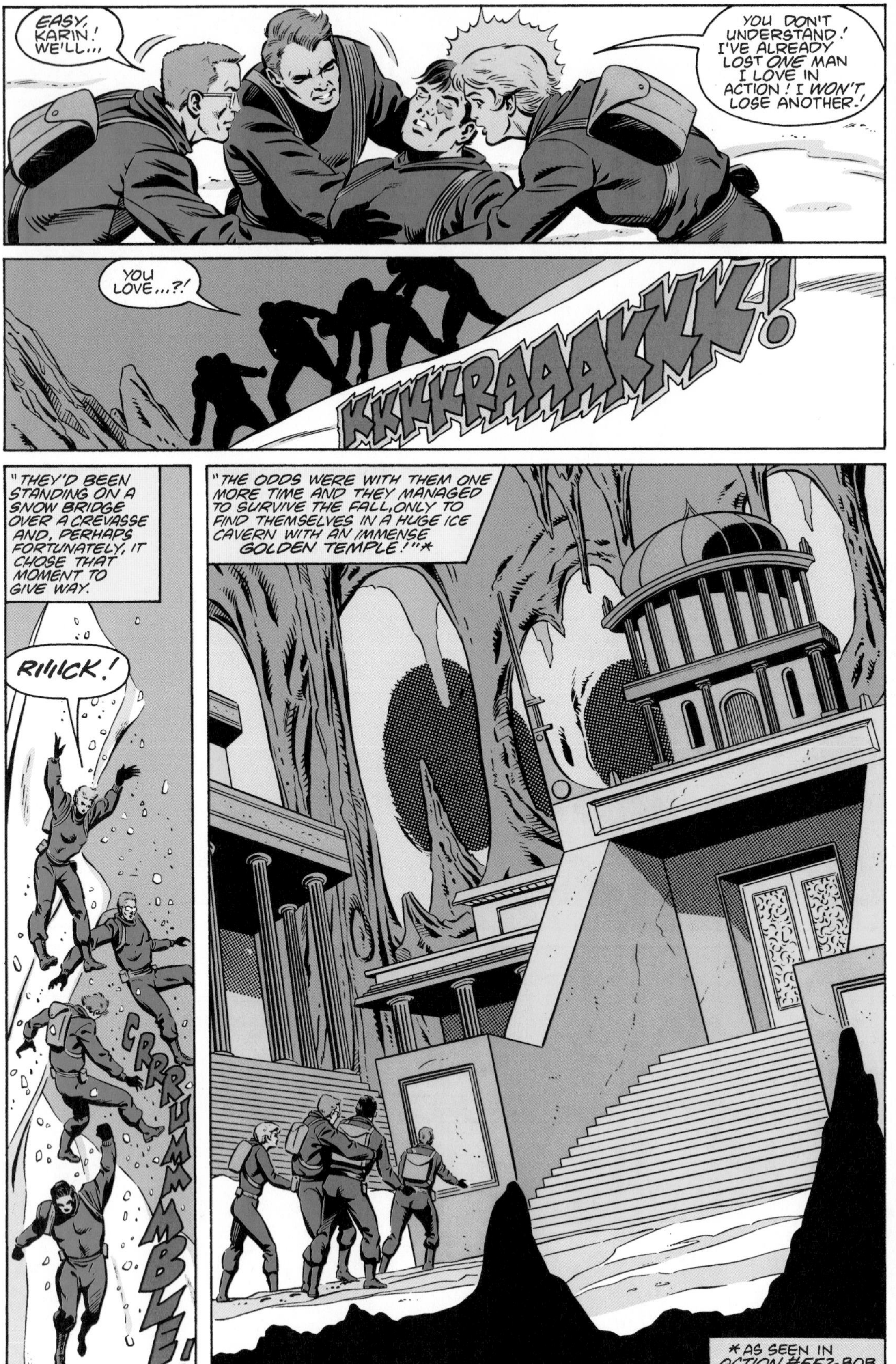
EASY, KARIN! WE'LL...
YOU DON'T UNDERSTAND! I'VE ALREADY LOST ONE MAN I LOVE IN ACTION! I WON'T LOSE ANOTHER!
YOU LOVE...?!
KKKKRAAAKKK!
"THEY'D BEEN STANDING ON A SNOW BRIDGE OVER A CREVASSE AND, PERHAPS FORTUNATELY, IT CHOSE THAT MOMENT TO GIVE WAY.
RIIICK!
CRRRUMMMBLE!
"THE ODDS WERE WITH THEM ONE MORE TIME AND THEY MANAGED TO SURVIVE THE FALL, ONLY TO FIND THEMSELVES IN A HUGE ICE CAVERN WITH AN IMMENSE GOLDEN TEMPLE!"*
*AS SEEN IN ACTION #552-BOB

"KARIN'S CONCERN FOR RICK HAD NOT GONE UNREMARKED OR MISUNDERSTOOD."

YOU AND FLAG-- THIS HAS BEEN GOING ON SINCE WE BEGAN, HASN'T IT, KARIN?

OH, PLEASE, JEFF! NOT NOW!

KARIN... DON'T... THE *TEAM*....!

HUSH, DARLING! IT'S OUT NOW!

WHY COULDN'T YOU JUST *TELL* US?

RICK... WE FELT IT WAS *BETTER* THIS WAY! FOR THE SAKE OF THE *TEAM*! HUGH, I'M *SORRY*!

HONESTY WOULD'VE BEEN BEST FOR THE TEAM, NOT PLAYING US FOR *FOOLS*!

YOU CAN TAKE THE TEAM AND *SHOVE* IT! WHEN WE GET BACK, I'M *THROUGH*!

IT'S HAPPENING JUST LIKE I *FEARED*. OR IS IT, DEEP DOWN, THE WAY THAT I ALWAYS WANTED ?!

THE SQUAD WAS MY *DUTY*, NOT MY *DREAM*.

DEEP DOWN, HAVE I SET US UP FOR THIS FALL?

"ANGER, DOUBT, GUILT-- THE SUICIDE SQUAD WAS STARTING TO CRACK.

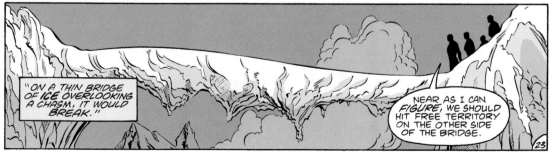

"ON A THIN BRIDGE OF ICE OVERLOOKING A CHASM, IT WOULD *BREAK*."

NEAR AS I CAN *FIGURE*, WE SHOULD HIT FREE TERRITORY ON THE OTHER SIDE OF THE BRIDGE.

23

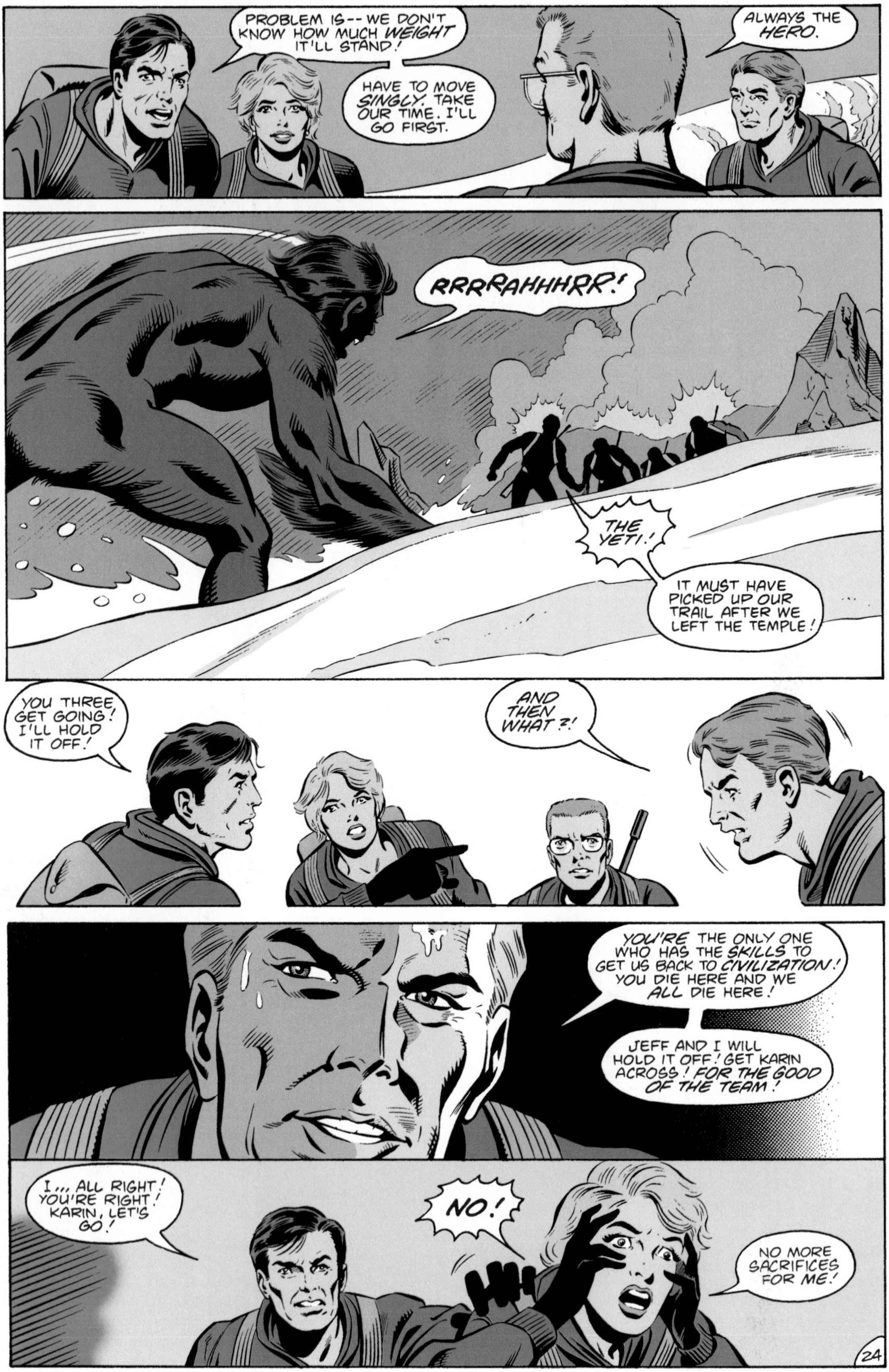

PROBLEM IS-- WE DON'T KNOW HOW MUCH WEIGHT IT'LL STAND!
HAVE TO MOVE SINGLY. TAKE OUR TIME. I'LL GO FIRST.
ALWAYS THE HERO.
RRRRAHHHRR!
THE YETI!
IT MUST HAVE PICKED UP OUR TRAIL AFTER WE LEFT THE TEMPLE!
YOU THREE GET GOING! I'LL HOLD IT OFF!
AND THEN WHAT?!
YOU'RE THE ONLY ONE WHO HAS THE SKILLS TO GET US BACK TO CIVILIZATION! YOU DIE HERE AND WE ALL DIE HERE!
JEFF AND I WILL HOLD IT OFF! GET KARIN ACROSS! FOR THE GOOD OF THE TEAM!
I... ALL RIGHT! YOU'RE RIGHT! KARIN, LET'S GO!
NO!
NO MORE SACRIFICES FOR ME!
24

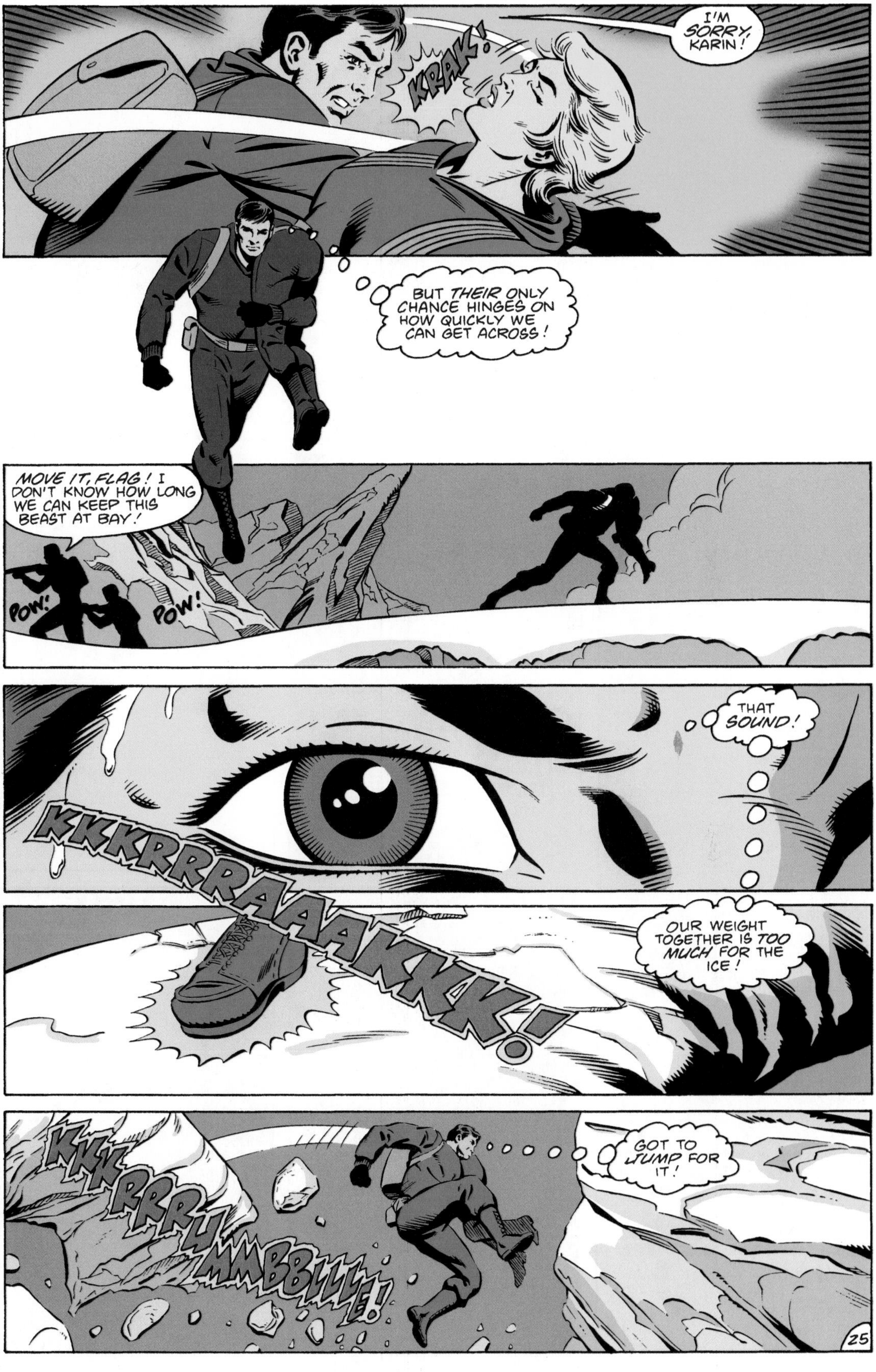
KRAK!
I'M SORRY, KARIN!
BUT THEIR ONLY CHANCE HINGES ON HOW QUICKLY WE CAN GET ACROSS!
MOVE IT, FLAG! I DON'T KNOW HOW LONG WE CAN KEEP THIS BEAST AT BAY!
POW!
POW!
THAT SOUND!
KKKRRRRAAAAKKKK!
OUR WEIGHT TOGETHER IS TOO MUCH FOR THE ICE!
KKKRRRRUMMBBLLLE!
GOT TO JUMP FOR IT!
25

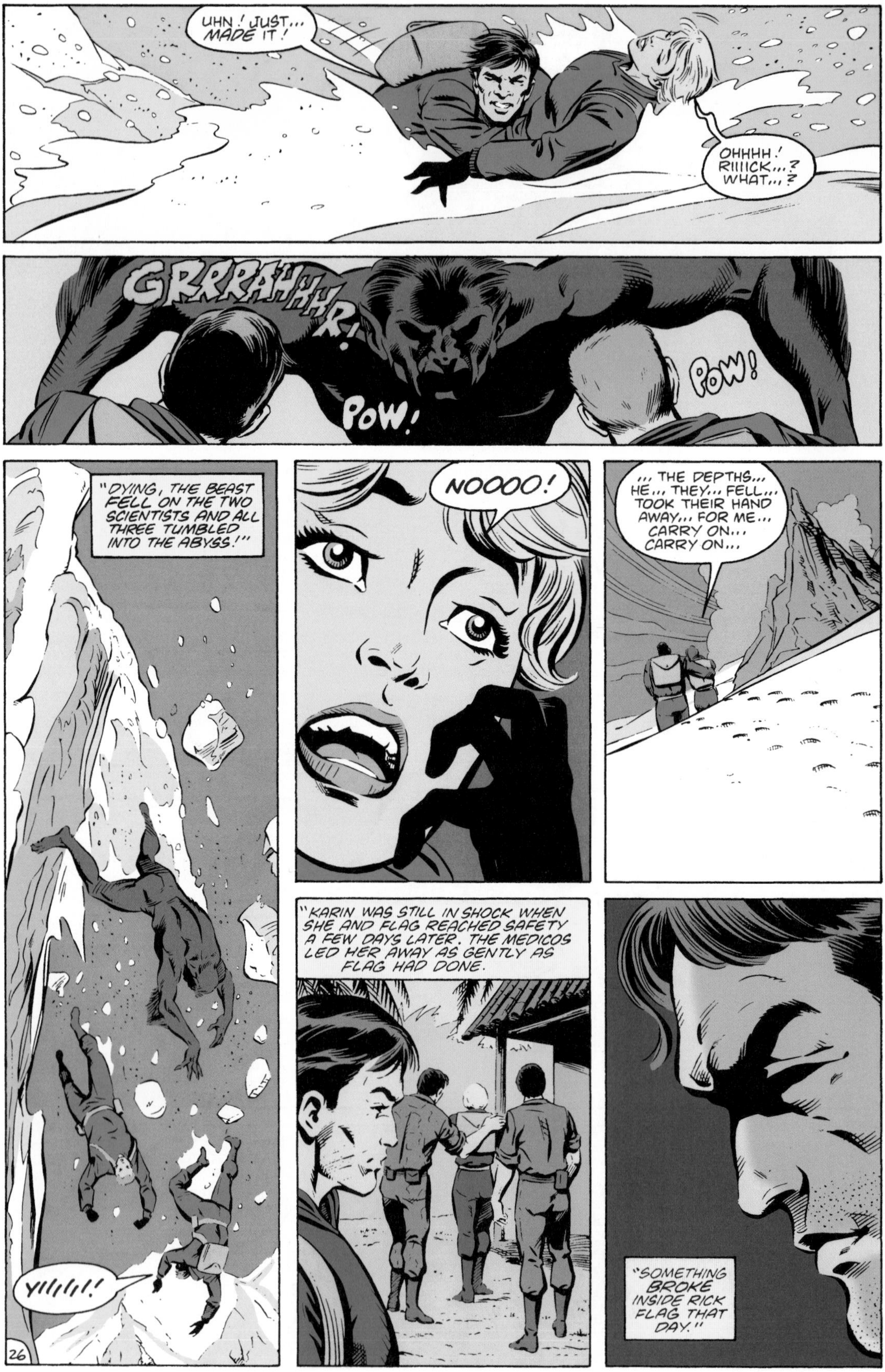
UHN! JUST... MADE IT!
OHHHH! RIIICK...? WHAT...?
GRRRAHHHR!
POW!
POW!
"DYING, THE BEAST FELL ON THE TWO SCIENTISTS AND ALL THREE TUMBLED INTO THE ABYSS!"
YIIII!
26
NOOOO!
... THE DEPTHS... HE... THEY... FELL... TOOK THEIR HAND AWAY... FOR ME... CARRY ON... CARRY ON...
"KARIN WAS STILL IN SHOCK WHEN SHE AND FLAG REACHED SAFETY A FEW DAYS LATER. THE MEDICOS LED HER AWAY AS GENTLY AS FLAG HAD DONE.
"SOMETHING BROKE INSIDE RICK FLAG THAT DAY."

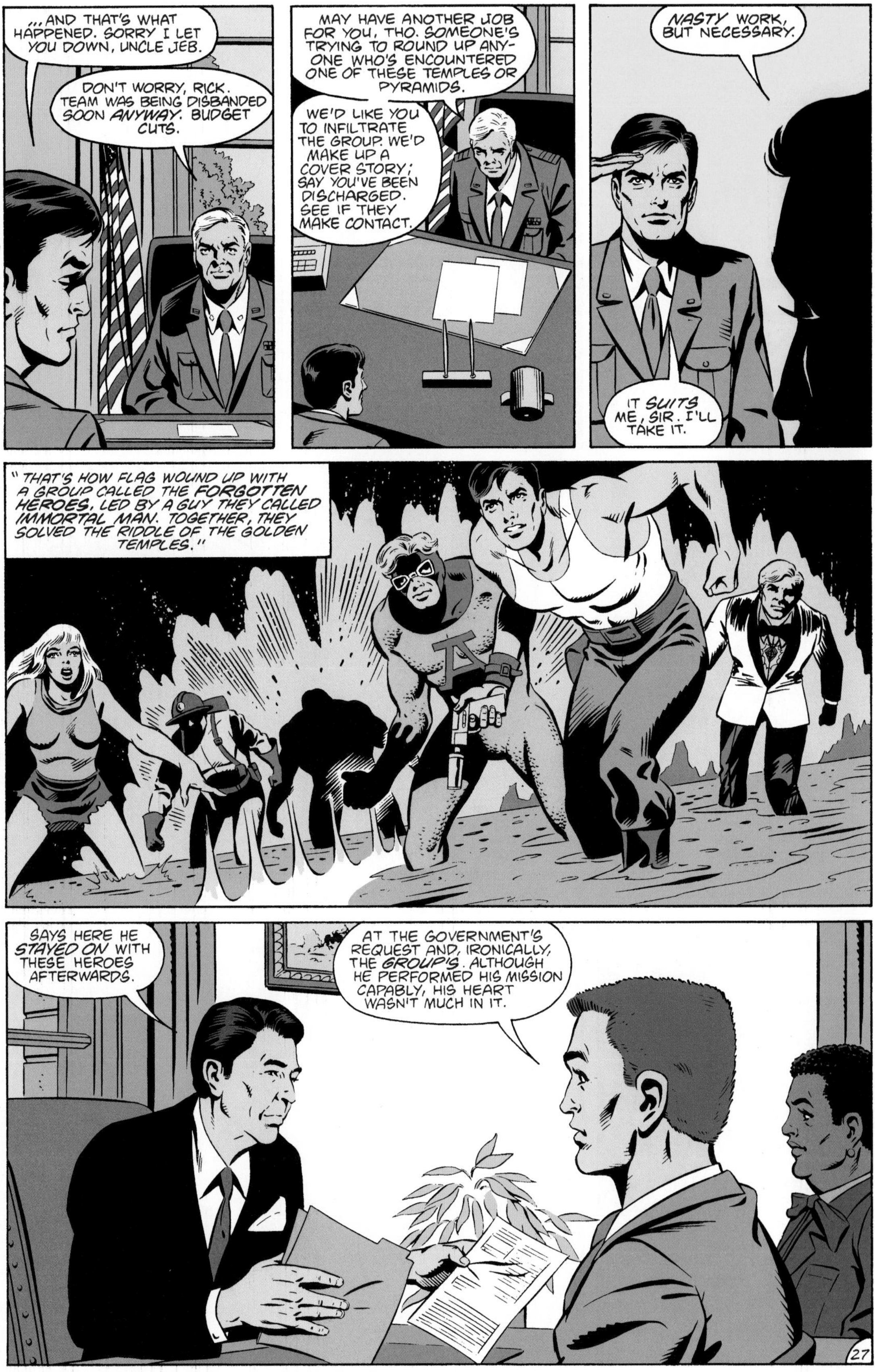
...AND THAT'S WHAT HAPPENED. SORRY I LET YOU DOWN, UNCLE JEB.
DON'T WORRY, RICK. TEAM WAS BEING DISBANDED SOON ANYWAY. BUDGET CUTS.
MAY HAVE ANOTHER JOB FOR YOU, THO. SOMEONE'S TRYING TO ROUND UP ANYONE WHO'S ENCOUNTERED ONE OF THESE TEMPLES OR PYRAMIDS.
WE'D LIKE YOU TO INFILTRATE THE GROUP. WE'D MAKE UP A COVER STORY; SAY YOU'VE BEEN DISCHARGED. SEE IF THEY MAKE CONTACT.
NASTY WORK, BUT NECESSARY.
IT SUITS ME, SIR. I'LL TAKE IT.
"THAT'S HOW FLAG WOUND UP WITH A GROUP CALLED THE FORGOTTEN HEROES, LED BY A GUY THEY CALLED IMMORTAL MAN. TOGETHER, THEY SOLVED THE RIDDLE OF THE GOLDEN TEMPLES."
SAYS HERE HE STAYED ON WITH THESE HEROES AFTERWARDS.
AT THE GOVERNMENT'S REQUEST AND, IRONICALLY, THE GROUP'S. ALTHOUGH HE PERFORMED HIS MISSION CAPABLY, HIS HEART WASN'T MUCH IN IT.
27

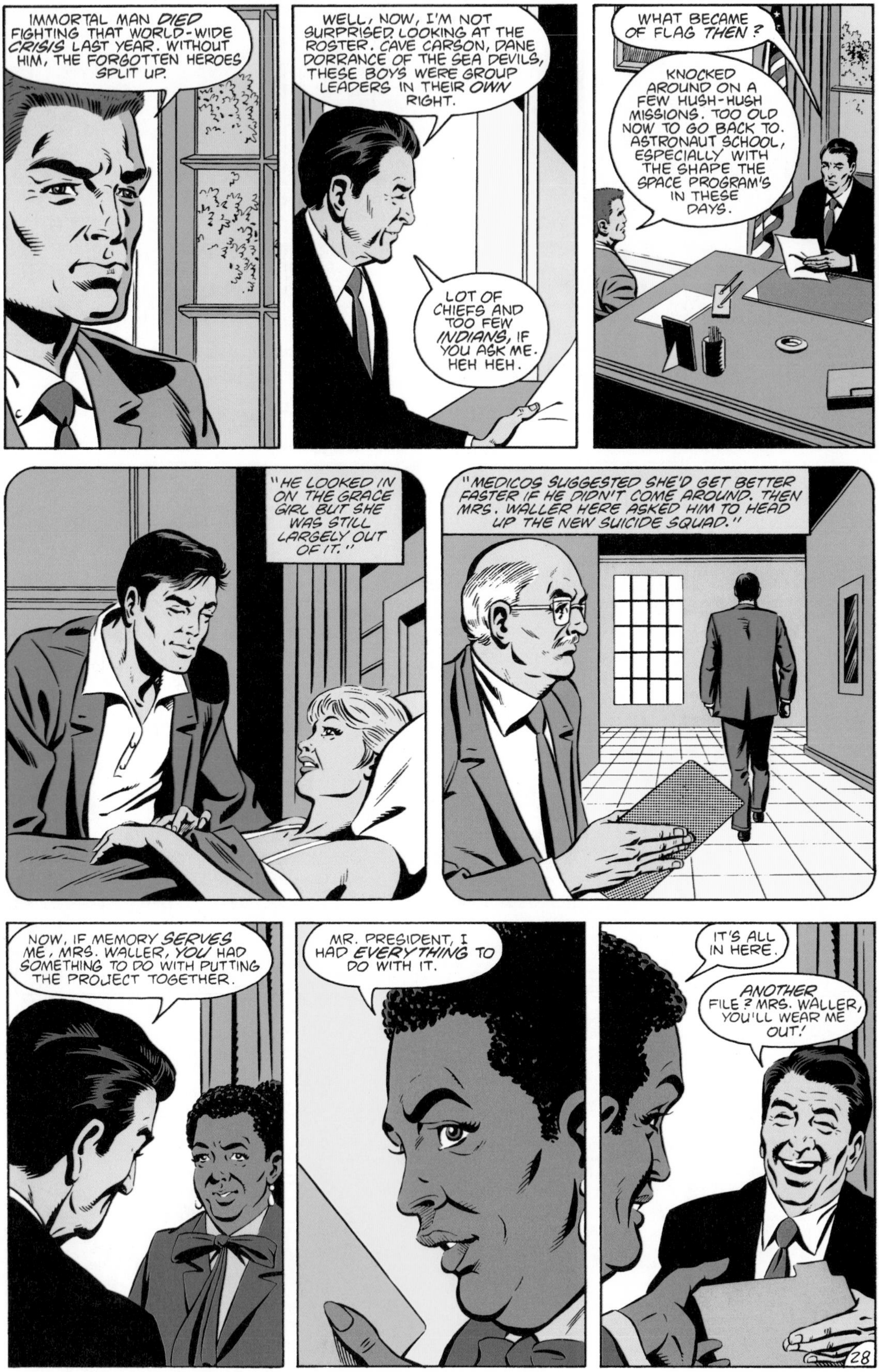
IMMORTAL MAN DIED FIGHTING THAT WORLD-WIDE CRISIS LAST YEAR. WITHOUT HIM, THE FORGOTTEN HEROES SPLIT UP.
WELL, NOW, I'M NOT SURPRISED LOOKING AT THE ROSTER. CAVE CARSON, DANE DORRANCE OF THE SEA DEVILS, THESE BOYS WERE GROUP LEADERS IN THEIR OWN RIGHT.
LOT OF CHIEFS AND TOO FEW INDIANS, IF YOU ASK ME. HEH HEH.
WHAT BECAME OF FLAG THEN?
KNOCKED AROUND ON A FEW HUSH-HUSH MISSIONS. TOO OLD NOW TO GO BACK TO ASTRONAUT SCHOOL, ESPECIALLY WITH THE SHAPE THE SPACE PROGRAM'S IN THESE DAYS.
"HE LOOKED IN ON THE GRACE GIRL BUT SHE WAS STILL LARGELY OUT OF IT."
"MEDICOS SUGGESTED SHE'D GET BETTER FASTER IF HE DIDN'T COME AROUND. THEN MRS. WALLER HERE ASKED HIM TO HEAD UP THE NEW SUICIDE SQUAD."
NOW, IF MEMORY SERVES ME, MRS. WALLER, YOU HAD SOMETHING TO DO WITH PUTTING THE PROJECT TOGETHER.
MR. PRESIDENT, I HAD EVERYTHING TO DO WITH IT.
IT'S ALL IN HERE.
ANOTHER FILE? MRS. WALLER, YOU'LL WEAR ME OUT!
28

WON'T KEEP YOU LONG FROM YOUR *NAP*, SIR. JUST A *SHORT* AND *BITTER* STORY. MINE.

THE REPORTS OF THE CRIME AND VIOLENCE THAT OCCUR IN CHICAGO'S *CABRINI-GREEN* ARE ALL TRUE. PLACE IS ALSO HOME TO LOTS OF GOOD, *DECENT* FOLKS TRYING TO FIND A WAY *OUT* OF THE CYCLE OF POVERTY.

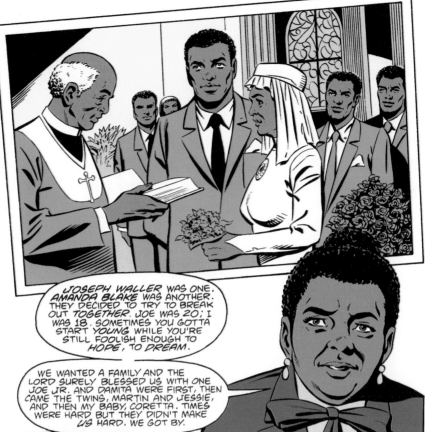

JOSEPH WALLER WAS ONE. AMANDA BLAKE WAS ANOTHER. THEY DECIDED TO TRY TO BREAK OUT *TOGETHER*. JOE WAS 20; I WAS 18. SOMETIMES YOU GOTTA START *YOUNG* WHILE YOU'RE STILL FOOLISH ENOUGH TO *HOPE*, TO *DREAM*.

WE WANTED A FAMILY AND THE LORD SURELY BLESSED US WITH ONE. JOE JR. AND DAMITA WERE FIRST, THEN CAME THE TWINS, MARTIN AND JESSIE, AND THEN MY BABY, CORETTA. TIMES WERE HARD BUT THEY DIDN'T MAKE *US* HARD. WE GOT BY.

OF COURSE, IN THOSE DAYS WE HAD SOME SOCIAL PROGRAMS TO FALL BACK ON. YOU *DO* REMEMBER SOCIAL PROGRAMS, DON'T YOU, MR. PRESIDENT?

NOW, NOW, MRS. WALLER...

29

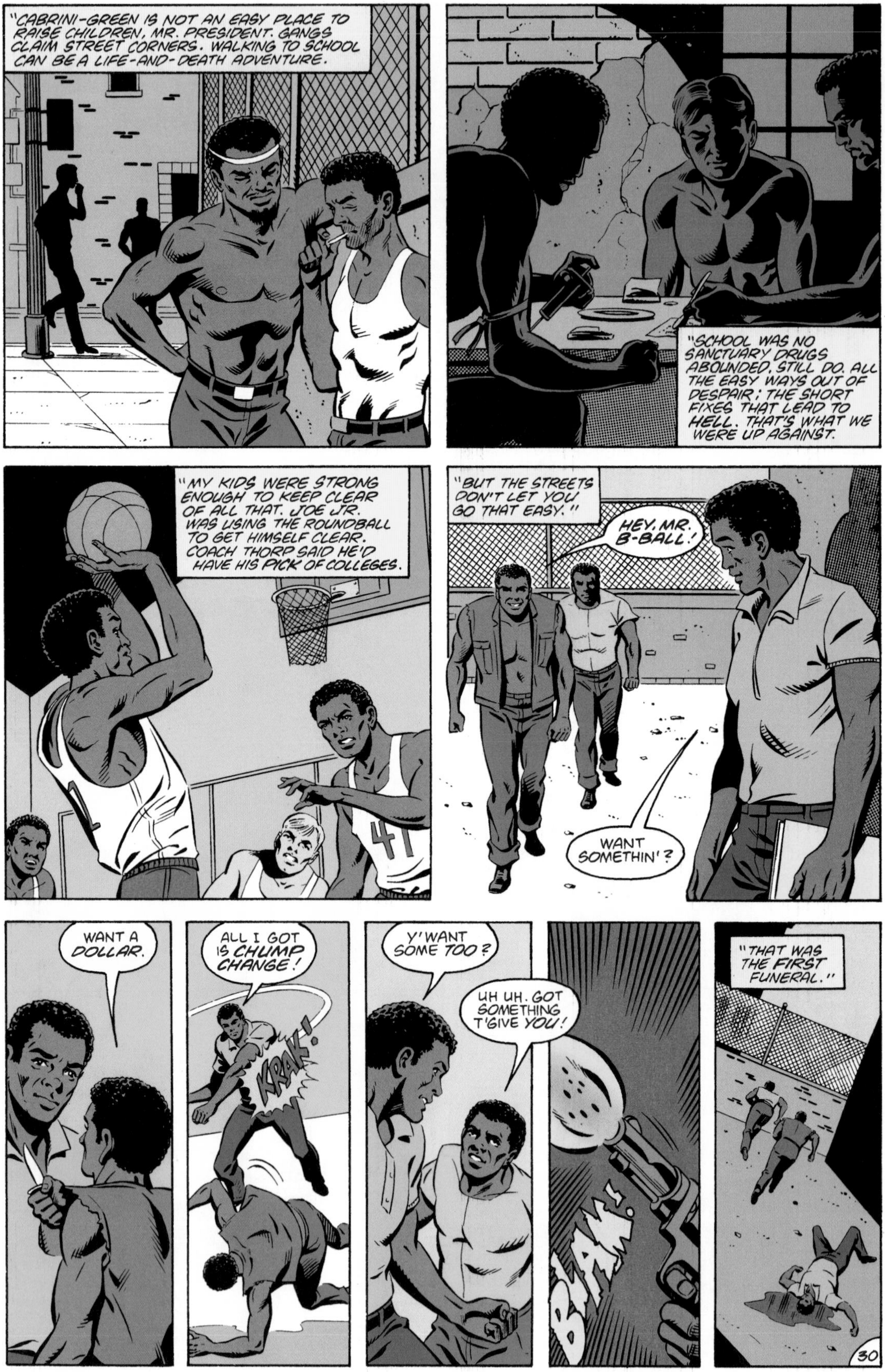
"CABRINI-GREEN IS NOT AN EASY PLACE TO RAISE CHILDREN, MR. PRESIDENT. GANGS CLAIM STREET CORNERS. WALKING TO SCHOOL CAN BE A LIFE-AND-DEATH ADVENTURE.
"SCHOOL WAS NO SANCTUARY. DRUGS ABOUNDED, STILL DO. ALL THE EASY WAYS OUT OF DESPAIR; THE SHORT FIXES THAT LEAD TO HELL. THAT'S WHAT WE WERE UP AGAINST.
"MY KIDS WERE STRONG ENOUGH TO KEEP CLEAR OF ALL THAT. JOE JR. WAS USING THE ROUNDBALL TO GET HIMSELF CLEAR. COACH THORP SAID HE'D HAVE HIS PICK OF COLLEGES.
41
"BUT THE STREETS DON'T LET YOU GO THAT EASY."
HEY, MR. B-BALL!
WANT SOMETHIN'?
WANT A DOLLAR.
ALL I GOT IS CHUMP CHANGE!
KRAK!
Y'WANT SOME TOO?
UH UH. GOT SOMETHING T'GIVE YOU!
BLAM!
"THAT WAS THE FIRST FUNERAL."
30

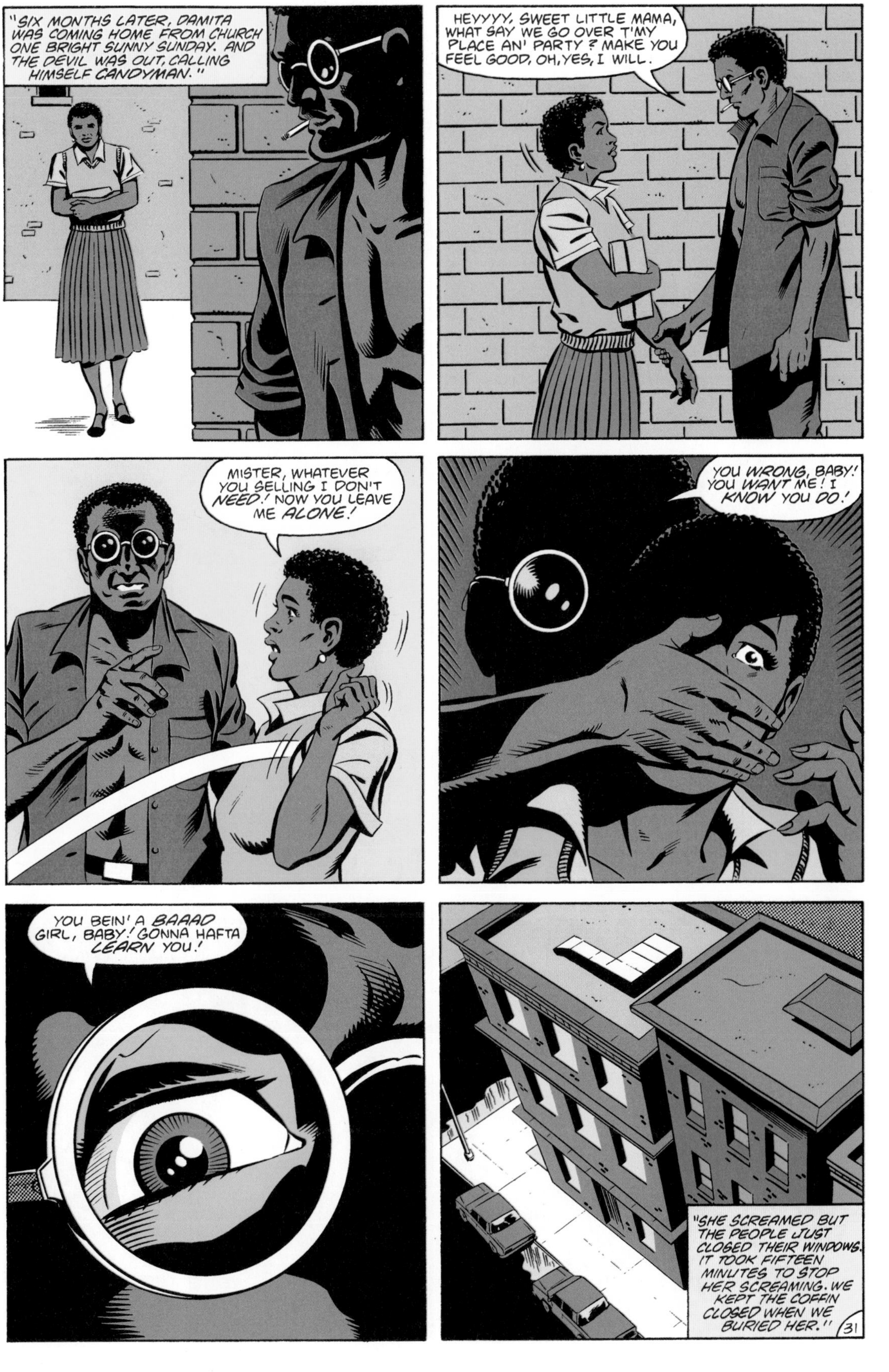
"SIX MONTHS LATER, DAMITA WAS COMING HOME FROM CHURCH ONE BRIGHT SUNNY SUNDAY. AND THE DEVIL WAS OUT, CALLING HIMSELF CANDYMAN."
HEYYYY, SWEET LITTLE MAMA, WHAT SAY WE GO OVER T'MY PLACE AN' PARTY? MAKE YOU FEEL GOOD, OH, YES, I WILL.
MISTER, WHATEVER YOU SELLING I DON'T NEED! NOW YOU LEAVE ME ALONE!
YOU WRONG, BABY! YOU WANT ME! I KNOW YOU DO!
YOU BEIN' A BAAAD GIRL, BABY! GONNA HAFTA LEARN YOU!
"SHE SCREAMED BUT THE PEOPLE JUST CLOSED THEIR WINDOWS. IT TOOK FIFTEEN MINUTES TO STOP HER SCREAMING. WE KEPT THE COFFIN CLOSED WHEN WE BURIED HER."
31

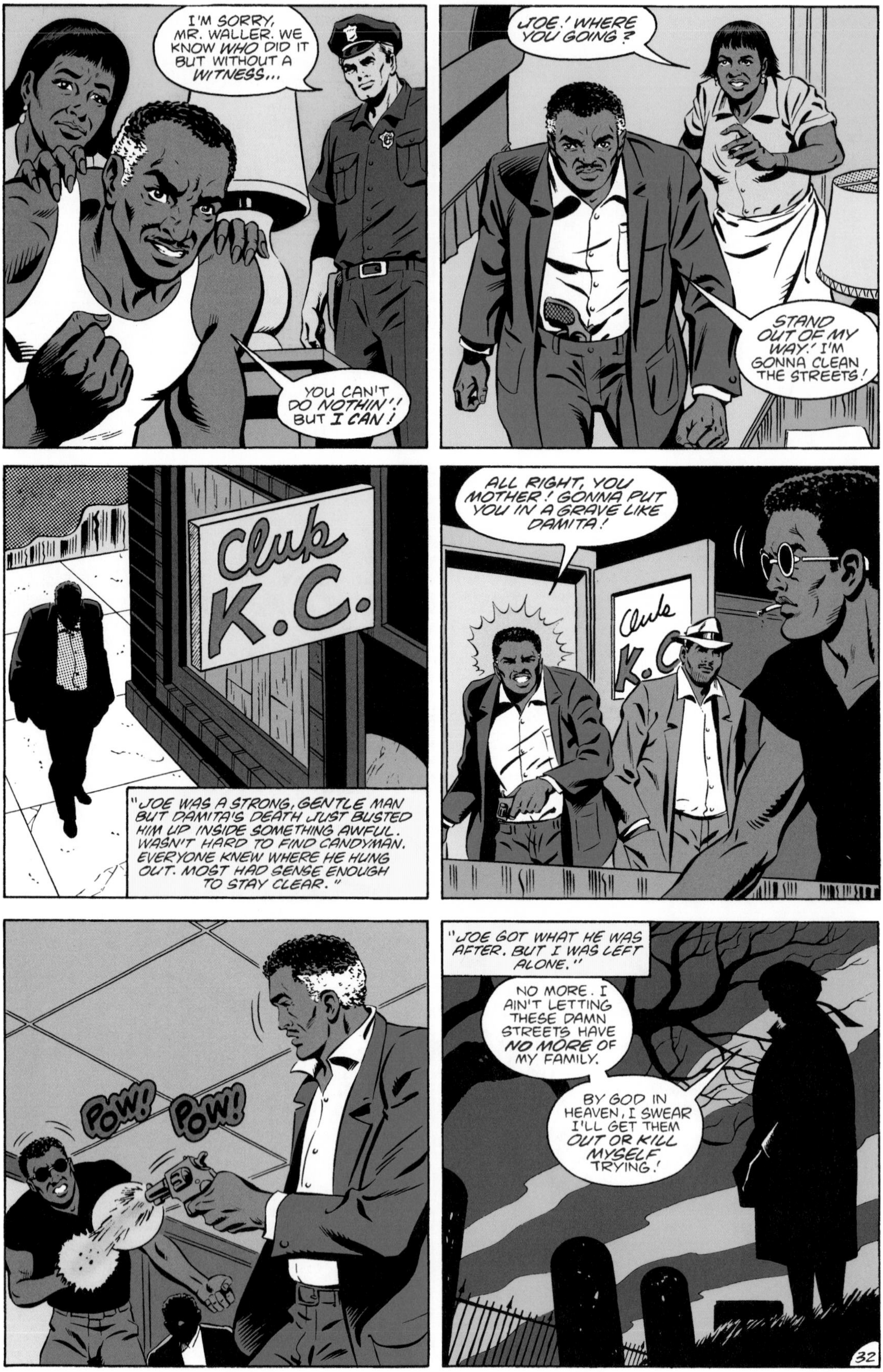
I'M SORRY, MR. WALLER. WE KNOW WHO DID IT BUT WITHOUT A WITNESS...
YOU CAN'T DO NOTHIN'! BUT I CAN!
JOE! WHERE YOU GOING?
STAND OUT OF MY WAY! I'M GONNA CLEAN THE STREETS!
Club K.C.
"JOE WAS A STRONG, GENTLE MAN BUT DAMITA'S DEATH JUST BUSTED HIM UP INSIDE SOMETHING AWFUL. WASN'T HARD TO FIND CANDYMAN. EVERYONE KNEW WHERE HE HUNG OUT. MOST HAD SENSE ENOUGH TO STAY CLEAR."
ALL RIGHT, YOU MOTHER! GONNA PUT YOU IN A GRAVE LIKE DAMITA!
POW! POW!
"JOE GOT WHAT HE WAS AFTER. BUT I WAS LEFT ALONE."
NO MORE. I AIN'T LETTING THESE DAMN STREETS HAVE NO MORE OF MY FAMILY.
BY GOD IN HEAVEN, I SWEAR I'LL GET THEM OUT OR KILL MYSELF TRYING!
32

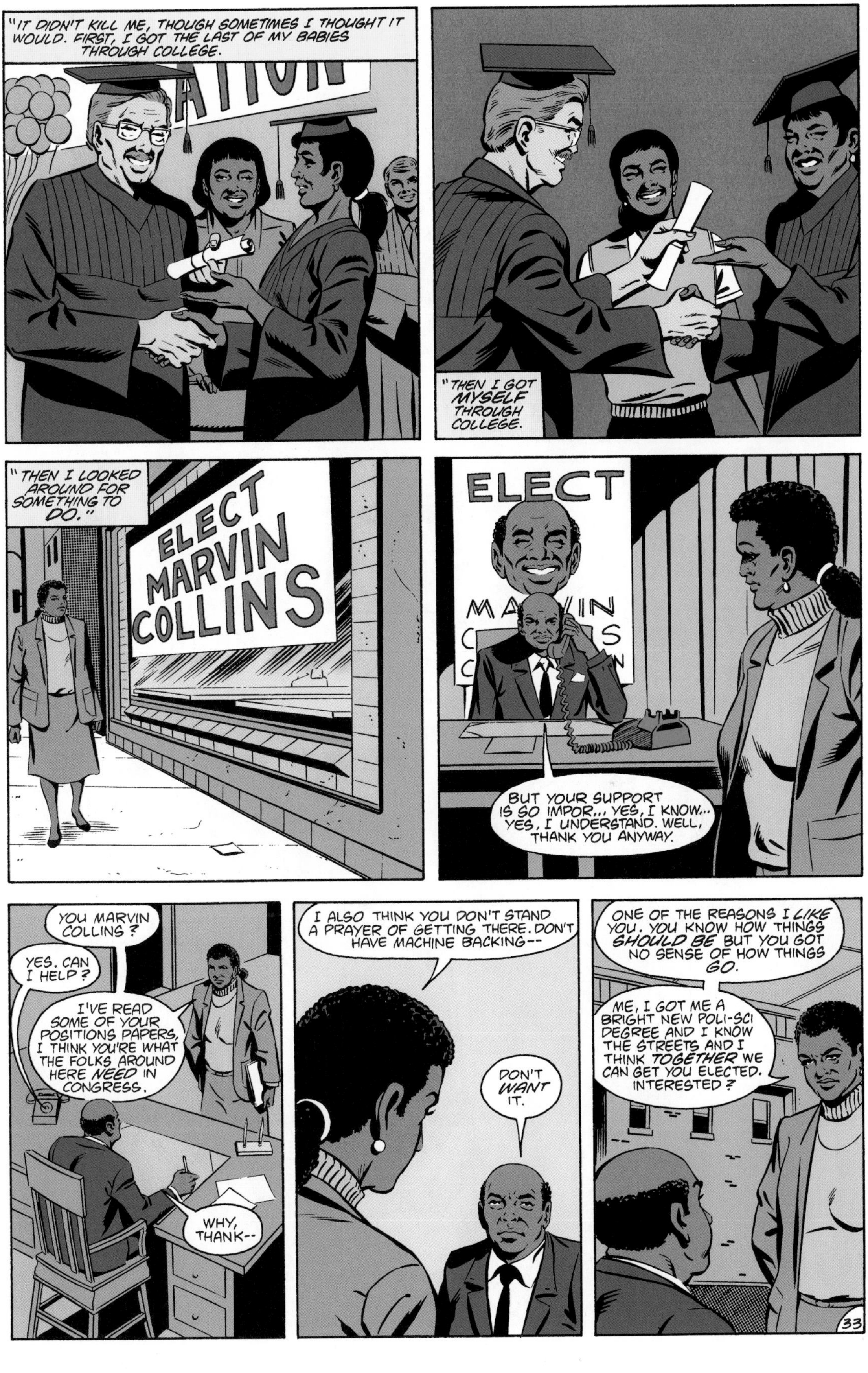
"IT DIDN'T KILL ME, THOUGH SOMETIMES I THOUGHT IT WOULD. FIRST, I GOT THE LAST OF MY BABIES THROUGH COLLEGE.
"THEN I GOT MYSELF THROUGH COLLEGE.
"THEN I LOOKED AROUND FOR SOMETHING TO DO."
ELECT MARVIN COLLINS
ELECT
BUT YOUR SUPPORT IS SO IMPOR... YES, I KNOW... YES, I UNDERSTAND. WELL, THANK YOU ANYWAY.
YOU MARVIN COLLINS?
YES. CAN I HELP?
I'VE READ SOME OF YOUR POSITIONS PAPERS, I THINK YOU'RE WHAT THE FOLKS AROUND HERE NEED IN CONGRESS.
WHY, THANK--
I ALSO THINK YOU DON'T STAND A PRAYER OF GETTING THERE. DON'T HAVE MACHINE BACKING--
DON'T WANT IT.
ONE OF THE REASONS I LIKE YOU. YOU KNOW HOW THINGS SHOULD BE BUT YOU GOT NO SENSE OF HOW THINGS GO.
ME, I GOT ME A BRIGHT NEW POLI-SCI DEGREE AND I KNOW THE STREETS AND I THINK TOGETHER WE CAN GET YOU ELECTED. INTERESTED?
33

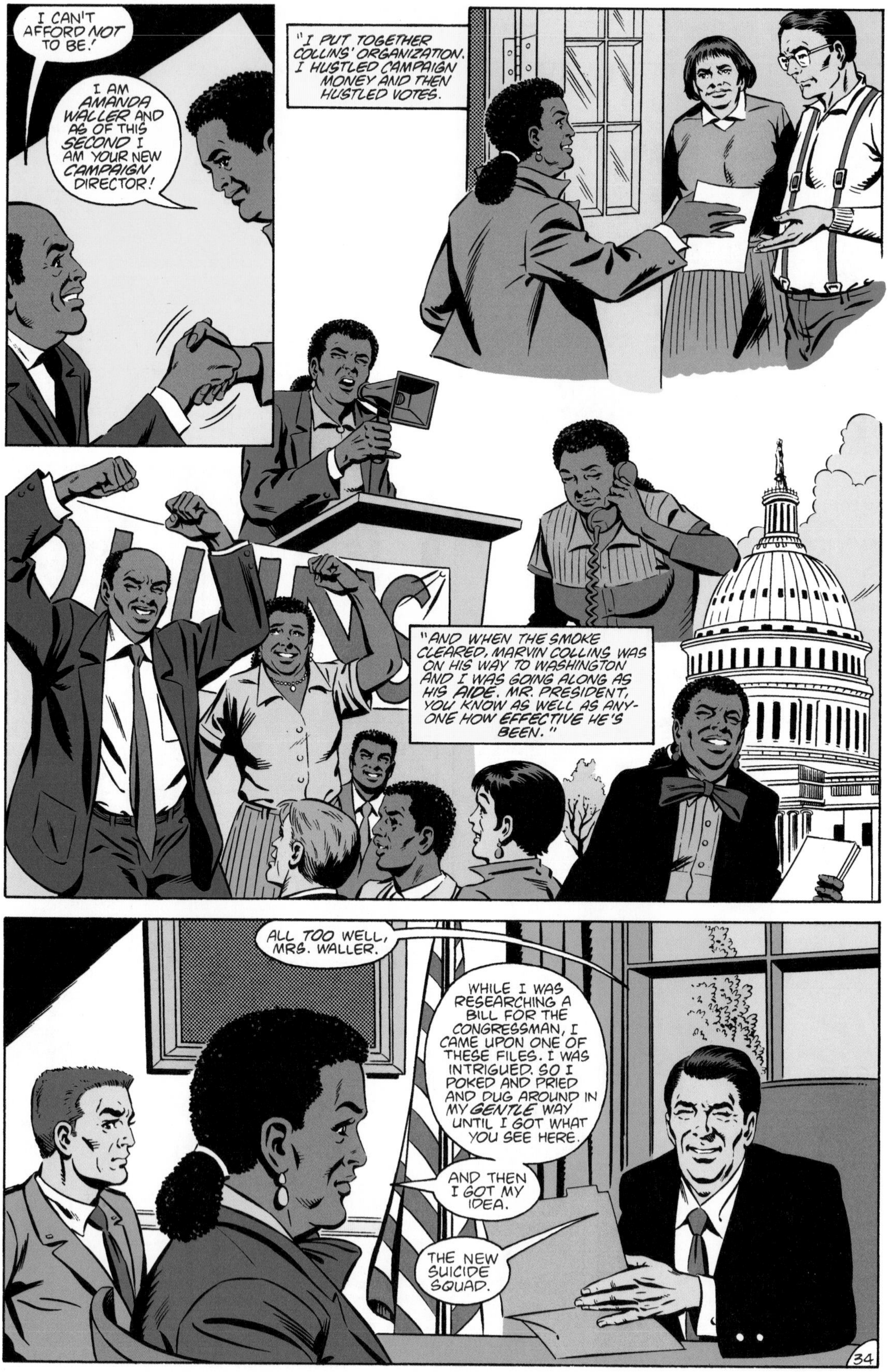
I CAN'T AFFORD NOT TO BE.'
I AM AMANDA WALLER AND AS OF THIS SECOND I AM YOUR NEW CAMPAIGN DIRECTOR!
"I PUT TOGETHER COLLINS' ORGANIZATION. I HUSTLED CAMPAIGN MONEY AND THEN HUSTLED VOTES.
"AND WHEN THE SMOKE CLEARED, MARVIN COLLINS WAS ON HIS WAY TO WASHINGTON AND I WAS GOING ALONG AS HIS AIDE. MR. PRESIDENT, YOU KNOW AS WELL AS ANYONE HOW EFFECTIVE HE'S BEEN."
ALL TOO WELL, MRS. WALLER.
WHILE I WAS RESEARCHING A BILL FOR THE CONGRESSMAN, I CAME UPON ONE OF THESE FILES. I WAS INTRIGUED, SO I POKED AND PRIED AND DUG AROUND IN MY GENTLE WAY UNTIL I GOT WHAT YOU SEE HERE.
AND THEN I GOT MY IDEA.
THE NEW SUICIDE SQUAD.
34

SIR, I'M A PRACTICAL WOMAN. I SEE A PROBLEM, I WANT IT SOLVED. THERE ARE THINGS, HERE AND ABROAD, THAT NEED DOING, BUT FOR ONE REASON OR ANOTHER, THE GOVERNMENT CANNOT DO THEM.
THAT'S FINE. I UNDERSTAND THAT. BUT THOSE THINGS STILL NEED DOING.
WHAT'S NEEDED IS A COVERT GROUP OF AGENTS-- UTTERLY RUTHLESS, TOTALLY EXPENDABLE.
PRISONS ARE FULL OF THOSE KIND OF PEOPLE AND IT COSTS TO KEEP THEM THERE. ESPECIALLY THE SUPER-VILLAINS. SO WHY NOT LET THEM CONTRIBUTE TO THEIR COUNTRY?
MAKE THEM A DEAL: DO WHAT NEEDS DOING, SUCCEED AND SURVIVE, AND KEEP YOUR TRAP SHUT, AND WE'LL COMMUTE YOUR SENTENCES TO TIME SERVED.
"GOT ENOUGH INTEREST TO FIELD A PILOT TEAM--CAPTAIN BOOMERANG, THE ENCHANTRESS, BLOCKBUSTER, AND DEADSHOT. RICK FLAG WAS BROUGHT BACK AS FIELD COMMANDER AND THE BRONZE TIGER WAS ADDED TO KEEP OUR LOSERS IN LINE.
"WE GOT CALLED SOONER THAN WE PLANNED-- TO BATTLE BRIMSTONE. THE SUICIDE SQUAD TOOK HIM OUT; NOT THE JLA, AND NOT FIRESTORM. WE DID, THOUGH IT COST US BLOCKBUSTER'S LIFE!*
*LEGENDS #3 --BOB
35

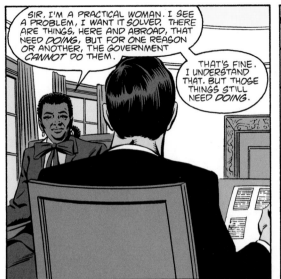

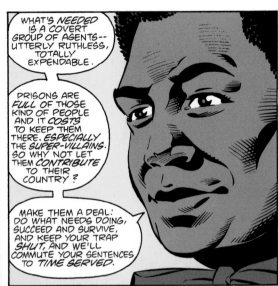

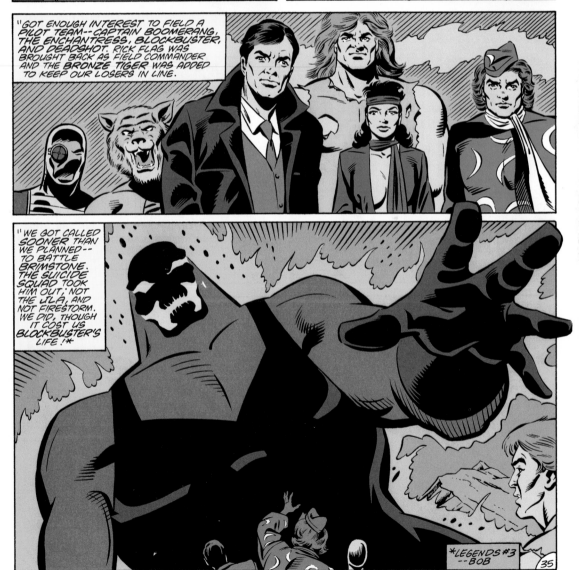

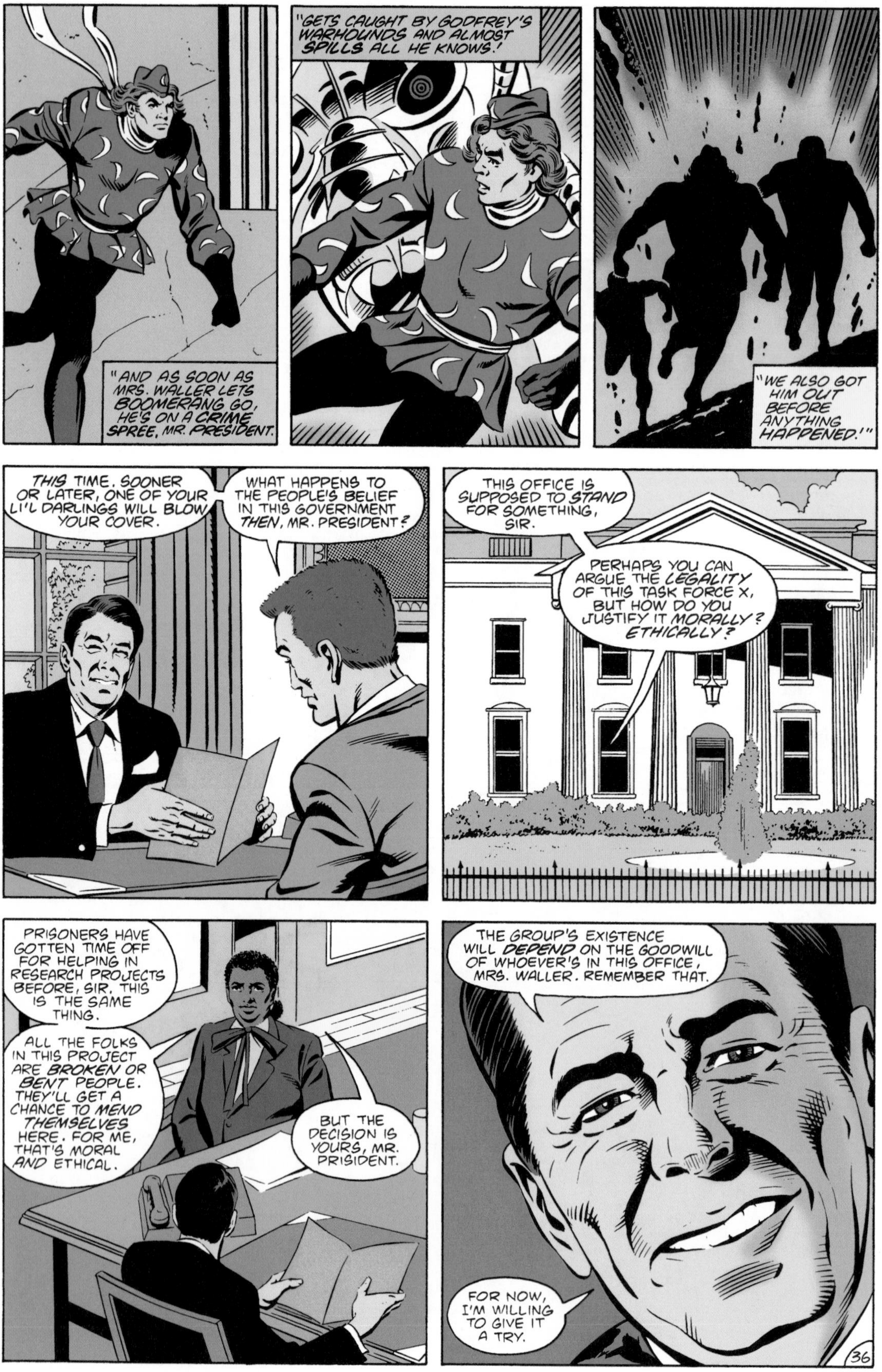
"AND AS SOON AS MRS. WALLER LETS BOOMERANG GO, HE'S ON A CRIME SPREE, MR. PRESIDENT.
"GETS CAUGHT BY GODFREY'S WARHOUNDS AND ALMOST SPILLS ALL HE KNOWS.'
"WE ALSO GOT HIM OUT BEFORE ANYTHING HAPPENED!"
THIS TIME. SOONER OR LATER, ONE OF YOUR LI'L DARLINGS WILL BLOW YOUR COVER.
WHAT HAPPENS TO THE PEOPLE'S BELIEF IN THIS GOVERNMENT THEN, MR. PRESIDENT?
THIS OFFICE IS SUPPOSED TO STAND FOR SOMETHING, SIR.
PERHAPS YOU CAN ARGUE THE LEGALITY OF THIS TASK FORCE X, BUT HOW DO YOU JUSTIFY IT MORALLY? ETHICALLY?
PRISONERS HAVE GOTTEN TIME OFF FOR HELPING IN RESEARCH PROJECTS BEFORE, SIR. THIS IS THE SAME THING.
ALL THE FOLKS IN THIS PROJECT ARE BROKEN OR BENT PEOPLE. THEY'LL GET A CHANCE TO MEND THEMSELVES HERE. FOR ME, THAT'S MORAL AND ETHICAL.
BUT THE DECISION IS YOURS, MR. PRISIDENT.
THE GROUP'S EXISTENCE WILL DEPEND ON THE GOODWILL OF WHOEVER'S IN THIS OFFICE, MRS. WALLER. REMEMBER THAT.
FOR NOW, I'M WILLING TO GIVE IT A TRY.
36

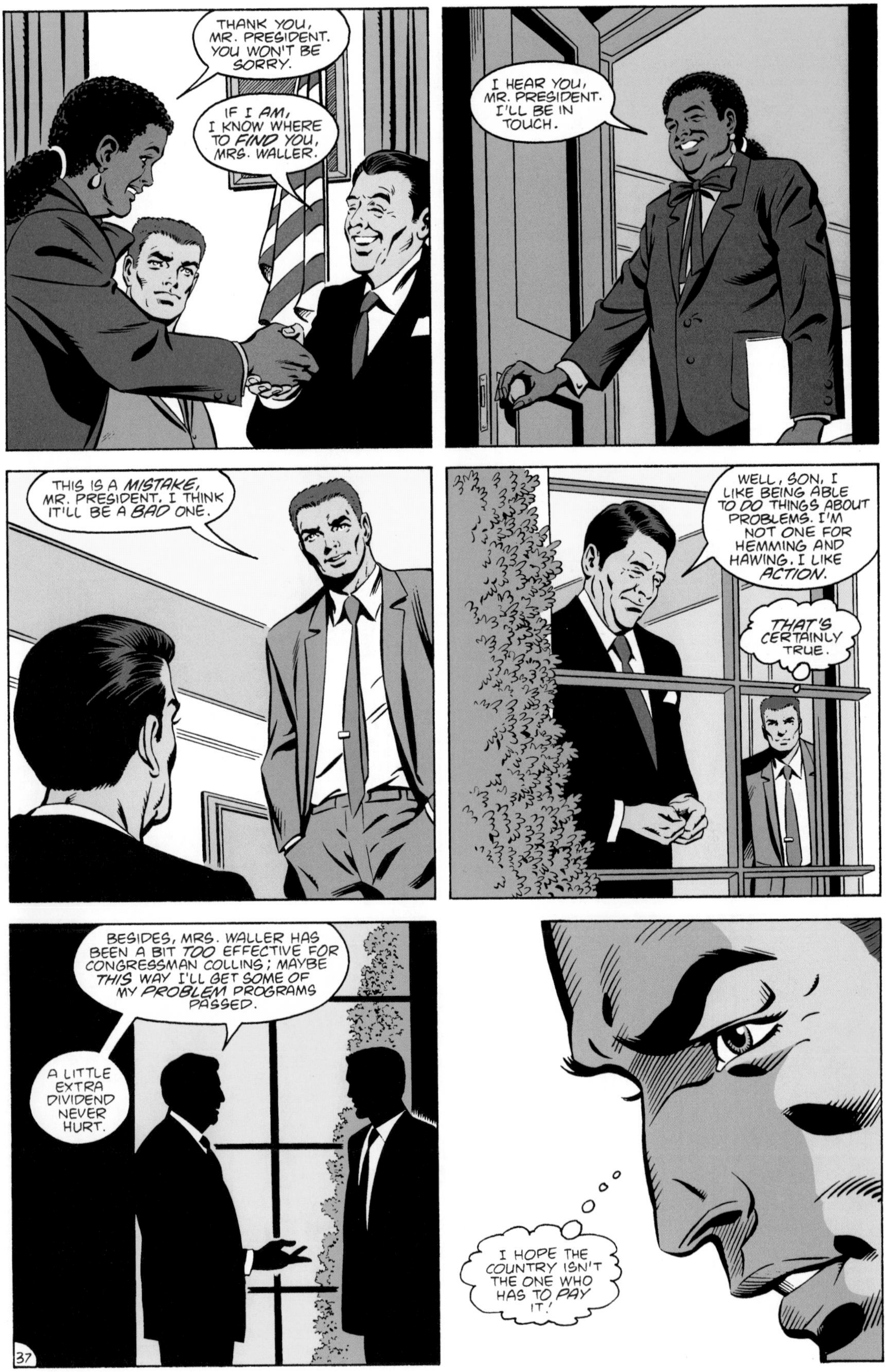
THANK YOU, MR. PRESIDENT. YOU WON'T BE SORRY.
IF I AM, I KNOW WHERE TO FIND YOU, MRS. WALLER.
I HEAR YOU, MR. PRESIDENT. I'LL BE IN TOUCH.
THIS IS A MISTAKE, MR. PRESIDENT. I THINK IT'LL BE A BAD ONE.
WELL, SON, I LIKE BEING ABLE TO DO THINGS ABOUT PROBLEMS. I'M NOT ONE FOR HEMMING AND HAWING. I LIKE ACTION.
THAT'S CERTAINLY TRUE.
BESIDES, MRS. WALLER HAS BEEN A BIT TOO EFFECTIVE FOR CONGRESSMAN COLLINS; MAYBE THIS WAY I'LL GET SOME OF MY PROBLEM PROGRAMS PASSED.
A LITTLE EXTRA DIVIDEND NEVER HURT.
37
I HOPE THE COUNTRY ISN'T THE ONE WHO HAS TO PAY IT!

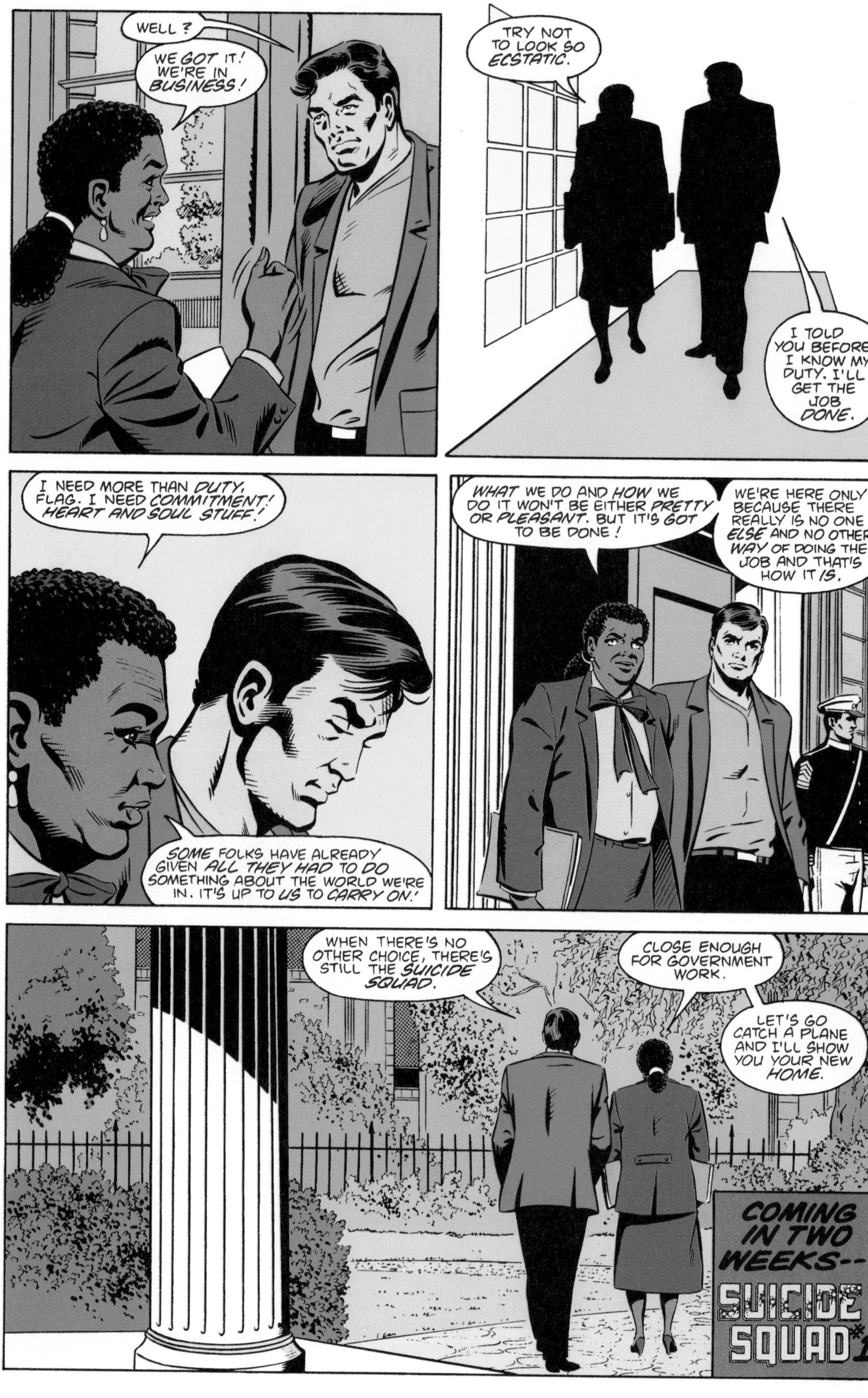
WELL?
WE GOT IT! WE'RE IN BUSINESS!
TRY NOT TO LOOK SO ECSTATIC.
I TOLD YOU BEFORE; I KNOW MY DUTY. I'LL GET THE JOB DONE.
I NEED MORE THAN DUTY, FLAG. I NEED COMMITMENT! HEART AND SOUL STUFF!
SOME FOLKS HAVE ALREADY GIVEN ALL THEY HAD TO DO SOMETHING ABOUT THE WORLD WE'RE IN. IT'S UP TO US TO CARRY ON!
WHAT WE DO AND HOW WE DO IT WON'T BE EITHER PRETTY OR PLEASANT. BUT IT'S GOT TO BE DONE!
WE'RE HERE ONLY BECAUSE THERE REALLY IS NO ONE ELSE AND NO OTHER WAY OF DOING THE JOB AND THAT'S HOW IT IS.
WHEN THERE'S NO OTHER CHOICE, THERE'S STILL THE SUICIDE SQUAD.
CLOSE ENOUGH FOR GOVERNMENT WORK.
LET'S GO CATCH A PLANE AND I'LL SHOW YOU YOUR NEW HOME.
COMING IN TWO WEEKS--
SUICIDE SQUAD #1

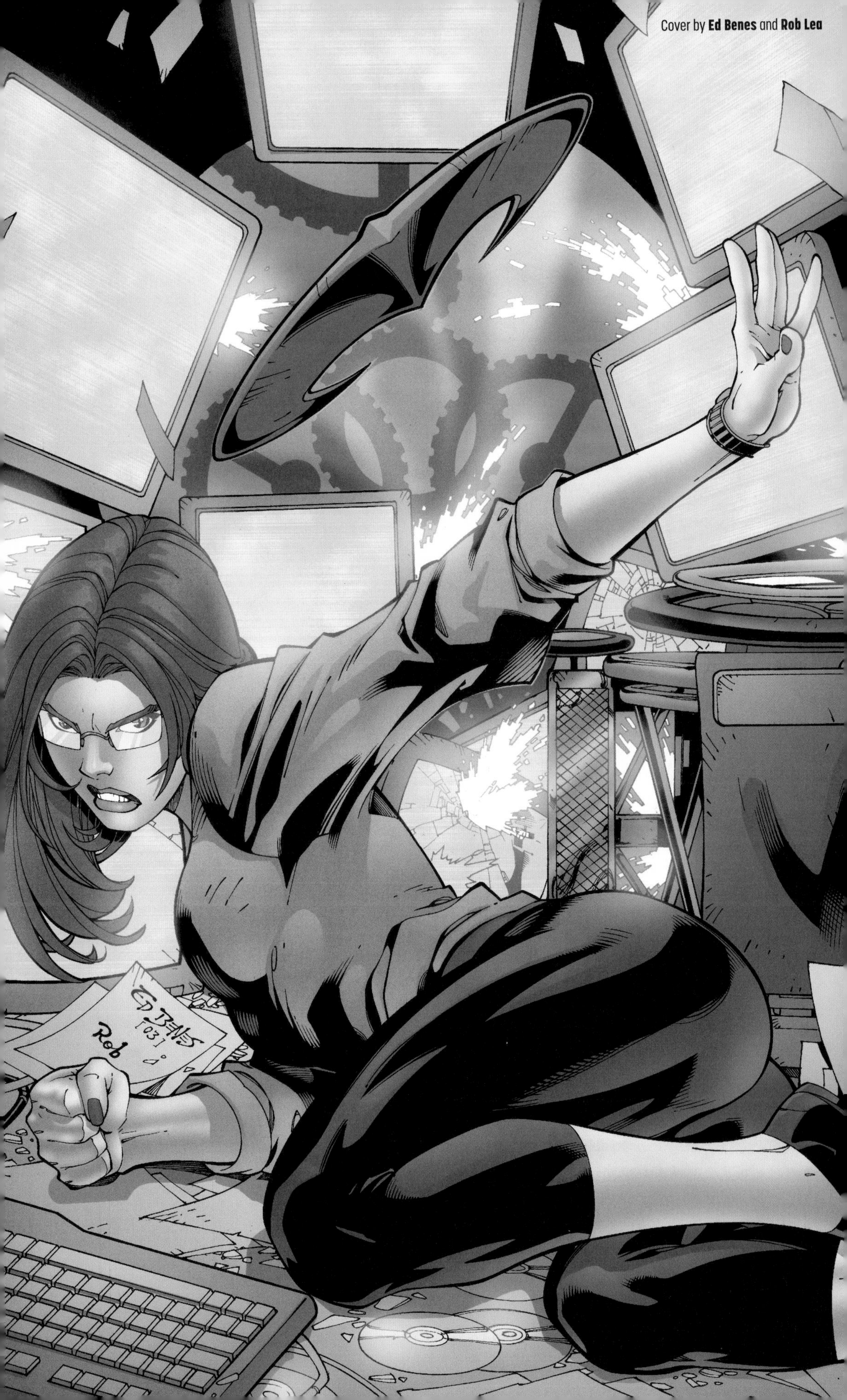

Cover by **Ed Benes** and **Rob Lea**

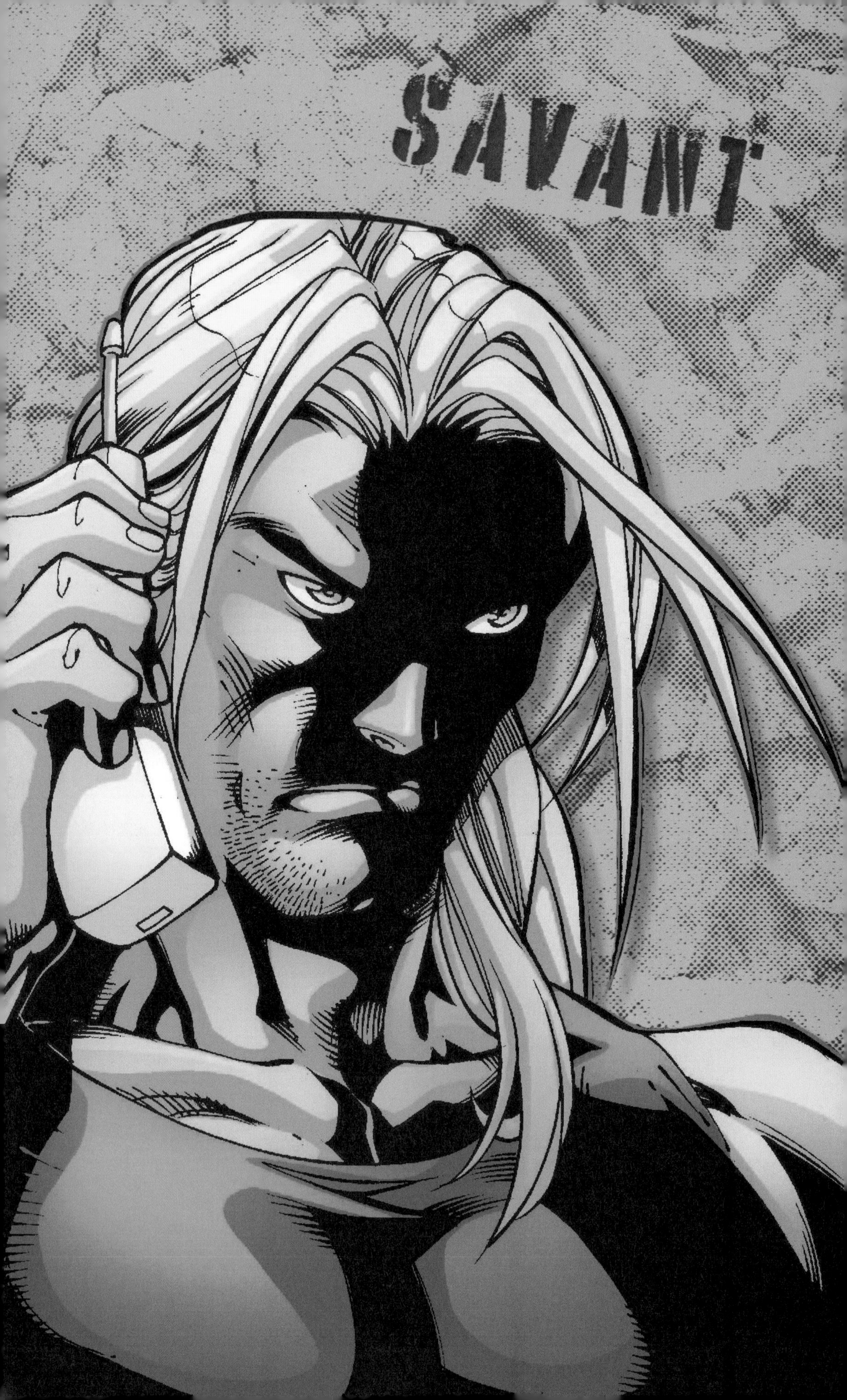
SAVANT

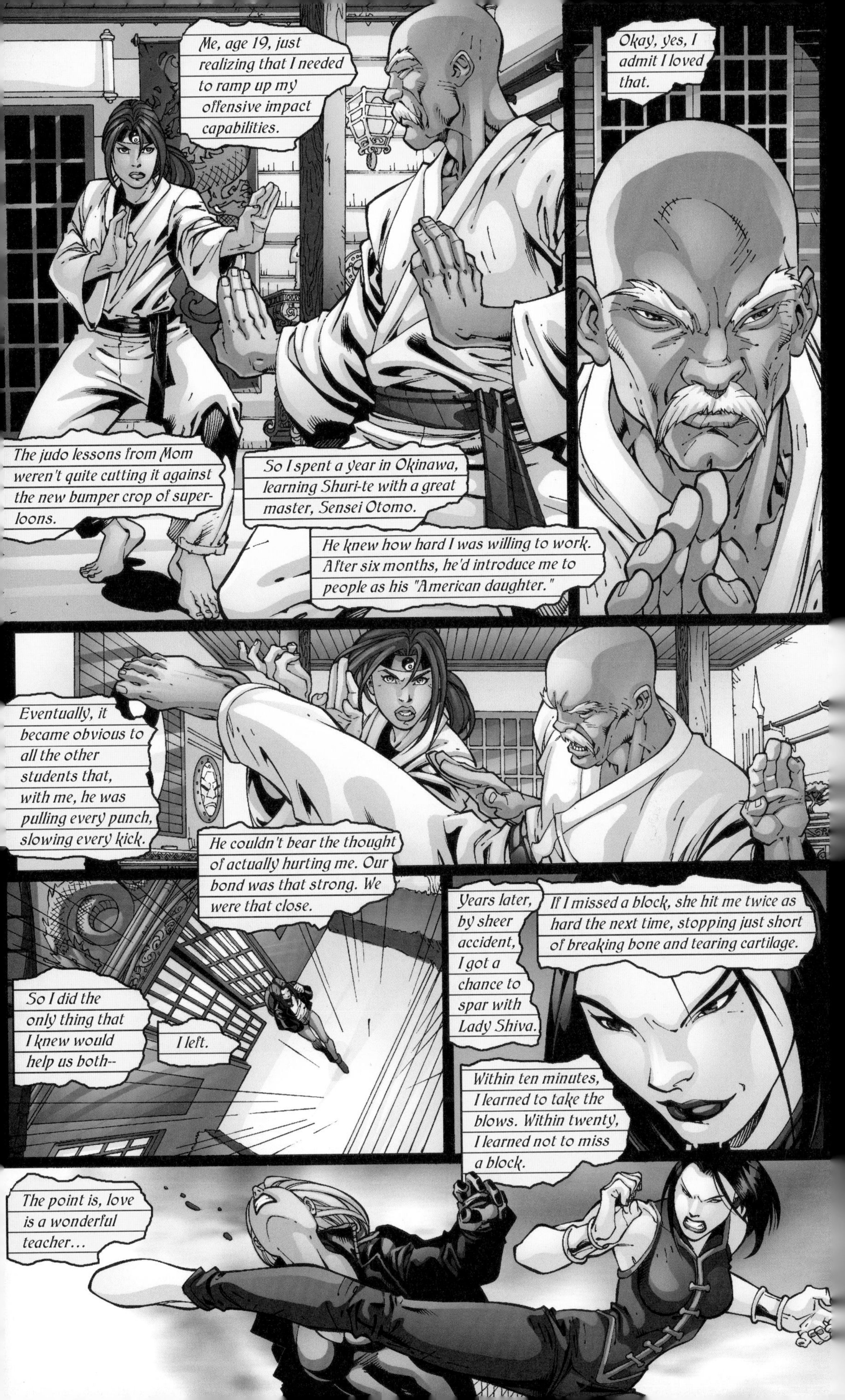
Me, age 19, just realizing that I needed to ramp up my offensive impact capabilities.
Okay, yes, I admit I loved that.
The judo lessons from Mom weren't quite cutting it against the new bumper crop of super-loons.
So I spent a year in Okinawa, learning Shuri-te with a great master, Sensei Otomo.
He knew how hard I was willing to work. After six months, he'd introduce me to people as his "American daughter."
Eventually, it became obvious to all the other students that, with me, he was pulling every punch, slowing every kick.
He couldn't bear the thought of actually hurting me. Our bond was that strong. We were that close.
So I did the only thing that I knew would help us both--
I left.
Years later, by sheer accident, I got a chance to spar with Lady Shiva.
If I missed a block, she hit me twice as hard the next time, stopping just short of breaking bone and tearing cartilage.
Within ten minutes, I learned to take the blows. Within twenty, I learned not to miss a block.
The point is, love is a wonderful teacher...

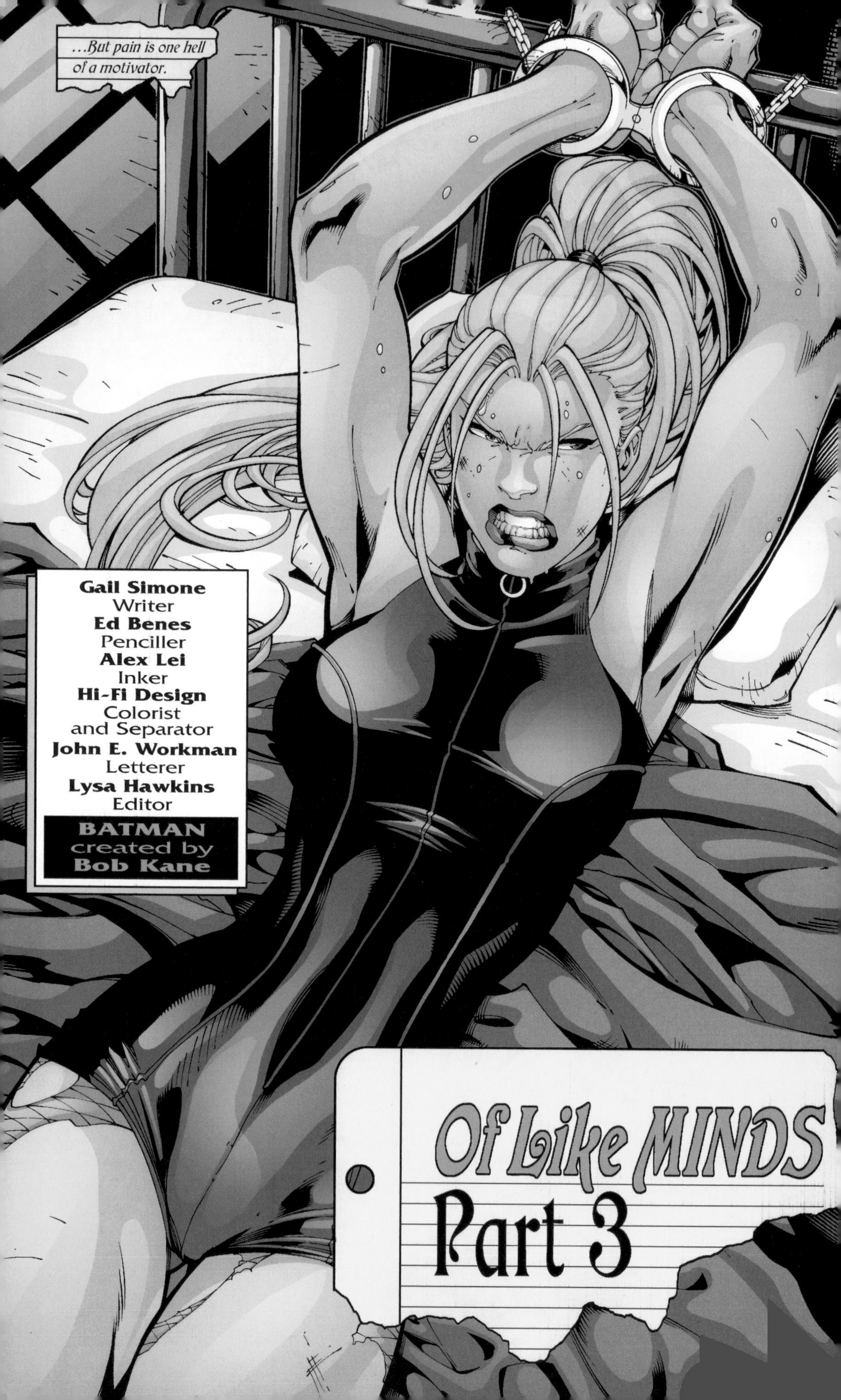

...But pain is one hell of a motivator.
Gail Simone Writer
Ed Benes Penciller
Alex Lei Inker
Hi-Fi Design Colorist and Separator
John E. Workman Letterer
Lysa Hawkins Editor
BATMAN created by Bob Kane
Of Like MINDS
Part 3

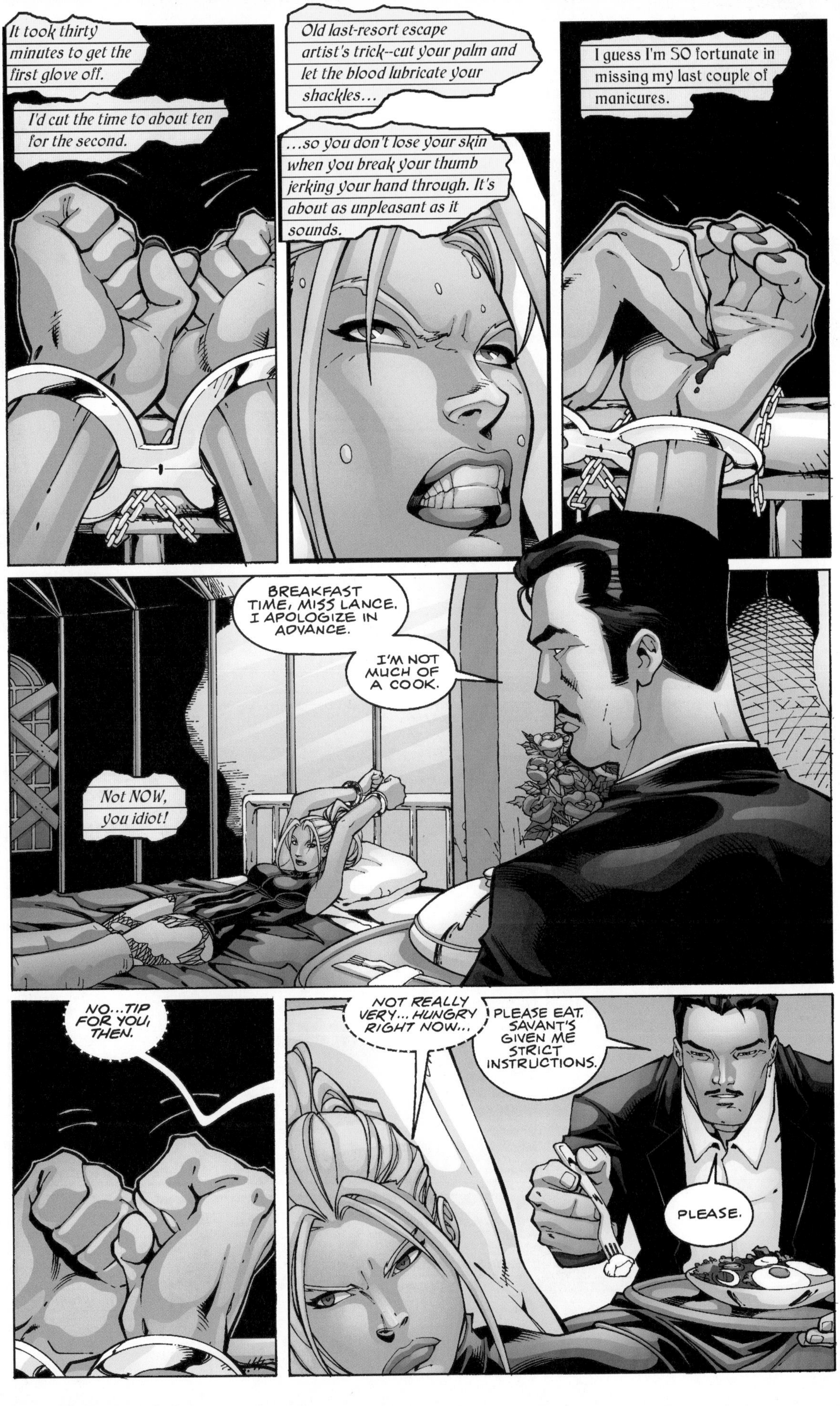

It took thirty minutes to get the first glove off.
I'd cut the time to about ten for the second.
Old last-resort escape artist's trick--cut your palm and let the blood lubricate your shackles...
...so you don't lose your skin when you break your thumb jerking your hand through. It's about as unpleasant as it sounds.
I guess I'm SO fortunate in missing my last couple of manicures.
BREAKFAST TIME, MISS LANCE. I APOLOGIZE IN ADVANCE.
I'M NOT MUCH OF A COOK.
Not NOW, you idiot!
NO...TIP FOR YOU, THEN.
NOT REALLY VERY... HUNGRY RIGHT NOW...
PLEASE EAT. SAVANT'S GIVEN ME STRICT INSTRUCTIONS.
PLEASE.

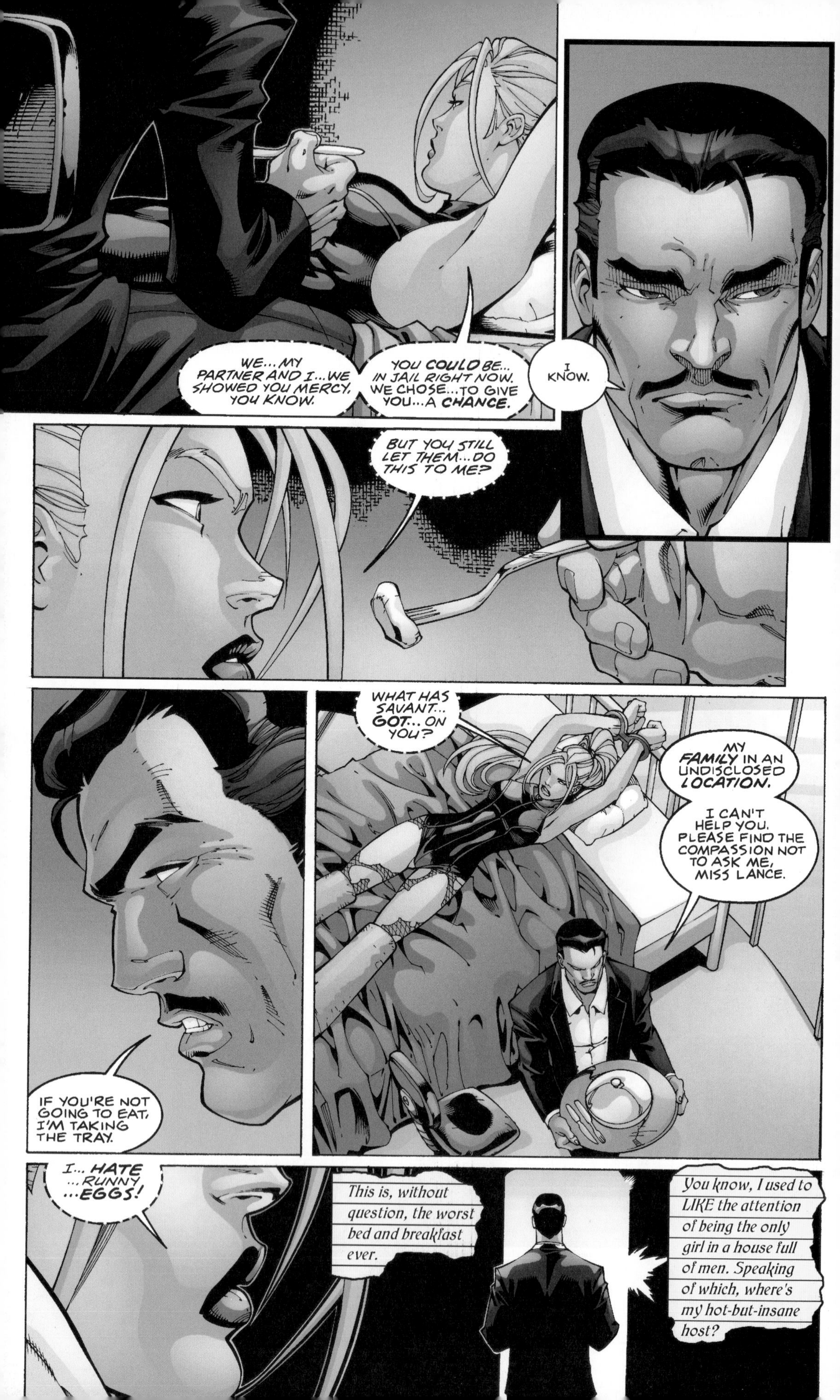
WE... MY PARTNER AND I... WE SHOWED YOU MERCY, YOU KNOW.
YOU COULD BE... IN JAIL RIGHT NOW. WE CHOSE... TO GIVE YOU... A CHANCE.
I KNOW.
BUT YOU STILL LET THEM... DO THIS TO ME?
WHAT HAS SAVANT... GOT... ON YOU?
MY FAMILY IN AN UNDISCLOSED LOCATION.
I CAN'T HELP YOU. PLEASE FIND THE COMPASSION NOT TO ASK ME, MISS LANCE.
IF YOU'RE NOT GOING TO EAT, I'M TAKING THE TRAY.
I... HATE ...RUNNY ...EGGS!
This is, without question, the worst bed and breakfast ever.
You know, I used to LIKE the attention of being the only girl in a house full of men. Speaking of which, where's my hot-but-insane host?

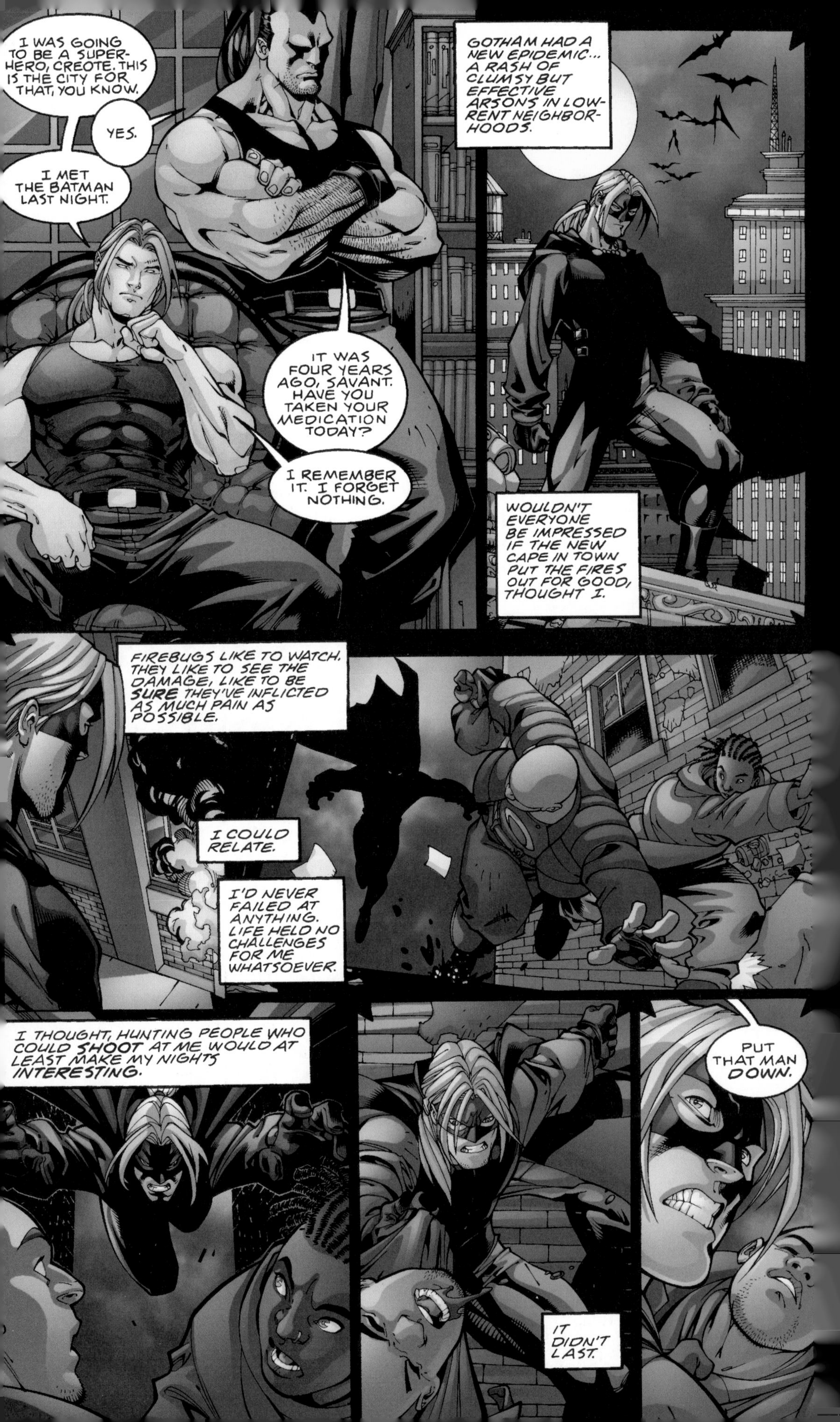
I WAS GOING TO BE A SUPER-HERO, CREOTE. THIS IS THE CITY FOR THAT, YOU KNOW.
YES.
I MET THE BATMAN LAST NIGHT.
IT WAS FOUR YEARS AGO, SAVANT. HAVE YOU TAKEN YOUR MEDICATION TODAY?
I REMEMBER IT. I FORGET NOTHING.
GOTHAM HAD A NEW EPIDEMIC... A RASH OF CLUMSY BUT EFFECTIVE ARSONS IN LOW-RENT NEIGHBORHOODS.
WOULDN'T EVERYONE BE IMPRESSED IF THE NEW CAPE IN TOWN PUT THE FIRES OUT FOR GOOD, THOUGHT I.
FIREBUGS LIKE TO WATCH. THEY LIKE TO SEE THE DAMAGE, LIKE TO BE SURE THEY'VE INFLICTED AS MUCH PAIN AS POSSIBLE.
I COULD RELATE.
I'D NEVER FAILED AT ANYTHING. LIFE HELD NO CHALLENGES FOR ME WHATSOEVER.
I THOUGHT, HUNTING PEOPLE WHO COULD SHOOT AT ME WOULD AT LEAST MAKE MY NIGHTS INTERESTING.
IT DIDN'T LAST.
PUT THAT MAN DOWN.

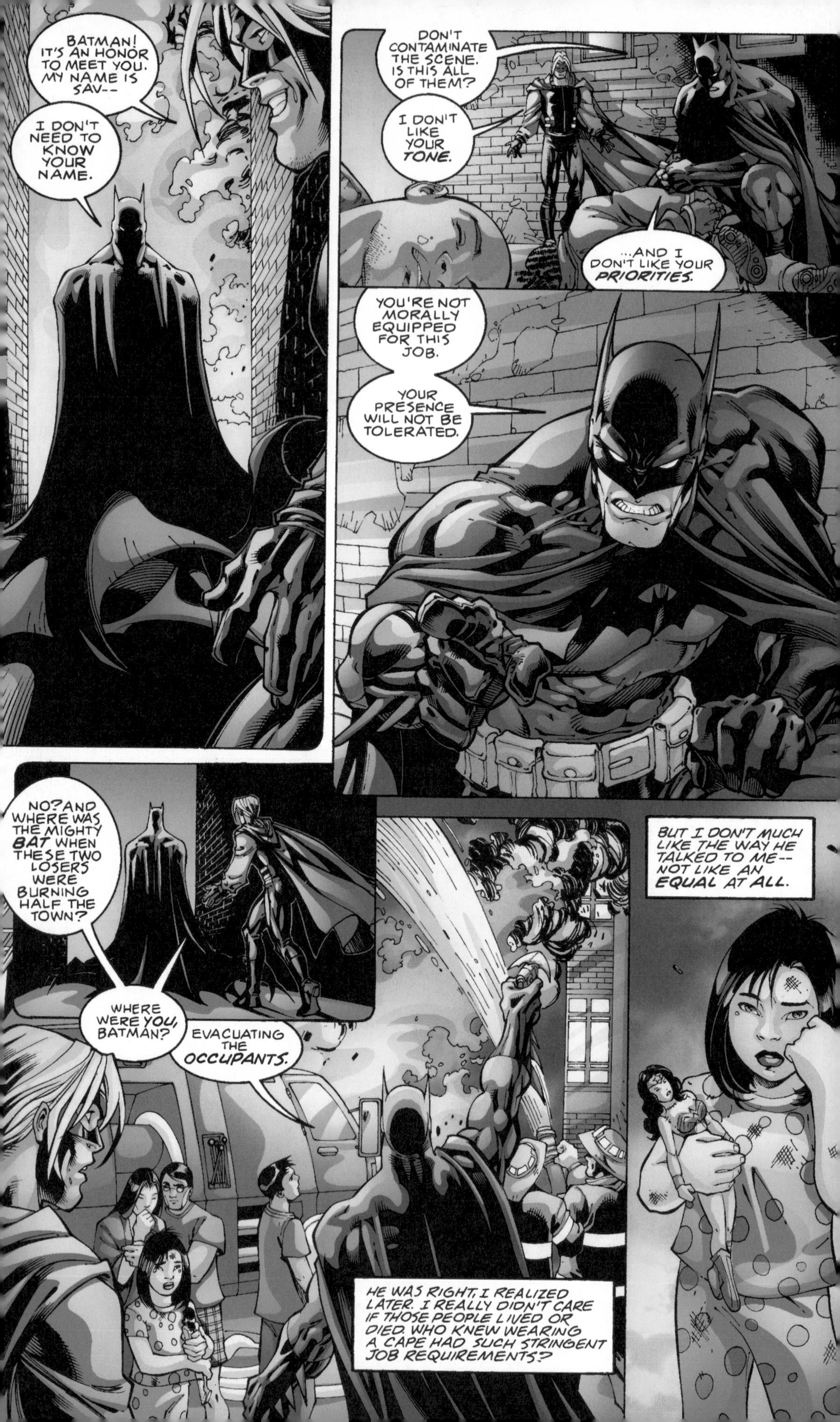
BATMAN! IT'S AN HONOR TO MEET YOU. MY NAME IS SAV--
I DON'T NEED TO KNOW YOUR NAME.
DON'T CONTAMINATE THE SCENE. IS THIS ALL OF THEM?
I DON'T LIKE YOUR TONE.
...AND I DON'T LIKE YOUR PRIORITIES.
YOU'RE NOT MORALLY EQUIPPED FOR THIS JOB.
YOUR PRESENCE WILL NOT BE TOLERATED.
NO? AND WHERE WAS THE MIGHTY BAT WHEN THESE TWO LOSERS WERE BURNING HALF THE TOWN?
WHERE WERE YOU, BATMAN?
EVACUATING THE OCCUPANTS.
BUT I DON'T MUCH LIKE THE WAY HE TALKED TO ME-- NOT LIKE AN EQUAL AT ALL.
HE WAS RIGHT, I REALIZED LATER. I REALLY DIDN'T CARE IF THOSE PEOPLE LIVED OR DIED. WHO KNEW WEARING A CAPE HAD SUCH STRINGENT JOB REQUIREMENTS?

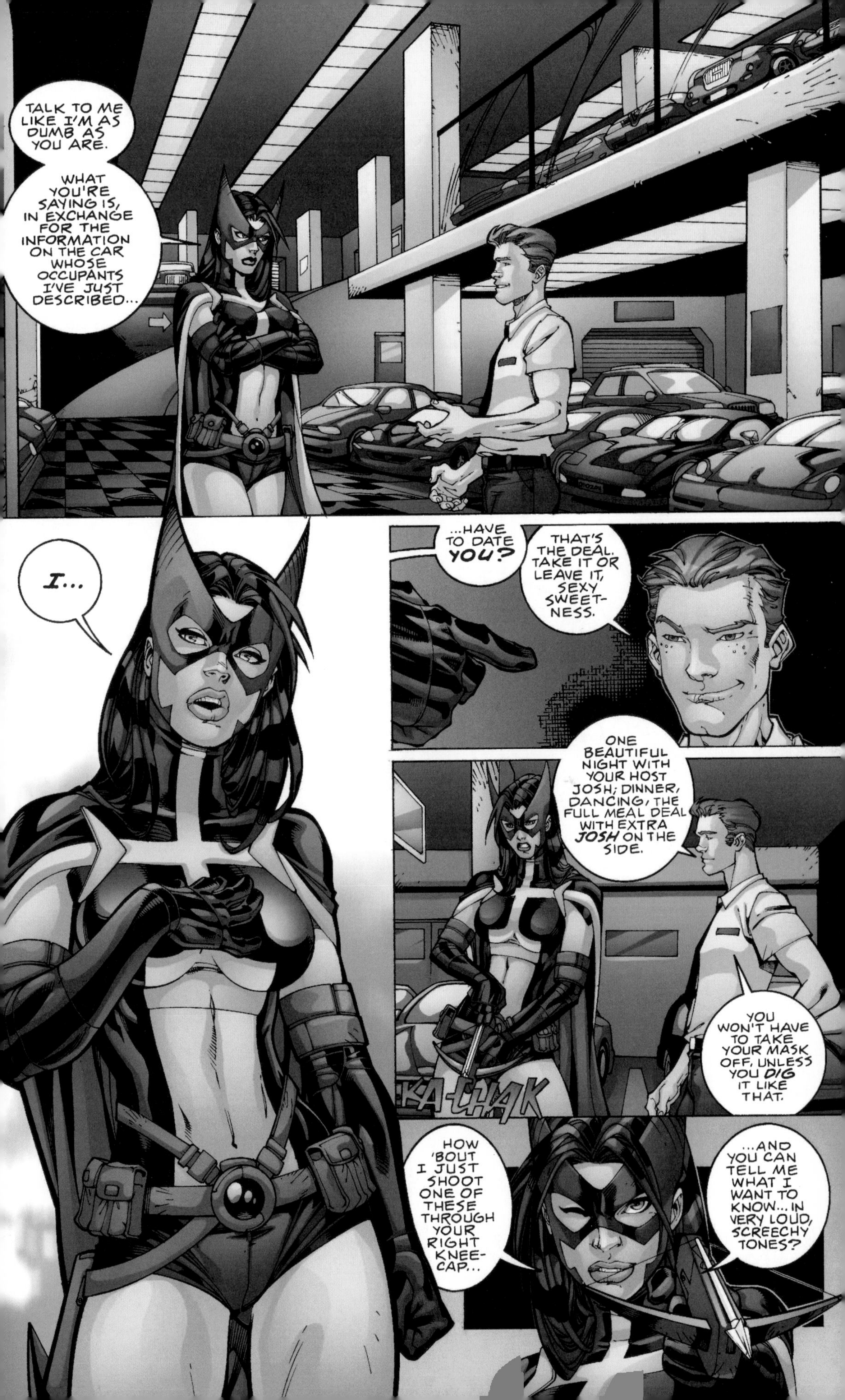
TALK TO ME LIKE I'M AS DUMB AS YOU ARE.
WHAT YOU'RE SAYING IS, IN EXCHANGE FOR THE INFORMATION ON THE CAR WHOSE OCCUPANTS I'VE JUST DESCRIBED...
I...
...HAVE TO DATE YOU?
THAT'S THE DEAL. TAKE IT OR LEAVE IT, SEXY SWEET-NESS.
ONE BEAUTIFUL NIGHT WITH YOUR HOST JOSH; DINNER, DANCING, THE FULL MEAL DEAL WITH EXTRA JOSH ON THE SIDE.
YOU WON'T HAVE TO TAKE YOUR MASK OFF, UNLESS YOU DIG IT LIKE THAT.
KA-CHAK
HOW 'BOUT I JUST SHOOT ONE OF THESE THROUGH YOUR RIGHT KNEE-CAP...
...AND YOU CAN TELL ME WHAT I WANT TO KNOW... IN VERY LOUD, SCREECHY TONES?

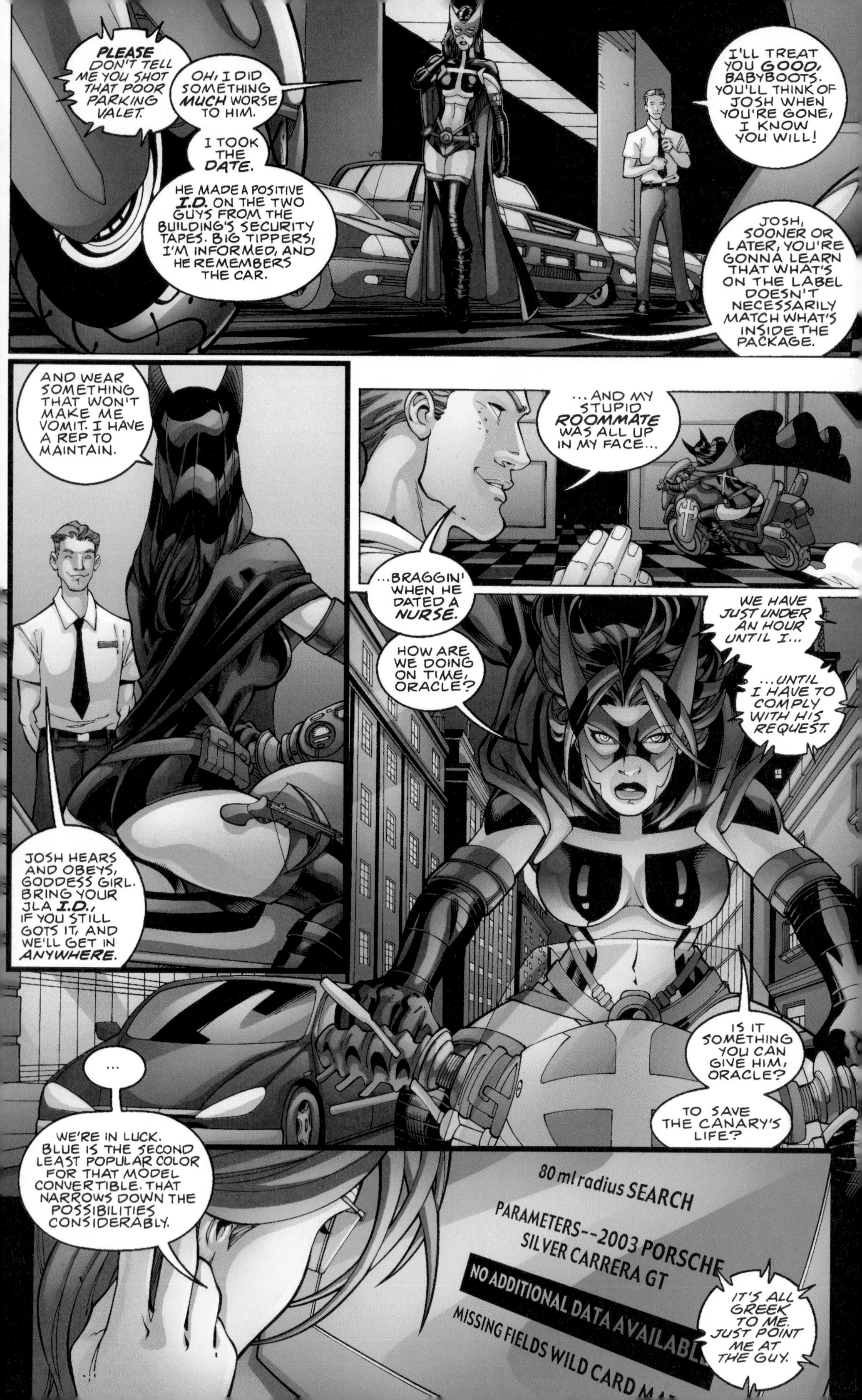
PLEASE DON'T TELL ME YOU SHOT THAT POOR PARKING VALET.
OH, I DID SOMETHING MUCH WORSE TO HIM.
I TOOK THE DATE.
HE MADE A POSITIVE I.D. ON THE TWO GUYS FROM THE BUILDING'S SECURITY TAPES. BIG TIPPERS, I'M INFORMED, AND HE REMEMBERS THE CAR.
I'LL TREAT YOU GOOD, BABYBOOTS. YOU'LL THINK OF JOSH WHEN YOU'RE GONE, I KNOW YOU WILL!
JOSH, SOONER OR LATER, YOU'RE GONNA LEARN THAT WHAT'S ON THE LABEL DOESN'T NECESSARILY MATCH WHAT'S INSIDE THE PACKAGE.
AND WEAR SOMETHING THAT WON'T MAKE ME VOMIT. I HAVE A REP TO MAINTAIN.
JOSH HEARS AND OBEYS, GODDESS GIRL. BRING YOUR JLA I.D., IF YOU STILL GOTS IT, AND WE'LL GET IN ANYWHERE.
...AND MY STUPID ROOMMATE WAS ALL UP IN MY FACE...
...BRAGGIN' WHEN HE DATED A NURSE.
HOW ARE WE DOING ON TIME, ORACLE?
WE HAVE JUST UNDER AN HOUR UNTIL I...
...UNTIL I HAVE TO COMPLY WITH HIS REQUEST.
IS IT SOMETHING YOU CAN GIVE HIM, ORACLE?
TO SAVE THE CANARY'S LIFE?
...
WE'RE IN LUCK. BLUE IS THE SECOND LEAST POPULAR COLOR FOR THAT MODEL CONVERTIBLE. THAT NARROWS DOWN THE POSSIBILITIES CONSIDERABLY.
80 ml radius SEARCH
PARAMETERS--2003 PORSCHE SILVER CARRERA GT
NO ADDITIONAL DATA AVAILABLE
MISSING FIELDS WILD CARD MA
IT'S ALL GREEK TO ME. JUST POINT ME AT THE GUY.

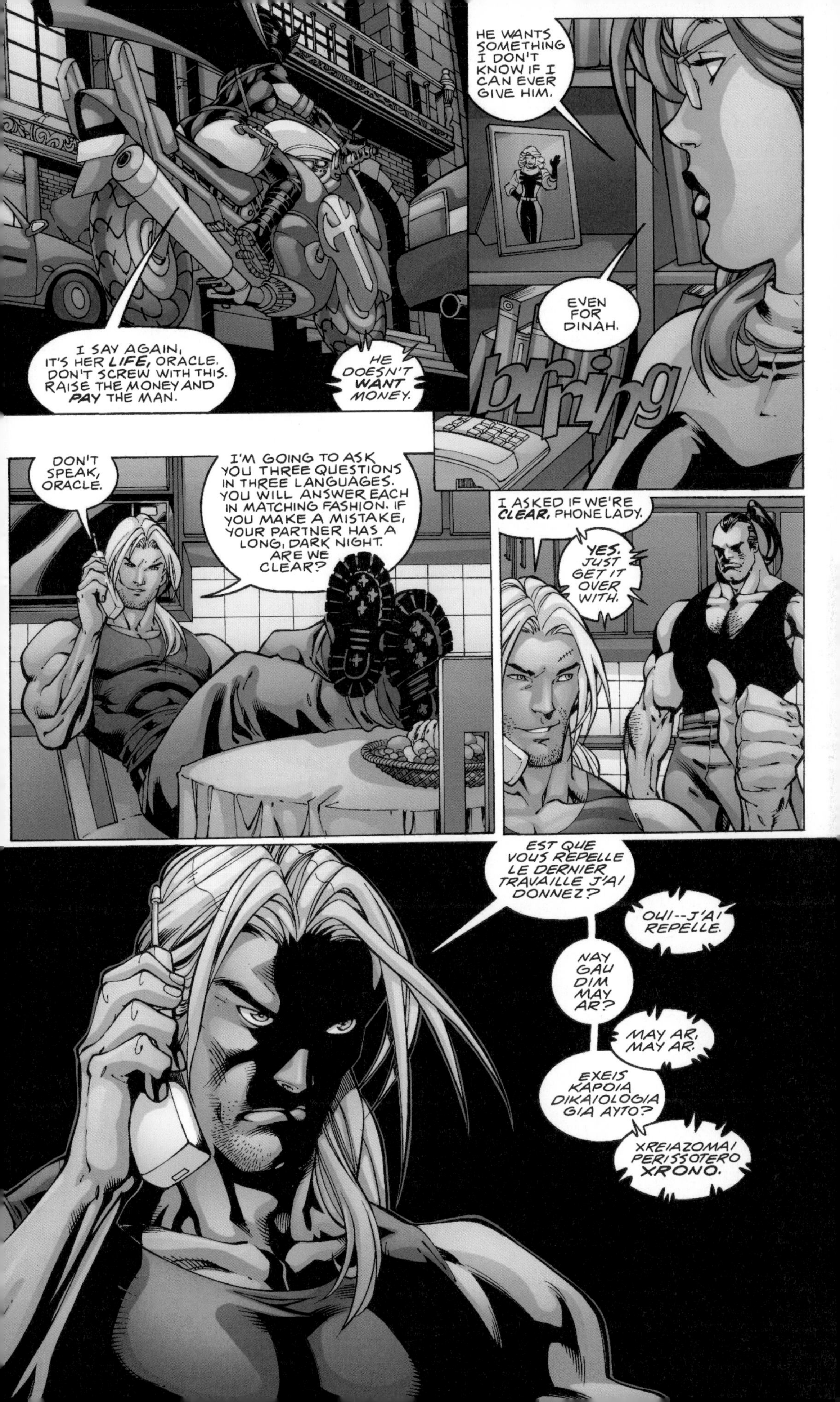
I SAY AGAIN, IT'S HER LIFE, ORACLE. DON'T SCREW WITH THIS. RAISE THE MONEY AND PAY THE MAN.
HE DOESN'T WANT MONEY.
HE WANTS SOMETHING I DON'T KNOW IF I CAN EVER GIVE HIM.
EVEN FOR DINAH.
brring
DON'T SPEAK, ORACLE.
I'M GOING TO ASK YOU THREE QUESTIONS IN THREE LANGUAGES. YOU WILL ANSWER EACH IN MATCHING FASHION. IF YOU MAKE A MISTAKE, YOUR PARTNER HAS A LONG, DARK NIGHT. ARE WE CLEAR?
I ASKED IF WE'RE CLEAR, PHONE LADY.
YES. JUST GET IT OVER WITH.
EST QUE VOUS REPELLE LE DERNIER TRAVAILLE J'AI DONNEZ?
OUI--J'AI REPELLE.
NAY GAU DIM MAY AR?
MAY AR, MAY AR.
EXEIS KAPOIA DIKAIOLOGIA GIA AYTO?
XREIAZOMAI PERISSOTERO XRONO.

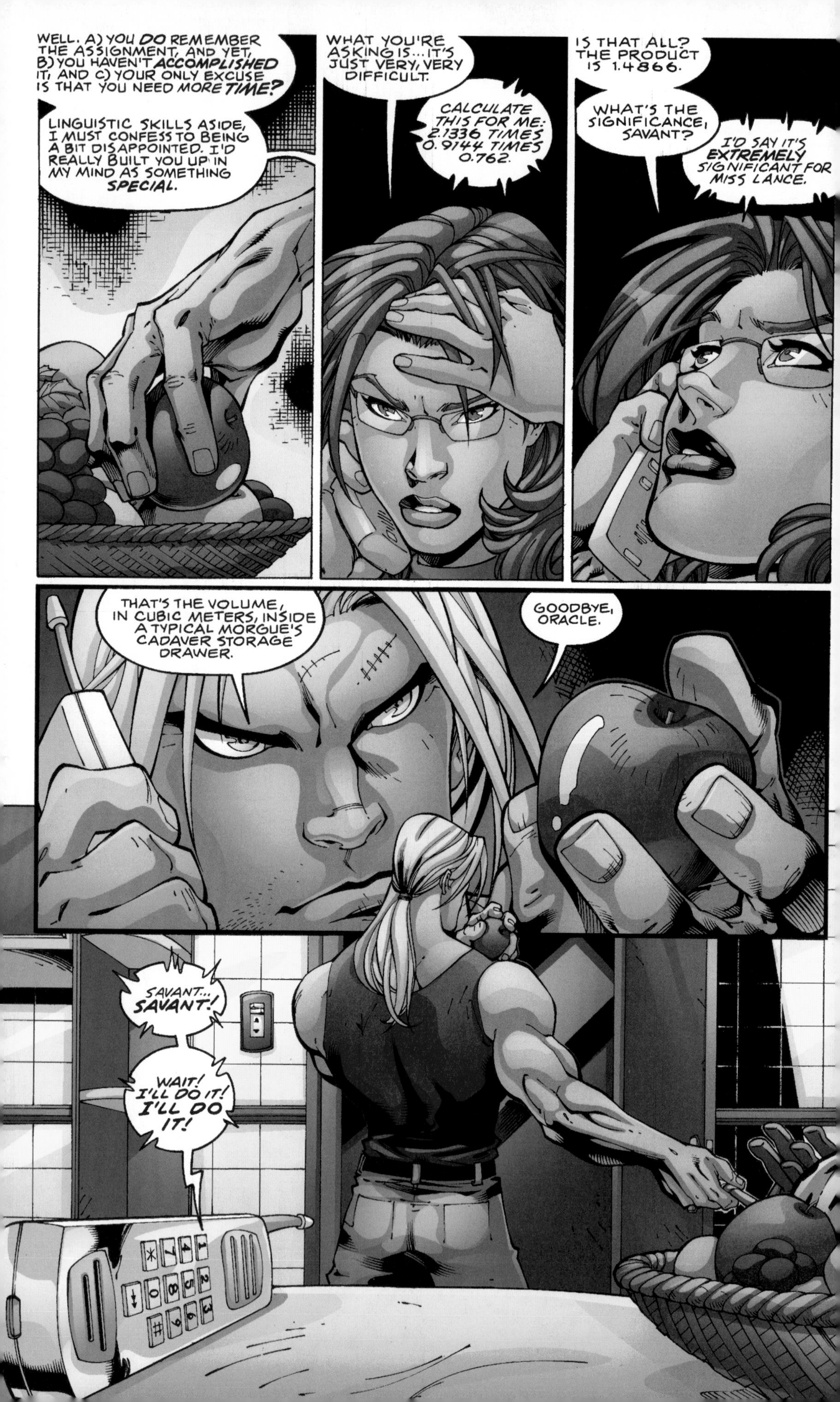
WELL. A) YOU DO REMEMBER THE ASSIGNMENT, AND YET, B) YOU HAVEN'T ACCOMPLISHED IT, AND C) YOUR ONLY EXCUSE IS THAT YOU NEED MORE TIME?
LINGUISTIC SKILLS ASIDE, I MUST CONFESS TO BEING A BIT DISAPPOINTED. I'D REALLY BUILT YOU UP IN MY MIND AS SOMETHING SPECIAL.
WHAT YOU'RE ASKING IS... IT'S JUST VERY, VERY DIFFICULT.
CALCULATE THIS FOR ME: 2.1336 TIMES 0.9144 TIMES 0.762.
IS THAT ALL? THE PRODUCT IS 1.4866.
WHAT'S THE SIGNIFICANCE, SAVANT?
I'D SAY IT'S EXTREMELY SIGNIFICANT FOR MISS LANCE.
THAT'S THE VOLUME, IN CUBIC METERS, INSIDE A TYPICAL MORGUE'S CADAVER STORAGE DRAWER.
GOODBYE, ORACLE.
SAVANT... SAVANT!
WAIT! I'LL DO IT! I'LL DO IT!

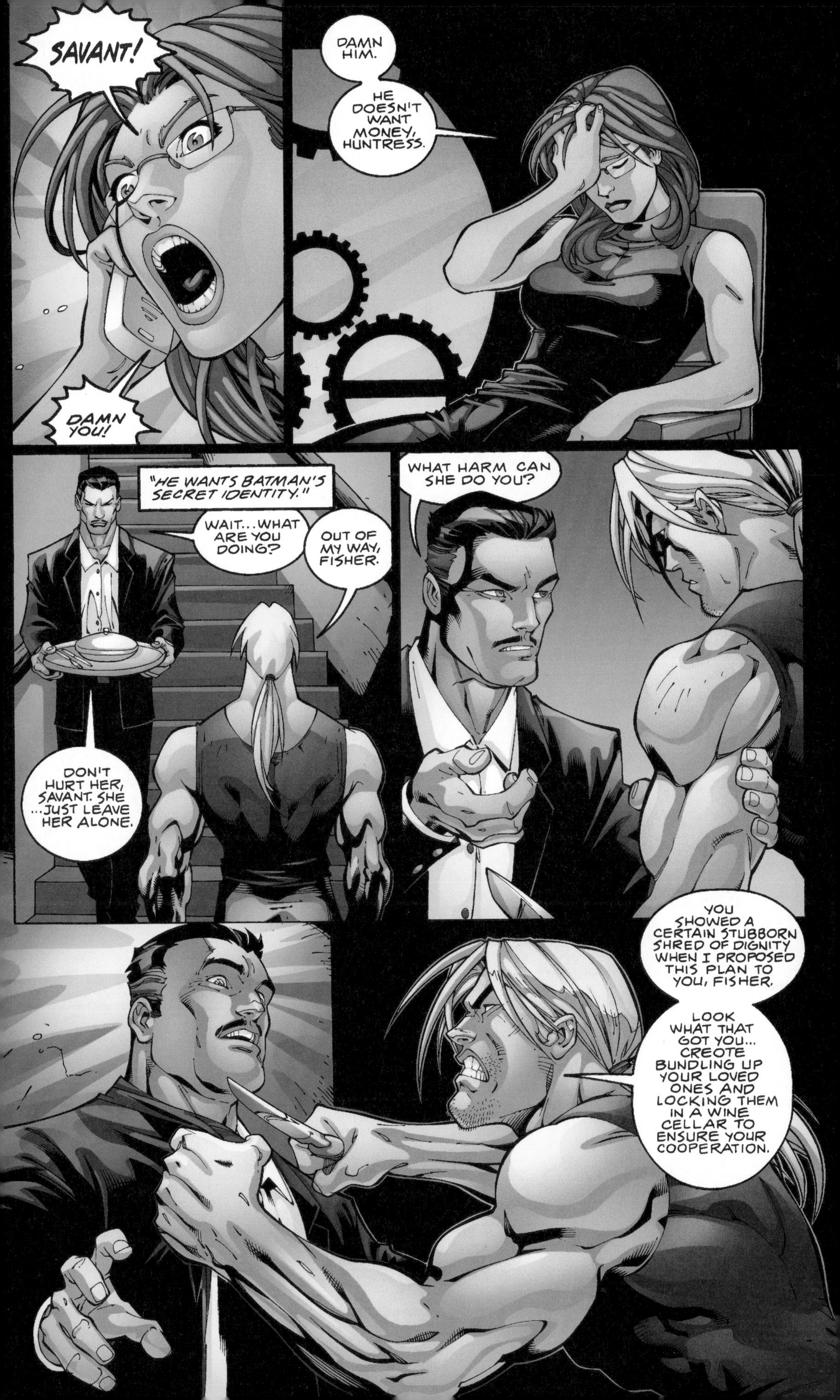
SAVANT!
DAMN YOU!
DAMN HIM.
HE DOESN'T WANT MONEY, HUNTRESS.
"HE WANTS BATMAN'S SECRET IDENTITY."
WAIT... WHAT ARE YOU DOING?
OUT OF MY WAY, FISHER.
DON'T HURT HER, SAVANT. SHE ...JUST LEAVE HER ALONE.
WHAT HARM CAN SHE DO YOU?
YOU SHOWED A CERTAIN STUBBORN SHRED OF DIGNITY WHEN I PROPOSED THIS PLAN TO YOU, FISHER.
LOOK WHAT THAT GOT YOU... CREOTE BUNDLING UP YOUR LOVED ONES AND LOCKING THEM IN A WINE CELLAR TO ENSURE YOUR COOPERATION.

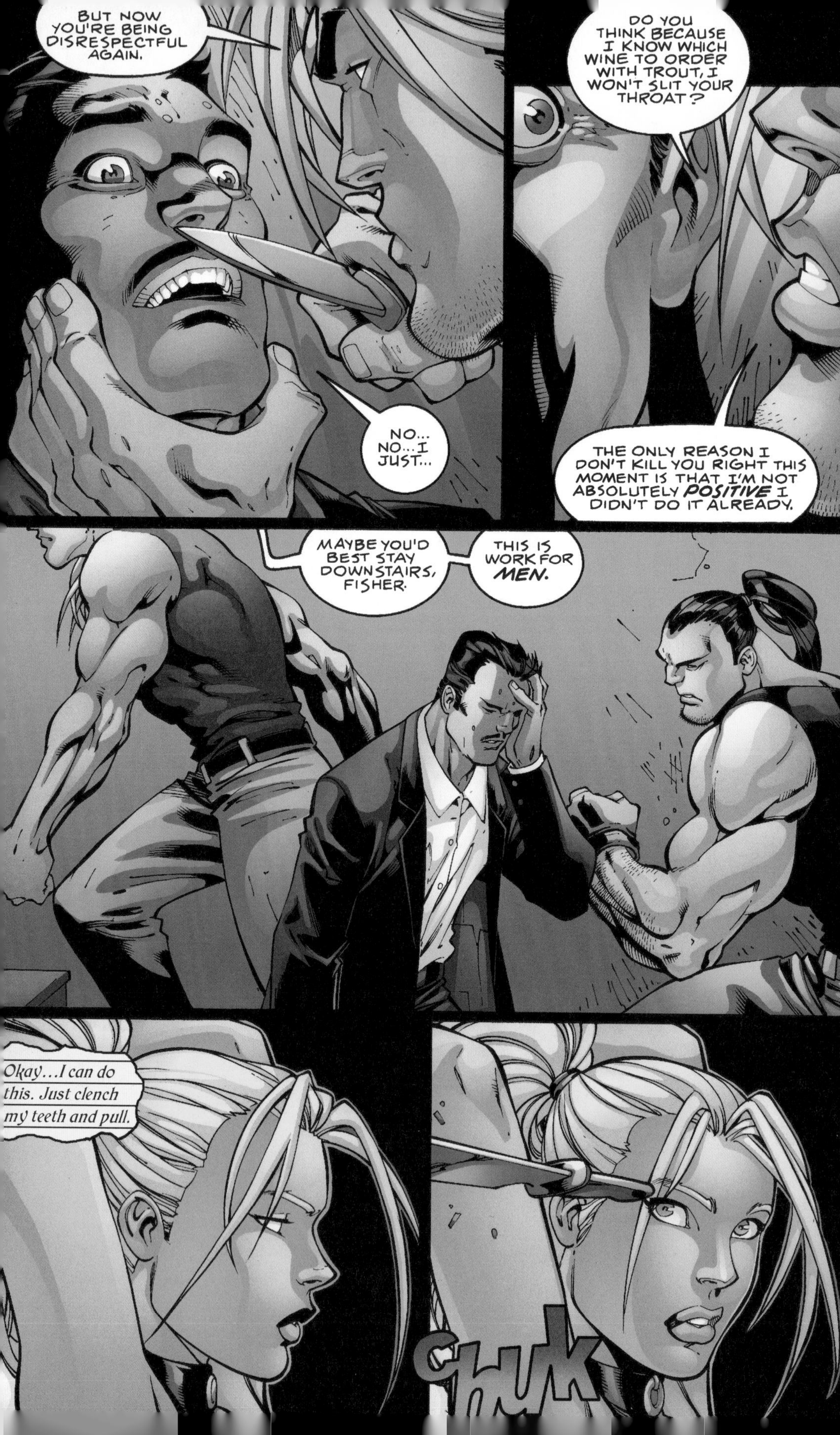
BUT NOW YOU'RE BEING DISRESPECTFUL AGAIN.
NO... NO... I JUST...
DO YOU THINK BECAUSE I KNOW WHICH WINE TO ORDER WITH TROUT, I WON'T SLIT YOUR THROAT?
THE ONLY REASON I DON'T KILL YOU RIGHT THIS MOMENT IS THAT I'M NOT ABSOLUTELY POSITIVE I DIDN'T DO IT ALREADY.
MAYBE YOU'D BEST STAY DOWNSTAIRS, FISHER.
THIS IS WORK FOR MEN.
Okay...I can do this. Just clench my teeth and pull.
CHUK

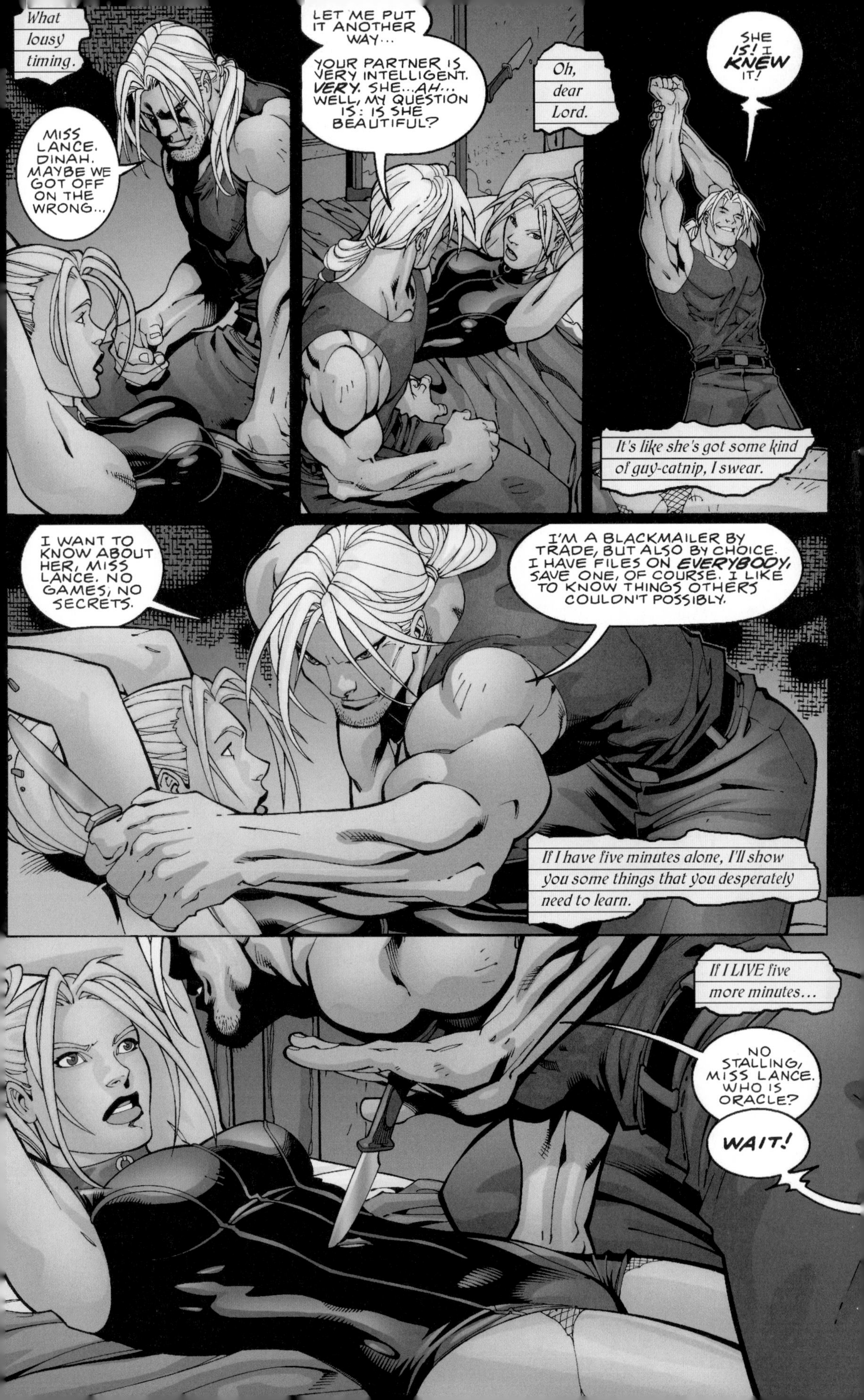

What lousy timing.
MISS LANCE. DINAH. MAYBE WE GOT OFF ON THE WRONG...
LET ME PUT IT ANOTHER WAY...
YOUR PARTNER IS VERY INTELLIGENT. VERY. SHE...AH... WELL, MY QUESTION IS: IS SHE BEAUTIFUL?
Oh, dear Lord.
SHE IS! I KNEW IT!
It's like she's got some kind of guy-catnip, I swear.
I WANT TO KNOW ABOUT HER, MISS LANCE. NO GAMES, NO SECRETS.
I'M A BLACKMAILER BY TRADE, BUT ALSO BY CHOICE. I HAVE FILES ON EVERYBODY, SAVE ONE, OF COURSE. I LIKE TO KNOW THINGS OTHERS COULDN'T POSSIBLY.
If I have five minutes alone, I'll show you some things that you desperately need to learn.
If I LIVE five more minutes...
NO STALLING, MISS LANCE. WHO IS ORACLE?
WAIT!

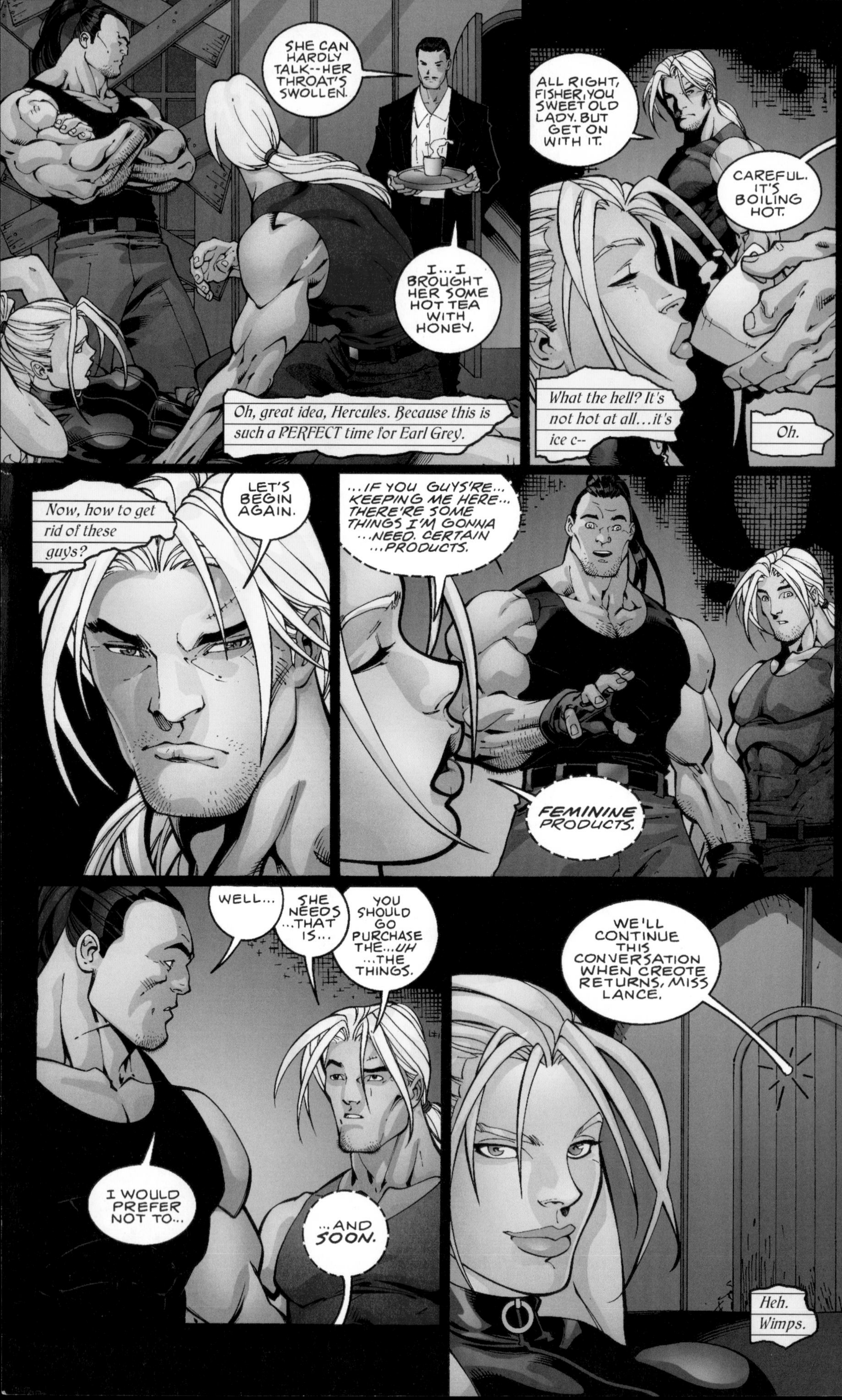
SHE CAN HARDLY TALK--HER THROAT'S SWOLLEN.
I... I BROUGHT HER SOME HOT TEA WITH HONEY.
Oh, great idea, Hercules. Because this is such a PERFECT time for Earl Grey.
ALL RIGHT, FISHER, YOU SWEET OLD LADY. BUT GET ON WITH IT.
CAREFUL. IT'S BOILING HOT.
What the hell? It's not hot at all...it's ice c--
Oh.
Now, how to get rid of these guys?
LET'S BEGIN AGAIN.
...IF YOU GUYS'RE... KEEPING ME HERE... THERE'RE SOME THINGS I'M GONNA ...NEED. CERTAIN ...PRODUCTS.
FEMININE PRODUCTS.
WELL...
SHE NEEDS ...THAT IS...
YOU SHOULD GO PURCHASE THE...UH ...THE THINGS.
I WOULD PREFER NOT TO...
...AND SOON.
WE'LL CONTINUE THIS CONVERSATION WHEN CREOTE RETURNS, MISS LANCE.
Heh. Wimps.

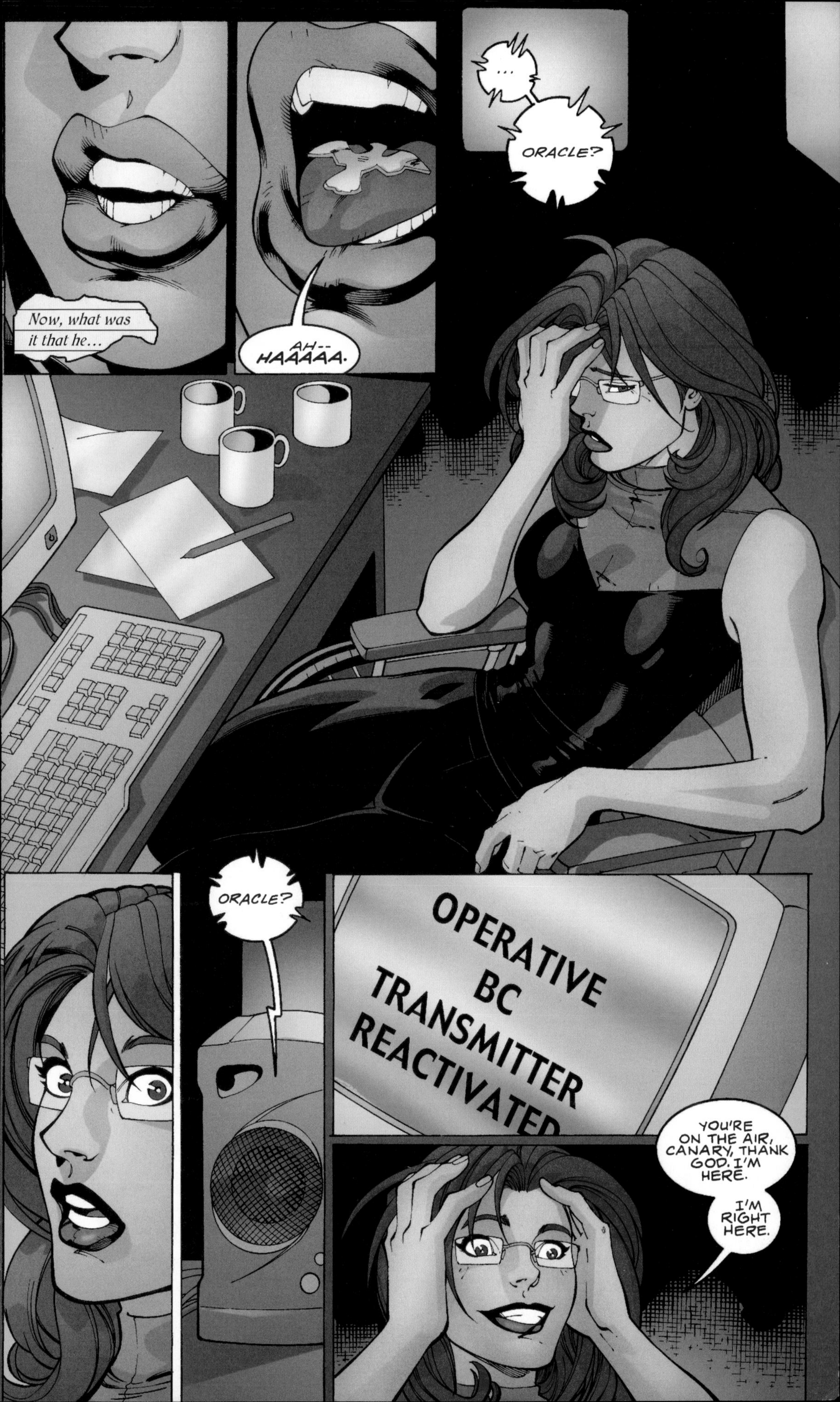

Now, what was it that he…
AH-- HAAAAA.
...
ORACLE?
ORACLE?
OPERATIVE BC TRANSMITTER REACTIVATED
YOU'RE ON THE AIR, CANARY, THANK GOD. I'M HERE.
I'M RIGHT HERE.

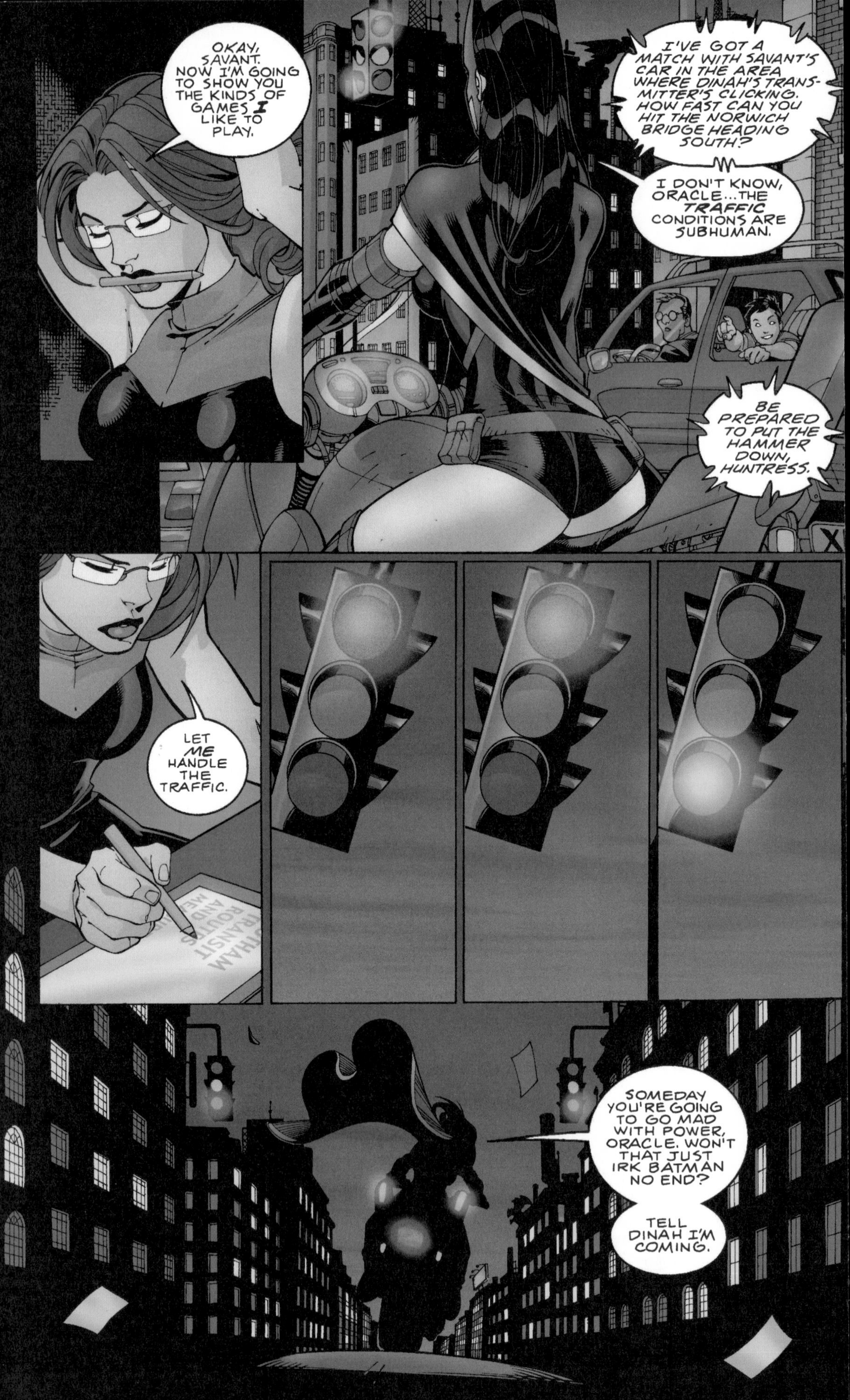
OKAY, SAVANT. NOW I'M GOING TO SHOW YOU THE KINDS OF GAMES *I* LIKE TO PLAY.
I'VE GOT A MATCH WITH SAVANT'S CAR IN THE AREA WHERE DINAH'S TRANS-MITTER'S CLICKING. HOW FAST CAN YOU HIT THE NORWICH BRIDGE HEADING SOUTH?
I DON'T KNOW, ORACLE...THE *TRAFFIC* CONDITIONS ARE SUBHUMAN.
BE PREPARED TO PUT THE HAMMER DOWN, HUNTRESS.
LET *ME* HANDLE THE TRAFFIC.
SOMEDAY YOU'RE GOING TO GO MAD WITH POWER, ORACLE. WON'T THAT JUST IRK BATMAN NO END?
TELL DINAH I'M COMING.

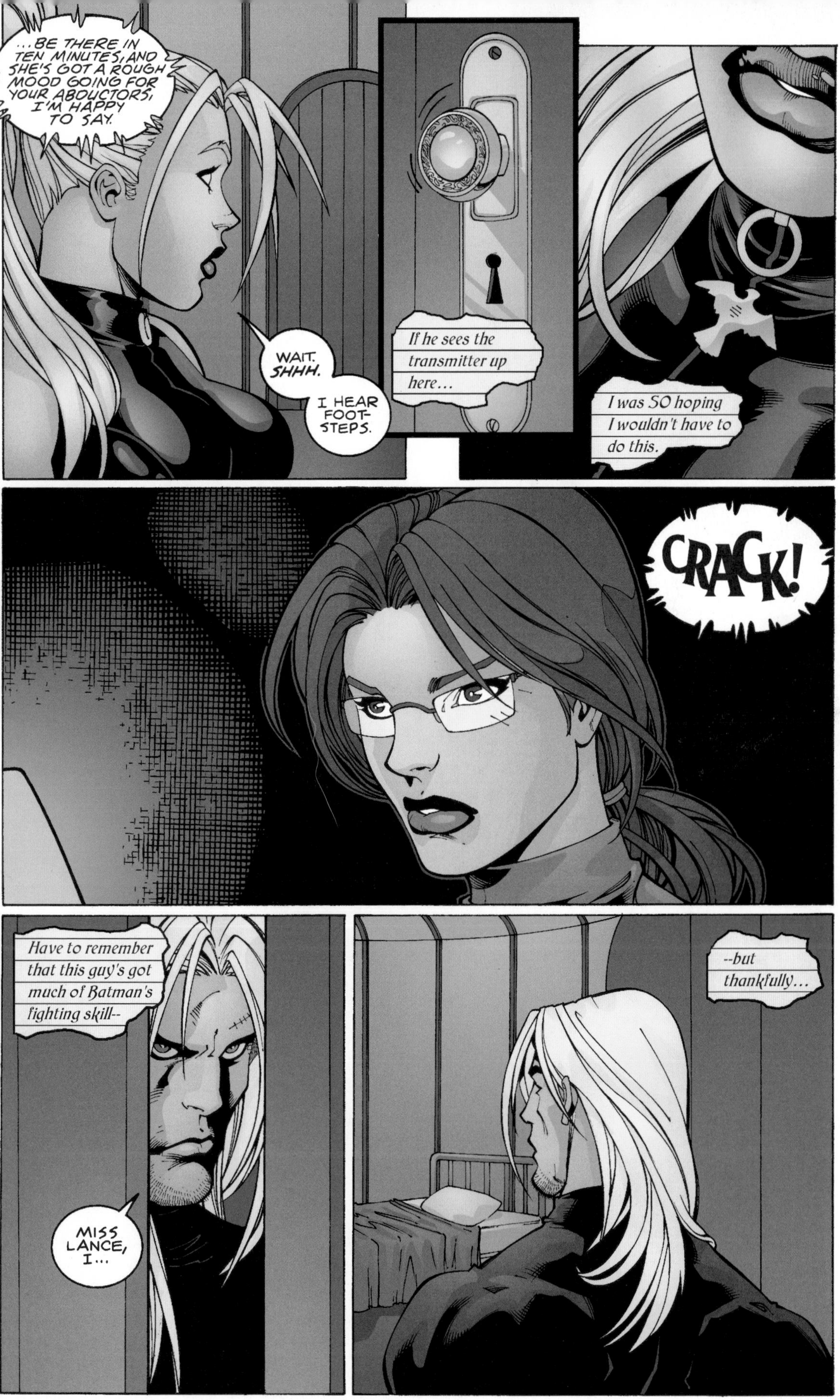

...BE THERE IN TEN MINUTES, AND SHE'S GOT A ROUGH MOOD GOING FOR YOUR ABDUCTORS, I'M HAPPY TO SAY.
WAIT. SHHH.
I HEAR FOOT-STEPS.
If he sees the transmitter up here...
I was SO hoping I wouldn't have to do this.
CRACK!
Have to remember that this guy's got much of Batman's fighting skill--
MISS LANCE, I...
--but thankfully...

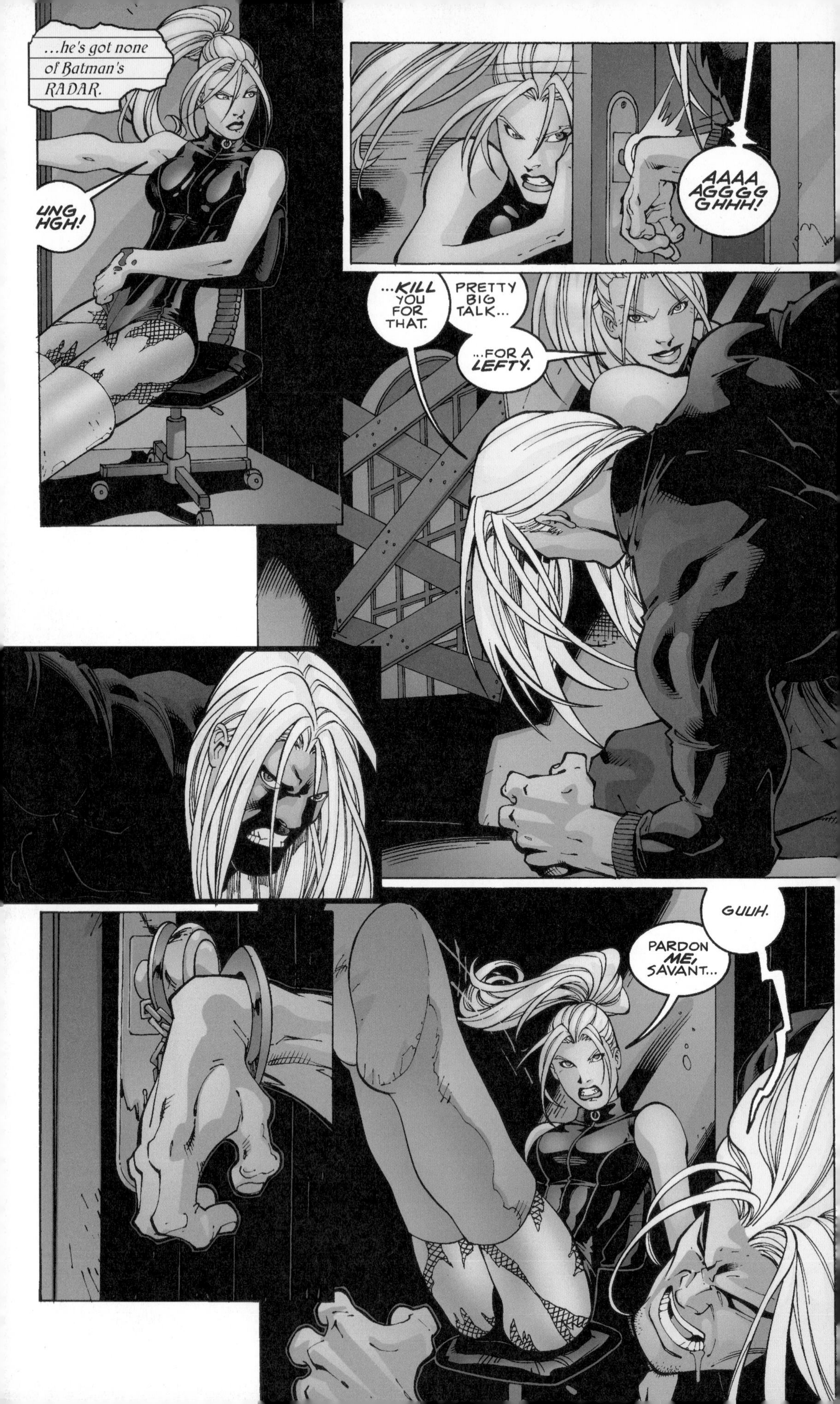

...he's got none of Batman's RADAR.
UNG HGH!
AAAA AGGGG GHHH!
PRETTY BIG TALK...
...KILL YOU FOR THAT.
...FOR A LEFTY.
GUUH.
PARDON ME, SAVANT...

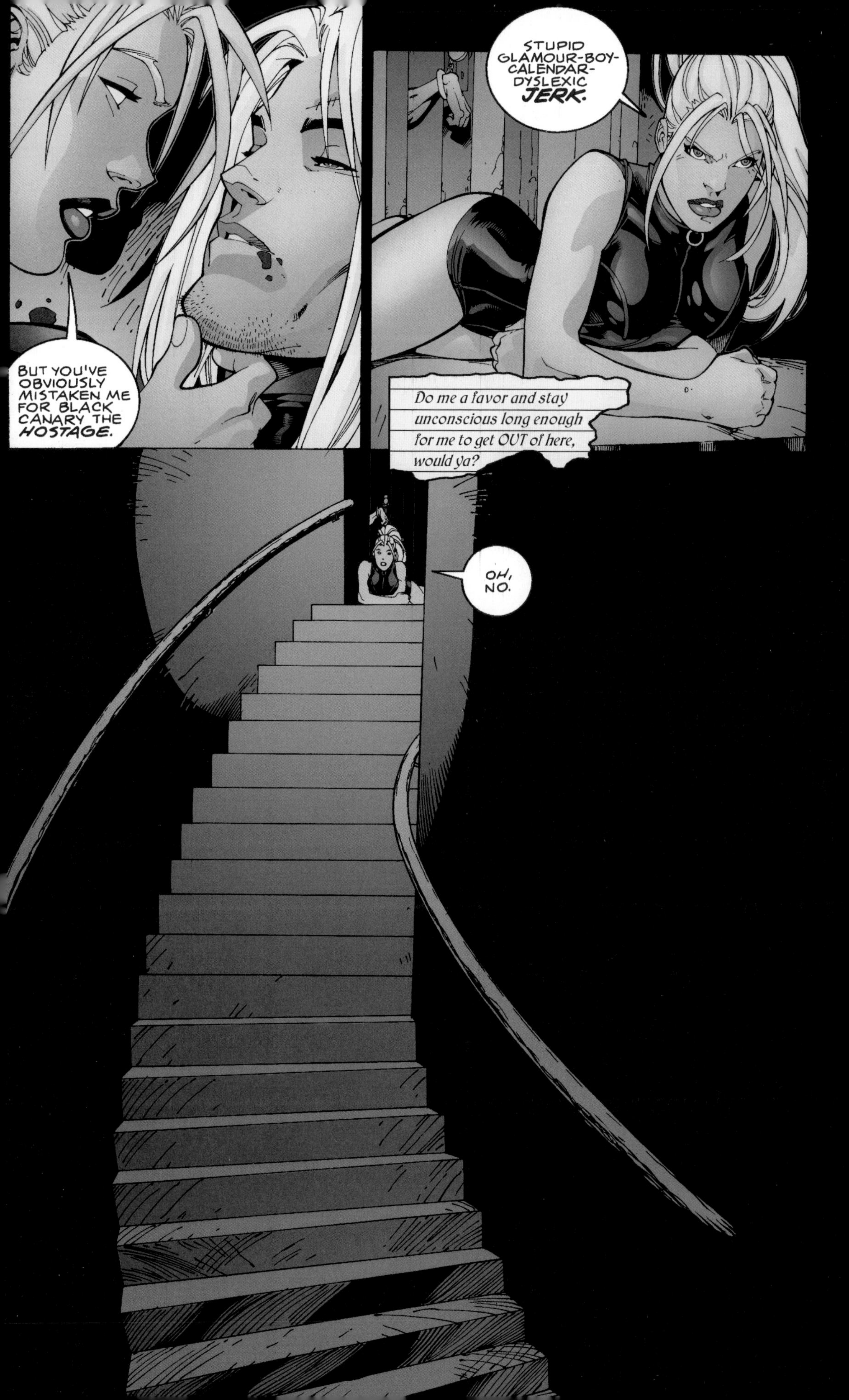
BUT YOU'VE OBVIOUSLY MISTAKEN ME FOR BLACK CANARY THE HOSTAGE.
STUPID GLAMOUR-BOY-CALENDAR-DYSLEXIC JERK.
Do me a favor and stay unconscious long enough for me to get OUT of here, would ya?
OH, NO.

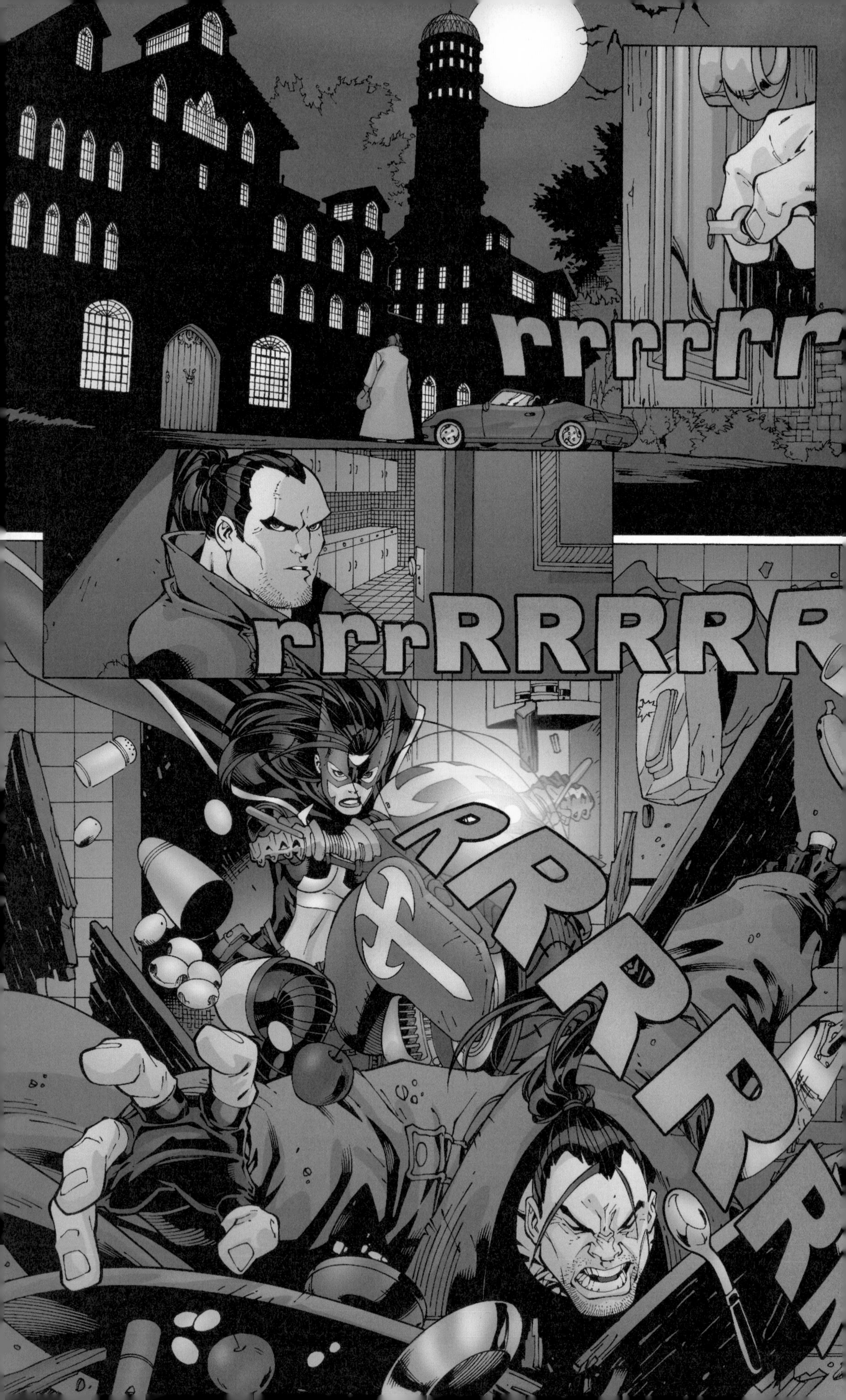
rrrrrr
rrrRRRRRR
RRRRR

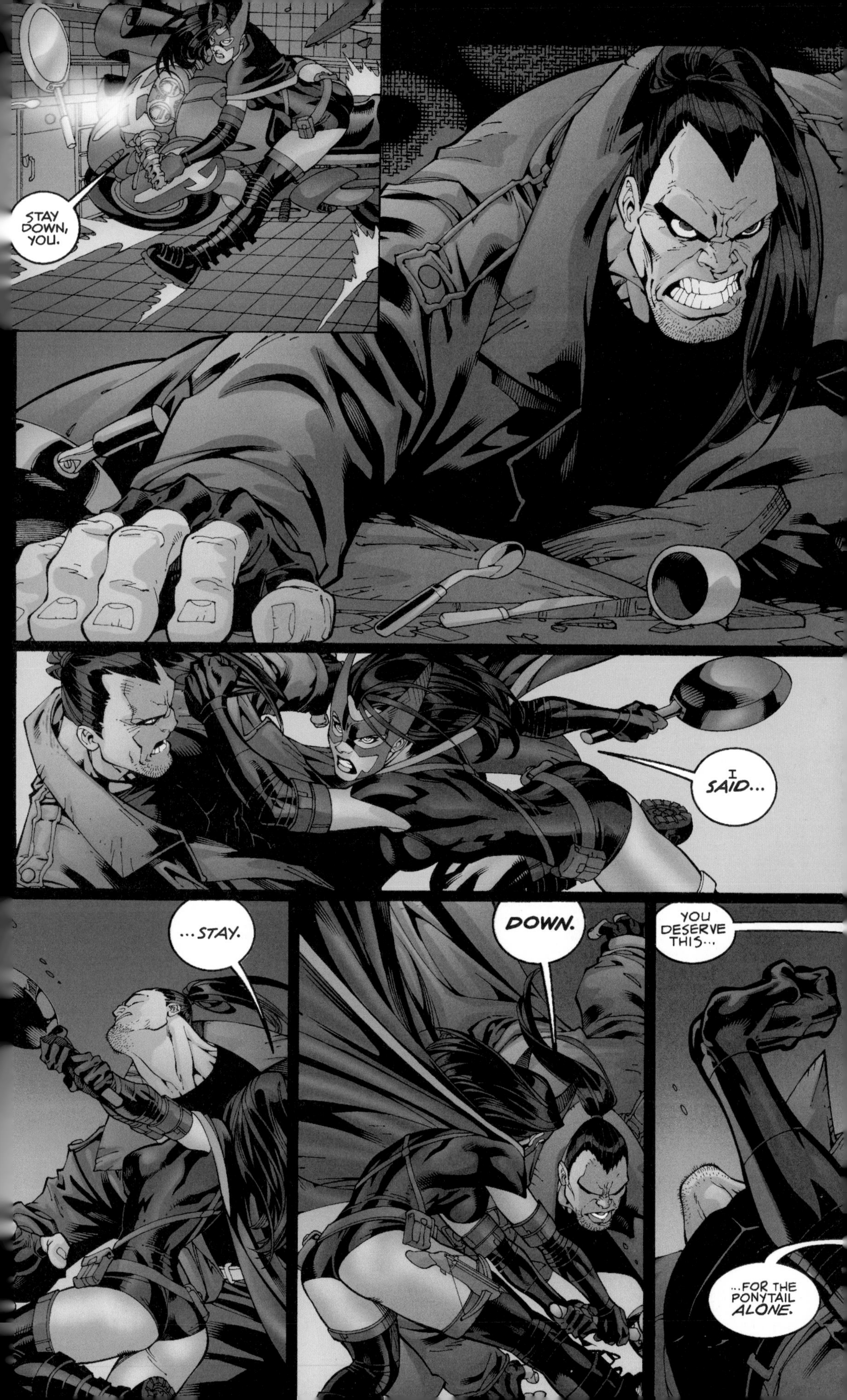
STAY DOWN, YOU.
I SAID...
...STAY.
DOWN.
YOU DESERVE THIS...
...FOR THE PONYTAIL ALONE.

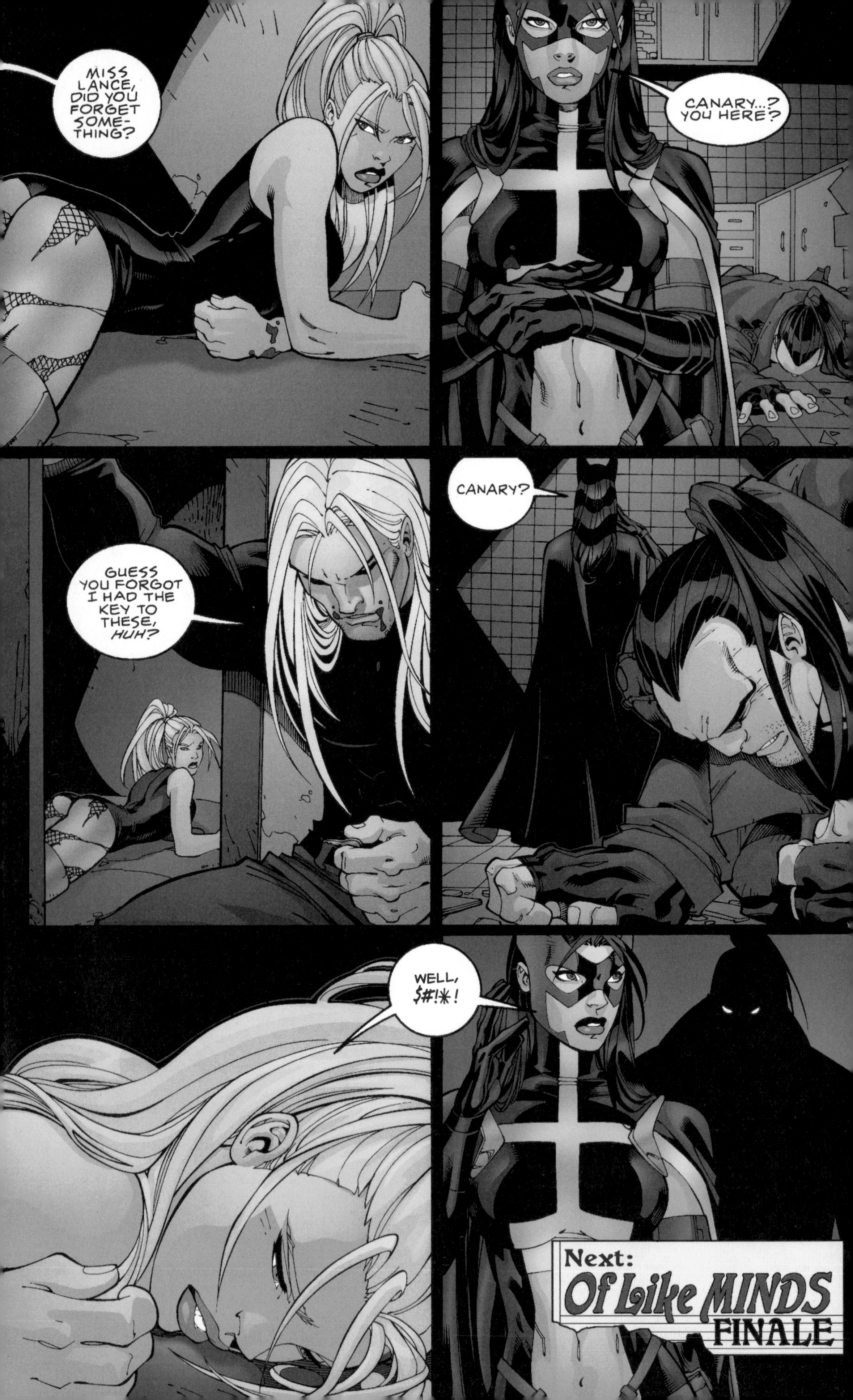
MISS LANCE, DID YOU FORGET SOME-THING?
CANARY...? YOU HERE?
GUESS YOU FORGOT I HAD THE KEY TO THESE, HUH?
CANARY?
WELL, $#!*!
Next:
Of Like MINDS
FINALE

SUICIDE SQUAD

VOL. 1: KICKED IN THE TEETH

ADAM GLASS with FEDERICO DALLOCCHIO

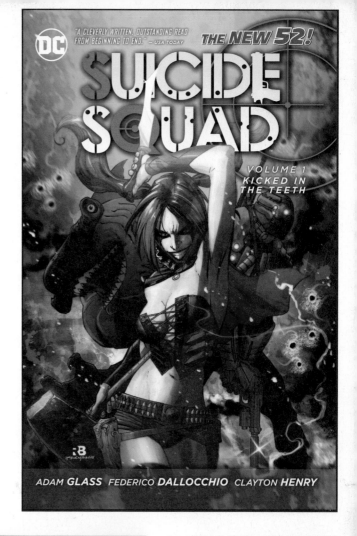

SUICIDE SQUAD
VOL. 2: BASILISK RISING

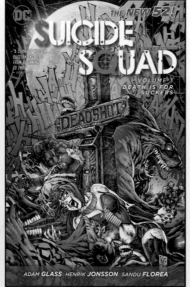

SUICIDE SQUAD
VOL. 3: DEATH IS FOR SUCKERS

READ THE ENTIRE EPIC!

SUICIDE SQUAD VOL. 4:
DISCIPLINE AND PUNISH

SUICIDE SQUAD VOL. 5:
WALLED IN

"It's nice to see one of the best comics of the late '80s return so strongly."
– Comic Book Resources

"It's high energy from page one through to the last page." **– BATMAN NEWS**

DC UNIVERSE REBIRTH

SUICIDE SQUAD

VOL. 1: THE BLACK VAULT

ROB WILLIAMS
with JIM LEE and others

VOL.1 THE BLACK VAULT
ROB WILLIAMS • JIM LEE • PHILIP TAN • JASON FABOK • IVAN REIS • GARY FRANK

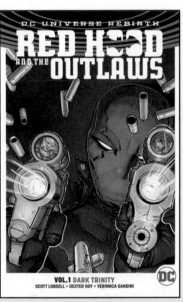

THE HELLBLAZER VOL. 1:
THE POISON TRUTH

RED HOOD AND THE OUTLAWS VOL. 1:
DARK TRINITY

HARLEY QUINN VOL. 1:
DIE LAUGHING